The Collector's Guide to
CLASSIC CAMERAS
1945–1985

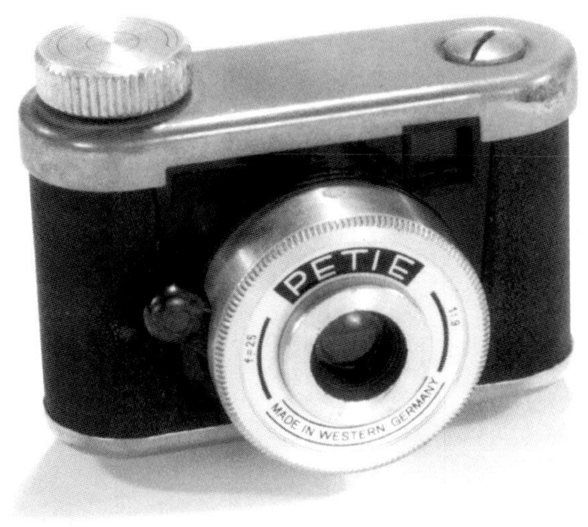

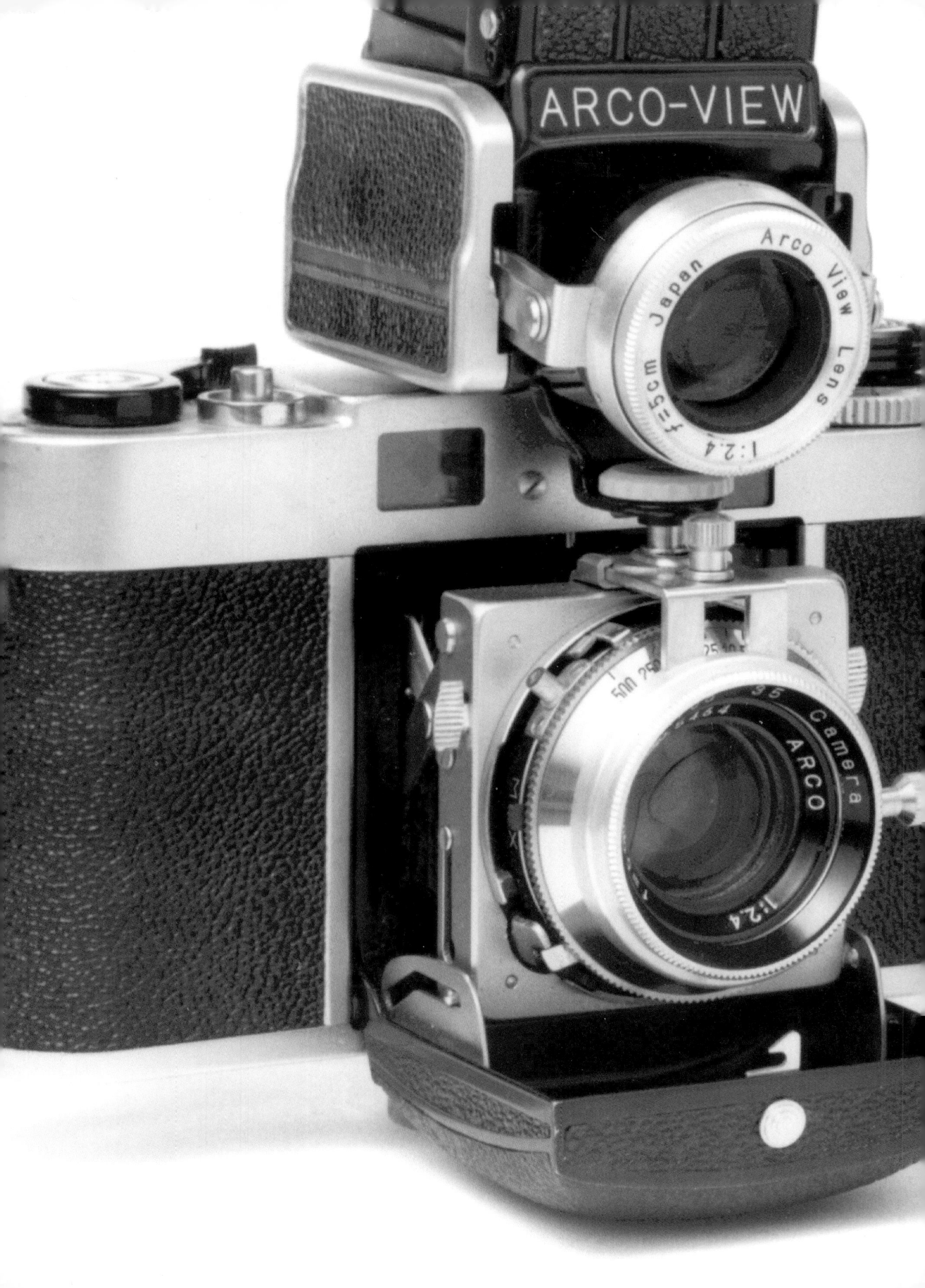
ARCO-VIEW
Arco View Lens
Japan
f=5cm
1:2.4
Camera
ARCO
1:2.4

The Collector's Guide to CLASSIC CAMERAS 1945–1985

John Wade

HOVE BOOKS

First English Edition March 1999

Published by
Hove Books Ltd
30 The Industrial Estate, Small Dole
West Sussex BN5 9XR UK
Fax. No 01273 494992

ISBN 1 897802 11 0

Design by TT Designs
Henfield, West Sussex U.K.

Printed in Hong Kong by Midas Printing Ltd

British Library Cataloguing in Publication Data
A catalogue record for this book is available from the British Library

U.K.Book Trade Distribution
Fountain Press Ltd
2 Gladstone Road
Kingston upon Thames
Surrey KT1 3HD
Fax No. 0181 547 3022

Distribution in Photo Trade U.S.A.
The Saunders Group
21 Jet View Drive
Rochester N.Y. 146244996
Fax (716) 328-5078

Contents

Introduction

THIS IS A BOOK for camera collectors. Well, you probably guessed that from the title. But it's worth reiterating because today there are people who collect cameras, but who aren't true camera collectors. Not in my book, anyway.

My definition of a camera collector is someone who collects cameras because he or she wants to know how different models have evolved; someone who is fascinated by the hundreds of different designs that have come and gone over the years; who is interested in seeing the genesis of certain well known styles; who is ready to be amazed and amused by the unusual and, very often, downright crazy concepts that some manufacturers thought would work, and which quite clearly never would. If that sounds like you, then read on.

This is a not a book for investors. That is to say, it's not aimed at the person who believes that the only reason for buying an old camera is to wrap it up and put it carefully in a cupboard until the day that it matures and reaps a vast profit from its sale. Real collectors don't hide their cameras away because they like to look at them and play with them. They don't sell their cameras because they love them too much!

It would, of course, be foolish to suggest that camera collections don't appreciate in value, but for the true collector, the value is of secondary importance to the interest factor. Of course some of the most interesting cameras around are, by their very nature, also some of the most expensive. So I freely acknowledge that a camera might be expensive because it is interesting. But start assuming that a camera is only interesting simply because it is expensive and you've taken a wrong turning somewhere.

Likewise, a camera doesn't have to be rare to be collectable. In 1963, Kodak launched the Instamatic system. It was a great success and Instamatics were made by the million, so that today you can pick them up for next to nothing at flea markets and in secondhand shops. But the first Instamatic, by the very nature of it being the first of its kind, is a landmark camera, which makes it collectable. The same goes for a camera like the Polaroid Automatic 100. The model is common, cheap and easy to buy. It was also the world's first camera with an electronic shutter coupled to an automatic exposure system. So it's a landmark and it's collectable, despite the fact that it isn't at all rare.

So, in this book, you will find the rare and expensive alongside the common and cheap. What earns each a place on these pages is the fact that they have something innovative about them, something interesting, unusual or strange... something that makes them collectable.

Neither is this a book for the person who wants to know every last detail of the history of every camera ever made. It's not a book full of databases of serial numbers and dates of manufacture. Instead, I have tried to look in detail at the designs, specifications and quirks of what I freely admit to be a fairly subjective range of cameras. I'm looking in a fair amount of detail, for example, at the Leica M3, because it was a landmark of its time. But that doesn't mean that I have then gone on to look at the M1, M2, M4, M4-2, M4-P, M5 and M6 in the same amount of detail. If that's what you want, then read a book on Leica.

So yes, there will be cameras that I've left out. But usually they will be cameras that are well known and well documented elsewhere. In their place I've hopefully added other cameras that you might not have heard of, or which you might not previously thought of as collector's items. I haven't detailed the serial number range of every model or how the number of screws in the accessory shoe varies from the Model A to the Model B. Instead, I am giving you information based on observation, from someone who has actually handled these cameras and delights not just in the innovation that is apparent in them, but equally in the peculiarities of design that are often overlooked elsewhere.

The other thing that differentiates this book from many others is the dates that it covers: 1945 to 1985. It's a 40-year timespan that is beginning to appeal to a new generation of camera collectors. Camera collecting began to be taken seriously in the 1970s, at which time most collectors were interested only in the very early equipment. Many drew a line at 1939, picking the start of the Second World War as the last date that they would accept as a collector's item. But time moves on and, since those days, a new generation of collectors, interested in newer cameras, has emerged, not least because the early equipment that was fairly easy to buy in the 1970s is now very expensive. And the 1970s themselves have now become a collectable era.

The only place where I have ventured outside this period is in a single chapter on collecting amateur cine cameras. This a branch of collecting that is only now beginning to take off, appealing to the new generation at whom this book is aimed. Since amateur cine photography is not freely covered in other books on collecting, it seemed appropriate here to journey back a further 20 years or so and cover the subject from its beginnings.

But back on the still camera side, there is now a strong interest in cameras made after the Second World War, and not just because they are easier to buy; there is a lot of interesting innovation in this period too.

The 1950s saw tremendous changes in camera design. It was a period in which, for a while at least, it seemed that 16mm was going to become the new miniature format in place of 35mm; a decade that started with box cameras still being sold new and ended with the Nikon F, the first true system 35mm single lens reflex.

As technology improved, cameras evolved faster and faster. The 1960s saw the real emergence of the Japanese into the Western marketplace and, with them, came a range of new, unusual and - today - highly collectable cameras. The 1970s saw new ideas in single lens reflex design emerge and die within a few years.

In the 1980s, technology was all, but cameras were conforming more and more to very similar basic styles, with each manufacturer out to ape and improve on the style of his rivals. Cameras had become extremely clever but, for the collector, rather dull and uninteresting. It seemed like a good place to draw a line and I've drawn it at 1985, the year the Minolta 7000 was launched. As the first body-integral autofocus single lens reflex, it set a style that marked the beginning of a new era in camera design and the end of one for the collector... until, of course, the next generation of camera collectors comes along.

John Wade,
March 1999

A Brief History

WHILE IT IS NOT the intention of this book to tell the complete history of photography, collectors should learn something about the more important landmarks that shaped different styles of camera through the various ages of photography. The following brief history gives a basic understanding of the how that development took place

1826: Joseph Nicéphore Niépce takes what has come to be accepted as the first photograph. Until then, 'cameras', were actually camera obscuras, apparatus used by artists as an aid to sketching and an understanding of perspective. The camera used by Niépce was probably made by a French optician and the exposure, using Niépce's methods based on his knowledge of lithography, took all day.

1839: Louis Jacques Mandé Daguerre announces the daguerreotype process. This was the first viable method of photography, which resulted in a positive image on a silver-plated copper plate. Daguerre's camera, specially made for the process, was the world's first commercially successful photographic camera.

1840: William Henry Fox Talbot announces the Calotype process. His process, unlike those of Niépce and Daguerre, utilised an intermediary negative, made on paper. His early cameras, made by a village carpenter, were no more than 6cm square, using microscope lenses and became known as mousetrap cameras, a name coined by Talbot's wife Constance.

1850: Frederick Scott Archer reveals the wet collodian process. It took photography onto glass plates, but they had to be specially prepared in a nearby or mobile darkroom, immediately prior to exposure.

1855: The first dry plate process is announced by French chemist J.M. Taupenot. For the first time, plates could be purchased with emulsions that would keep until required for picture taking. With the emulsions now rated at constant speeds, exposure measuring devices started to appear.

1881: Marion's Academy is the first twin lens camera. It wasn't actually a twin lens reflex because the image was projected onto the viewing screen at the back, parallel with the lens, rather than onto view finder on the top of the camera as in a true TLR.

1885: George Eastman introduces the Eastman-Walker roller slide. This device contained a roll of paper film that fitted to the back of a camera, converting it from use with plates to rollfilm.

1888: George Eastman launches the Kodak. The first camera to bear this illustrious name was also the first purpose made rollfilm model. It took 100 exposures to a roll and had to be returned to the factory for processing.

1892: Launch of the Bulls-Eye. This one was the first camera with a red window to read film numbers. It came from the Boston Manufacturing Company, who soon sold the idea to George Eastman for his Kodak cameras. Until he bought the company, Eastman had to pay a Royalty to the Boston Manufacturing Company every time he fitted one of his own cameras with the famous red window.

1897: The Chromographoscope becomes the first camera to take colour pictures. It shot the same scene through red, green and blue filters, on three different monochromatic plates that were combined optically for viewing.

1900: Kodak launch the No. 3 Folding Pocket Kodak. With a bed that dropped down from the body, along which a lens panel was pulled on rails, this set the style for folding cameras throughout the first half of the 20th Century.

1903: Launch of the Autochrome process. This process, on glass plates, used minute grains of coloured potato starch to filter the light and resulted in the first viable method of colour photography.

1912: Kodak launch the Vest Pocket Kodak. This was the first camera to use 127 film.

1914: Kodak launch the Autographic back. With this unusual device, a trapdoor could be opened in the camera back and a stylus used to write on the backing paper. The action broke a membrane between the backing paper and the film, allowing light to fog the film in the shape of the writing and so allow the photographer to add written details to negatives between frames.

1816: Kodak launch the No.3A Autographic Special. It had the style of a folder of the time, but featured the first coupled rangefinder, situated beneath the lens.

1922: The Ensign Cupid is launched. The camera was the first to produce 16 exposures on 120 film, a style that became very popular a decade later, often with 120 film, but more often using 127.

1925: Leitz introduce the first Leica. The camera, which made its inaugural appearance at the Leipzig Spring Fair and which soon became known as the Leica I was the first really viable 35mm camera.

1928: Franke and Heidecke launch the Rolleiflex. The original model was the first rollfilm twin lens reflex and set a style that would remain popular for half a century or more.

1932: Zeiss Ikon launch the first Contax . This was the first serious rival to the Leica.

1933: Ihagee launch the Exakta. This was the first truly compact rollfilm single lens reflex.

1935: Kodak launch Kodachrome. Produced to make colour transparencies, this soon became the first commercially successful amateur colour film.

1936: Ihagee launch the Kine Exakta. This is generally accepted as the first 35mm single lens reflex, although another school of thought suggests that the Russian GOMZ factory launched a 35mm SLR called the Sport in 1935. Recent evidence, however, points to the fact that the Sport came a few years later, making the Kine Exakta the first. Either way, this was the camera that set the style for the 35mm SLR of the future.

1938: Zeiss Ikon launch the Twin Lens Contaflex. This was the first camera with a built-in exposure meter.

1938: Kodak launch the Super Kodak Six-20. This camera was the first with automatic exposure control.

1947: The Hungarian Gamma company launch the Duflex. This is reckoned to be the first single lens reflex with an instant return mirror. It is, however, a very rare camera and the better known Asahiflex IIb, made by Asahi in 1954, is more often credited with the feature. There was also a plate camera, called the Vanneck, which had a very early form of instant return mirror as far back as 1890.

1948: Polaroid launch the Model 95. This marked the introduction of instant photography.

1948: Launch of the Contax S. This was the first 35mm SLR with a pentaprism viewfinder.

1959: Nikon launch the Nikon F. This quality camera was the first system SLR, produced from the start to accept a motor drive.

1959: Voigtlander launch the Vitrona. It held a set of batteries in a long hand grip and was notable for being the first camera with a built-in electronic flashgun.

1959: Canon launch the Canon P. This was the world's first quality camera to be mass produced on an assembly line.

1960: Feinwerk Technik introduce the Mec 16SB. This 16mm camera was the world's first with through the lens metering

1963: Topcon launch the RE Super. With this, through the lens metering appeared in an SLR for the first time.

1963: Kodak launch the Instamatic. This was the first camera to use the 126 size drop-in film cartridge. It influenced amateur snapshot camera design for the next decade.

1963: Polaroid launch the Automatic 100. This was the first camera with a fully automatic electronic shutter.

1968: Konica launch the Autoreflex. This one was the first automatic SLR. It used shutter priority automation.

1972: Kodak launch their Pocket Instamatic cameras. These were the first to use 110 film and, as with 126 snapshot cameras, manufacturers the world over fell in line to produce their own versions.

1976: Canon launch the AE-1. This was the first SLR with a central processing unit.

1978: Konica launch the C35AF. This 35mm compact was the first autofocus camera.

1978: Polaroid launch the SX-70 Sonar AutoFocus. This was an instant camera and the world's first autofocus single lens reflex.

1978: Konica launch the FS-1. This was a 35mm SLR and was the first with a built-in electric motor drive.

1980: Ricoh launch an autofocus lens. It used a K-mount to fit to Ricoh, Pentax and other SLRs of the day. Canon launched their own version the same year for Canon FD-mount cameras.

1981: Kodak launch the Disc. Once again, the Kodak system became a standard for other manufacturers of snapshot cameras.

1982: Sony announce the Mavica. The name was a corruption of Magnetic Video Camera and it was the first digital camera to record images on magnetic disc, rather than film. The camera never went into production

1985: Canon Launch the T80. This SLR used similar technology to that found in the Canon autofocus lens, creating the first autofocus SLR.

1985: Minolta launch the Minolta 7000. With this, the autofocus mechanism was taken into the body, rather than the lens, making it the first really viable autofocus 35mm SLR.

1986: Pentax launch the Zoom 70. This was the first compact with a zoom lens.

1988: Fuji launch the Quicksnap. This is the camera that started the craze for throwaway cameras.

1989: Canon launch the ION. The initials stood for Image Online Network and this was the first commercially available electronic camera, marking the start of a new era in the history of photography.

How and where to buy Collectable Cameras

BUYING COLLECTABLE cameras is a lot easier today that it was when the hobby first began. In those days, there were no specialist dealers or camera fairs. On the other hand, it was possible to find bargains in unexpected places: camera shops with old stock that had been hanging around their shelves for years; antique shops who wanted to get rid of items which, at that time, were not yet considered collectable, junk shops among piles of rubbish.

Today, many camera shops sell what have become known as modern classics, cameras from the recent past which some amateur photographers buy secondhand in preference to modern, do-everything, fully-automatic equipment. Among these it's possible to find some of the later cameras that are now becoming collectable in their own right, although prices usually reflect the fact that they are being sold as usable cameras. Very few general photographic stores today sell cameras older than 15 or 20 years, however, so the collector has to look elsewhere.

One method is to join one of the many clubs that have now grown up for collectors. Here you will meet like minded people who are ready to buy, sell and exchange collectable equipment, usually at reasonable prices to fellow collectors. Another method is to advertise in the wanted section of local newspapers. Look too at the classified advertisements of mail order photo dealers who advertise in photographic magazines. Very often, among the modern equipment, you will find a section on collectables.

Today, there is good and bad news for the collector. The good news is that it has never been easier to find places to buy. The bad news is that in some ways the hobby has been a victim of its own success. Its popularity has spawned a number of recognised price guides, so that many more people who have something to sell know its so-called value, and there is less chance of finding a bargain.

Nevertheless, there are still interesting and unusual cameras out there to be had, if you know where to look. Here are the prime places where collectors buy, the differences between them and how to deal with each.

Camera fairs

If you're new to camera collecting and have never been to a fair, this is the ideal place start. Newcomers sometimes feel they are going to make fools of themselves, surrounded by experts on the subject, but nothing could be further from the truth. Camera collectors are a friendly bunch who love to impart information and will never make you feel small about your lack of knowledge - unless you start spouting off on a subject you know nothing about. Then they'll soon put you in your place.

If you want to buy a piece of equipment at a

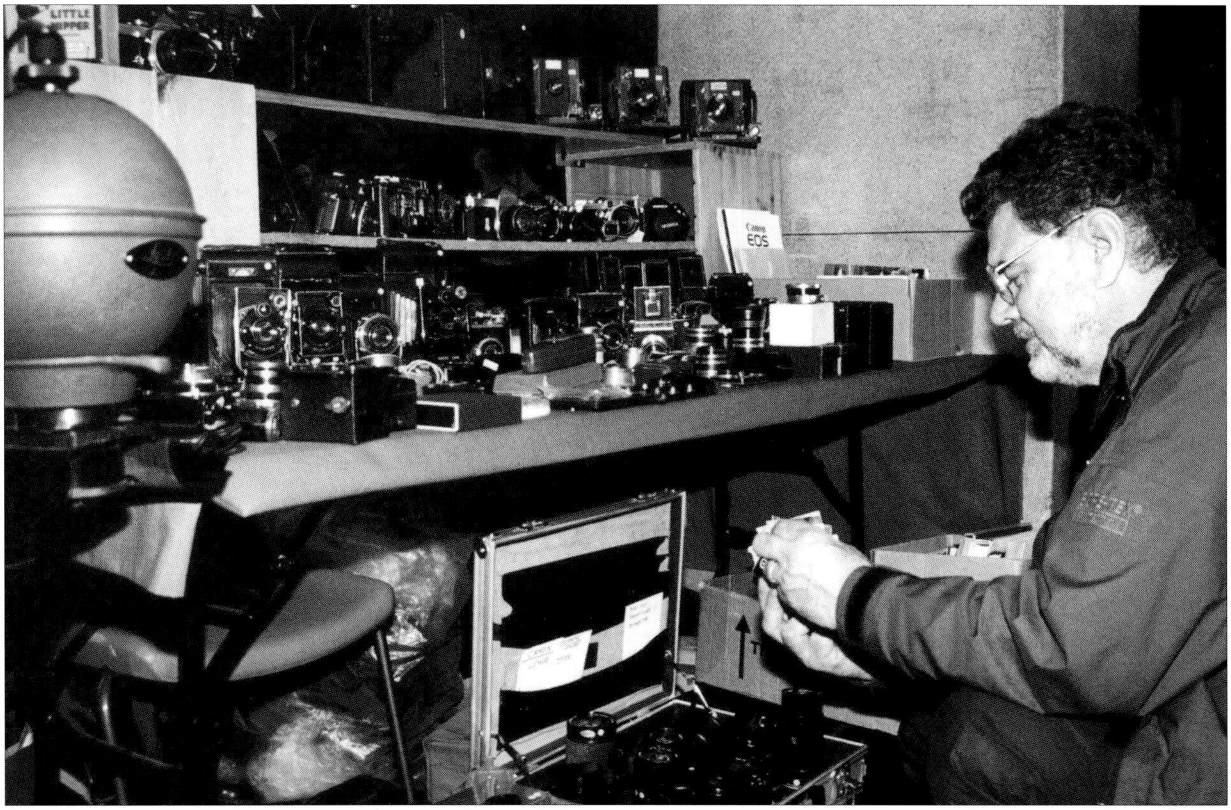

Camera fairs are excellent places to buy classic and collectable cameras.

camera fair, talk to the person selling it. Ask him about it. Ask him to show you how it works, what he knows of its history, what year it was made. It's how we all learn.

Camera fairs attract recognised dealers, but they also attract private collectors who take a stall as a way of meeting collector friends old and new and to sell off items that they might have duplicated in their collections, through buying better examples. These are the ideal people to buy from, because they are not there to make huge profits, only to charge a fair price, and because they have been collecting for so many years, they often have some fascinating cameras to sell on.

When you buy at a camera fair, you need to have a good look around first. There are very few real bargains to be had, because everyone with a stall or table knows the value of what is being sold. But you will find widely different prices, depending on the condition of the item. Some stall holders don't like to haggle. They claim the price they set is the price they want. The majority, however, are open to offers and, in fact, mark the cameras up, prepared to be knocked down. So don't be afraid to make an offer, preferably one that is slightly less than you are actually prepared to pay, so that there is the opportunity for the seller to make the usual reply: "Okay, I'll meet you half way."

You also stand a better chance of a bargain towards the end of the day than at the start, although if you leave things too late you run the risk of losing the very item that you had set your sights on from the moment you entered the fair. It's all part of the gamble of camera collecting.

Specialist dealers

The popularity of camera collecting has led to some photographic shops giving over a major part of their floor space to collectables, whilst other new dealerships have been set up specifically for selling classic and collectable equipment and nothing else.

The reason why some collectors tend to stay away from dealers is because of their prices,

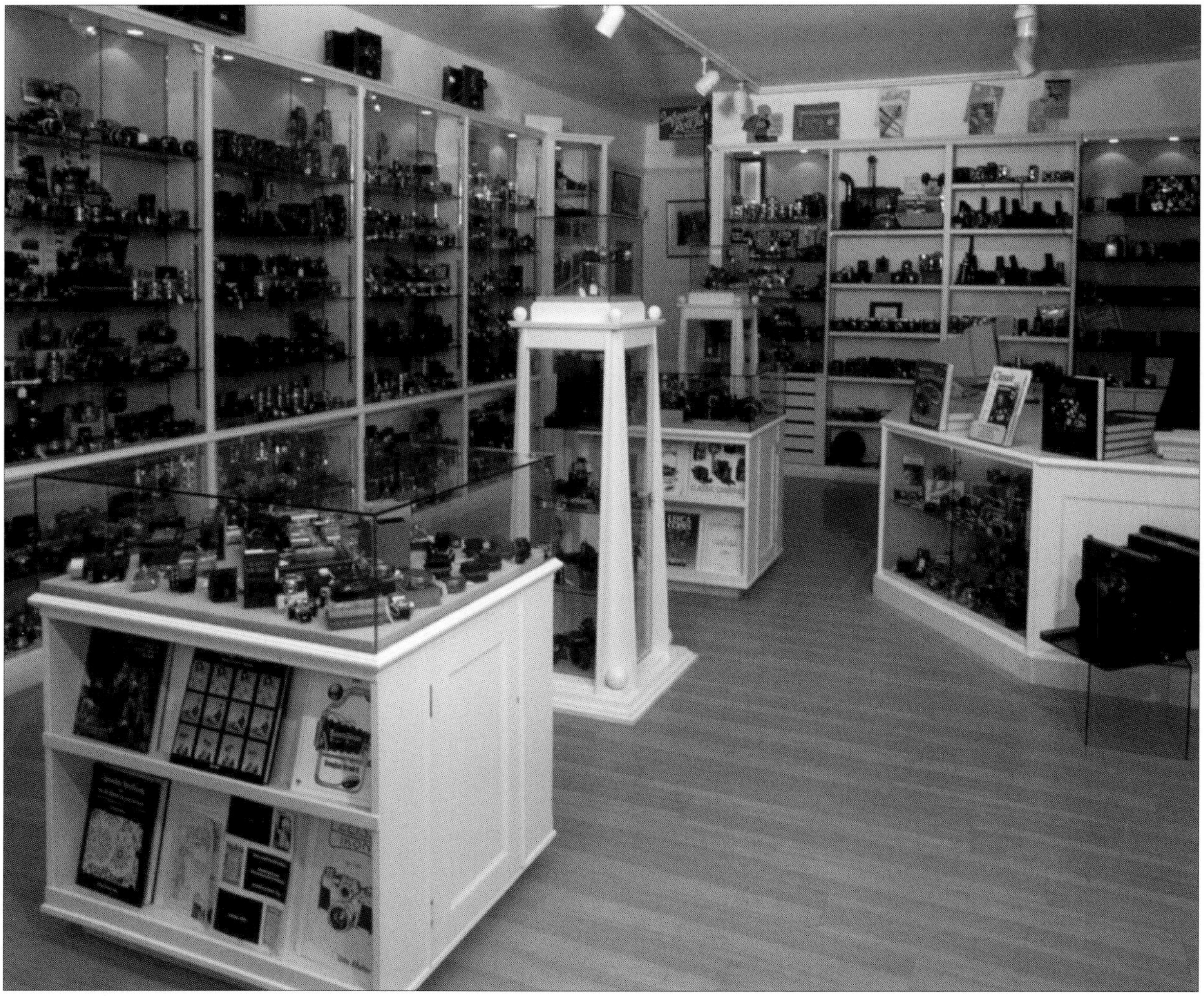

Specialist dealers offer a wide range of quality collectable cameras for sale.

and yes it's true that in most cases you'll pay more for a camera from a dealer than you would from, say, a fellow collector or at a camera fair. But there's a good reason for that.

Dealers have to make a living. They have overheads - rent, staff, lighting and heating - that others don't have to worry about if they merely want to sell a camera or two privately. Many of them also set prices that reflect the fact that they sell to foreign collectors, particularly in Japan, where they can demand higher prices.

So much for the bad news. Let's look at the positive side. First, the equipment sold by most specialist dealers is in top condition, and if there is anything wrong with it, they'll tell you, reducing the price accordingly. That's something you won't always get from a fellow collector! Then there's the fact that some dealers offer a camera search service to look for specific cameras on your behalf.

Also worth considering is the sheer range of equipment that they have available. Dealers can get their hands on equipment that ordinary collectors can only dream about finding elsewhere. They do this in a number of ways that are not available to others.

They have the finance to buy complete collections, selling off individual items. They are known to be buyers, so collectors with something unusual to sell go to them first. They have contacts, very often all over the world, who look out for cameras on their behalf. They go to fairs at home and abroad where they find cameras that might not always be available here in your home country.

It's also worth remembering that, because they have contacts among a great many collectors, they know who wants what and are consequently in a good position to offer you a decent price if you are selling or part exchanging. You'll rarely get a real bargain from a dealer because he knows his business too well. What you will get is a vast choice of good equipment at a fair price.

Auctions

There are two types of auction: the big, prestigious type organised by internationally known auction houses where you can find rare and wonderful cameras that you might never see anywhere else outside the really specialised dealers or even museums; and local auctions, where it's unusual to find anything really rare, but where you can pick up bargains.

Many collectors shy away from auctions because they don't understand how they work. Everyone has heard those stories about the man who sneezed at the wrong moment and ended up bankrupting himself by inadvertently buying something he neither wanted nor could afford. Actually, in real life, it's nothing like that. It's almost impossible to bid without meaning to, and whatever type of auction you go to, the procedure is much the same.

It starts with the viewing. Sometimes, the day before and usually up to just before the sale starts, you go to look at the lots. You'll buy a catalogue that lists them all, sometimes with the prices they are expected to achieve, and you take your time examining anything you are interested in.

At local auctions, the catalogue is often no more than a laser printed list. At larger auction houses you can subscribe to well illustrated catalogues that are often a wealth of information in their own right.

Before the start of the sale, you go to the registration desk. There, someone will take your name, address, possibly your telephone number and maybe proof of identity. Then they will give you a number. In the sale room (note, you call it the sale room, not the salesroom), the auctioneer calls up each lot and it is held up for inspection. Then he starts the bidding by suggesting a price. If you are interested, you let him know. And no, that doesn't mean you have to wink, blow your nose or tap your teeth with your pipe! You simply raise a hand or hold up your number.

The auctioneer will then increase the price and someone else will bid, and he raises the price again. It's not up to you to call out the price, it's the auctioneer who sets it, leaving it to you to register your interest. But beware. At the start, he will increase the price by only small amounts, but as bidding goes on and the value increases, so too will the amounts by which each bid is increased. The best way is to set a fixed price that you are prepared to pay in your mind and to drop out immediately the auctioneer goes above that price.

So you keep bidding until you are the last one in, at which point the item is knocked down to you. You then hold up your number. Afterwards, you go to the collection point, quote your number, pay your money and collect your goods. But, again, beware, because the price you bid might be less than the price you are asked to pay. That's because a buyer's premium - often as much as 12.5 per cent - is usually added to the price and, at the larger auction hoses, if the camera you are buying is subject to tax, that too could be added.

The sale room of the world famous Christie's auction house.

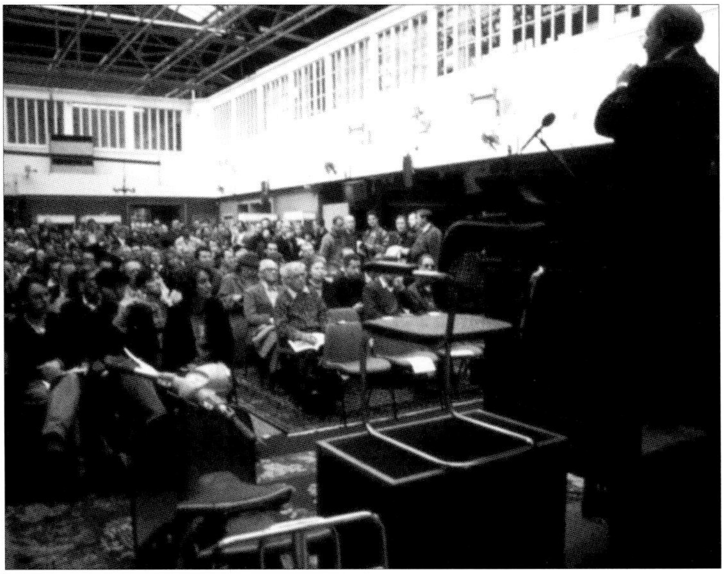

Much the same happens at local auctions, although the buyer's premium here will be lower - usually 10 per cent and at some places as low as 5 per cent. The lots are often made up from house clearances and things that people bring in on the day. These are the places where antique market people go to stock up their stalls and they will rarely bid more than 50 per cent of the price they hope to get for an item. If you bid 51 per cent, you're in with a chance... and a bargain.

Whichever type of auction you attend, prices only reflect the demand on the day and are reliant on who is there and who wants what. If two collectors are bidding and each is determined to get a camera, the price will be forced up and up until someone has to pay far more than they might have done, buying from a specialist dealer.

On the other hand, if you are the only one who wants a certain model of camera, you could get it at a low, low price, simply because no one else bids. It's what makes auctions so fascinating and so much fun.

Antique markets

Very occasionally, you find a camera specialist at a general antique market and his prices will be about what you'd pay at a camera fair. But mostly we're looking here at general dealers who sell anything and everything that's old. These people are rarely experts on cameras, although most of them have access to the various price guides available and can price a camera fairly accurately.

Not being specialists, however, they don't always see the minor and subtle distinction between some models that can often mean a leap in value.

The trick, when shopping at an antique market is to get there early and immediately do a very fast tour of all the stalls, training your eye to look for nothing but cameras. After that, you can relax and look at everything else at your leisure. They are often good places to look for accessories like exposure meters as opposed to actual cameras.

Flea markets and junk fairs

Here we are talking about places where ordinary people, as opposed to professional dealers, go to offload household items no longer of use. They are nearly always full of totally useless junk, but amongst the rubbish, you can sometimes find a gem. And because the sellers are rarely experts on what they are selling, you can get them for good prices too.

Arriving early and doing a fast tour of the tables is also the rule of the flea market. Note the starting time and turn up right as it opens, while items are still being unpacked. Then go round fast before someone else spots the bargain you were after. Another rule: if you see something you want, buy it there and then. Don't go back later for it because it will be gone.

Although you do hear stories of unbelievable bargains, it is actually quite rare to find anything really valuable at a junk fair or flea market. But for the camera collector, they are the ideal places for building up a collection of simple snapshot cameras. And, who knows, we all live in hope of that day when a real once in a lifetime bargain is going to turn up.

Prelude To An Era

By 1945, when the era we are considering in this book began, most major camera designs were already established and the era began with the basics already in place. Rangefinder cameras, 35mm and rollfilm single lens reflexes, twin lens reflexes, studio cameras, box cameras, folding cameras, stereo cameras, panoramic cameras... all had been invented or patented prior to the Second - and, in many cases, even the First - World War. The result was a series of unusual and interesting variations on the basic themes, many of which trod the path to success, but a lot of which followed the road to failure. Those are the cameras that this book is looking at in detail. But to understand where they came from, it does no harm to look back a little further at the genesis of many of the traditional designs, to see how they started and developed.

Camera movements

Sanderson cameras pioneered sophisticated camera movements.

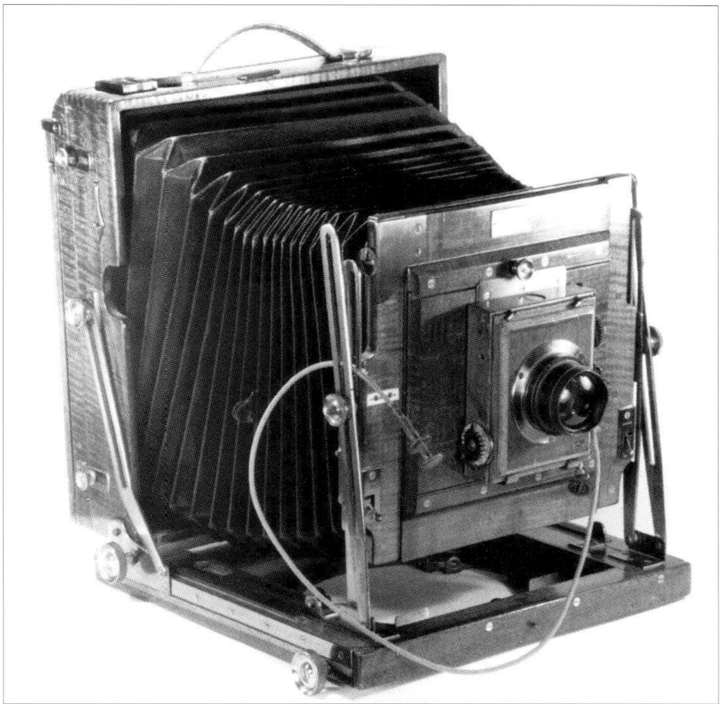

Field and studio cameras like the Linhof and MPP are notable for their camera movements: the way lens panels and cameras backs rise, shift, lift, swing and tilt in relation to one another to alter the shape of the image on film. The camera that was responsible for starting those movements was the Sanderson.

Frederick Sanderson was a cabinet maker and wood and stone carver, born in Cambridge, England in 1856. He became interested in photography early in life and was particularly keen on architecture, a subject that demanded camera movements. Many cameras at this time had rising and crossing lens panels, but Sanderson wasn't content with those two movements, so used his skills as a cabinet maker, combined with his knowledge of photography, to come up with a new design of camera, launched in 1895 and simply known as The Sanderson.

The secret of the camera's success lies in the way the front panel is slotted into twin arms pivoted to the front of the body, with a threaded stud passing through slots in each arm, topped by a knurled knob to clamp the panel into any position. With all four arms independently hinged, the front panel can be

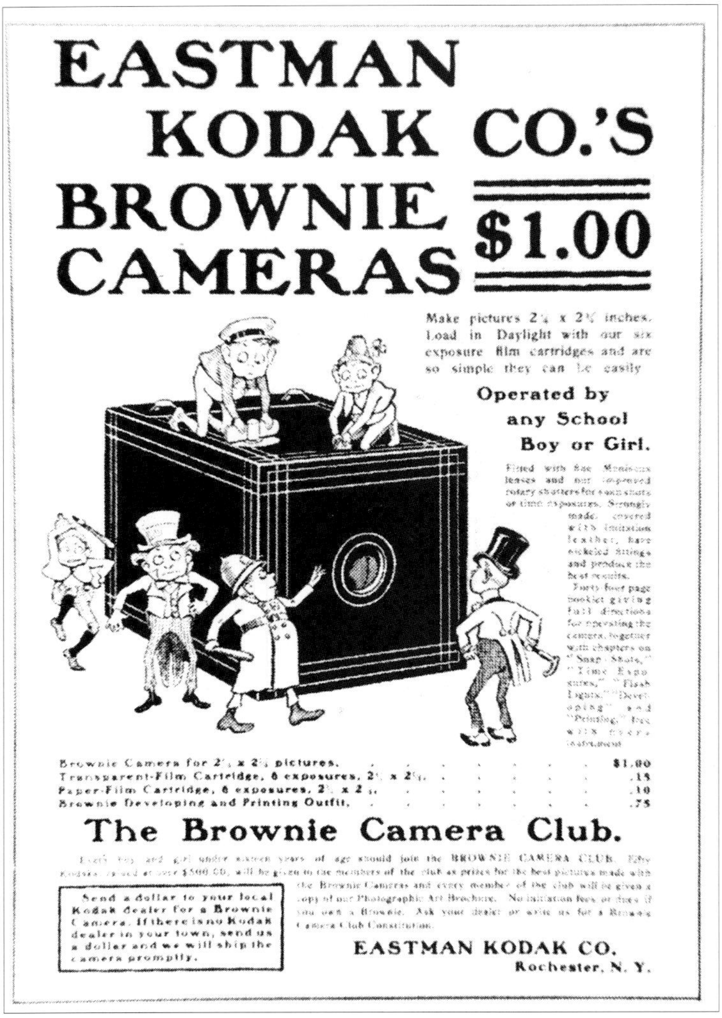

The first Kodak Brownie appeared in 1900.

locked totally out of square. Rise and fall, tilt and swing of the lens are all controlled by that one pair of knurled knobs. Holding them between the thumb and forefinger of each hand, the photographer can stand behind the camera to view the image on the ground glass screen, whilst shifting, swivelling or tilting the lens panel as desired before locking it firmly into the required position. The back of the camera is also hinged to the baseboard and that too can be tilted and locked in any position. The features were used on Sanderson cameras right through until the 1930s.

The first Brownies

The first Brownie was made by Kodak in 1900 and aimed at children. A Brownie, at that time in America, was a sort of pixie or elf and both the box and the advertisements for the camera showed these cute little fellows. The original model takes 117 film for 6 x 6 cm negatives. Within a few months of its launch, there was a new, slightly improved model known as the No.1 which became the first commercially successful Brownie. There was also a hybrid model made between these two. All the early cameras have separate viewfinders. In 1901, Kodak produced the No. 2 Brownie, which was the first camera to take 120 size film.

Early folders

One of the most popular styles of camera right through until as late as the 1960s was the roll-film folder. The style features a bed that drops down at right angles to the body to reveal rails along which the lens panel is drawn out. The camera that started it was the No. 3 Folding Pocket Kodak, launched in 1900. Early models have a leather-covered lens panel. The camera takes 118 size film and produces images 10 x 8 cm.

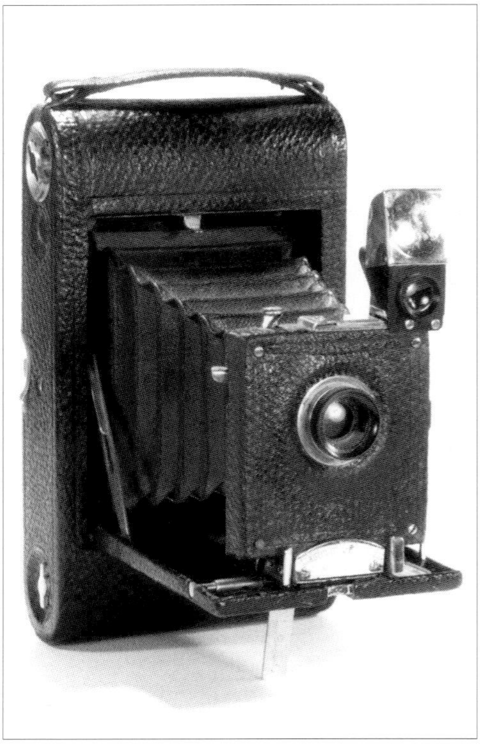

The No. 3 Folding Pocket Kodak launched a folding style that remained popular for more than half a century.

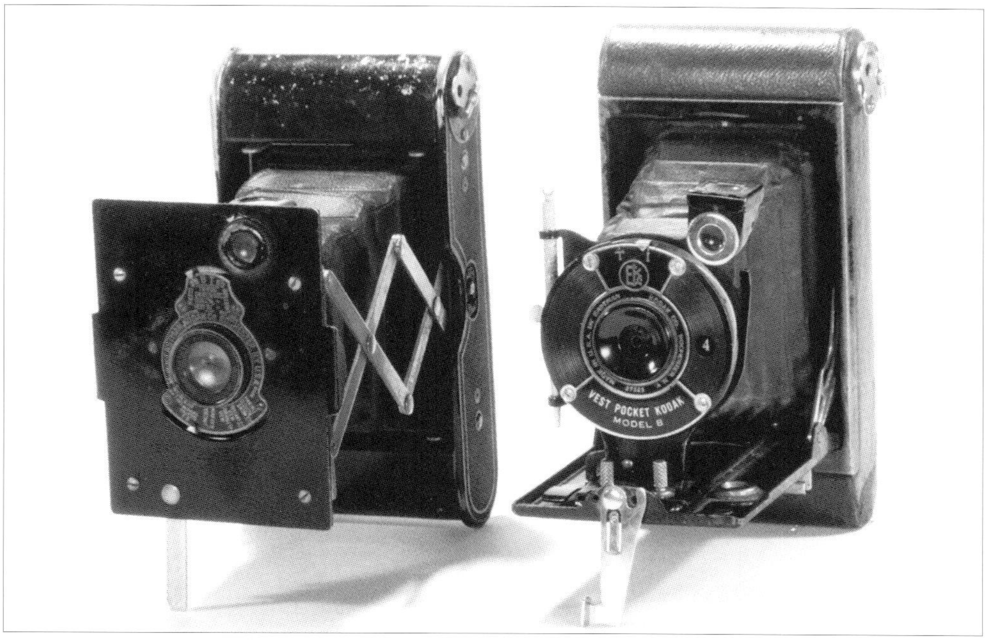

Vest Pocket Kodaks: the original style and the Model B.

The Kodak No. 3A Autographic Special, first camera with a built-in rangefinder.

First 127 camera

The first camera for 127 film was the Vest Pocket Kodak, made in 1912. It's a small camera with a lens panel that pulls forward on bellows, but is supported by criss-cross struts, known as lazy tongs. The first model sold between 1912 and 1914, then in 1915, Kodak introduced their Autographic back to the camera. It allowed the photographer to open a flap and write on the film's backing paper with a stylus. The action broke a thin membrane between the backing paper and film allowing light to fog the film and so expose the written words onto the emulsion. There was also the Vest Pocket Autographic Special, produced in 1915, with a Persian morocco leather covering.

The life of the Vest Pocket Kodak in that form ended in 1925, when Kodak launched the Model B. Still taking 127 film and with a fairly simple specification, this one follows the style of larger folding cameras with a bed that drops down from the body and a lens panel that pulls out on rails.

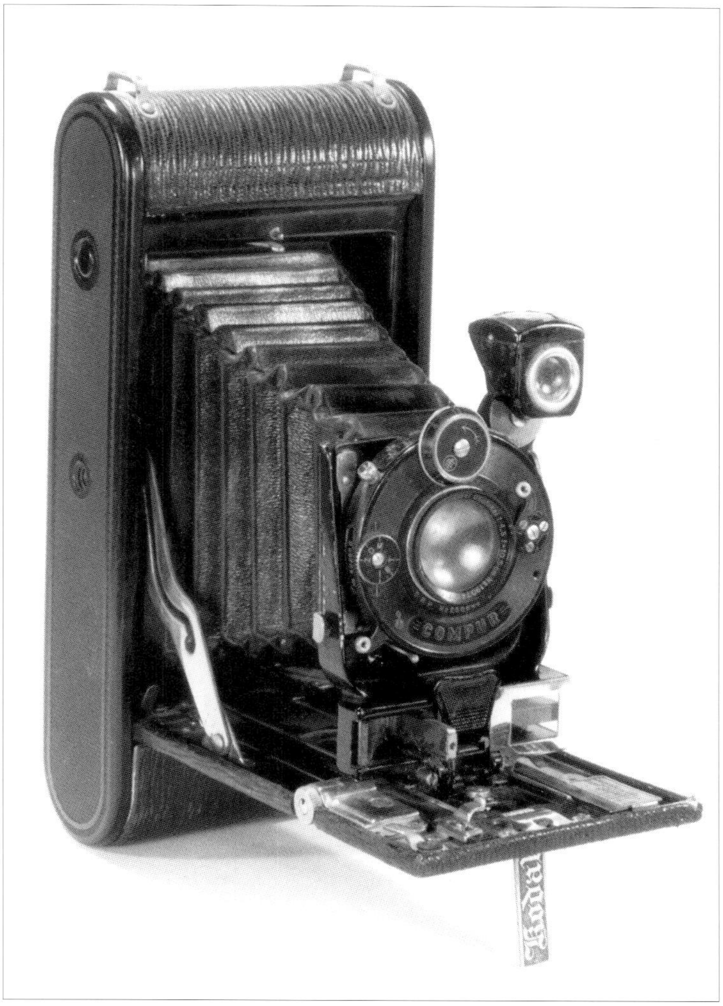

First rangefinder camera

At first, the Kodak No. 3A Autographic Special, launched in 1916, looks like almost

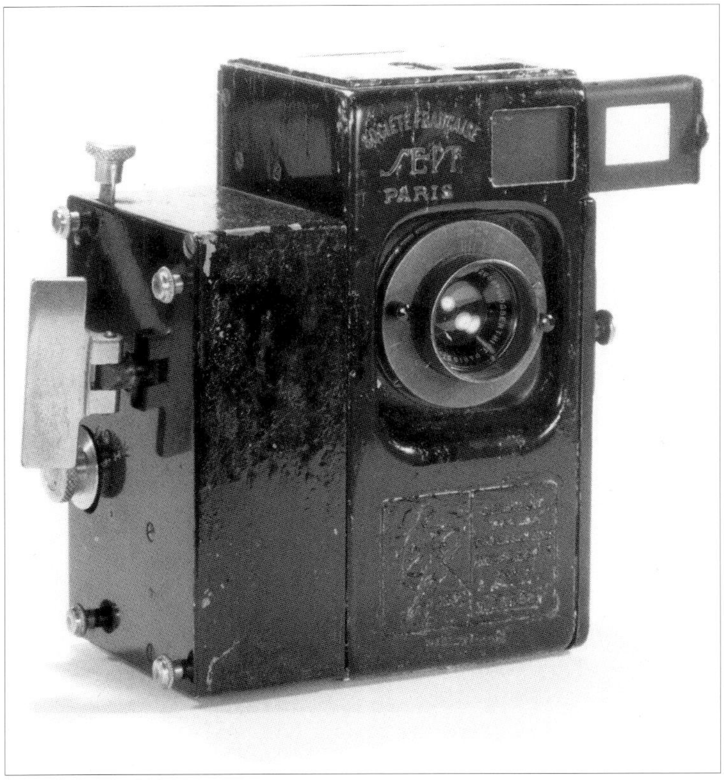

The Debrie Sept had a built-in motor drive in 1922.

any other folder of the time. But below the lens is what makes the Special special: two, small rectangular windows. This is the first camera with a coupled rangefinder. In use, the photographer stands at right angles to the subject, looking into the side of one of the windows and seeing the scene as a split image. Turning a knurled wheel on the opposite side of the baseboard focuses the lens and lines up the image, at which point the lens is in focus. The camera takes pictures 14 x 8 cm on 122 size film.

Built-in motor drives

The Debrie Sept was made in 1922. It's a 35mm camera, made three years before the Leica which really launched 35mm, and it has a built-in motor drive, driven by clockwork. Loading 17 ft of 35mm film in special cassettes provides a 15 second burst of movie action which, being a hand held camera, made it popular with newsreel photographers of the day. But the Sept is a still camera too. It takes around 250 pictures, 18 x 24 mm half frame size, either in a continuous sequence or one at a time, the clockwork motor winding the film automatically after each exposure. The single speed shutter provides instantaneous or time exposures and it is possible to combine several still exposures with perhaps a 10-second burst of movie action all on the same length of film.

Early 35mm cameras

The camera that gave 35mm its true start was the Leica, launched in 1925. There had been 35mm cameras before that date, the above mentioned Debrie Sept, the German Minigraph from around 1915 and the French Phototank from around 1921 to name but three examples. But it was the Leica that really began it.

The camera was the brainchild of Oskar Barnack, head of an experimental department at the Leitz Optical Company. He began by cutting down glass plates, but failed to get the

Pioneers of 35mm photography: the Leica I and the Contax I.

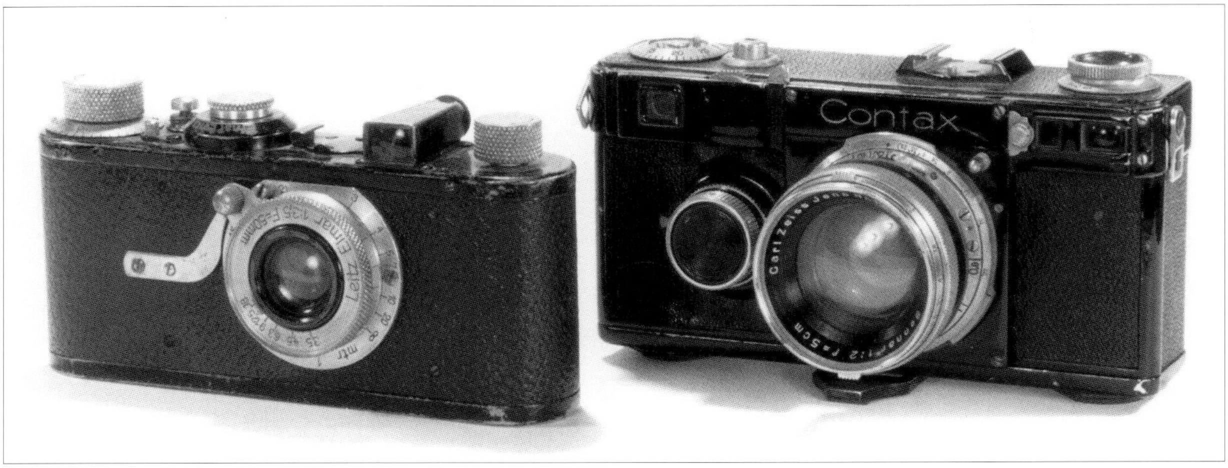

quality he needed and, in the end, he designed a still camera that used 35mm cine film. Cine cameras then, as now, used 35mm film running vertically to give a full frame across the width to produce a format of 18 x 24 mm. Barnack's still camera turned the film on its side to run horizontally and doubled the format to 24 x 36 mm - and so was born today's standard 35mm frame.

The next serious 35mm camera was the Contax, launched by Zeiss Ikon in 1932, the same year as the Leica II arrived. It's a very different design that is squarer than the Leica, with a bayonet interchangeable lens in place of Leica's screw mount and a metal focal plane shutter that runs vertically rather than horizontally as in the Leica. Like the Leica II, but unlike the Leica I, the Contax also has a coupled rangefinder. Six variations were produced until the launch of the Contax II in 1936.

The Leica and the Contax were extremely sophisticated models whose price put them out of reach of the average photographer. So it fell to Kodak to bring 35mm to the man in the street and the camera that did that was the Retina, first made by Kodak in Germany in 1934 and in slightly different styles into the 1950s. The first Retina looks like a folding rollfilm camera of old with a baseboard that folds out from the body, the lens automatically advancing along it as it folds down.

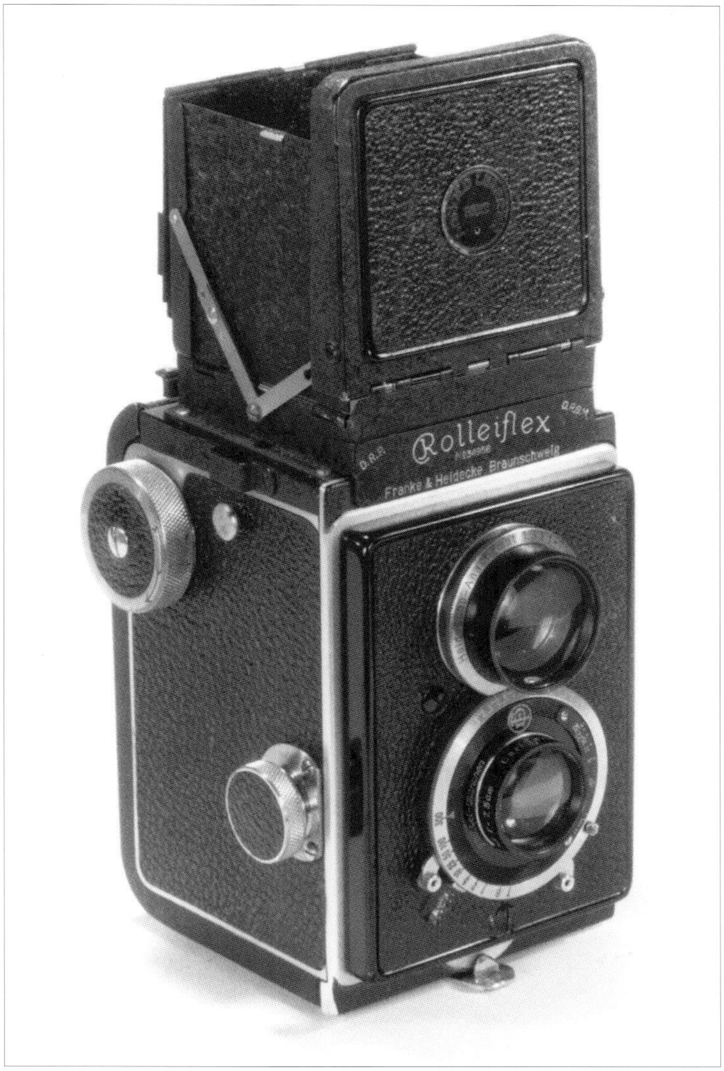

The original Rolleiflex.

The first rollfilm TLRs

The first twin lens camera is probably Marion's Academy from 1882. After that, twin lens reflexes that used plates were popular. But it wasn't until a rollfilm twin lens reflex arrived on the scene that the style became established as a major influence on future design. The company that produced that camera was Franke and Heidecke, the camera they launched in 1928 was the first Rolleiflex.

Franke and Heidecke had been making a stereo camera called the Rolleidoscop, which was the main influence for the Rolleiflex. Turned on its end and with one lens removed, it became the first rollfilm TLR.

This original model is easily identifiable because it has a knob to wind the film, rather than the crank seen on later Rolleis. Like the Rolleidoscop, it takes 117 film, six pictures to a roll, although you might find some today that have been converted for 120. The camera was introduced with an f/4.5 Tessar, which was almost immediately replaced by an f/3.8 version.

Early 16-on cameras

With the growing popularity of 35mm film, manufacturers of rollfilm cameras in the 1930s began to look at new ways to economise and offer more shots to the roll. A favourite

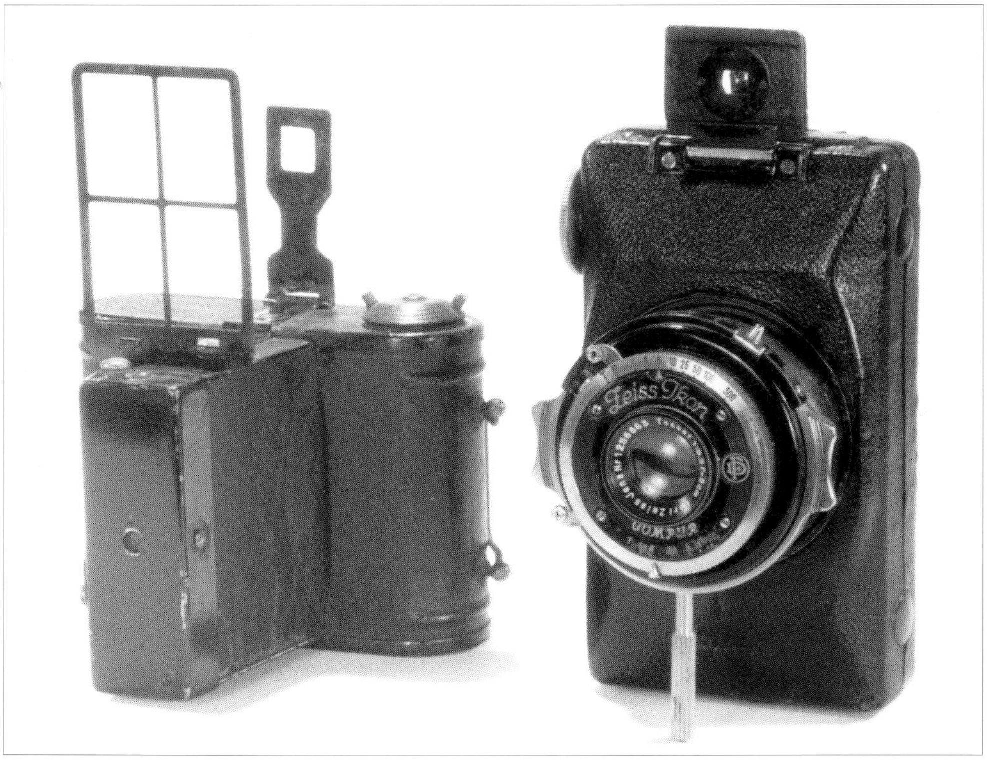

The Ensign Cupid which pioneered 16-on cameras and the Kolibri which popularised the style.

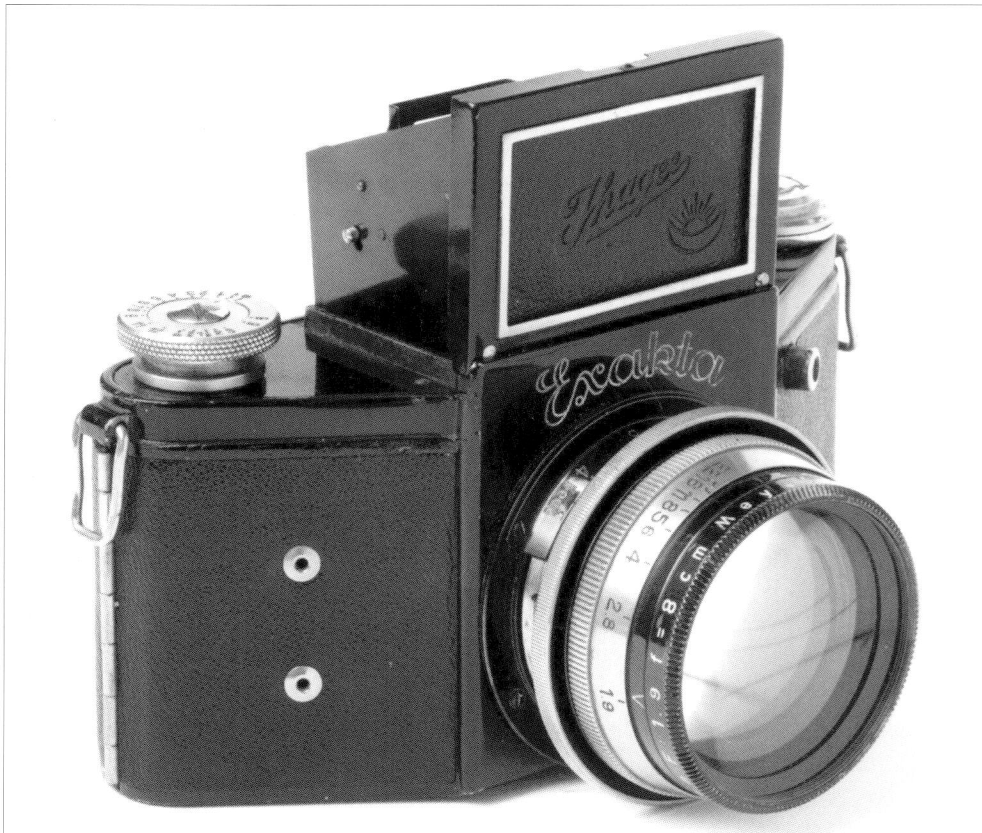

The Exakta pioneered rollfilm SLRs.

method was to double the number of exposures that could be obtained from a film by reducing the format and adding two red windows. The film was wound until the figure '1' appeared in the first window, the exposure was made, then the film was wound again until '1' appeared in the second window. After that exposure, the film was wound again until '2' appeared in the first window... and so on until 16 exposures had been made.

The Ensign Cupid, made in 1923, was the first 16-on camera and used 120 film. But the camera that really popularised the style was the first to use the same idea with 127 film. That was the Kolibri, made by Zeiss Ikon in 1930.

As with any half-frame camera, the Kolibri produces images deeper than they are wide when held in the usual horizontal fashion and, to counteract that, the camera is designed to be held vertically, with the film wound from bottom to top to produce landscape-shaped pictures. To use it, the lens is drawn out on a metal tube that locks into position at the infinity setting. Further focusing is carried out by a lever that rotates above the lens to rack the lens and Compur shutter out to a minimum focusing distance of 3ft 6in.

At the time of its launch, the Kolibri became known as the poor man's Leica.

The first rollfilm SLR

The first truly compact rollfilm single lens reflex was the Exakta, made by Ihagee of Dresden in 1933. A year later, a second model was introduced similar to the first but with the addition of slow shutter speeds. The new version was called the Exakta B and only then did the first version take on the name Exakta A.

These early Exakta are unusual in shape, triangular with the sides of the camera sloping away from the lens. The shutter release is on the front of the body, not the top, and it is released with the left hand. Focusing is by a helical screw around the lens barrel. The viewfinder is a waist-level type and there is a sports finder too. The first Exakta takes 127 film, eight pictures to a roll.

The first built-in meter

The first camera with a built-in photo electric exposure meter was the Twin Lens Contaflex of 1935. Unusually for a TLR, it takes 35mm film and offers interchangeable lenses. It was made by Zeiss Ikon.

The meter's cell is under a flap above the viewing lens, comprising a series of prisms that concentrate the cell on the same angle of view as the standard lens. Three scales are engraved beneath the cell. The lower shows film speed, the next shows apertures and an arrow on this second scale is set against the appropriate speed setting below. Beside the focusing hood, a meter needle floats in a window and a lever on the right of the camera is turned to bring

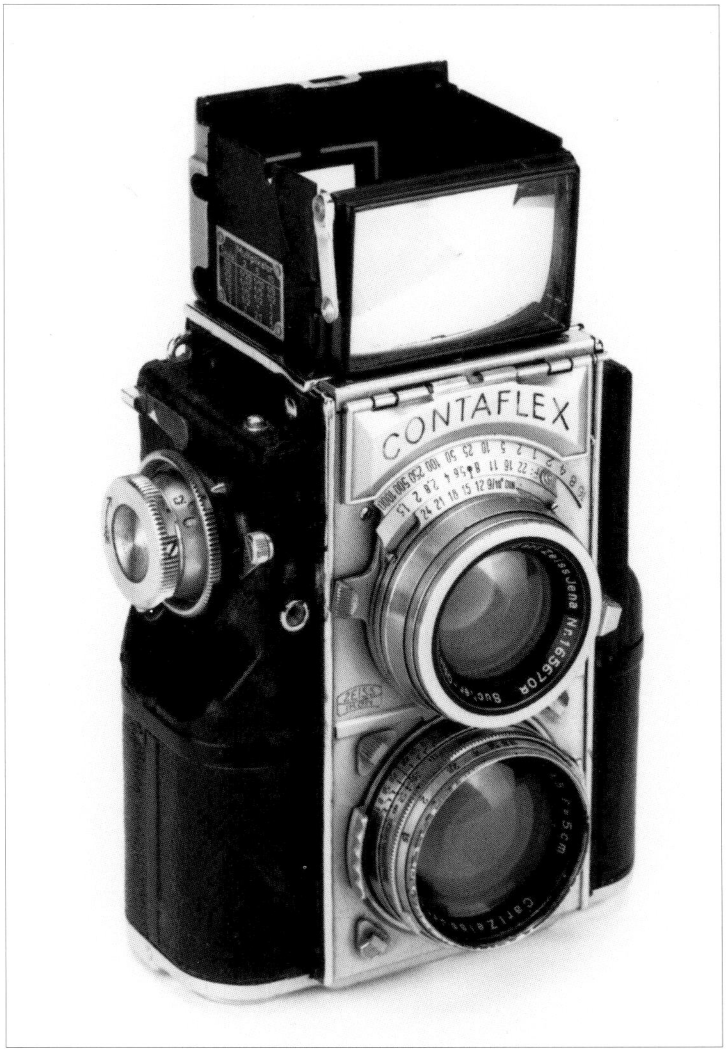

The Twin Lens Contaflex was first with a built-in photo electric exposure meter.

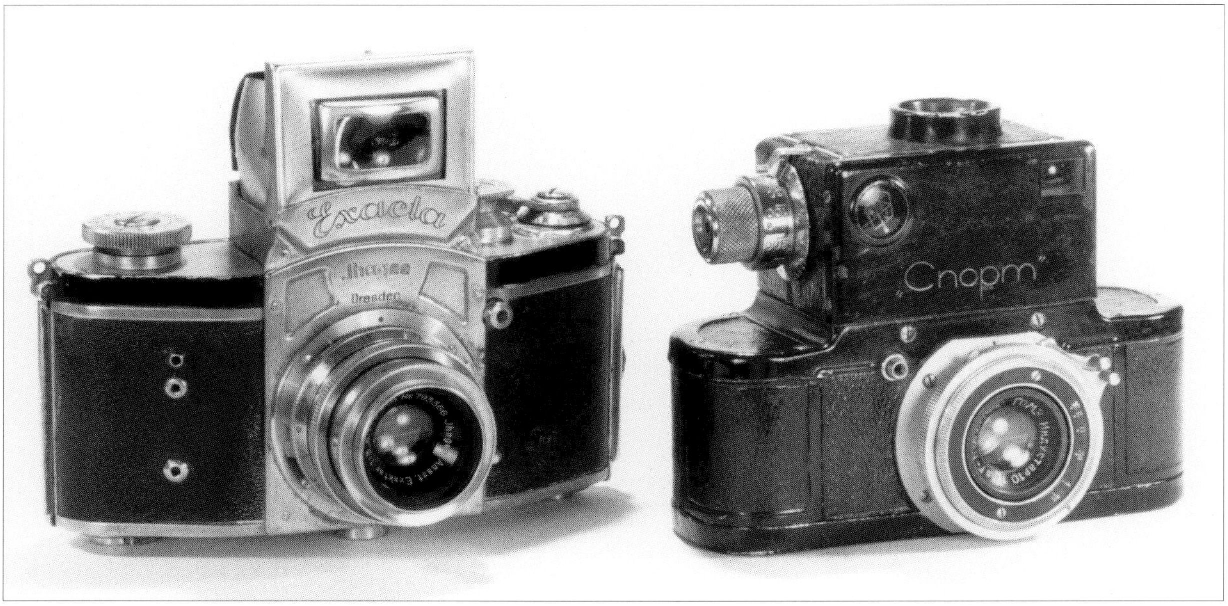

Early 35mm SLRs: the Kine Exakta and Sport.

the needle to a central mark. At that point, shutter speeds are read off against apertures on the two scales above the lens and transferred manually to the camera.

The first 35mm SLR

There is contention over what was actually the first 35mm SLR. The camera which is best known is the Kine Exakta. It was launched by Ihagee in 1936 and is basically a reworking of the original Exakta, but made for 35mm film.

There is a school of thought, however, that says it wasn't the first. Around the same time, a camera called the Sport was made in Russia, but there is conflicting evidence about its true date of origin. Some claim it to have been first made in 1935, in which case it is the first 35mm SLR. Others say it was made later, maybe around 1938. The Sport was made by GOMZ and looks like a small 35mm camera with a huge box on the top to house the reflex system. It is used at eye level, but by looking down into the eyepiece on the top of the box, and also features an eye-level direct vision viewfinder.

The Sport may or may not have been the first 35mm SLR, but, either way, it was the Kine Exakta that set the style and had the influence over future cameras.

The first auto exposure camera

Automatic exposure came from Kodak in 1938 with the introduction of the Super Kodak Six-20. It's a large folding camera with a meter cell above the lens. The output from the cell moves a meter needle and, once it has reached its appropriate setting, the shutter release is lightly pressed to move a comb-like mechanism that traps the needle where it stands. A spring-loaded connection on the aperture control then moves until it comes up against the locked needle, adjusting the aperture as it moves. Further pressure on the shutter release then exposes the film.

Masks adjust the light reaching the cell as the shutter speeds are changed and the camera is automatic between 1/25 second and 1/200 second. For longer exposures, settings have to be adjusted by hand. The meter is calibrated only for the speed of Kodak Verichrome film.

First pentaprism

The pentaprism, which made eye level viewing a viable proposition on 35mm cameras and so led to the 35mm single lens reflex as we know it today, came with the arrival of two cameras, first shown in 1948 and manufactured from

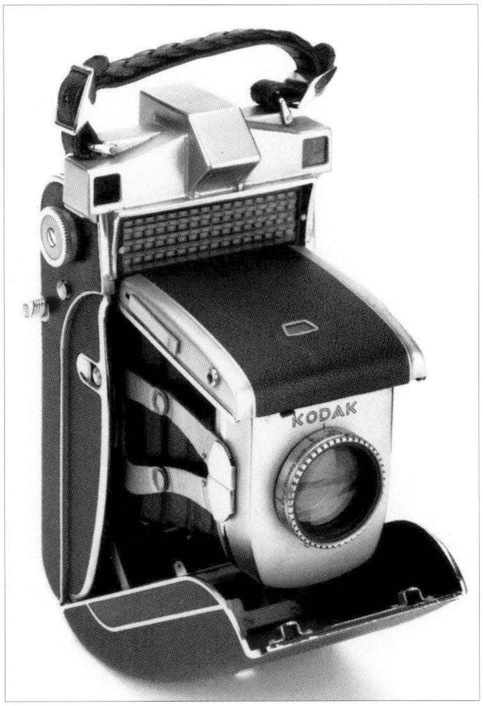

The Kodak Super Six-20 was first with auto exposure.

1949. They were the Contax S and the Rectaflex. Each lays claim to being the first, but the Contax has the earlier patent date and was probably launched just ahead of its rival, if only by a few weeks.

The Contax S was made by the VEB Zeiss Ikon company in East Germany, after a split which had taken Zeiss Ikon proper to West Germany after the Second World War. It was also the first camera with the 49mm screw thread that became extremely popular among later Japanese SLRs, particularly Pentax, which is why, it is often referred to as the Pentax screw.

The Rectaflex was made in Italy and there were two models, one with a top shutter speed of 1/1000 second, the other with 1/1300 second. The camera also had two small cross prisms cemented into the focusing screen to produce a split image rangefinder.

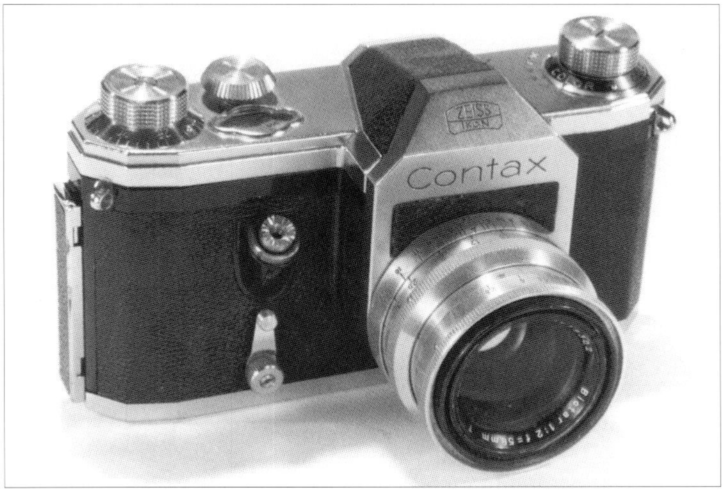

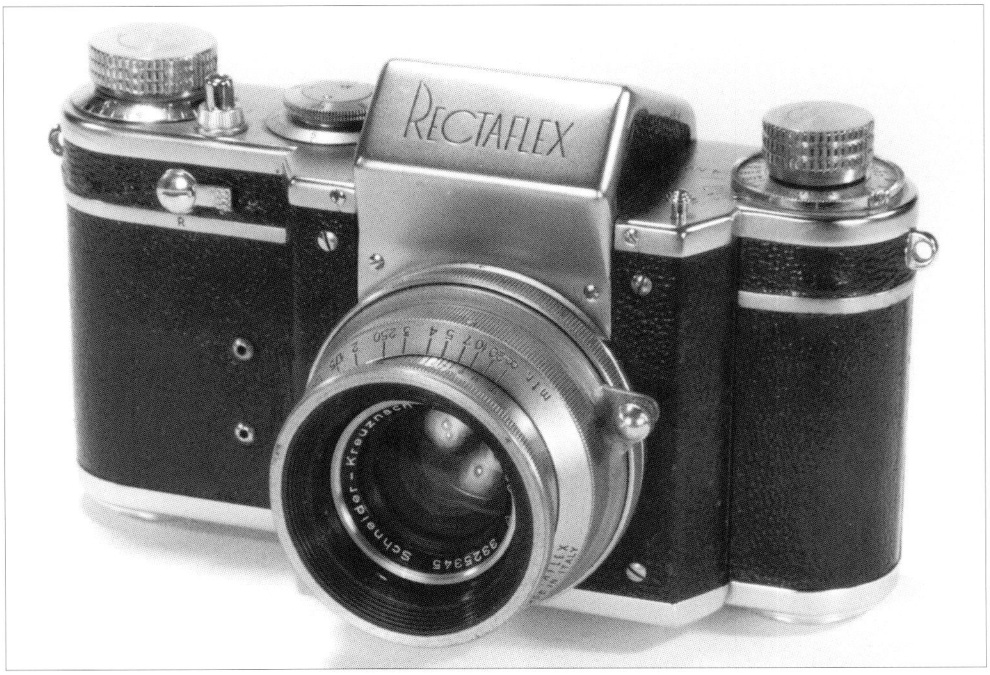

First 35mm SLRs with pentaprisms: the Contax S and the Rectaflex.

Unusual, Impractical and Very Collectable

DOWN THROUGH the ages of photography there have always been manufacturers who tackled basic camera design in unusual and often weird or wonderful ways. Sometimes the ideas led to real innovation and the start of a whole new style of camera. Other times, they led to no more than dead ends that went nowhere at all. Not all of the following designs were total dead ends, but none of them really caught on in a big way or influenced the future of camera design. For the collector, however, these are the very cameras that often prove to be of the most interest.

Gravity shutters

Purma cameras were among a select few that used gravity shutters, in which the shutter speed changes depending on how the camera is held.

They work by means of a metal focal plane shutter, in which one blind opens, to allow light to the film, followed by the second blind closing to cut it off. The speed with which the second blind follows the first, therefore, controls the exposure and, to that end, the second blind is fitted with a swivelling weight.

With the camera held horizontally, the weight does very little, simply moving across the focal plane with the blind and governing it to give a medium shutter speed. When the camera is held vertically, however, the weight swivels down and drags that second blind down faster, giving a briefer shutter speed. Turn the camera up the other way and that same weight swivels round again to hold the

The Purma Special and Purma Plus use gravity shutters.

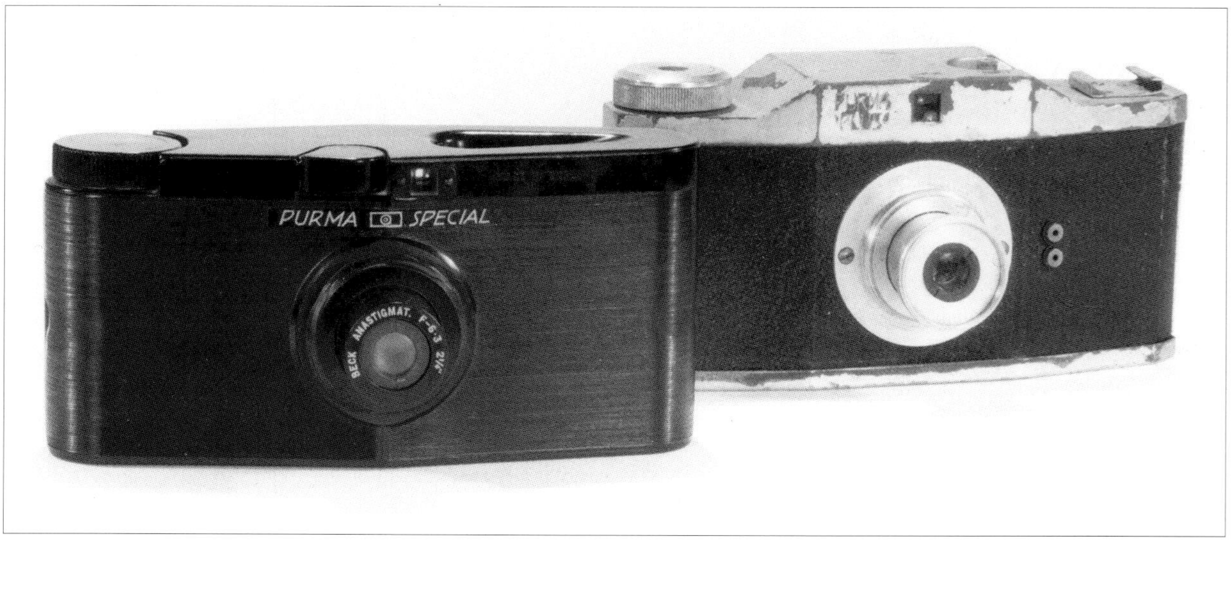

second blind back, resulting in a slow shutter speed.

The first model was called the Purma Special and made of Bakelite by the English firm of R.F. Hunter in the 1930s. In 1951, Hunter produced a new, all-metal version called the Purma Plus. Both have the same kind of shutter, use a curved film plane to make up for aberrations in the cheap lenses and take 16 square pictures, 32 x 32 mm on 127 film.

Incidentally, the Purma Special has also gone down in history for the first use of plastic in a viewfinder.

Focusing methods

The simple expedient of moving a lens back and forth to focus its image on the film has been handled in many different ways by camera manufacturers.

Take Contax. The first model was launched by Zeiss Ikon in 1932, but variations on it were still being produced post war and they all use a similar method of focusing. Instead of turning the lens itself, as was the case with the Leica that Zeiss originally set out to rival, the Contax uses a small serrated wheel that protrudes from the front of the camera and stands just a little proud of the top plate. Raising the camera to the eye and placing the right index finger on the shutter release, the third finger falls naturally on this wheel, which can be easily rotated with the camera to the eye. The wheel is geared to the lens barrel and the whole thing controls a rangefinder for accurate focusing.

The Ensign Commando, a dual format camera for either eight or 16 pictures to a roll of 120, was produced in 1945, the year the Second World War ended, and was based on a design developed during the war for military use. Its unusual method of focusing couples the rangefinder to a focusing knob on the top of the body, but turning the knob doesn't move the lens. Instead, it moves the film plane backwards and forewords inside the body. A similar focusing method was used in the Stereo Realist (see page 104).

The Ilford Sportsmaster, made in 1960, has not one, but four shutter buttons, each one marked with a focusing symbol and distance: infinity, 13ft, 8ft and 5ft. The top button, marked for infinity, merely releases the shutter. The other three also release the shutter, but not before they have moved the front element of the lens by different degrees to focus it at the designated distance just before the shutter is released.

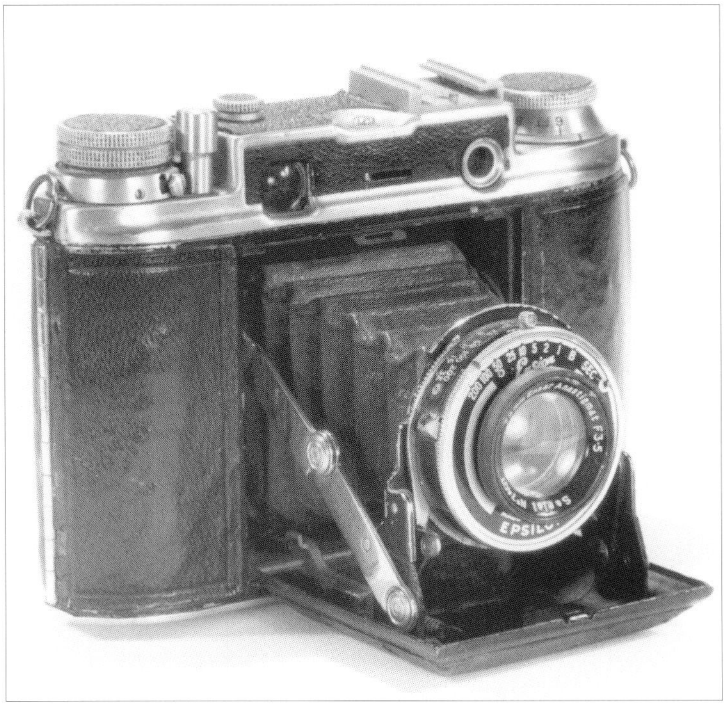

The Ensign Commando moves the film to focus.

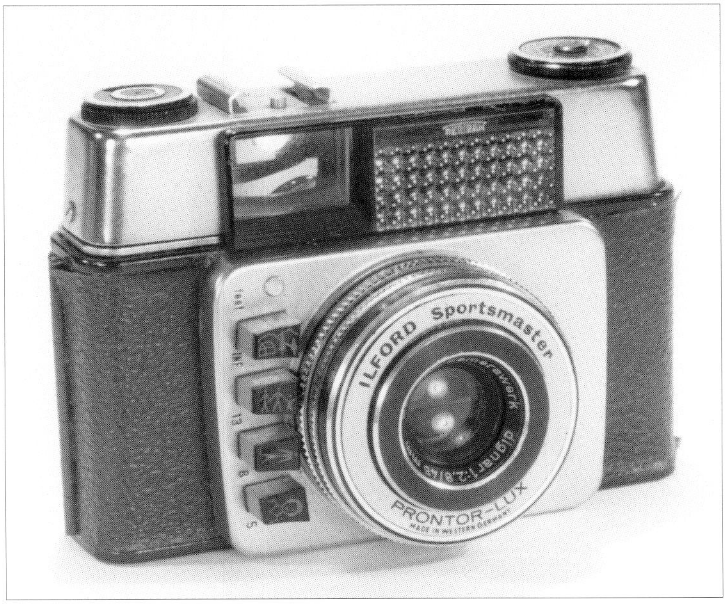

The Ilford Sportsmaster has four shutter releases, each for a different focusing distance.

Focusing on the Graphic 35 is by levers either side of the lens.

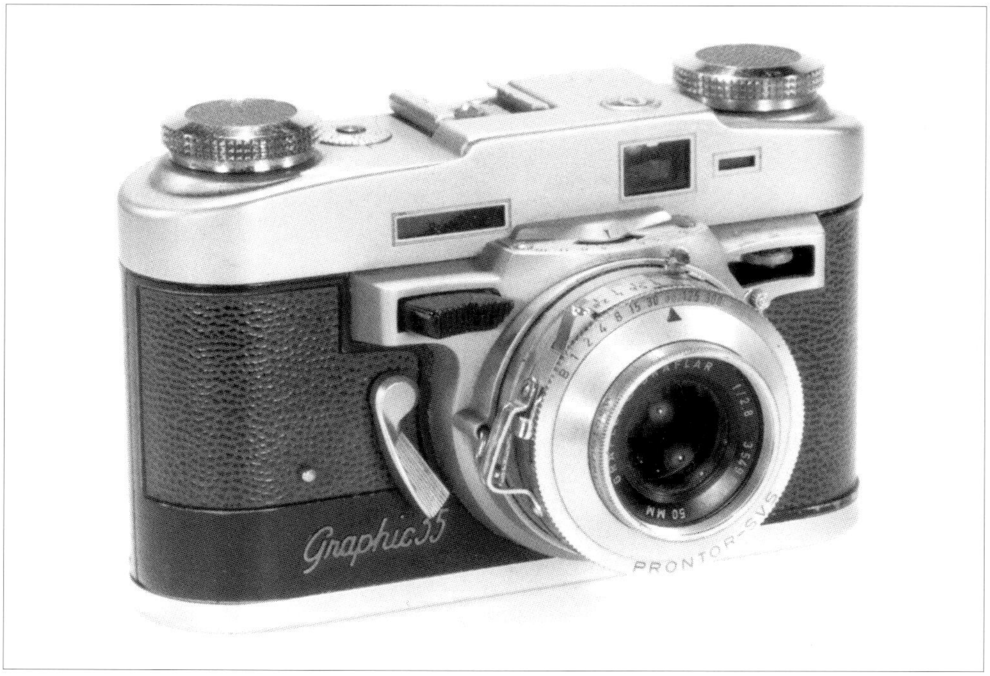

Although the Sportsmaster had the English film manufacturer's name on it, the camera was made for Ilford by Dacora in Germany, and they produced their own version in 1961, calling it the Dacora-Matic 4D. Watch out too for the Electra-II, yet another version of the same camera, still made by Dacora, but this time for Hanimex.

Graflex was a company that often took a different look at camera deign and the Graphic 35, made in America in 1955 with a lens and shutter imported from Germany, is no exception. With the camera at eye level, the photographer's two index fingers fall on a couple of buttons, one on each side of the lens. Pushing the right one focuses the lens towards infinity, pushing on the left one, brings it back towards the close focusing distances and focusing can be checked by a split image rangefinder that sits in a small window to the left of the viewfinder.

And the shutter release? That's beneath one of those focusing buttons, just beside the lens. It is released by flicking it sideways with the middle finger and without having to remove the index fingers from the focusing buttons, making focusing and shutter release very fast indeed.

Film wind on the Graflex Century 35 is by a lever beneath the lens.

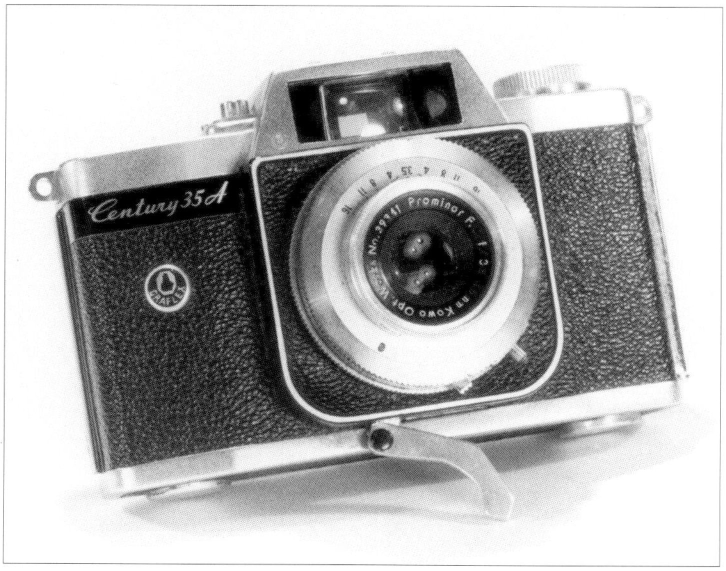

Winding methods

Graflex also had some interesting ideas about film winding. The Century 35A was made for the company in Japan by Kowa and uses a curved lever that folds down from beneath the lens to advance the film. Operated by the left hand whilst the right hand releases the shutter, it provides an interesting method of rapid fire and wind.

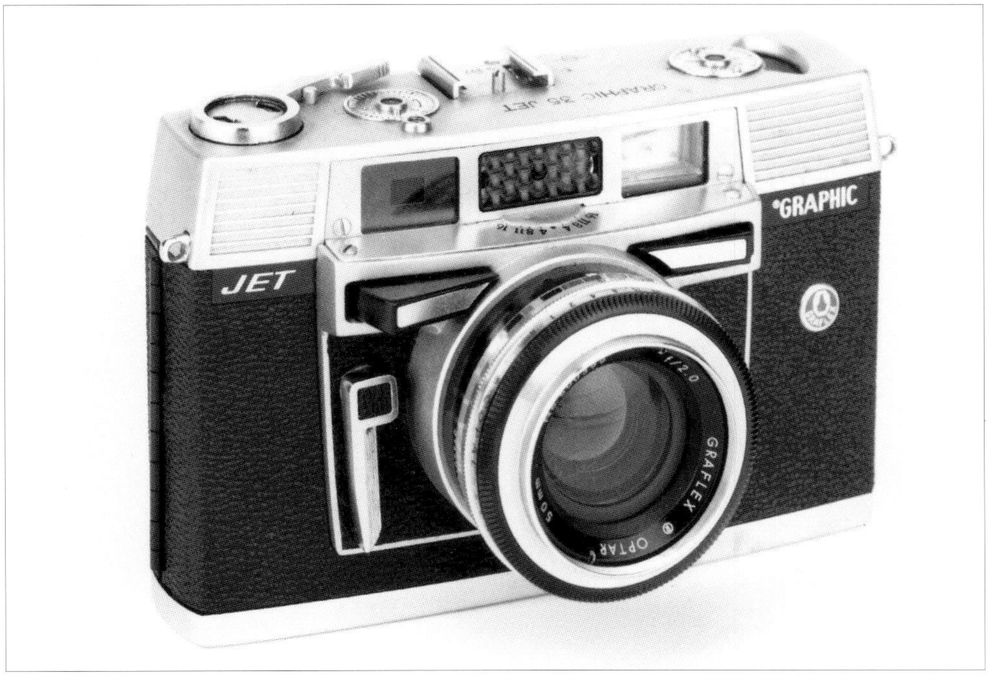

The Graphic Jet uses gas to advance the film.

Centre: Film wind on the Werra is by a collar around the lens.

Below: The rod protruding from the side of the Penti advances the film.

But Graflex's most unusual method of film winding came with the Graphic 35 Jet, also made for the company by Kowa in 1961. This one uses a mechanism driven by small cylinders of carbon dioxide. If you can find one still working today, you have a rare and valuable camera, but in most that are found on the collector's market the mechanism has long since stopped working.

More reliable - and a lot easier to buy today - is the Werra, made by Carl Zeiss Jena in the 1950s. At first sight there's no sign at all of the film wind because this 35mm camera has its winding mechanism built into a ring around the lens barrel. Twist it just under a quarter turn and the film advances one frame.

The half-frame Penti, made by Pentacon around 1959, is similar in so far as it appears at first to have no visible method of winding the film. That is, until the shutter is pressed, when a rod springs out from one end of the body. Push it in again and the film winds to the next frame.

A similar, but better made, system is used in Voigtlander's series of Vitessa cameras that first appeared in the 1950s in which a plunger protruding from the top plate is depressed to advance the film. The Vitessa T, made in 1957,

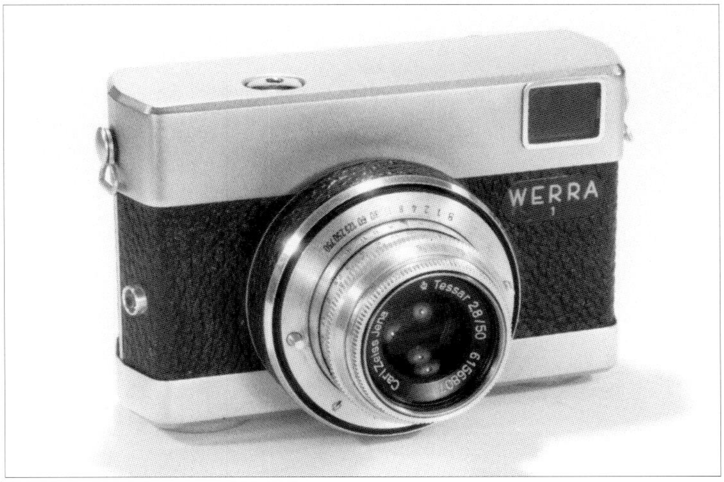

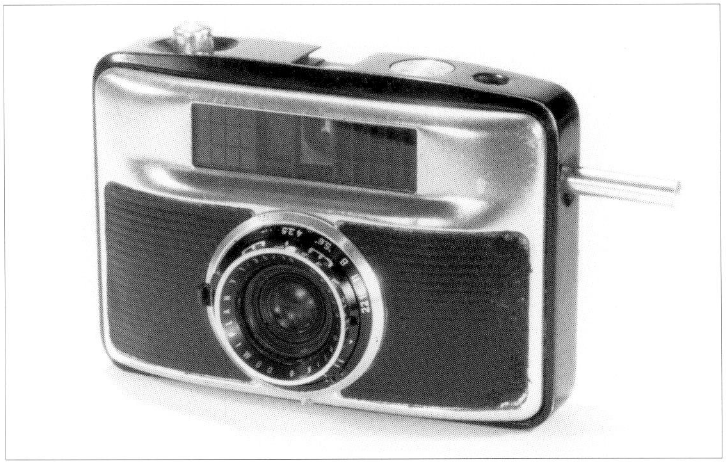

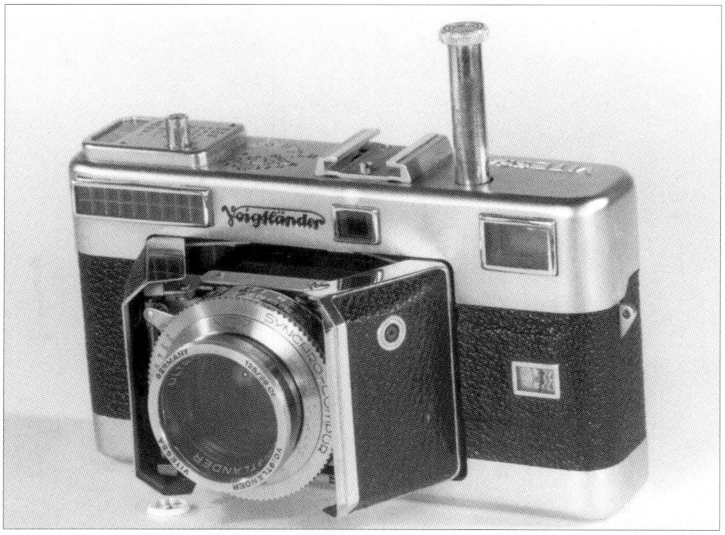

The Vitessa uses a plunger to wind the film.

has a rigid body. Other models - which include the original Vitessa, the Vitessa L and Vitessa N - use double doors that spring open to reveal the lens. These are often called barn doors or sometimes referred to as bomb doors.

The Agimatic, made by the English company Agilux in 1956, combines the wind lever with the shutter release. The lever is to the side of the lens and is depressed with the index finger of the right hand. First pressure releases the shutter, but then continuing the downward stroke winds the film as well. The actual wind-on mechanism is by way of a sprocket that engages the film and a friction driven take-up spool. However, when the lever is in its rest position, just prior to releasing the shutter, both the take-up spool and the sprocket are free to move backwards, thus doing away with the necessity of a rewind button to release them. A disc, mounted on the feed shaft and seen through a window in the top plate, revolves as the film is wound in either direction. Rewind is by a lever, rather than the usual knob.

The Agimatic offers interchangeable lenses via a bayonet mount that is interesting because it's the mount that rotates, not the lens. The standard lens is a 45mm f/2.8 Agilux, but an 85mm medium tele was also available, when a mask incorporated in the viewfinder could be slid into place to give the field of view.

The camera has a built-in rangefinder in the viewfinder, but it is non coupled and its settings have to be transferred manually to the focusing ring. A second window in the back of the camera incorporates a built-in extinction meter.

Mercury II

Everything about the Mercury II is impractical... which is what makes it such a collectable item today. The camera was made by the Universal Camera Corporation in America, a company that seemed to have the knack of producing new concepts in design that failed to impress the public (see the Minute 16 on page 94). They introduced the first model Mercury in 1938 with a very similar design to the model II, but using a special 35mm size film, wound onto a spool with backing paper. That didn't go down too well so, in 1945, they introduced the second model for use with standard 35mm cassettes - about the only thing about the camera that was conventional.

The first thing that sets the Mercury II apart from other cameras is the strange semi-circular hump protruding from the top plate. It's engraved on both sides with a scale, labelled 'Depth Of Focus'. The reason for the hump is the camera's rotary shutter - a metal disc that revolves in the film plane, and because it is circular in shape, it protrudes from the top of the camera inside that hump.

The next unusual design concept is the two knobs on the front of the body, one each side of the lens. The one on the left is the film wind knob, unusual but not unique because the Contax I had its film wind knob in the same place in 1932. Unlike the Contax, however, this one is geared to a disc to its side that rotates as the film is wound to indicate the number of exposures that have been made.

The knob on the other side of the lens sets the shutter speed by pulling and turning, but only after the film has been advanced. Doing that turns the shutter speed knob as well and the indicated setting is accurate only when the film has been wound on. Before that, the indicator points to the wrong speed on the dial. It

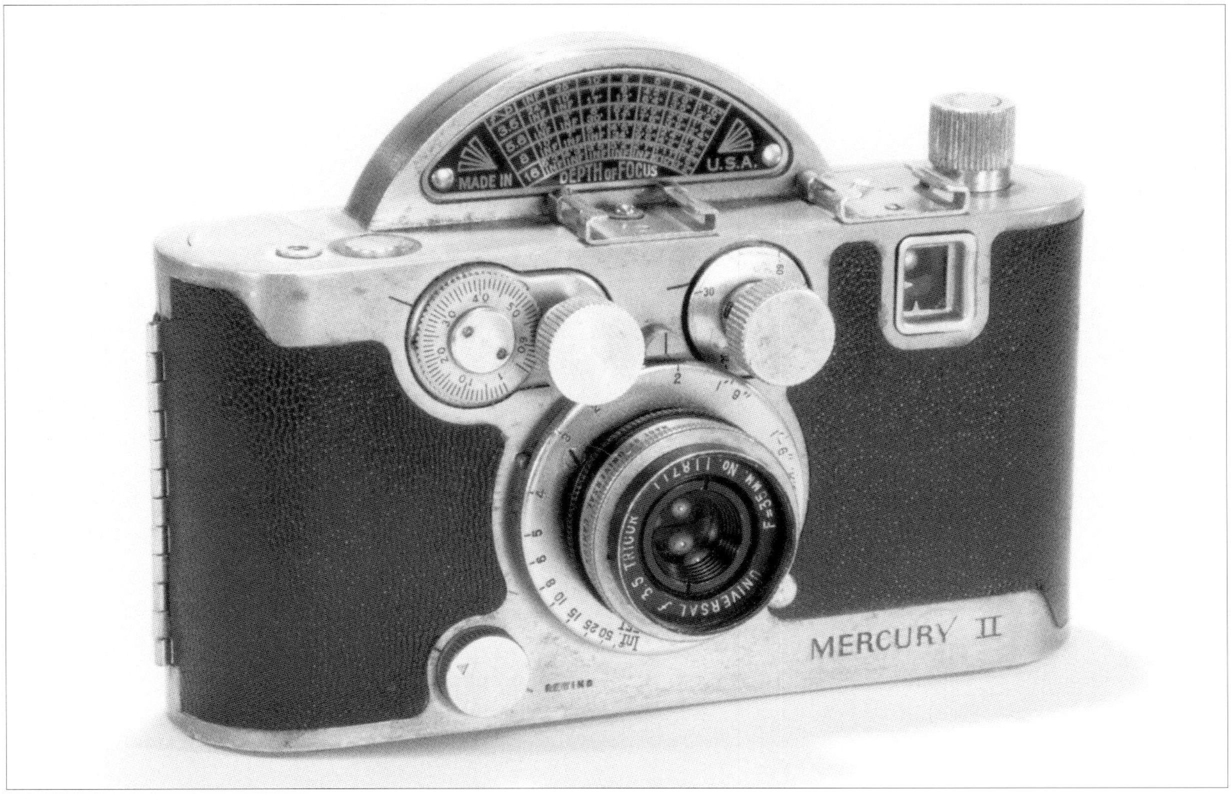

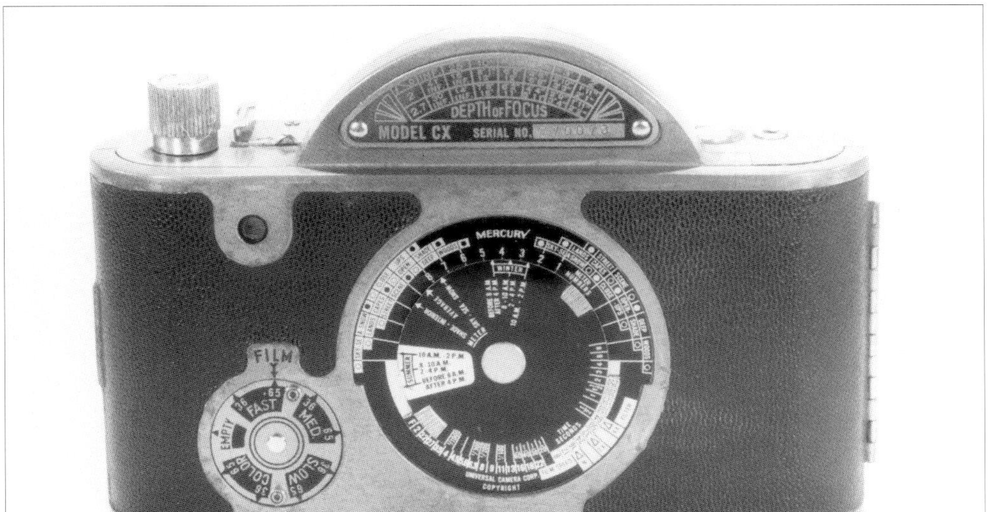

The Mercury II, an unusual design from the Universal Camera Corporation.

The complicated exposure calculator built into the back of the Mercury II.

comes as no surprise to discover that the shutter speeds run in a strangely erratic sequence: 1/20, 1/30, 1/40, 1/60, 1/100, 1/200, 1/300 and 1/1000 seconds. There are also T an B settings. Surprisingly, the aperture setting around the lens and the focusing, by means of a lever that rotates the lens mount, screwing the lens back and forth, are quite conventional.

The film format, however, isn't. Despite being a fairly large camera, measuring 14 x 9 x 3.5 cm, the format is half frame. So you can expect 72 frames out of a 36-exposure cassette. Wrong. The counter only goes up to 65.

And the way the back is opened is a little

worrying too. It involves pressing a small button on the baseplate, in exactly the same place as, and looking exactly like, the usual rewind button. Photographers of the 1940s must have found that a little confusing when, after taking their 65 pictures, they decided to rewind the cassette and found they'd popped open the back of the camera instead! The real rewind control isn't a button at all. It's a knob, on the front of the body, just below and to the left of the lens, that turns through a full 180 degrees.

On the top, there's a shutter release button, but the threaded socket for a cable release that you usually expect in the middle of the button is actually beside it embedded in the top plate.

There are two accessory shoes. The one in the middle of the top plate has a stud in its centre which makes a connection with a flashgun - an early form of hot-shoe, but one that was designed for bulb flashguns, not electronic flash. The other shoe is to the side but you can't put a conventional rangefinder in it because it bumps into that hump on one side or the rewind knob on the other, and the hump would either block the eyepiece or prevent use of the distance measuring dial. That is why the Mercury's own rangefinder was designed to be used verically, not horizontally. The second shoe also houses the Mercury II's own exposure meter.

Then there is the exposure calculator, mounted on the back of the camera beside a film type reminder. The calculator takes the form of three, flat metal discs, one embedded in the camera back, the other two revolving on top of it. First move is to set the film speed by turning the middle disc so that the speeds engraved on the lower part of it line up against one of three arrows on the bottom disc. There's the option of setting the speed against 'N' for normal, or against '2x' or '4x' to allow for filter factors. Setting film speed 100 against the '2x' mark, for example, resets film speed 50 against the 'N' mark. In other words, it's compensating by giving an extra stop of exposure when a filter with a 2x factor is fitted.

As the top of the three discs is rotated, it turns the middle one too, so that the film speed setting remains constant. On this middle disc are found the options of working on the 'Summer' side or the 'Winter' side. Choosing, for example, the segment marked 'Summer' the photographer now has the choice of three times of day, each identified by a small arrow: '10 a.m. - 2 p.m.', '8 a.m. - 10 a.m. and 2 p.m. - 4 p.m.', or 'before 8 a.m. and after 4 p.m.' The time of day is set against one of several scenarios detailed on that lower disc. These include 'sky, sea and snow', 'close-ups', 'landscapes', 'open shade', 'street scenes', and 'deep woods'. With all of that completed, shutter speeds are then read off against apertures on the lower part of the disc.

Simple when you know how!

Canon Dial

In 1963, Canon produced a camera in a unique design never seen before or since. It was called the Canon Dial, the name taken from ten lens-like windows that surround the main lens, making it resemble an old telephone dial.

Behind them is a series of different sized apertures, and turning a milled ring around the lens rotates these apertures in front of a cell, making it more or less sensitive. In that way the film speed is set on the camera's in-built meter.

The meter is needed because the Dial is a shutter priority camera. Set the shutter speed on a scale around the lens between 1/30 second and 1/250 second and the camera automatically sets the required aperture between f/2.8 and f/22. Pull out a knob on the front of the camera and you can use it to set the same apertures manually, their setting indicated by a needle moving across a display in the viewfinder.

The Dial is a half frame camera, taking 35mm in standard cassettes to give an image size of 18 x 24 mm. Most half-frame cameras that run the film horizontally through the body end up with an upright image format with the camera having to be turned on its side to shoot the more conventional landscape shot. The Canon Dial, however, differs from most in running the film vertically through the body from top to bottom, so that the image is landscape shape when the camera is held in its normal shooting position.

The way the film is advanced and rewound is also unusual, utilising a built-in clockwork motor drive whose spring is housed in a short, stubby handle on the base of the camera. When the back is open, this handle turns the take-up spool to facilitate film loading. But with the back shut, it becomes the winding mechanism for the clockwork motor. Wind it until it stops, press the shutter button and the film advances one frame after each exposure. Press the rewind button on the side and the film is wound back into the cassette.

Argus C3

If there was a prize for silly camera designs, the Argus C3 would be a prime contender. It's an American 35mm camera that was made for nearly 30 years from 1939 onwards, a brick-shaped design with a thumb wheel coupled, via an intermediary cog wheel, to the lens for focusing. Shutter speeds are set on a dial on the camera's front, apertures on a rotating scale that is inset around the front element of the lens... and therein lies the design anomaly that makes the C3 interesting. Used without any accessories, the camera controls are easy to set. But add a filter or a lens hood and the aperture setting ring is immediately obscured, making it impossible to adjust.

Any other manufacturer might have re-thought their design at this point, but not Argus. Instead, they added a couple of little metal pimples to the aperture ring. Then they sold a special accessory, Y-shaped with two small holes at the end of each arm, designed to fit over the pimples.

Now when a filter or lens hood is used, the Y-shaped accessory is fitted first, so that its tail sticks out the side and can be used to turn the ring beneath the accessories to adjust apertures. Unfortunately, it's still almost impossible to read the settings because the scale is all but hidden beneath the lens hood.

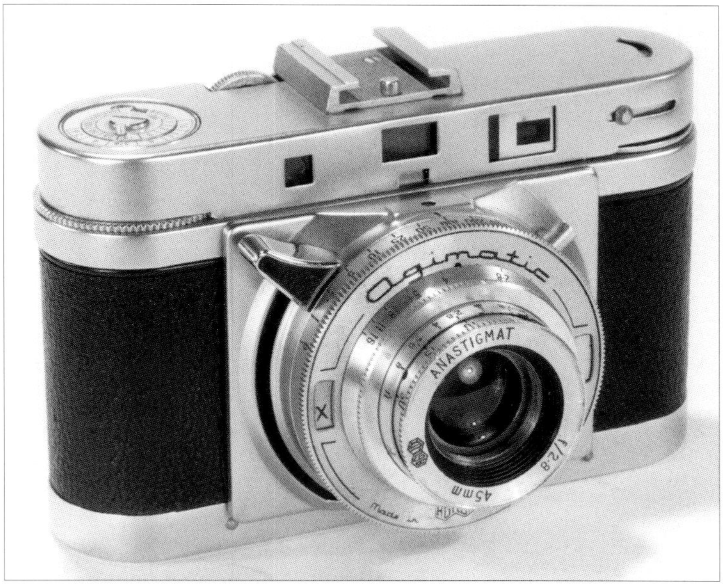

Film wind and shutter release are on a single lever with the Agimatic.

Flash Pixie

Back in the 1950s there was a craze for making sub-miniature cameras (see pages 91-100). There seemed to be no end to how small manufacturers could make their models, but what happened when they wanted to add accessories like flashguns - especially when the camera itself wasn't much larger than a flashbulb of the time?

The result, in one case, was the beautifully ridiculous Flash Pixie, a plastic subminiature made in America by William R Whittaker for

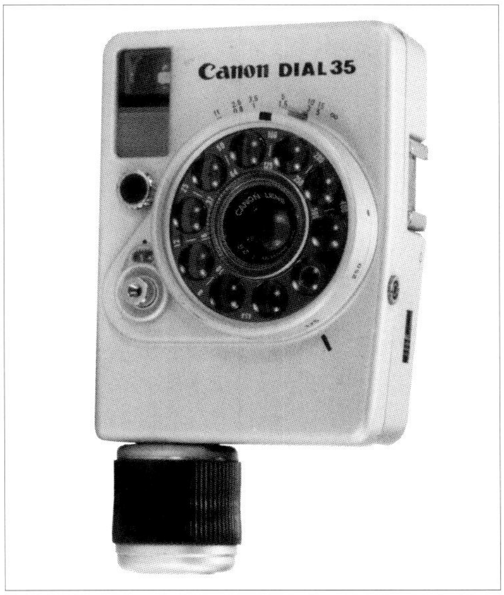

Canon's one-off design for the Dial.

16mm film. It has a fixed focus f/6.3 lens and three apertures designated for 'bright', 'dull' and 'colour'. The version without the flash measures 50 x 35 x 30mm. But a second version adds a flashgun whose battery compartment alone is nearly as big as the camera itself... and the flashgun is three times the size of the camera!

The Flash Pixie's flashgun is bigger than the camera.

Akarette

The Akarette was made by Apparate und Kamerabau in Germany and launched in 1952. Its unusual feature is that it has two viewfinders, side by side: one for the standard 50mm lens, the other for a medium telephoto 75mm. The viewfinders are selected by a switch on the front of the camera which opens one whilst masking the other and, at the same time, putting a red dot in the front window of the one not in use

In 1953, the Akarette was renamed the Akarelle and made with a lever wind in place of the knob on the Akarette. It was slightly modified again in 1955.

Sirius Action Tracker

A lot of manufacturers produced half frame cameras, delivering two images to a standard 35mm frame. But how about quarter frame - four tiny images on a 35mm 24 x 36 mm frame? That's the format used by the Sirius

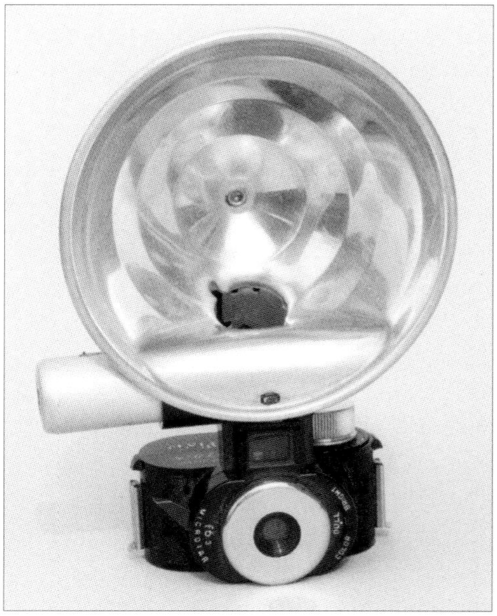

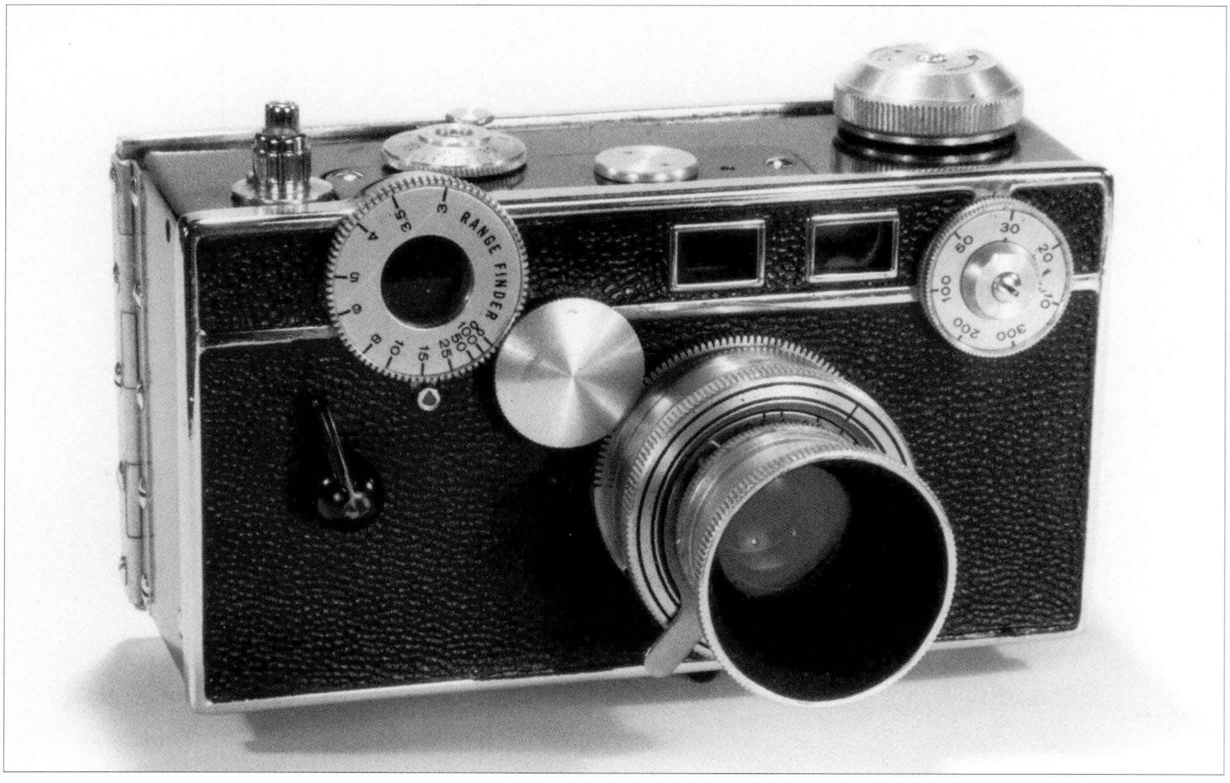

The Argus C3 found a novel way to set apertures.

Action Tracker, a camera very much of the 1980s. It features four lenses, each with its own shutter and, as the release is pressed, each one is fired in turn, one after the other. The idea is to capture sporting sequences, but it never really took off and, a few years after its launch, the Action Tracker was being sold off at under £5 a time by photo dealers who were stuck with them on their shelves. Today, it's a collector's item.

Mimosa I

Although cameras in general have adopted all sorts of different shapes and sizes, the 35mm camera, after a few experiments with style in the early days, gradually settled down to a fairly conventional and easily recognisable shape. But there were exceptions, and one of them is the Mimosa, a 35mm model that looks more like a box camera.

The Mimosa was made by Mimosa AG in Dresden, the first model in 1947, a second model in 1950. The easiest way of telling the two apart is to look at the viewfinders. A small frame finder folds up from the top of the model I, whereas the model II has an optical viewfinder built into the body. The first model has a range of shutter speeds from 1 second to 1/250 second, an f/2.9 lens that stops down to f/16 and focusing from 0.6 metres to infinity.

The camera attains its box like appearance by placing the film chambers much closer to the lens than usual, coupled with a deeper than expected body. It means a sharper than normal turn for the film to make as it emerges from the cassette, near enough 90 degrees in fact. To counteract the bowing effect this might cause in the film as it travels across the film plane, a trapdoor hinges down from the top of the inside of the camera and locks at the base, holding the film tight against its built-in back plate. This trapdoor is snapped into position and locked before the back of the camera is attached.

Comet III and Comet 3

Here we have two cameras with the same basic design, each with the same name, but differen-

The Akarette has two viewfinders for different lenses.

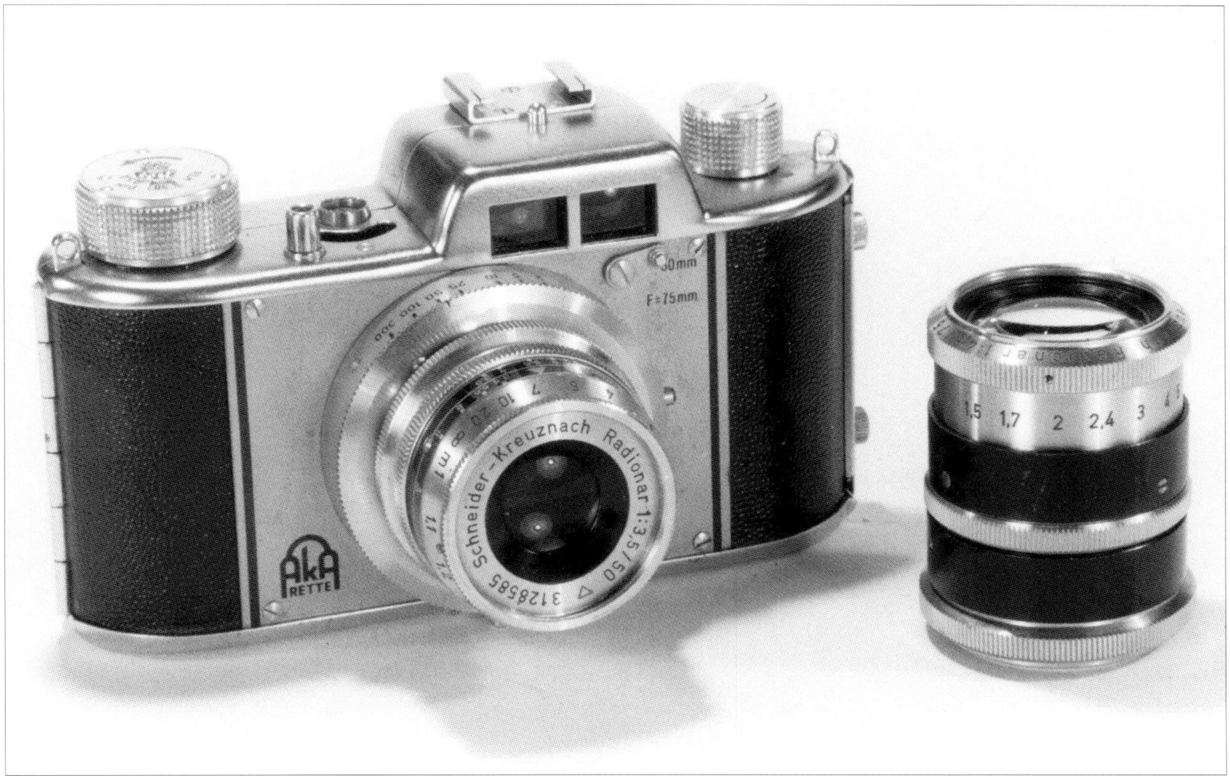

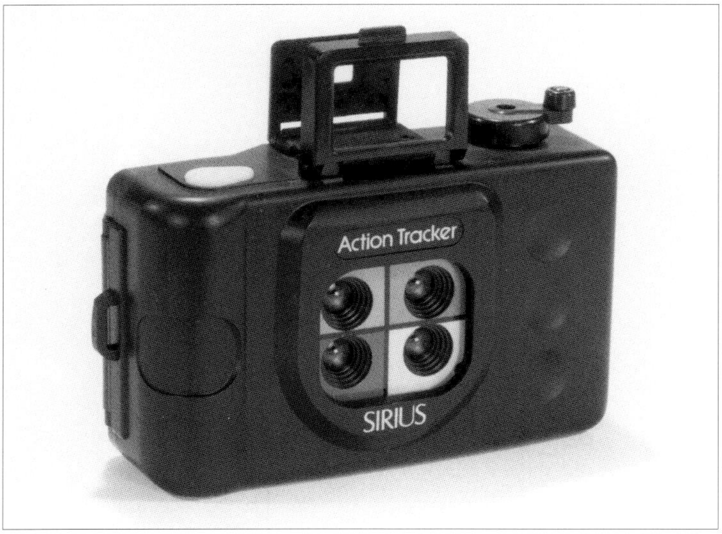

The Sirius Action Tracker shoots four images on a single frame of 35mm film.

Below: The Mimosa is one of the more unusually designed 35mm cameras.

Below right: The Comet III, not to be confused with the Comet 3.

tiated by the use of Roman numerals on one and Arabic on the other. And if that isn't unusual enough, the camera itself is of a weird design, looking more like a small cine camera than a still one.

Comet cameras were made by Bencini in Italy. The Milan-based company made many different types for 126 cartridge film, 35mm, 127 and 120, several of which carried the Comet name. The first model and the Comet II were small but conventionally shaped 127 cameras, the second model differing only from the first by its use of a focusing lens. They were produced in 1948 and 1951 respectively. Then came the third Comet in 1953 - and a radical departure from traditional style.

It's a 127 camera, taking 16 exposures to a roll. But the design is for a tall body with the film running vertically from the bottom to the top. This means that, with the camera held in its correct taking position, the format is horizontal, unlike many 16-on cameras which produce a vertical format from film running side to side through the body.

It's the lens that differentiates the two models. On the Comet 3 it is fixed focus, whilst on the Comet III, it focuses down to 3ft. The shutter offers only 1/50 second and 'B', with the shutter release taking the form of a large lever attached to a wheel that is embedded in the top half of one side of the body. The result is a camera that has a lot of style, despite its unusual design.

Janus

The Janus is two cameras, taking two different types of film, in one body. Point it one way, it's an 8mm cine camera; point it the other way, it's a 35mm still camera. For those twin purposes it has two viewfinders, one on each side of the body.

The Janus was made in Russia during the early 1960s and probably got no further than

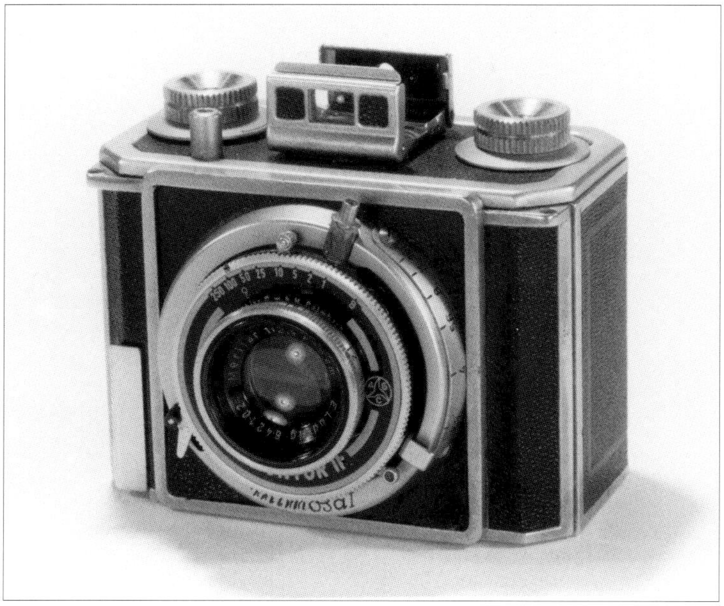

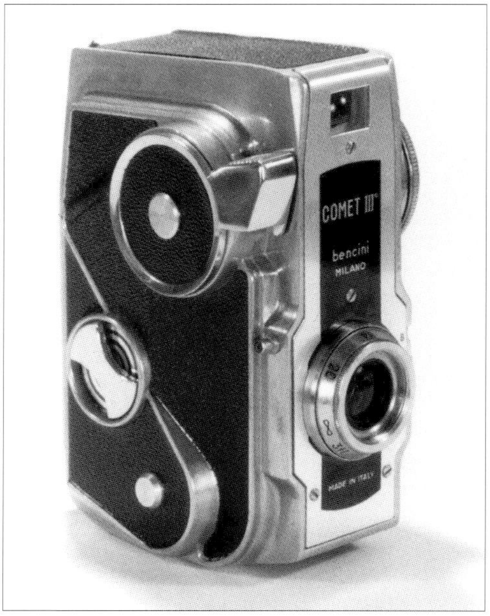

the prototype stage. On the still side, it has a lens and shutter assembly similar to Smena cameras, which gives it an association with the GOMZ factory in Leningrad where Start cine cameras were also made. The lens for the still camera is designated as a 4cm f/4.5 T-22 and shutter speeds run from 1/10 second to 1/200 second plus 'B'. It takes 24 x 36 mm pictures on standard 35mm film.

Turning the camera round, the cine side has an unnamed 10mm f/1.8 lens and the battery-driven motor runs at 16 frames per second. It takes Standard-8 film.

A few cine cameras of the past doubled as still cameras (see pages 171, 177, and 182), but by taking both cine and still frames on the same film. The Janus is probably the first and last example of a model that combined the two functions separately in one camera.

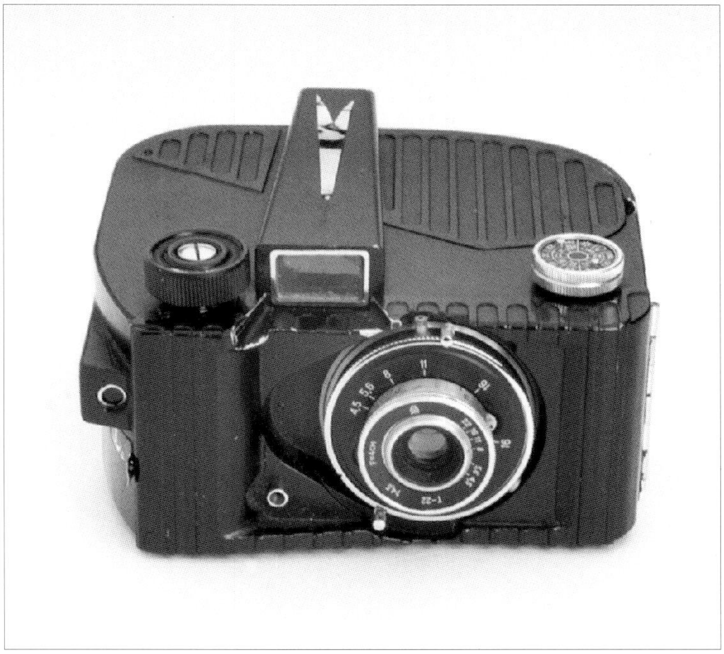

The Janus as a still camera.

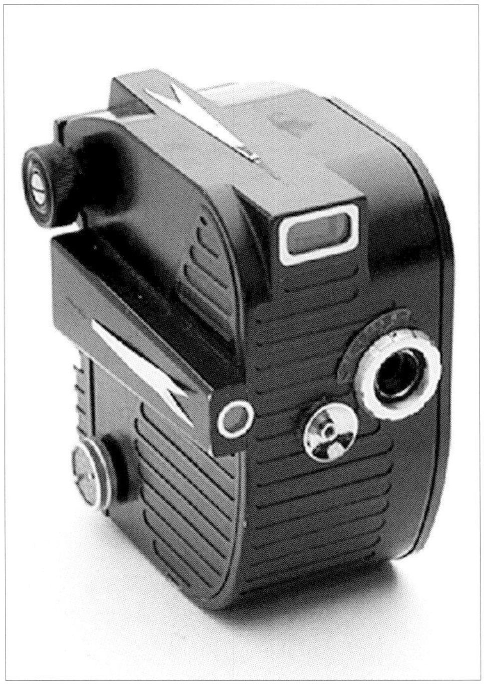

The Janus as a cine camera.

Fotochrome

A very few cameras were made to run the film at right-angles to the lens, with the image projected via a 45 degree mirror. The Tessina (see page 56) was one, the Fotochrome was another.

This unusual-looking beast was made by the Japanese Petri company in 1965, specifically for Fotochrome Inc. in America, who used it for promotional advertising, the cameras being sold door-to-door.

The film runs across the base of the body and, when processed by Fotochrome, yielded direct colour prints, 5.5x8cm in size, without the need for an intermediary negative. The film was originally supplied in its own special cartridges and was made with a single sprocket hole for each frame. As the film is wound across the body, a small pin situated close to the film plane, jumps up into the hole and automatically stops the film at the correct position. As the shutter is pressed, the pin retracts, then moves forward again against the moving film, allowing it to be wound until it springs up again through the next hole, stopping the frame at the next picture-taking position,

The shutter release is on one side of a large hump that houses the lens, with a viewfinder on the other. The camera has a single speed shutter and a meter whose Selenium cell surrounds the lens, which focuses from 5ft to infinity.

The Fotochrome also has its own built-in bulb flashgun that is revealed when a small stud on the side of the lens hump is pushed to flip up the reflector.

The Fotochrome is unusual in having a film path that runs at right angles to the lens. It is shown here with its flip-up flash reflector in place.

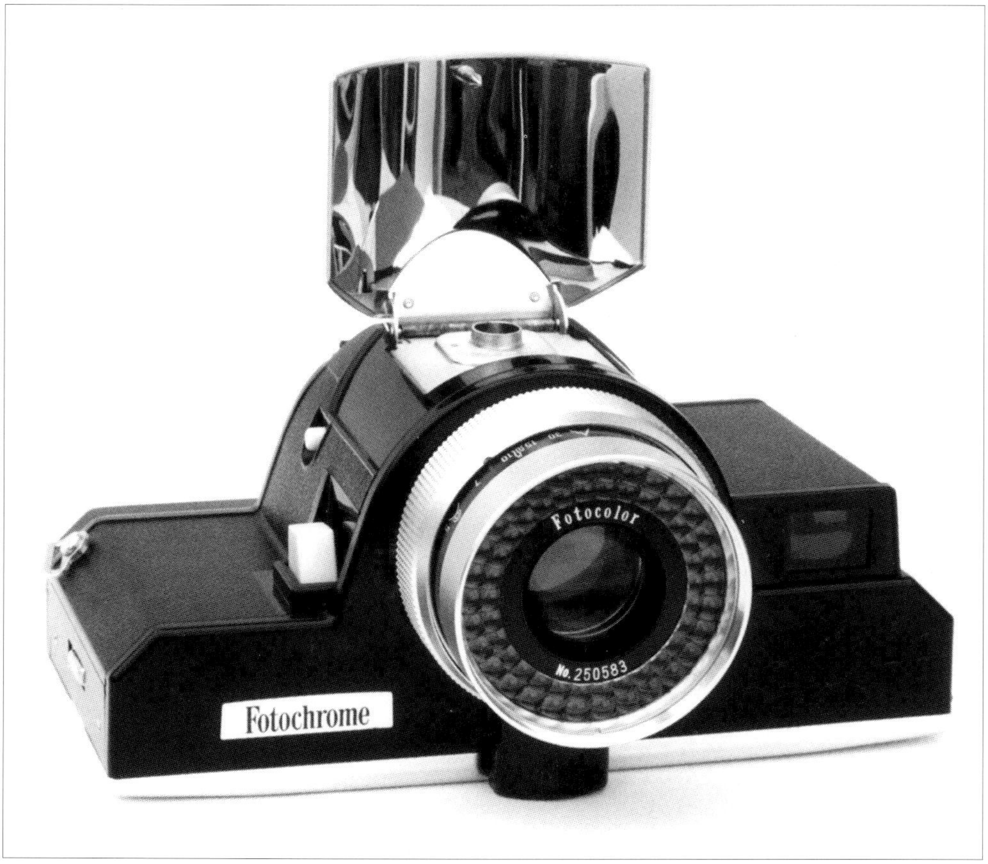

Donald Duck Camera

Mickey Mouse appeared on quite a few cameras, most notably on the Mick-a-Matic, shaped like Mickey's head (see page 121-122). Donald Duck, on the other hand, was a little rarer, but he did make an appearance on this camera, made in the 1970s by Toys Clan in Hong Kong.

It's in the shape of Donald's head, with a lens in one eye and a viewfinder in the other. Inside the head is a fairly basic, plastic 127 camera with twin red windows to produce 16 3x4cm images on a single roll of film. As each exposure is made, the number on the film's backing paper, designed for eight images to a roll, is wound first to window number one, then to window number two and so on throughout the film. The single speed shutter is released by a lever that doubles as Donald's tongue.

A few of these cameras came onto the market in the 1980s, to be bought not only by collectable camera fans, but also by Disney collectors. The supply then seemed to dry up and today the camera is rare.

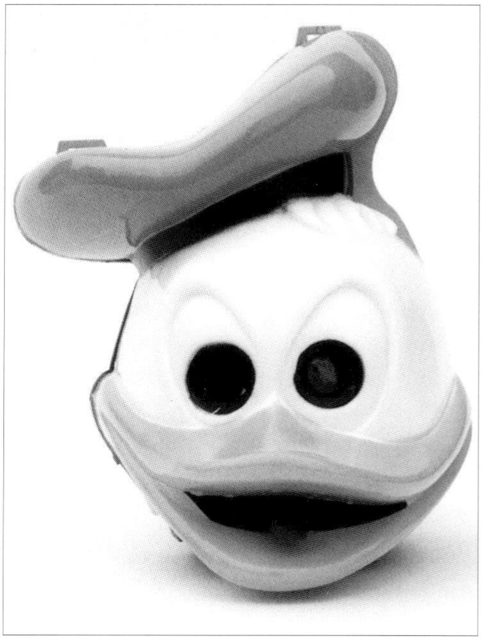

The Donald Duck Camera, collected by camera enthusiasts and Disney fans alike.

The Kookie

The Kookie Kamera might have found a home among the instant picture cameras (see pages 129-136) because it offers a method of both taking and developing a picture. But it's not really an instant picture camera in the Polaroid or Kodak sense. In fact, it isn't really like any other camera at all!

It was made by the American Ideal Toy Corporation around 1968. Shaped like a small Victorian plate camera, it stands on a 'tripod' made of brightly coloured gaspipes supported in a manhole cover. From one side, two hands protrude, one holding a flashgun, the other supporting a tray on which stands a can of tomato soup - or 'toymato' soup as the label suggests.

In fact, the soup can is actually the lens, which is fitted on the camera in place of the lens hood before the picture is taken, and it's no ordinary lens either. It's an anamorphic.

Anamorphic lenses are used mostly in the cinema. Fitted to the camera, they condense the image laterally onto film. Placed in position on the projector lens, they then expand the image again, producing the widescreen effect that comes with Cinemascope.

The Kookie uses the lens to simply condense or expand the image and so produce strangely distorted pictures of people. The instruction book describes these as 'tall skinny pictures' or 'short fat pictures', according to the angle at which the lens is fitted to the camera. With the lens fitted at an angle somewhere between the two, even more strangely distorted pictures are produced in which vertical lines lean to the side and horizontal lines slope diagonally across the frame.

The distorted pictures are what the Kookie's instruction book calls Photogoofs. For indoor photography, the flashgun - or 'flashpot' in Kookie talk - takes flashcubes.

If you actually manage to take a picture with the Kookie, the next step is development, and that takes place in a tank that's fitted below the camera, using the special Kookie film and developer. After exposure, the 'sniper bolt' on the side of the camera is pulled out and a knob turned to advance the film into the tank of developer below. The 'snipper bolt' is then pushed back, cutting the film from the roll.

With the tank removed from the camera, an egg timer fitted to the side of the body and complete with running sand, is adjusted to time development. The tank is gently shaken while the sand runs through the timer for three minutes, after which the developed print can be removed, washed in running water and left to dry.

And as if all this isn't enough, the Kookie was originally sold with a set of paper disguises that included a top hat, false ears, mask and moustache for unfortunate victims to wear as they held a poster with a funny body on it under their chin.

Who says camera collecting isn't fun?

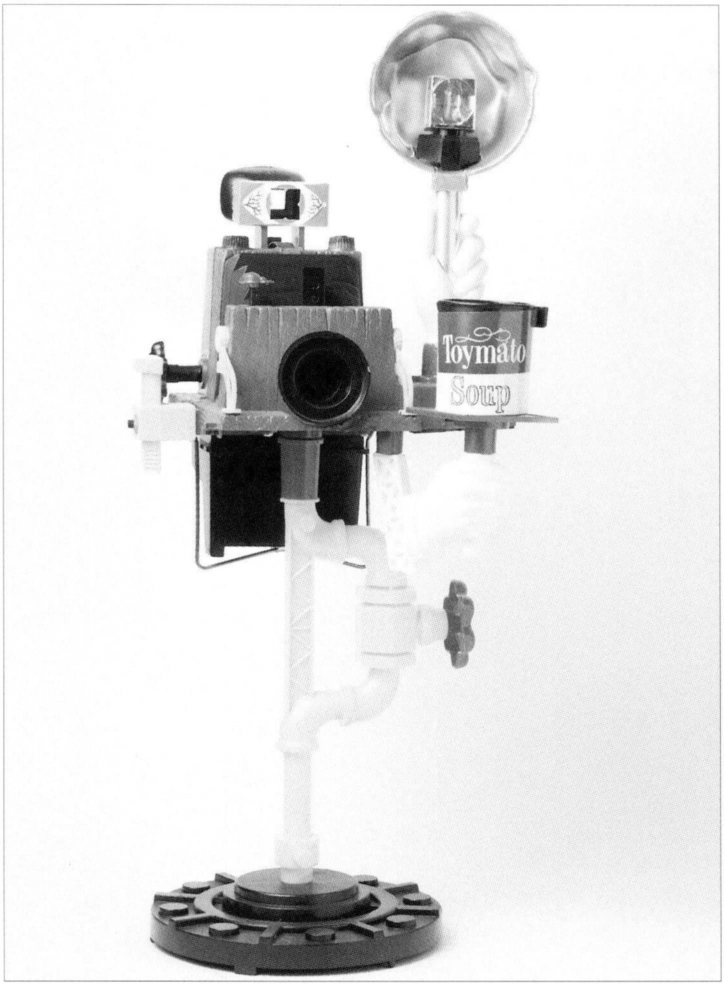

The Kookie takes and develops it own pictures.

Unconventional SLRs

The single lens reflex is probably one of the most popular designs of all time. Most follow similar lines of style, but occasionally there have been radical departures from both design and film format. Here are a few of the more unusual SLRs produced after 1945.

Zeiss Contaflexes

Two features epitomise the 35mm single lens reflex: a focal plane shutter and interchangeable lenses. Contaflex cameras, made by Zeiss starting in the early 1950s, did away with the first and found a different way of tackling the second.

The Contaflex name wasn't new at this time. It had been used by Zeiss Ikon back in 1935 for an unusual 35mm twin lens reflex that was the world's first camera with a built-in photo electric meter. That Twin Lens Contaflex is very collectable today, but didn't win too much favour in its time, the camera being built only until 1939. So the Contaflex name died for awhile until it was resurrected in 1953.

Zeiss made many different Contaflex models right up until the early 1970s. Here, we'll concentrate on the first four, which were the real innovators.

The main thing that sets the Contaflex apart from other contemporary 35mm single lens reflexes is its shutter. Since an SLR allows light through the lens to reach the viewfinder, a method must be found of blocking that light from the film until the moment of exposure. The focal plane shutter was always considered the best method, giving a way of masking the film and timing exposure at the same time. But when Zeiss launched the Contaflex, they broke with that tradition and built the shutter into the lens... and the more you think about it, the more you realise how many problems that causes.

First of all, without the benefit of a blind across the focal plane, light coming through the lens to be reflected into the viewfinder can also leak onto the film. So a separate capping plate must be incorporated to shield the film while the shutter is open for viewfinding purposes.

The shutter must then close, blocking light off from the viewfinder, as the mirror and the plate over the film both swing out of the way. The aperture, which all this time has been fully open to make viewfinding easier, must now close down to its pre-set stop and, finally, the shutter must open then quickly close again to make the exposure. All in a fraction of a second.

All of which of course leads to a very complicated mechanism built into the lens. To provide interchangeable lenses in the usual way, then, would mean similar mechanisms built into each lens and complicated couplings between those lenses and the camera body. So instead of offering interchangeable lenses, the

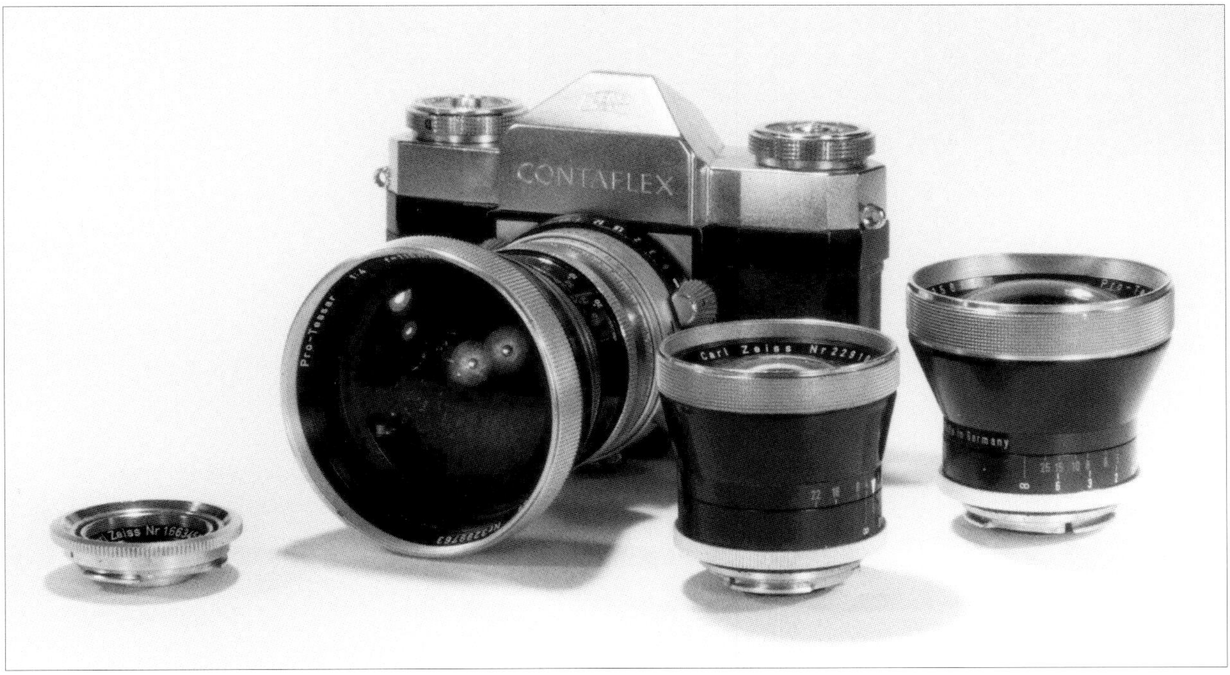

Contaflex III, front element removed and 115mm Pro-Tessar fitted. The other lenses shown are the 35mm and 85mm Pro-Tessars.

Contaflexes adapted the standard lens to produce different focal lengths

Let's look in more detail at how this works. First of all, that complicated shutter and aperture mechanism, which is controlled by the film wind knob and shutter release.

It begins when the film is wound to the next frame ready for shooting. As the film begins to advance, so too does the frame counter. At the same time, the capping plate folds down in front of the film to shield it from light which is about to arrive through the lens. Next, the reflex mirror folds down and into place and the iris diaphragm opens fully, at the same time tensioning a device which readies itself for closing the aperture down again to the correct stop when the picture is taken. The shutter then opens fully and the photographer is ready to view the subject through the reflex viewfinder.

All this happens in the time it takes to wind the film from one frame to the next. The sequence that follows happens as the shutter release is pressed

First the shutter closes. Then the pre-selector iris closes down to its appropriate f-stop. The mirror and the capping plate swing up to uncover the film. The shutter then opens for the set time and finally closes again. All of this takes no more than 1/50 second, whatever the set shutter speed. The design of the Compur shutter which made all this possible was later adopted by Hasselblad.

To get round the problem of having to produce wideangle and telephoto lenses with the built-in shutters, the Contaflex offered adapters in place of complete lenses. On the first two models, this means no more than a telephoto adapter which fits to the front of the standard lens via a special attachment holder. It is called the Teleskop 1.7x, which gives an idea of the magnification it provided. The Steritar stereo prism can also be fitted in the same way.

But on the third and fourth models, Zeiss went for something a little more sophisticated. They made the front element interchangeable on a bayonet mount. To switch to shorter or longer focal lengths, then, the front element is removed, leaving the rear optics and the shutter still firmly attached to the camera body. In place of the front element, a converter is fitted, to combine with the exiting optics and so change the focal length.

The converters include Pro-Tessar 35mm wideangles, 85mm and 115mm telephotos.

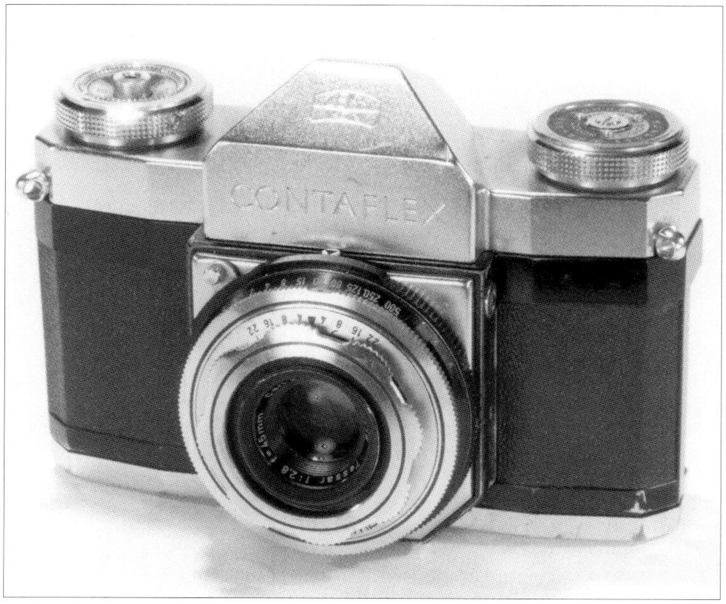

Contaflex I.

The first four Contaflexes look fairly similar, so here's a guide to how to tell them apart.

The Contaflex I was made in 1953 with a 4.5cm f/2.8 Tessar lens and Synchro-Compur shutter speeded from 1 second to 1/500 second. It offers X and M synchronisation which, like all the other Contaflexes that have done away with the focal plane shutter, can be synchronised at any speed. Shutter speeds and apertures are set independently on two rings around the lens. Early models show the shutter speeds unevenly placed around the lens and have no delayed action. On later models, the shutter speeds are evenly spaced and a delayed action device is added.

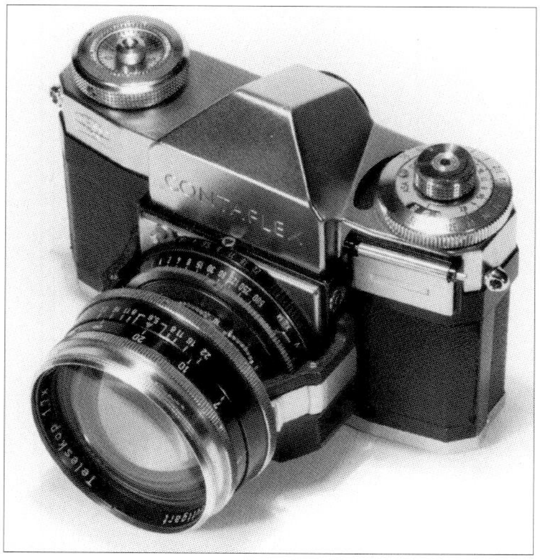

The Contaflex II with Teleskop lens and attachment holder in place.

The Contaflex II, which appeared in 1954, has the same specification but adds a built-in exposure meter. The cell is on the front of the camera just below the rewind knob around which is an adjustable ring marked with shutter speeds on one side and numbers from 1 to 8 on the other. It revolves against an inner scale containing apertures. As the camera is pointed at the subject, a needle moves across a numbered scale inset into the camera's top plate. The appropriate number is then set on one side of the ring above and the engravings on the other side indicate the appropriate shutter speed against each aperture. These are then manually transferred to the controls around the lens.

The Contaflex III, made in 1957, has a 5cm f/2.8 Tessar lens in a Synchro-Compur shutter. But the apertures and shutter speeds - the same as on the first two models - are linked so that, changing a shutter speed automatically adjusts the aperture and vice versa. In order to change the shutter speed relative to the aperture, a small lug on the aperture dial is pulled back, which frees the mechanism and allows the two scales to move independently of one another. When they are linked, exposures can also be set by an EV scale which runs from 2 to 18 in red at 90 degrees to the aperture scale which is marked in black.

Focusing is made easier by the addition of two knobs, one on each side of the lens, and linked to the focusing ring. In use, as the camera is held to the eye with the index finger of the right hand on the shutter release, the two middle fingers fall naturally onto these knobs, giving a fast and accurate method of fine tuning the focus. The Contaflex IV is similar, but adds another built-in exposure meter, this one calibrated in EV numbers to make it easier to set exposures by the EV scale on the side of the lens.

All four models have split image rangefinders; all four position their shutter releases in the centre of the film wind knob and frame counter. Each can be used with a standard cassette of 35mm film which is rewound in the normal way at the end of the roll, or with

Contax Cassettes, the second one in place of the take-up spool, so that the film winds from one to the other and doing away with the necessity for rewinding.

Other Contaflexes, made after the first four, include the Contaflex Alpha, which is similar to the III, but with a Pantar 45mm f/2.8 lens; the Contaflex Beta, which adds an exposure meter to the Alpha specification; the Contaflex Rapid, which has lever wind in place of a knob; and the Contaflex Prima which adds an exposure meter. Then came the Contaflex Super, Super B and Super BC, identified by meter cells in the front of the pentaprism housing; the Contaflex S Automatic and the Contaflex 126, which moved away from 35mm and used the Kodak 126 Instamatic cartridge (see page 119).

Contaflex cameras are beautifully crafted but are not as sought after as the rather more conventional Contarex cameras that began to arrive in 1959. The unusual way in which the Contaflexes tackle shutter speeds and lens interchangeability, however, makes them very desirable to the collector who is interested in the unusual.

Olympus Pen F

From the late 1950s, through to the early 1960s, Olympus flirted with the half frame format - 18 x 24 mm on standard 35mm film. First came the Olympus Pen in 1959, followed by the likes of the Pen S, EE, EES and D, between 1960 and 1962. Then, in 1963, the Pen-F arrived and became the world's first half frame single lens reflex.

The Olympus Pen-F is a system camera, originally sold with a range of accessories that included wideangle, tele and zoom lenses, bellows, copy stand and even a microscope adapter.

It's an extremely sleek little camera, measuring only 12.5 x 7x 7 cm, and with a top plate that shows no trace of the tell-tale hump that houses the pentaprism on a more conventional SLR. That's because it doesn't use a pentaprism, but instead gets the light from the lens to the viewfinder with a series of mirrors that take a rather unusual path.

Remove the bayonet-mounted lens and, inside, the reflex mirror is pivoted vertically so that it moves from side to side, rather than up and down, reflecting its image onto a fresnel screen directly to the left. From there, the image is reflected from a second mirror, up to a third, which turns it right to a fourth mirror that reflects it back and out of the viewfinder. Because this is a half-frame camera with the film running horizontally, the viewfinder image - and the image shape on film - is upright. It takes two strokes of the lever wind to advance one frame

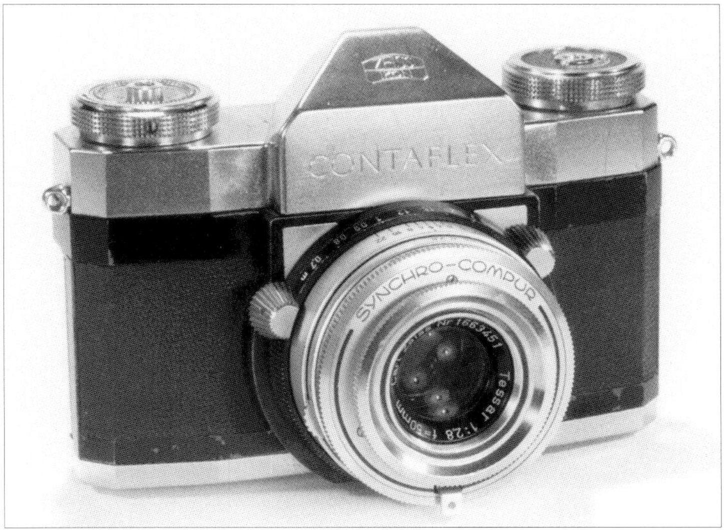

Contaflex III.

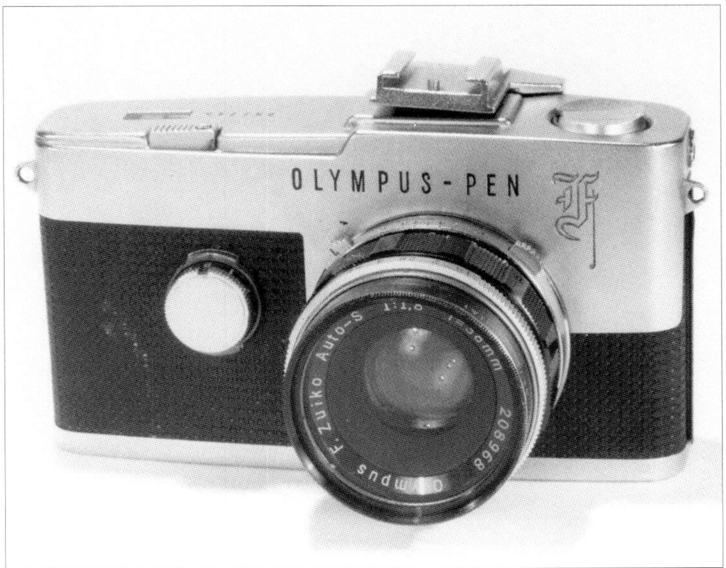

Olympus Pen-F half frame SLR.

The shutter is unusual too. It's a rotary type, made of embossed titanium foil with a semi-circular aperture cut in it. Press the release and the disc spins, stopping momentarily when the aperture is at the focal plane to give the appropriate shutter speed, from 1 second to 1/500 second. Since that aperture is a constant size for all speeds, the Pen-F is unusual among SLRs in being able to synchronise flash at any speed.

You will often find the Pen-F on the collector's market with its own meter. This is a device that bayonets directly onto the shutter speed knob situated on the front of the body beside the lens, after which the camera's shutter speed is set by turning a knob on the meter which connects with the speed control beneath and the speed set is displayed on a rotating scale behind a window in the top of the meter. Pressing a catch on the side frees the knob from the shutter speed scale, allowing it to be turned to select the film speed, indicated in a window on the meter's side.

Pressing a stud on other the side of the meter opens an iris in front of the cell for the reading to be taken. A needle swings across the scale to indicate the appropriate aperture which should be used against the speed that has already been selected. The indicated aperture is then set manually on the lens.

Actually, the meter is rather an eyesore which ruins the smooth lines of the body, which is maybe why it didn't last long. In 1966, Olympus introduced the Pen-FT, which sports the same smooth lines as the Pen-F, but with the attraction of a built-in, through the lens meter.

The Mecaflex

A good few collectable cameras use the square 24 x 24 mm format on 35mm, but only one has ever used this image shape and size in a single lens reflex. The camera is the Mecaflex, made by Metz in 1953 to take 50 pictures on a standard length of 35mm film.

The Mecaflex was designed by Heinz Kilfitt, a watch maker from Munich, who also designed the first Robot camera, which he sold to Otto Berning and Co. in Dusseldorf. (Interestingly, this early example of a camera with built-in clockwork motordrive, launched

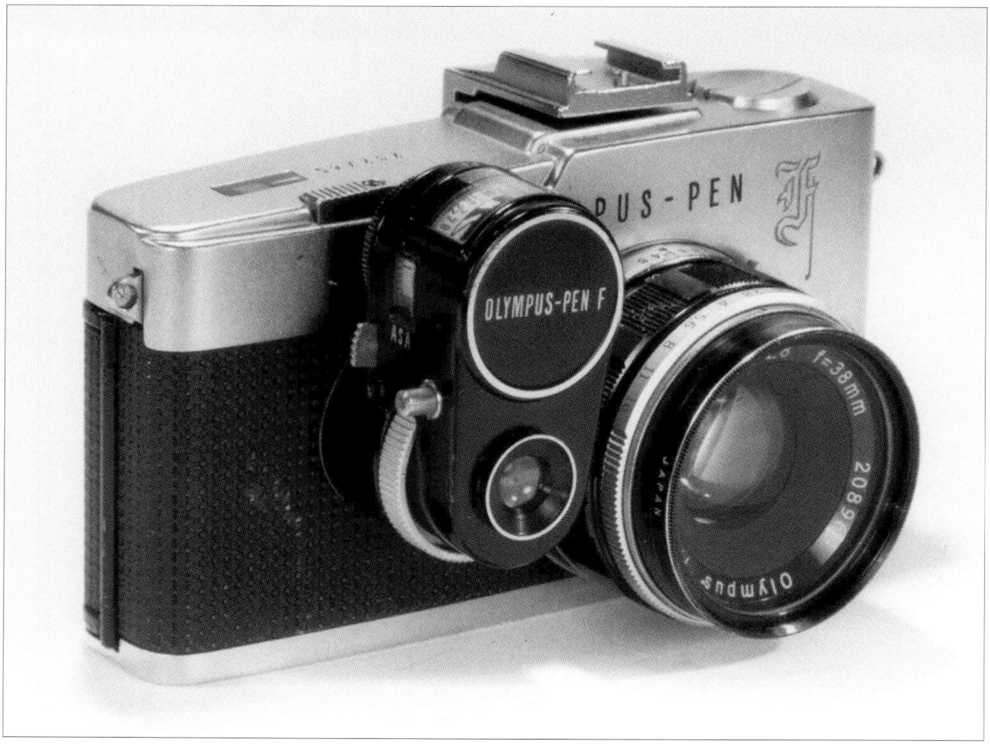

The Pen -F's meter rather spoils the camera's sleek looks.

in the 1930s, also used the 24 x 24 mm format on 35mm.)

Kilfitt sold the Mecaflex design to Metz, better known at that time as radio and television manufacturers. Metz made the bodies while Kilfitt supplied the lenses. Unfortunately the deal went sour, leaving Kilfitt with a lot of lenses and no cameras to put them on. So he had more bodies made in Monacco. Most models were made in satin chrome with black covering and a few were made with brown lizard skin covering. All the cameras are of strong interest to the collector, but those lizard skin versions are the rarest and most collectable of all.

Measuring only 10 x 6 x 6.5 cm, the Mecaflex is a small camera that sits comfortably in the palm of the hand and at first sight, it appears to have no visible controls. In fact, they are hidden beneath a top plate that hinges up at 90 degrees. As that is lifted, a metal focusing hood unfolds and a large, square magnifier clicks into place just above the small ground-glass screen. Unlike most waist level finders, this magnifier, which covers the whole area of the focusing screen, is not designed to be held close to the eye. Instead, the camera is held at waist height in the normal position for using a waist-level finder without magnifier. The magnifier then shows the whole image, which is a boon to composition, but not very good for fine focusing. A square aperture, the same size as the image, can also be opened in the front of the now vertical top plate which couples with an opening in the back of the focusing hood to form a direct vision, eye-level viewfinder.

Also under that top plate, alongside the focusing screen, are the shutter release and single stroke film wind lever with an inset frame counter on the right; a rewind knob, incorporating a film type reminder, on the left.

Moving round to the front of the camera, most controls fall in their expected places. A lever racks the interchangeable lens in and out for focusing, while shutter speeds and apertures are set on their own rings around the lens. A lever at the base of the lens is turned through about 30 degrees to rotate six lugs inside the mount and so release the lens. If you find one of these unusual cameras, look out for two standard lenses: the Kilar 40mm f/3.5 and 40m f/2.8. If you are very lucky, you might also find the 105mm f/4 Tele-Kilar, which for some time was thought never to have been made, but a few of which have turned up in recent years.

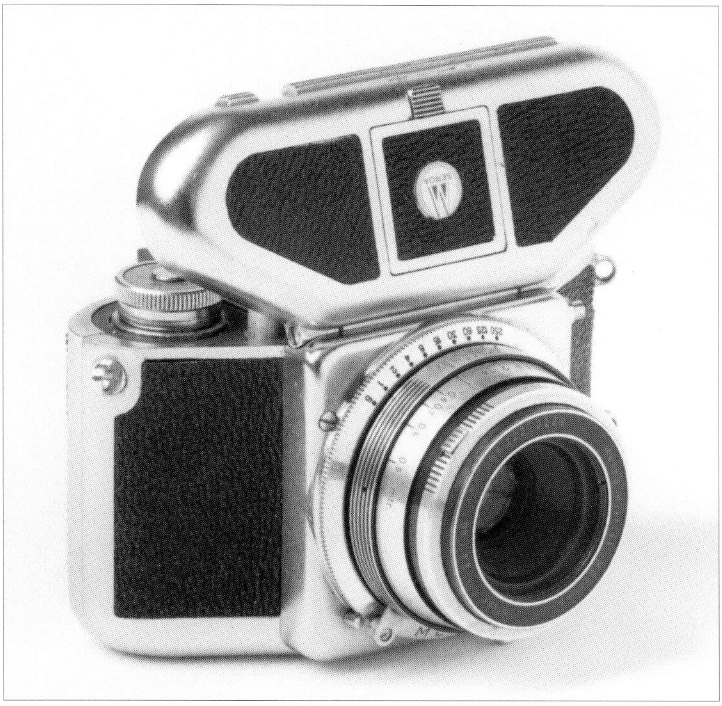

The unusual and very collectable Mecaflex.

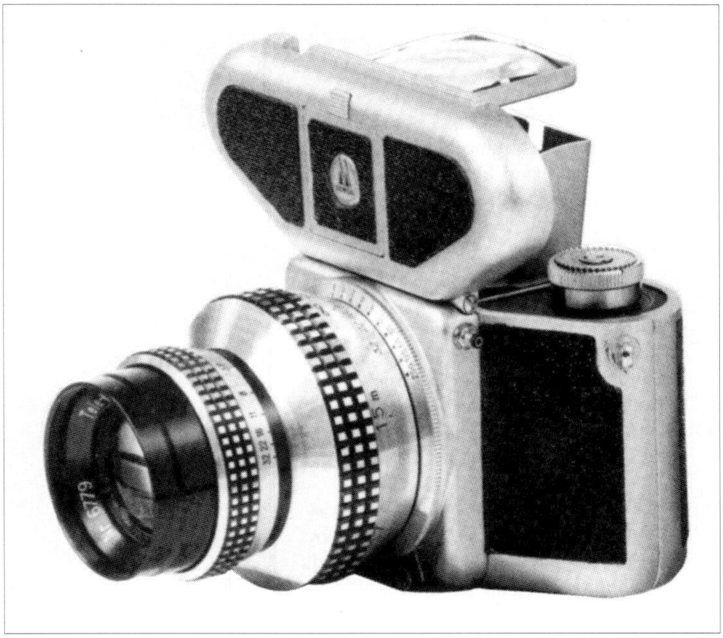

The Mecaflex with its rare 105mm telephoto lens.

Although the controls for setting shutter speeds and apertures are fairly conventional, the way each operates is a little out of the ordinary. The Mecaflex has an early form of automatic aperture stop-down by means of an ingenious series of mechanical linkages between the body and the lens. Here's how it works.

First the film is wound, bringing the reflex mirror into place at the same time. The aperture is then opened to its widest setting to give the brightest image on the focusing screen. To do this, the photographer has to press in a small catch on the aperture setting ring, keeping it depressed as the ring is turned against the tension of a spring. All the time this catch is depressed, the spring pulls the setting ring back towards the smallest aperture, but with the aperture at its widest setting, the catch is released and the ring locks in place.

As the aperture ring reaches its widest setting a quiet click indicates that a small lever beneath the lens had been moved very slightly to one side, allowing a pin to spring out from the body and block its return. Now, when the f-stop required for taking the picture is re-set on the control ring around the lens, the actual aperture remains wide open for easy focusing. As the picture is taken, first pressure on the shutter release retracts the pin, allowing the lever to move back and causing the aperture setting to spring to its pre-set f-number, just before the mirror flips up and the shutter fires. It then remains at this smaller aperture setting until the whole sequence is repeated for the next picture, but doesn't work unless the film has first been wound.

From the rear, the Mecaflex with its eye-level viewfinder fitted.

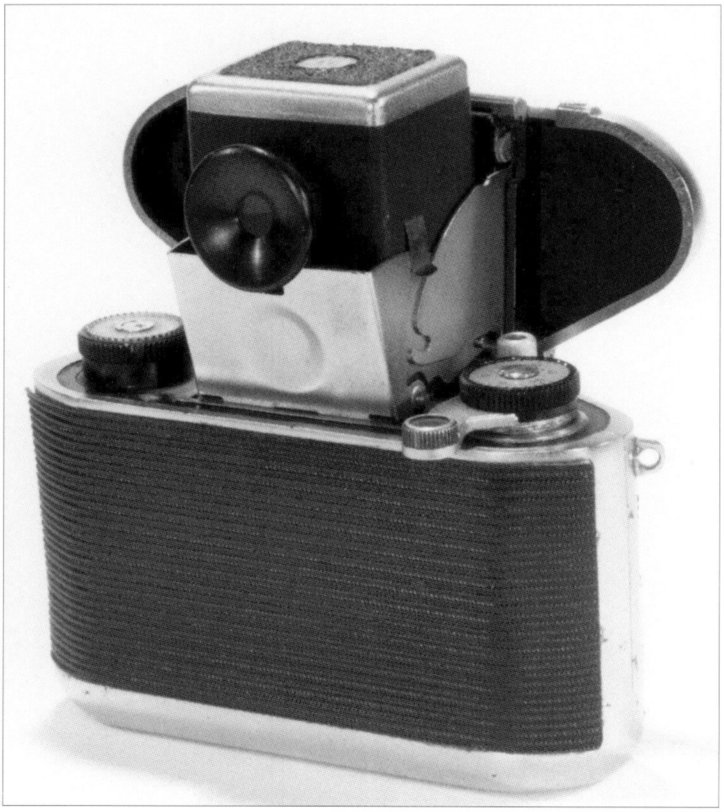

The shutter is a Prontor with X and M synchronisation for electronic and bulb flash respectively, but it is not the focal plane type that might be expected in a single lens reflex. In its place, there is an iris, set into the camera body, behind the lens. As the film is wound, the mirror is lowered and the iris opens to bring an image to the viewfinder, while the lowered mirror blocks light from the film. As the exposure is made, the mirror springs up and the shutter fires, much in the same way as the Contaflex.

With only a few exceptions, SLRs of the early 1950s were mostly built with waist-level, rather than eye-level, viewfinders and the Mecaflex was no exception. It was, however, unusual in offering an accessory viewfinder that fits over the ground-glass screen to convert the camera for eye-level viewfinding. This, now very rare, accessory is little more than a metal box with an angled mirror inside and a lens in an eyepiece to allow viewing of the camera's focusing screen at right angles. It doesn't attempt to correct the laterally reversed image on the screen the way a pentaprism would and if the camera is held vertically, the image turns upside down as with any waist-level reflex, but it did give an early and adequate method focusing a single lens reflex at eye level.

Today, the Mecaflex is a rare collector's item, sometimes to be found in France and occasionally in the south of England. In the mid-1950s, the camera was being distributed by the English firm of J.J. Silber, but there is a theory, by no means substantiated, that the Mecaflex was originally distributed by a company in Hampshire on England's south coast. The company is thought to have gone bankrupt and the salesmen paid off in stock, which many of them sold locally. The story may or may not be true, but the interesting fact remains that collectors and photographers have discovered a fair few of these rare cameras in and around the same English south-coast town.

The Hapyucc

The Russian-made Hapyucc is 16mm single lens reflex which is often regarded as a camera of the mid-1960s, but that is only when it became popular in the West. In fact its Russian origins can be traced back well into the 1950s, when it was first manufactured and tested on the market. At that time, however, it failed to sell and was forgotten about. But the idea failed to die and, a few years later, it was resurrected to gain a small measure of the acclaim it had always deserved.

The camera's first appearance outside of Russia was at the 1961 Soviet Exhibition in London, where it generated a fair amount of interest, after which it disappeared again, leaving behind one of the very few in existence at the premises of Technical and Optical Equipment Limited, the UK-based importers and distributors of Russian photographic equipment.

A British photographic journalist, on a trip to Russia a few years later learned that the Russians, disappointed with the quality of the camera's images, had discontinued it. But in fact, the camera was capable of remarkably good quality and the Russians' disappointment was probably founded more in the quality of subminiature film available to them at that time than in the mechanics or optics of the camera itself.

The journalist, writing in the British Journal of Photography in 1966, describes how he pleaded with the manufacturers to reconsider their decision to scrap the Hapyucc and, maybe swayed by his arguments, perhaps influenced by the fact that the camera still received intermittent favourable mentions in the Western press, the Russians relented and released the slightly redesigned version we

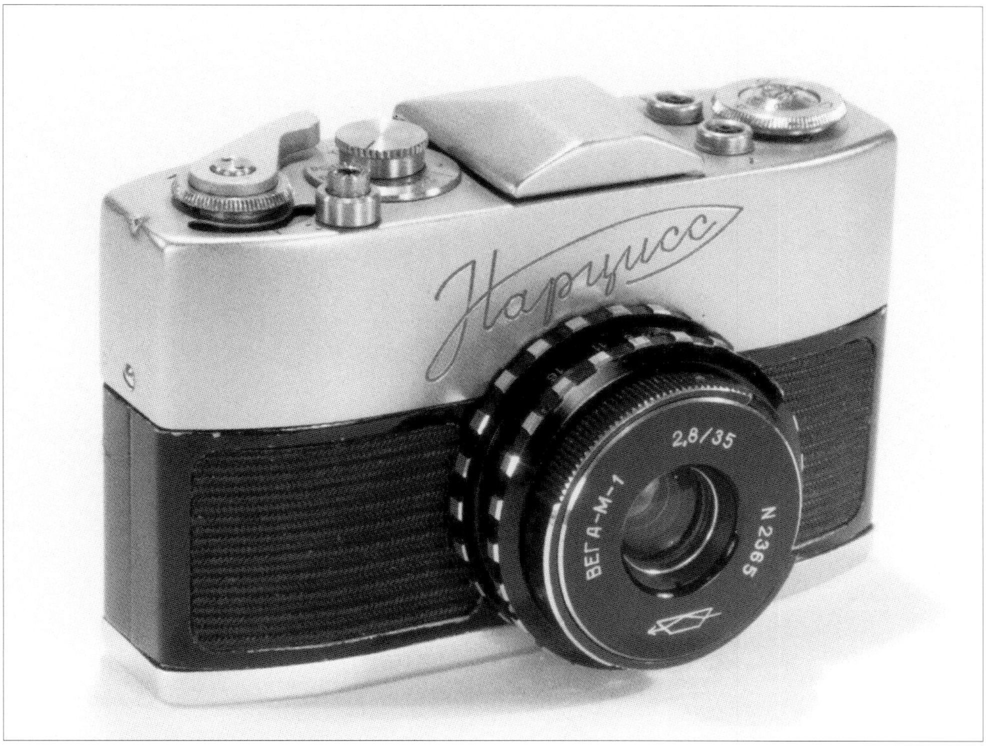

The Hapyucc or Narciss is an unusual 16mm SLR.

now know in 1965.

The word 'Hapyucc' is, in fact, an English corruption of the Cyrillic letters that make up the Russian name on the front of the camera. For export purposes, it was given a different name, the Narciss, a derivation of the word 'Narcissus'.

The Hapyucc is the only single lens reflex built for 16mm film and it is a true system camera, featuring interchangeable viewfinders and lenses. The camera was manufactured by Krasnogorsk Mekanicheski Zavod (Krasnogorsk Mechanical Factory) at Krasnogorsk, a suburb of Moscow. The same factory made many other cameras including the Zorki and Zenith, as well as the FT-2 and Horizont panoramic models and several cine cameras.

The vast majority of 16mm cameras use a twin cassette system in which film is wound from one to the other, but the Hapyucc follows the style of 35mm cameras with film, loaded into its own miniature cassette, slotted into the left of the camera body, wound onto a take-up spool on the right and then rewound back into the cassette at the end of the roll. The original film had no sprocket holes and the image went right to the edge. Without a sprocket feed, the take-up spool was made extra large in an attempt to maintain consistency of frame separation, despite which, the distance between frames did widen towards the end of each roll.

If you buy one of these cameras today to use with modern 16mm cine film, you'll find the quality remarkably good, but beware of the rewind mechanism which can prove difficult for the unwary photographer. Just as with 35mm cameras, before rewinding the film, a button on the base plate has to be depressed to disengage the film transport mechanism and then turned to lock it into position. Once the film has been rewound, this button must be unlocked, allowing it to spring out again. It's all too easy, however, to forget to unlock the control so that the film transport mechanism is left disengaged and the new film fails to transport through the camera as the lever wind is advanced. What makes matters worse is that to load the camera, the back and base are removed in one piece, taking the rewind button with it, an action which frees the control mechanism inside the camera body. So, with the back off, the film advances and everything seems to be functioning correctly, but with the back replaced, the knob in the base once again disengages the film transport mechanism and the film fails to advance.

The format of the Hapyucc is an innovative one for 16mm film. Most 16mm cameras offer film formats of 10 x 14 mm, some are smaller at 10 x 10 mm and a few give 14 x 17 mm. But the Hapyucc produces a relatively massive 14 x 21 mm image, giving up to 30 exposures to a roll of film. In area the image size is about 75 per cent of the size of a 35mm half frame of 18 x 24 mm, and falls into the same 3 : 2 ratio as the standard 35mm format of 24 x 36 mm. The result is a viewfinder image with a familiar shape to a 35mm photographer.

The camera measures 10 x 5 x 5 cm. The pentaprism, which is proud of the top plate on a more conventional single lens reflex is actually sunk into the body, and features an eyesight correction lens that can be adjusted for individual eyesight within plus one and minus two dioptres. The pentaprism itself is removable for an interchangeable waist-level finder that was planned but seems never to have been built.

Although the majority of Hapyucc cameras feature a satin chrome body with black ruberine inset panels, some early models were made in chrome and white. It is thought that these could have been manufactured for use in operating theatres, a fact that seems to be corroborated by the fact that white cameras are to be found as part of a boxed kit, containing specialised medical accessories for use with the camera. Also, an easily removable pentaprism, revealing a ground-glass screen set deep into the body, means that the camera is suitable for mounting on a microscope.

Controls are very much like those on a 35mm single lens reflex, with the lever wind, rewind knob, shutter button and speed selector on the top plate. Inset into the rewind knob there is a film speed and type indicator, with symbols for colour, monochrome and artificial light films and speeds from 16-250 ASA. The cloth focal plane shutter is speeded from 1/2 second to 1/500 second plus B, but the selector knob is unusual in placing the 1/30 second speed after the B setting, rather than between the 1/15 second and 1/60 second markings as would be expected. To get an extended time exposure, the speed dial is set to B, the shutter released and the control button turned in an anti-clockwise direction to lock it open. Turning it back unlocks the mechanism and the shutter closes.

Also on the top plate are flash synch sockets for X and M synchronisation, the electronic flash synch speed being 1/60 second, but there is no accessory shoe to hold a flashgun.

Focusing distances from 50 cm to infinity and apertures from f/2.8 - f/16 are set around the lens, whose focal length of 35mm, gives an angle of view a little narrower than that of a standard 50mm lens on the 35mm format and looks like a short telephoto to a photographer used to 35mm cameras.

The standard lens is interchangeable and the two most common are a 35mm Industar-60 f/2.8 and 35mm Vega-M-1 f/2.8, both in a 23mm screw mount. Very rare today are a couple of 28mm lenses in the 23mm screw mount and originally planned by the Russians to be the standard lenses. These were the f/2 Mir-5 and the f/2.8 Mir-6. A 50mm f/2 Jupiter-17 telephoto was also originally planned by the Russians.

No other lenses seem to have been made specifically for the camera, but since the Hapyucc was made by the Krasnogorsk Mechanical Factory, makers of Zenith cameras, it was originally sold with an adapter ring that allows it to take the full range of Zenith 35mm SLR lenses in their 42mm mount, thus making the Hapyucc the most versatile 16mm camera around.

If you find a Hapyucc in its original outfit, together with the adapter ring, you might also find instructions, a lens cap, four cassettes for manual bulk loading of film, a second adapter to fit the camera lens to an enlarger, an enlarger masking frame for the miniature negative size and spool flange for a developing tank.

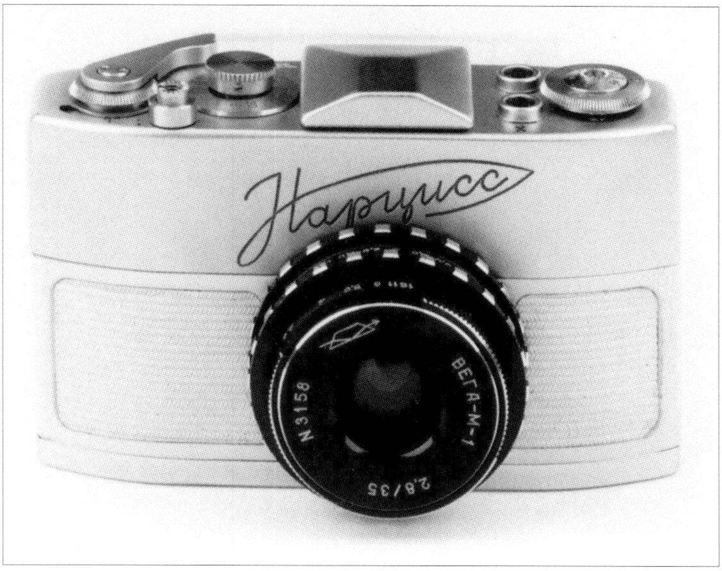

The white version of the Hapyucc may have been made for the medical world.

Test reports of the time suggested that the Hapyucc might point the way to the camera of the future and it isn't difficult to see why. Many manufacturers of the 1950s must have anticipated 16mm taking over from 35mm as the natural miniature format, in much the same way as 35mm had taken over from rollfilm a few decades before. If that had been the case, the Hapyucc or Narciss would not have been the only 16mm single lens reflex, it would more likely to have been the first of a whole new breed of camera.

Komaflex-S

Very few single lens reflexes were ever made for the 4 x 4 cm format on 127 film. In earlier times there had been the 1938 Supaflex Baby, a Japanese copy of the German Karmaflex, made by Karl Arnold in 1932, but these were fairly simple cameras. In 1960, the Japanese company of Kowa introduced a much more sophisticated and attractive camera to support the format and called it the Komaflex-S.

It's an attractive camera that looks a little like a miniature Hasselbald, measuring only 10 x 11 x 6 cm and made with a die-cast body in a grey anodized finish. The standard lens is a

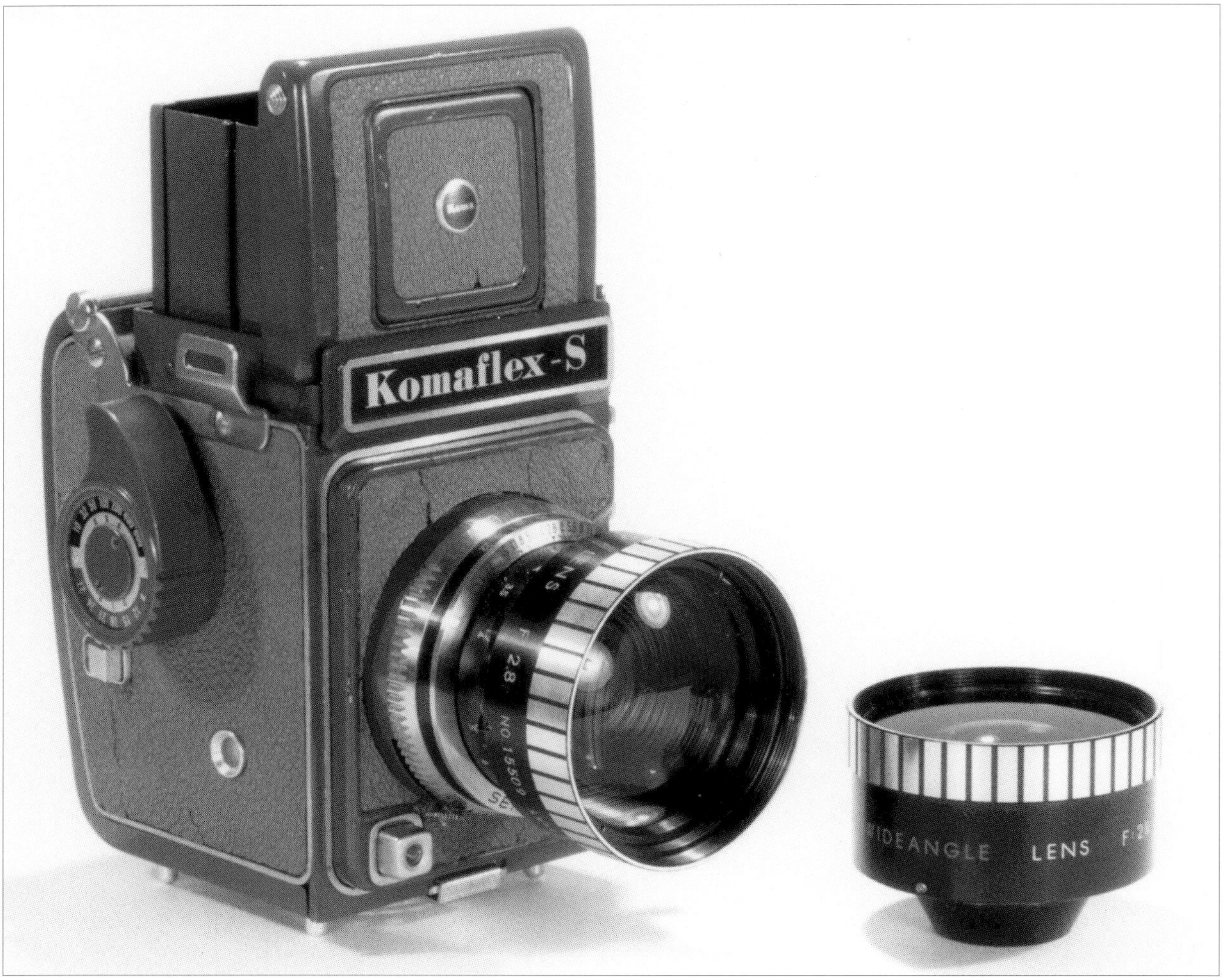

The Komaflex-S with telephoto auxiliary lens attached and wideangle converter beside it.

65mm f/2.8 Kowa Prominar, which incorporates its own shutter. The lens isn't interchangeable, but the focal length can be changed by the addition of two screw-on accessory lenses, made specially for the camera: the Koma auxiliary telephoto and the Koma auxiliary wideangle. Since this is a single lens reflex, their effect can be immediately seen in the viewfinder.

Shutter speeds and apertures are set on rings around the lens barrel and, between the scales, there is a third that links the two and shows EV numbers from 3 to 18.

An usual method of tensioning the shutter can leave the unwary confused. First the film is advanced by twisting a chubby lever on the side, which springs back to its original position after use. As well as winding the film, this also lowers the mirror. The shutter is then cocked by first pulling back on a small catch on the right side of the body, just below the winding mechanism, whilst at the same time pushing down on a lever to the left of the lens. The shutter is then released by a button at the base of the body beneath the lens.

Komaflex-S cameras are fairly rare and especially collectable if you can find one with its auxiliary lenses in their own padded leather case.

TLRs with a difference

THE HEYDAY of the rollfilm twin lens reflex was undoubtedly before the Second World War. It began with the first Rolleiflex in 1928 and, during the following decade, became one of the more popular styles of what were then known as miniature cameras. Following the war, the style continued, most notably with Rollei who still continued to turn out prestigious models, each of which today is not only a collector's item, but also a very usable camera.

The traditional shape, inspired by Rollei, continued most notably in Japan, where twin lens reflexes were made during the 1950s with names that began with almost every letter of the alphabet, from Accuraflex to Zenobiaflex. The reason why there are so many different names for these Japanese TLRs is because manufacturers were keen on changing names mid-way through a production run, so you end up with the same camera sporting several different names. The only letters that seem not to have been used during this period, are 'J', 'U' and 'X'. So if you find a Japanese TLR whose name begins with one of these, you have a rarity on your hands.

But it was in the years we are covering - after 1945 - that the TLR took a turn in direction as unusual new styles began to appear. The theory of having one lens to take the picture and another to reflect its image onto a ground glass screen on the top of the camera remained, but the shape of the camera bodies in many cases changed radically away from the traditional box shape, whilst film sizes veered in all sorts of directions away from the 120 format that had so often been associated with TLRs of the past.

Mamiya C3

The Mamiya C3 does take 120 film, but it earns its place here for being one of a rare breed of twin lens reflexes that takes interchangeable lenses. Until 1956, Mamiya had been making fairly traditional TLRs, but in that year, they launched the Mamiya C, with a different design to any of the others. It was followed, in 1957, by the C2, but the best of the early models is the Mamiya C3, which was launched in 1962.

Unlike other TLRs, the C3 has the taking lens and viewing lens fixed to a metal panel, held in place by a spring lock, which is unhooked to remove and change them. All lenses come in pairs, mounted on their own panels so that, as you change the taking lens, you also change the viewing lens, ensuring that the correct angle of view is always seen in the viewfinder. An eye level finder in the hood can be adapted with masks to show the different focal lengths as well.

Most 6 x 6 cm cameras use 80mm focal length lenses as standard, but the Mamiya C3's standard lens is 105m. An 80mm pair is also available, together with pairs of lenses covering 65mm and 180mm.

The next unusual aspect of the Mamiya is the way the lenses focus on bellows, allowing them to be racked out much further than usual.

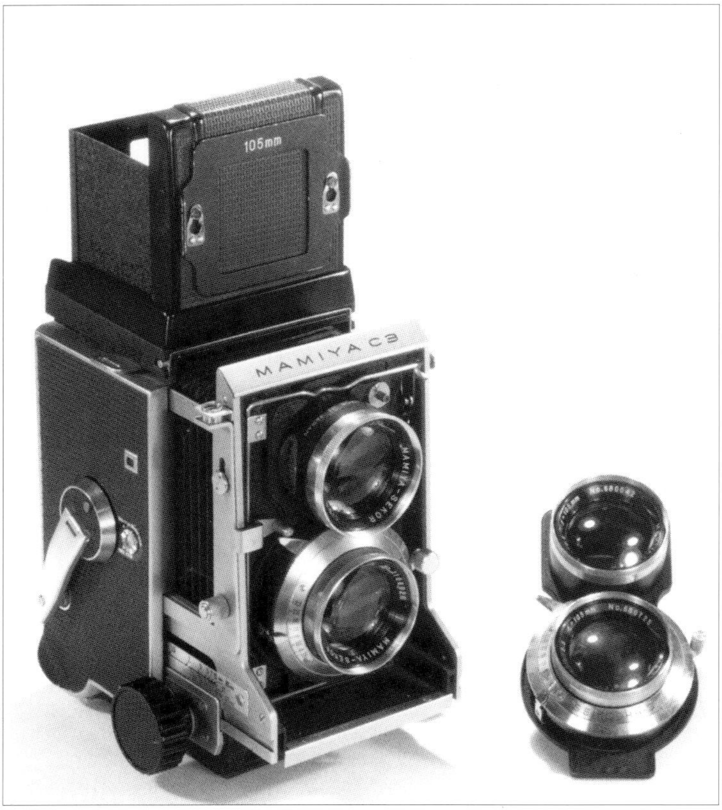

The Mamiya C3 is unusual among TLRs in having interchangeable lenses

On one side of the bellows, the C3 carries a panel marked with curves that refer to different focal lengths, lining up with a focusing scale that runs vertically beside them. In this way the camera indicates the appropriate focusing distances for the different lenses. At its longest extension, the 180mm lens focuses down to 3 ft, whereas, at the same extension, the 65mm lenses focus down to 4 inches, producing images more than life size. The ground glass screen has two horizontal etchings to indicate parallax correction at the closer distances. On the other side of the bellows, another scale indicates the increases in exposure needed at the closer focusing distances.

The film path on the C3 is also a little different from most TLRs in that it doesn't lead the film around bends but, instead, winds it straight from spool to spool. The film advance is by a crank lever, linked to the shutter release to prevent double exposures, but this can be freed by turning a knob beside the crank when multiple exposures are required. The setting is also used when a cut film back is fitted to the camera. Shutter speeds and apertures are selected on scales around the taking lens and each of these has its own shutter built in.

Various models of the Mamiya C series were made right up until the 1990s.

127 TLRs

The natural progression from the 120 TLR was to make one for 127 film, something Rollei did very successfully with the Baby Rolleiflex in 1931. Because 127 film was not numbered for 12 exposures at that time, Rollei introduced the crank wind with this model, an idea that was subsequently used on all their larger models later. Further examples of the Baby Rolleiflex continued to be launched after the Second World War as well. In 1957, another version was introduced, made in grey, with an f/3.5 Xenar lens. These are more common today than the pre-war models, but rarest of all is another black version, made in 1963. To check if you have the common one or the valuable one, look at the serial number. If it's above 2,000,000, you've got the rarer version.

The craze for 127 TLRs continued through the 1950s with Yashica getting in on the act with the Yashica 44, 44A and 44LM. You'll find them in a range of colours that includes black, grey, lavender, brown, blue and red, although not all models are found in all colours. Of the three models, the LM, made in 1959, is the only one with a built in meter. The cell above the viewing lens deflects a needle that swings across a scale of numbers which are transferred to an adjustable calculator set into the film wind knob. The resulting shutter speeds and apertures that are indicated are then set manually on the camera by means of two thumbwheels either side of the lens panel, between the taking and viewing lenses.

Ricoh leapt on the 127 TLR bandwagon in 1959 with the Ricoh Super 44. This one sports an f/3.5 Riken lens, shutter speeds from 1 second to 1/400 second and focusing from 1 metre to infinity. The knob which focuses the lenses works in conjunction with a depth of field scale.

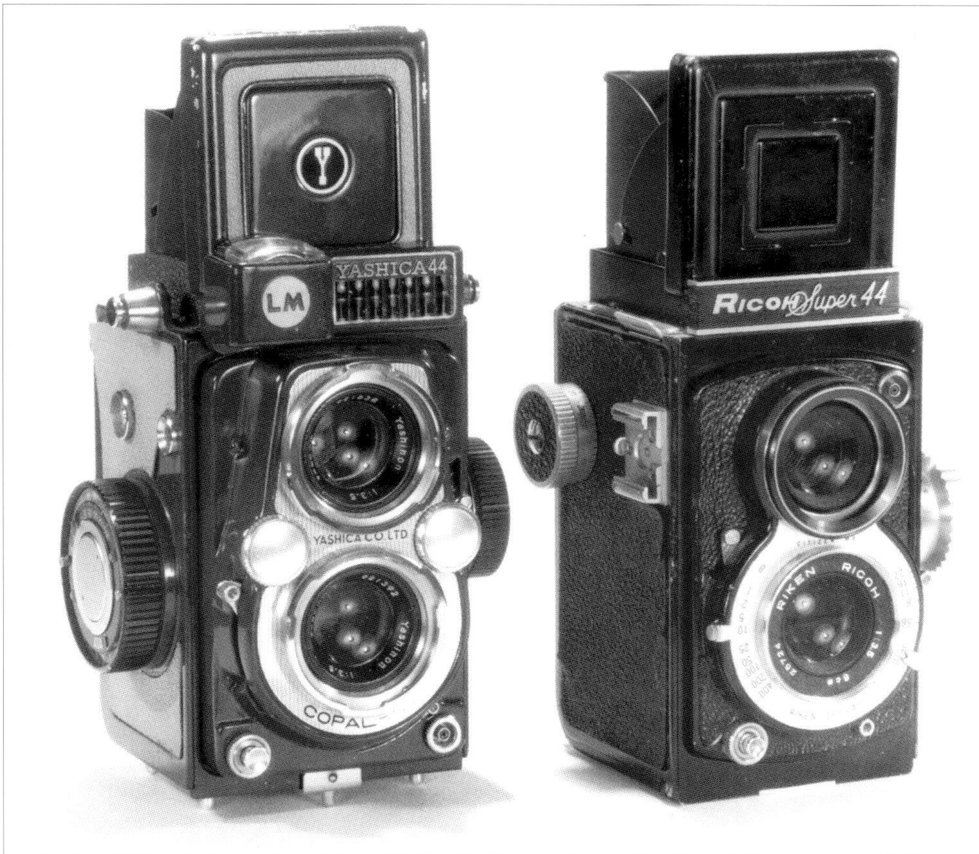

Two 4 x 4 cm twin lens reflexes: the Yashica 44LM and Ricoh Super 44.

Three more 4 x 4 cm TLRs: the Laqon-44, Walz Automat and Primo Jr.

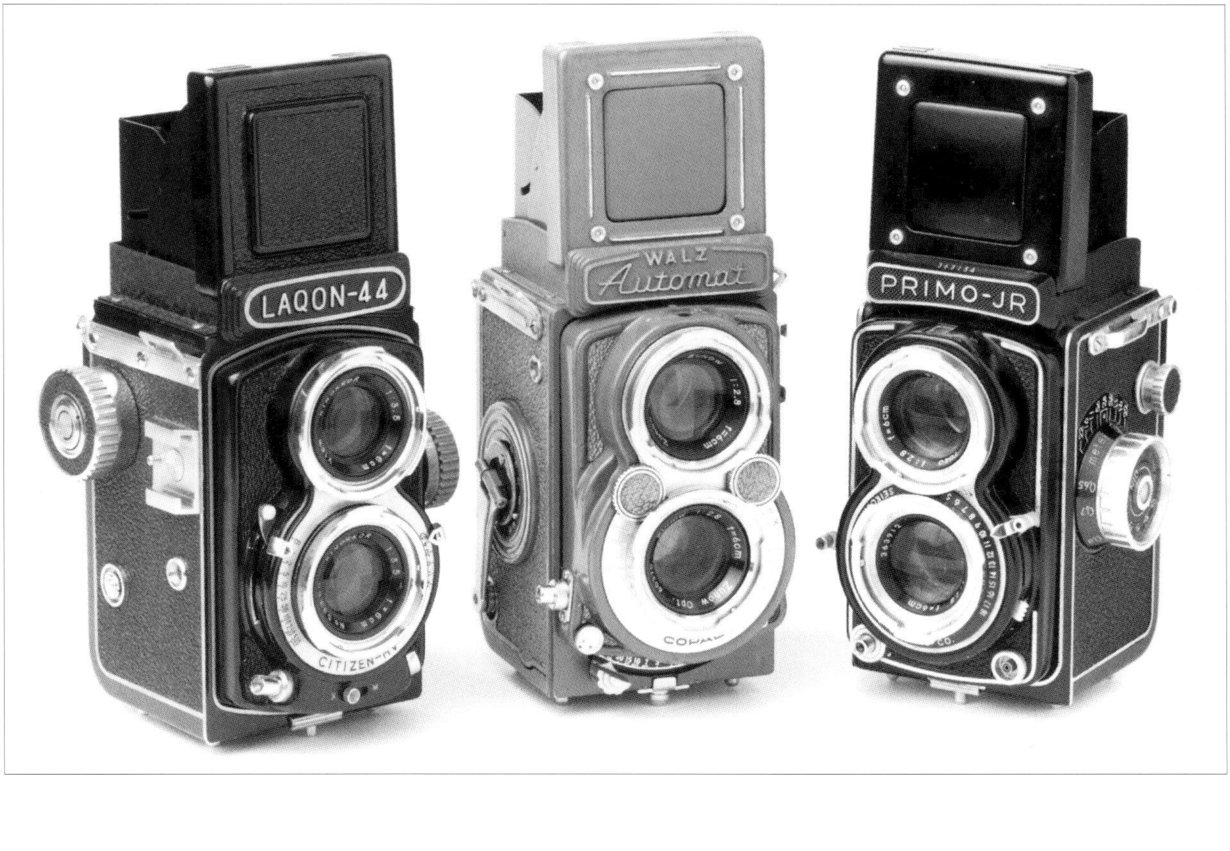

35mm TLRs

The best 35mm TLR was undoubtedly the Twin Lens Contaflex from Zeiss Ikon in 1938. That one offered interchangeable lenses from 35mm to 135mm and was, in fact, the first camera with a built-in exposure meter. But the 35mm TLR became about as popular as it ever got in the post-war years.

Bolsey C, C2 and C22

In 1950, the Americans came up with a 35mm TLR in the shape of the Bolsey C, the only low-cost 35mm reflex on the market at the time.

The Bolsey C is basically the Bolsey B (see pages 74-75) with a reflex finder and viewing lens added. So it features the usual Bolsey viewfinder and rangefinder in two separate windows, plus a reflex waist-level viewfinder on the top of the body. A flip-up magnifier in the finder hood aids more accurate focusing.

The Bolsey C22, a 35mm twin lens reflex, incorporating the Set-O-Matic automatic diaphragm feature.

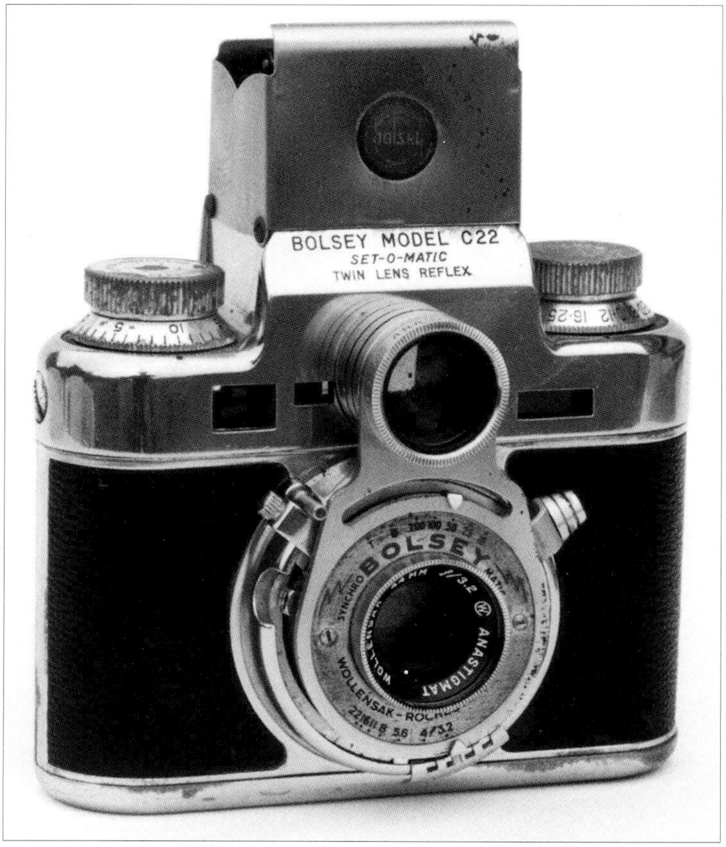

The addition of flash synchronisation resulted in the Bolsey C2 and then, in 1953, Bolsey produced the C22 model illustrated here. The new addition was what Bolsey called their Set-O-Matic automatic diaphragm setting for flash photography. It consists of a small strip with four slots in it, attached to the focusing collar which rotates beneath the lens. Lifting it forward allows the user to engage the aperture lever in any one of the slots so that now, as focusing is adjusted, so too is the aperture: the closer the distance the smaller the aperture, the greater the distance the larger the aperture. With the shutter set to 1/50 second, this then gives the correct aperture for flash, whatever the distance. Which of the four slots — marked A, B, C and D — is used depends on the speed of the film in use, together with the type and strength of the flashbulb, and the appropriate setting is indicated on a panel fixed to the back of the camera body.

The Bolsey C, C2 and C22 were rather ahead of their time and never really caught on with the public.

The Agfa Flexilette hails from 1960 and actually looks a lot like the accepted view of a 35mm camera with a waist-level finder. The difference is that there are two lenses where you expect to find only one. Because it's a TLR, the lower lens takes the picture and the upper one reflects its image onto a ground-glass screen. Both lenses are racked in and out simultaneously as a ring around them is rotated. To aid focusing on the small screen, the hood supports a magnifier and a split image rangefinder is built in.

The design was taken a stage further in 1962 with the Agfa Optima Reflex, which retains the twin lens reflex principle but adds a pentaprism for eye level viewing in place of the waist-level finder on the Flexilette. The Optima Reflex also has automatic exposure metering. Of the two cameras, this is the rarer.

The Japanese went through a stage of producing 35mm TLRs too. There's the Samocaflex (see page 148) and then there is the Toyoca 35 and the rarer Meisupi No.2 and No.3, which use twin lenses side by side on a

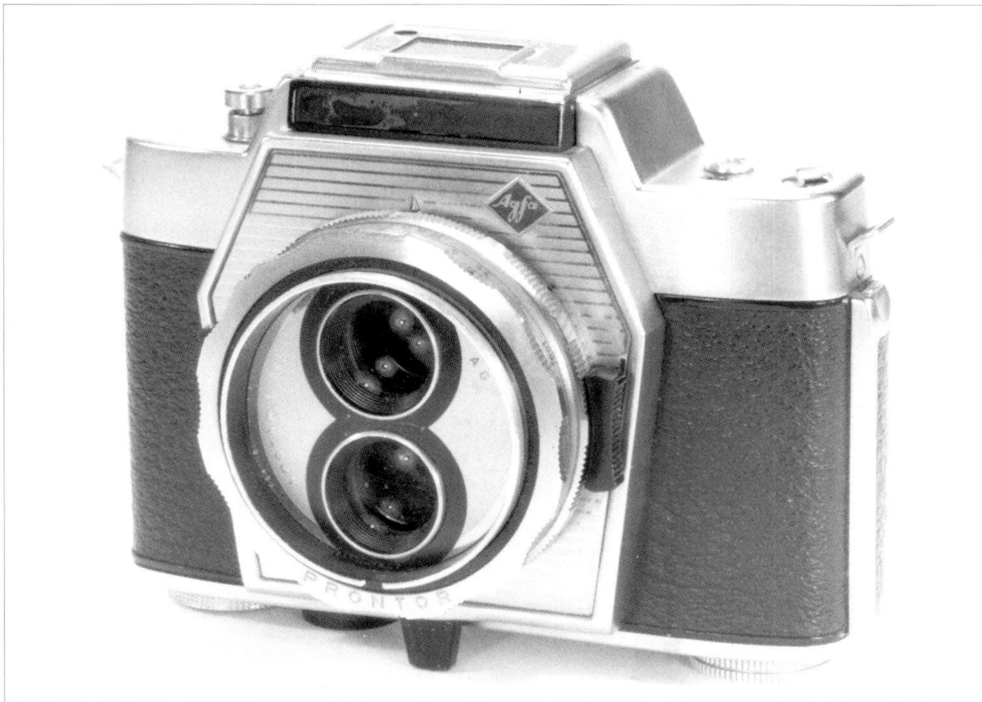

Agfa Flexilette 35mm TLR.

more traditionally shaped 35mm body - except that they don't take standard 35mm film. These cameras took 28 x 40 mm images on individual sheets of film contained in light-proof sheathes and which could be developed in daylight by use of a special red developer. Each sheet of film separated from its sheathe once immersed in the developer and, being

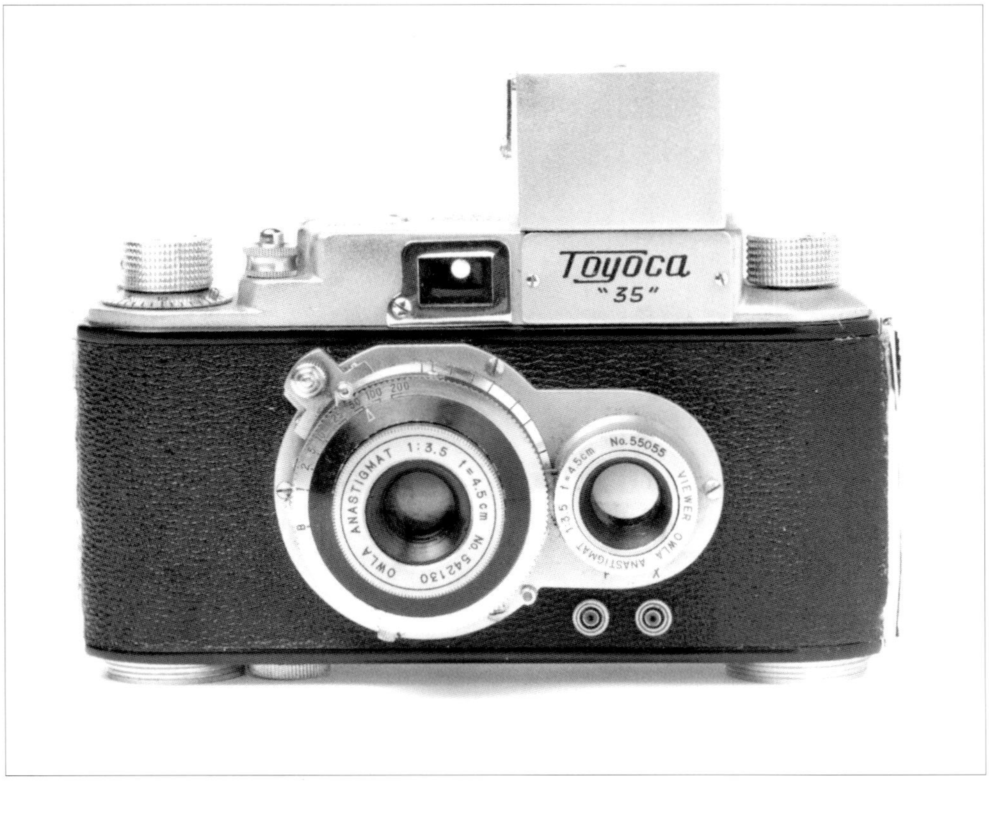

The Toyoca took a very different look at TLR design.

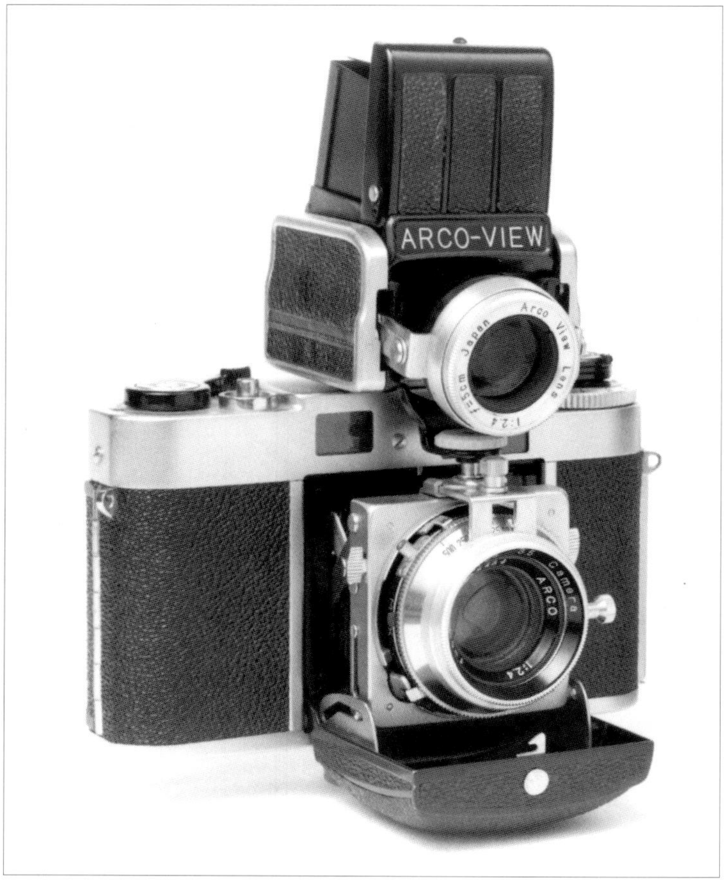

The Arco is a combination of rangefinder camera and TLR.

insensitive to red light, it was protected from fogging by the colour of the liquid.

In 1952 and 1956, another Japanese manufacturer took yet another look at 35mm TLRs with the Arco 35-I and the Arco Automat-D. These take the form of 35mm rangefinder cameras with lenses that extend on short bellows. But the addition of the Arco-View converts the cameras into twin lens reflexes, the viewfinder accessory coupling to the focusing mechanism

The Tessina

The Tessina is also a 35mm TLR, but it is worth separating from the others mentioned here because it is even more radical in its design. When it was launched in 1961, advertisements proclaimed: 'Your subminiature Tessina is an endless source of amusement. Unseen and unsuspected, it is the ideal camera for candid shots. In your hand it could be taken for your watch, hung round your neck it could be your exposure meter, and it is tiny enough to tuck into a lady's purse or a man's shirt pocket!'

The Tessina was made in Switzerland. At just 28 x 52 x 68 mm, it is about the size of a slightly slimmer than usual matchbox, made of satin chrome and with rounded ends. On the top (where a matchbox would have its label), there's a ground-glass focusing screen under a fold-up hood that doubles as a direct vision viewfinder. Beside that there's an accessory shoe that usually sports an exposure chart, but into which a small exposure meter can be slipped.

On the opposite side, there is a removable plate that contains brief instructions for the camera's use. It's removable because it can be replaced by another plate incorporating a strap so that the camera can be worn like a rather large wristwatch. In fact, there is a very rare accessory in the form of a real clockwork Swiss watch that can be slipped into the accessory shoe to complete the illusion.

When you open the Tessina by removing the whole of its base, the first thing you see is the back of the lens which appears to be exactly where you'd expect - directly opposite the film path. Except that it can't be, because that's where the viewfinder is. The lens is, in fact, on the narrow side of the body: if we are going to continue the matchbox analogy it's sunk into the surface where you would strike a match.

Closer examination of the inside of the camera, in fact, reveals that you are not looking directly at the back of the lens, but at its reflection in a 45 degree mirror.

The viewing lens is beside the one that actually takes the picture. Coupled to the taking lens for focusing, it reflects its image, via another 45 degree mirror, up to the ground glass screen on the top of the camera, while the taking lens reflects its image down to the film which runs at right angles across the base of the camera. The surprises don't end there either, because this miniature marvel also has a built-in motor drive, driven by a minute clockwork motor. On the back of the body, there are two knobs, one at each end. The one on the left is to rewind the film at the end of the roll, just as with any 35mm camera. The one on the right winds up the clockwork motor. Thereafter, as the shutter is released, the motor automatically advances the film, about ten exposures to a winding.

The Tessina takes standard 35mm film, but loaded into its own special slimline cassettes. When it was first sold, Adox black and white or Ektachrome colour films could be bought pre-loaded into the special cassettes and there were plans for further Tessina films with the Agfa, Ansco, Ferrania, Kodacolor, Kodachrome and Telcocolor names on them. Daylight film loaders were also available for photographers who wanted to load their own from standard 35mm cassettes to give up to 23 exposures of black and white or 18 of colour, due to the slight extra thickness of the film. The image size is 14 x 21mm, which is not much smaller than a 35mm half frame.

Other controls include a thumbwheel between those two knobs on the back, to adjust shutter speeds from 1/2 second to 1/500 second, plus 'B'; and a flash synch socket for M, F and X synchronisation. Two other dials on the top of the body, directly in front of the viewfinder and the accessory shoe, are for

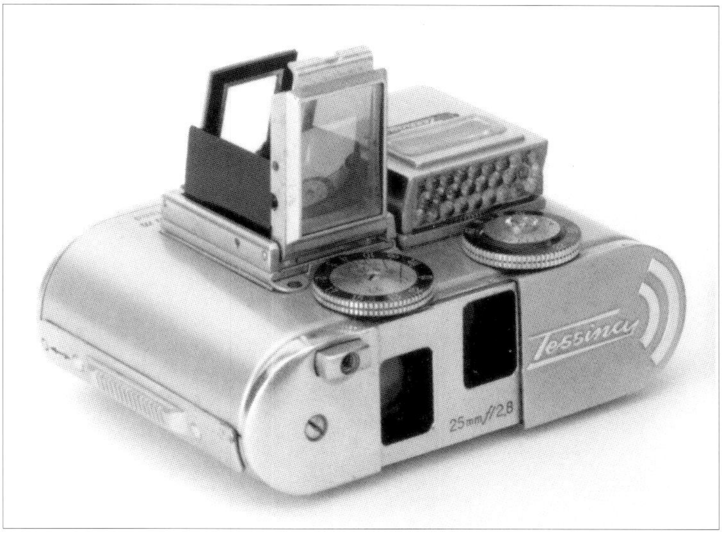

The Tessina is a 35mm TLR made in Switzerland.

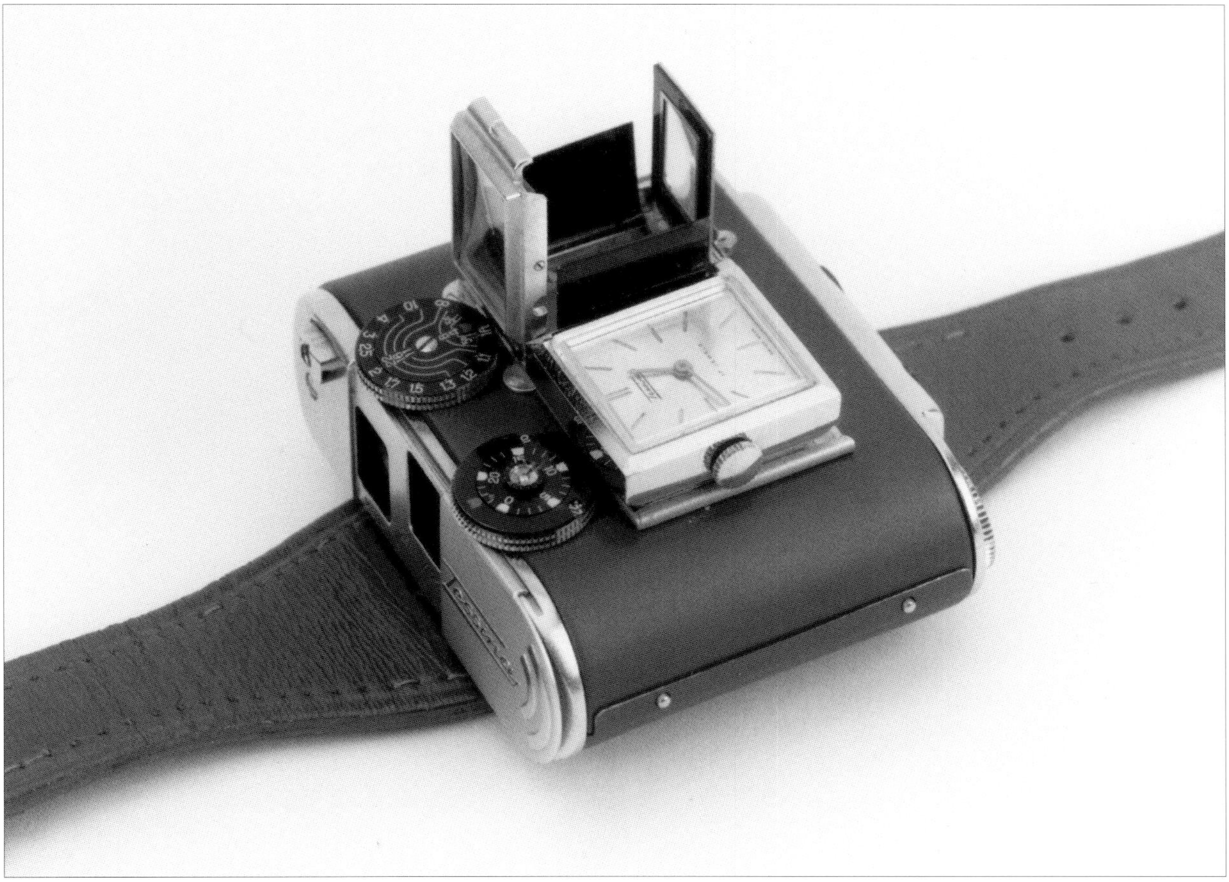

The Tessina with its rare watch accessory.

focusing the 25mm Tessinon lens down to 1 foot, and for adjusting apertures between f/2.8 and f/22. The focusing dial has a depth of field scale incorporated in its centre.

The Tessina was made by Concava SA, to similar standards associated with Swiss watches. It was the brainchild of an Englishman called Dr. Steineck, who had already given the world the Steineck ABC, a very simple camera the size and style of a wristwatch, back in 1940. The most common Tessina models are made in satin chrome but you'll also find cameras made in gold, red and black.

The Minicord is a twin lens reflex for 16mm film.

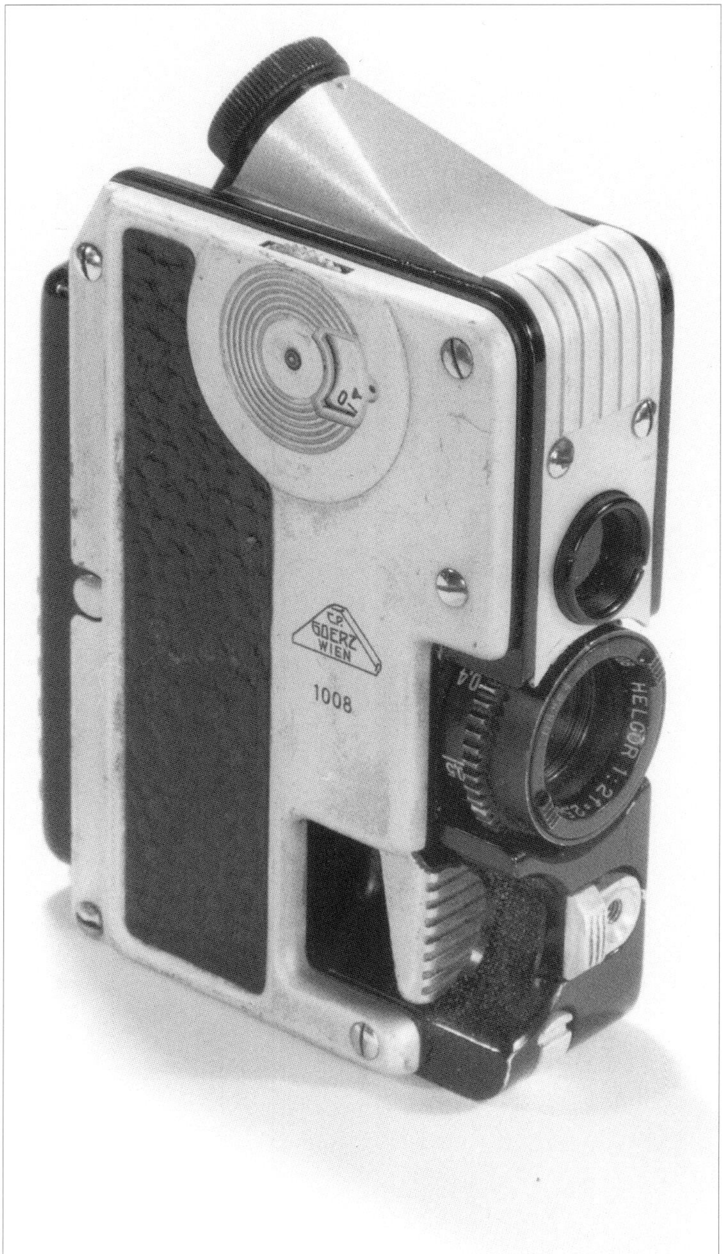

The Minicord

The Goerz Minicord is everything you least expect it to be. It looks like a small cine camera, but it isn't. It looks nothing like a twin lens reflex, but it is. It was made in Austria, a country not exactly renowned for camera manufacture. And it takes 16mm film.

The camera dates from 1951 and measures a mere 10 x 6.5 x 3 cm. Like any conventional TLR design, the camera has two lenses, one to take the picture, the second one above it to reflect its image onto a ground-glass screen. Unlike most other TLRs, the photographer views that screen through an eye-level, magnifying viewfinder, which is just as well since the actual image is so small. The viewfinder is fixed at about 45 degrees to the top of the camera and it is necessary to look down at an angle to see the scene straight in front of the lens.

Rotating the taking lens to focus also rotates the viewfinder lens, so that the image on the screen matches the one on the film. The viewfinder also has a focusing eyepiece that can be adjusted to suit individual eyesight.

The 16mm film used by the Minicord was originally loaded into a double cassette, separated by a metal frame, not unlike a more modern 110 cartridge, and the whole assembly drops into the back of the camera as a single unit.

Film wind is by means of a trigger-like plunger inset in the camera body just to the side of the shutter release. In operation, the photographer folds out a small finger grip from the base, hooks the middle finger of the right hand around it, then shoots and winds alternatively with the index finger, whilst focusing with the left hand. Given the knack, it's possible to get up to about one-and-a-half frames per second.

As the plunger is pressed, a claw mechanism inside the body grabs the film by a sprocket hole, pulls it from the lower cassette and pushes it up into the top one. With its original film, the camera gave 40 exposures.

The Minicord must be one of the quietest cameras ever made. It has a metal focal plane shutter that positively whispers across, especially at its slow settings, which go down to 1/10 second. The highest speed is 1/400 second and apertures, from f/2 to f/11, are set around the rim of the lens.

The size of a Minicord negative is just 10 x 10 mm, which isn't the easiest of things to handle in the darkroom, so back in the 1950s Goerz had the answer to that in the shape of a special enlarger called the Minilux.

Folding away into a small wooden case that doubles as the baseboard, the Minilux uses the Minicord as part of its construction. The camera is fitted to the enlarger's lamp house by way of its tripod bush, a spring clip holds the shutter open on the camera's 'B' setting and, with the normal cassettes removed, a special film carrying accessory is inserted. Illumination comes from a small 25-watt bulb, diffused through opal glass.

The Minicord is most commonly seen in chrome and black leather. But it can also be found in a brown leather covering and there are ultra rare models in gold metal with red or green leather.

Subminiature TLRs

The years around the 1950s saw several twin lens reflexes from Japan, made for subminiature film. The Gemflex was made in 1949 to take 14 x 14 mm frames on paper backed 17.5mm film. This little rarity is a true miniature TLR, complete with 25mm f/3.5 lenses, shutter speeds from 1/25 second to 1/100 second and apertures that were unusual in that their control was by a knob on the side of the body. Gemflex cameras are rare; accessories that include lens hoods and filters are even rarer.

The Babyflex, made in 1950, is similar but has a fixed focus lens, so isn't, strictly speaking, a TLR. But it does resemble a miniature TLR in style and uses the same film as the Gemflex.

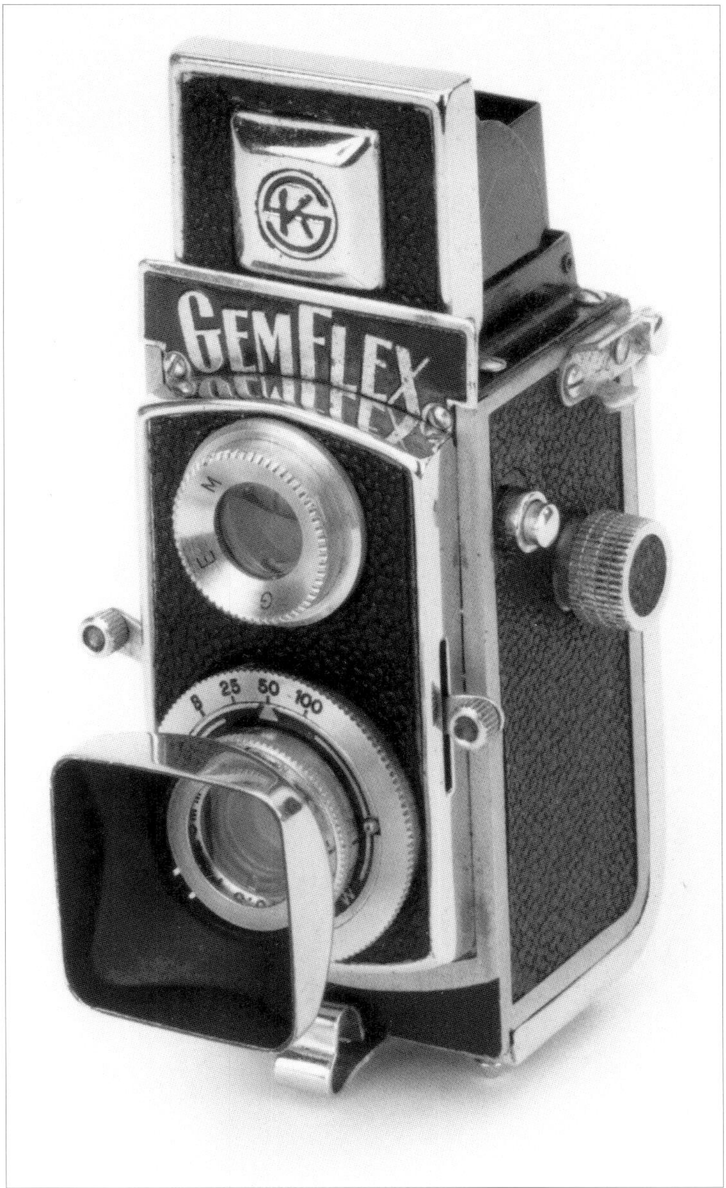

The Gemflex is a subminiature TLR.

There is also a second version called the Peace Babyflex, with similar features but with a different shutter.

TLR viewfinders

At one time it was also possible to convert almost any 35mm camera into a TLR by the addition of a special viewfinder. The Flexameter, made by Kühn in Wetzlar (where the Leicas come from) in Germany is a prime example.

The Flexameter sports its own 50mm f/2.8

The Flexameter reflex viewfinder, fitted here to an Edinex I.

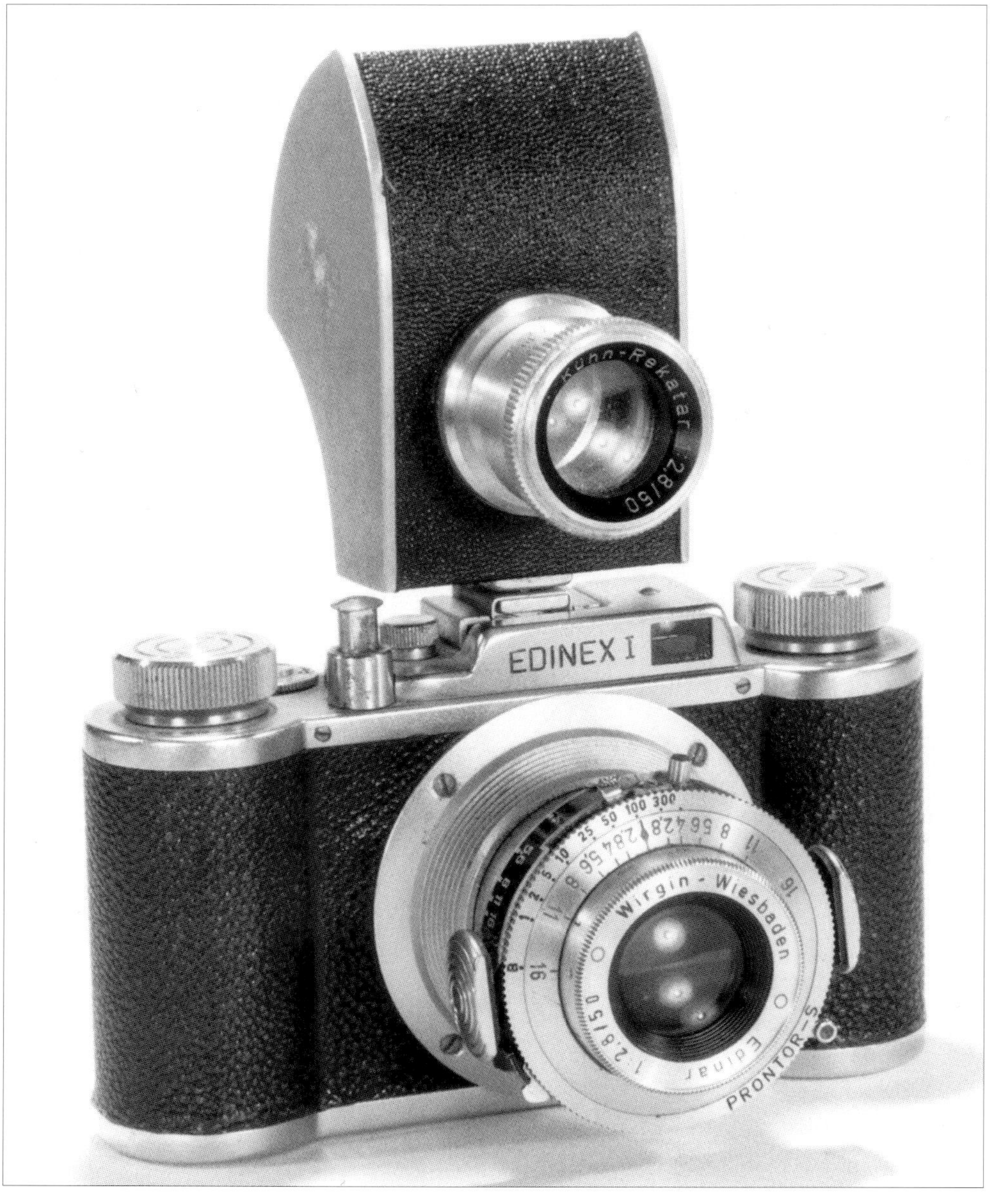

lens that reflects an image up to a neat little ground-glass screen, shielded by a metal hood. There was nothing new about the idea because similar, and more sophisticated, models with names like De Morenay Budd and Megoflex were being made for the likes of Leica and Contax before the war. The Flexameter, however, comes from the 1950s and is a lot simpler in design - making it a lot cheaper for today's collector.

Made to fit into a 35mm camera's accessory shoe, the lens on the Flexameter is focused on the screen in the normal way, then its reading is manually transferred to the camera lens which, naturally, must be of the same focal length. A separate magnifier was also available to clip onto the top of the hood, since the size of a 35mm image in a ground glass screen is a little small for accurate focusing.

What Happened to Box Cameras

BEFORE THE Second World War, the box camera was one of the most popular of simple camera designs. After the war, the box camera philosophy of an easy to use camera with the simplest possible shutter speed, aperture and focusing controls, continued but the shapes changed radically.

The Gnome Baby Pixie, beginning to move away from the traditional box camera image.

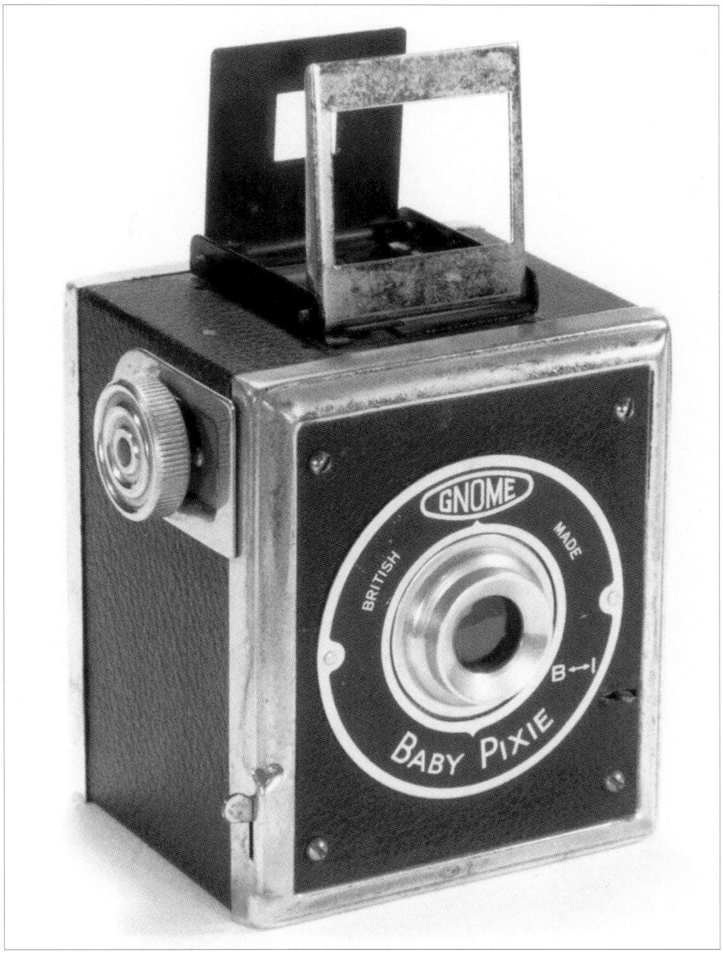

Some, like the Baby Pixie, made by Gnome in 1951, retained the box shape, although in a more compact form than the older, pre-war cameras, allowing 16 exposures on 620 film. Others, like the Wembley Sports, Agiflash or Ultra Fex moved away from the box form and more towards the traditional camera shape.

The Wembley Sports is a Bakelite camera, made in England in 1950. It takes eight pictures on 120 film. When not in use, the lens lies flat against the body, but to use the camera, the lens is wound out on a huge screw, also made of Bakelite, until it click-stops at infinity. Forcing it a little further, reveals three more click stops that rack the lens out even more for closer focusing, although there is no actual scale to say what distances these settings represent. The Sports has variable aperture settings from f/11 - f/22 and three shutter speeds from 1/25 second to 1/100 second.

The Ultra Fex is a similar style, but came from France in 1946 and is a little more stylish. Instead of the ugly Bakelite screw on the Sports, the lens is extended on a polished, rectangular metal tube. The rest of the body is Bakelite and there are a number of different variations on the theme with slightly different names, including the Fex, Elite-Fex, Fex 4.5, Fex 5.6 Cap Nord, Pari-Fex, Rubi-Fex and Superfex. The Ultra Fex takes eight pictures on 120 film. It has a three-speed shutter and two apertures charmingly designated as 'normal' and 'intense'.

The Agiflex is closer to the box camera concept in that it has a fixed aperture, shutter

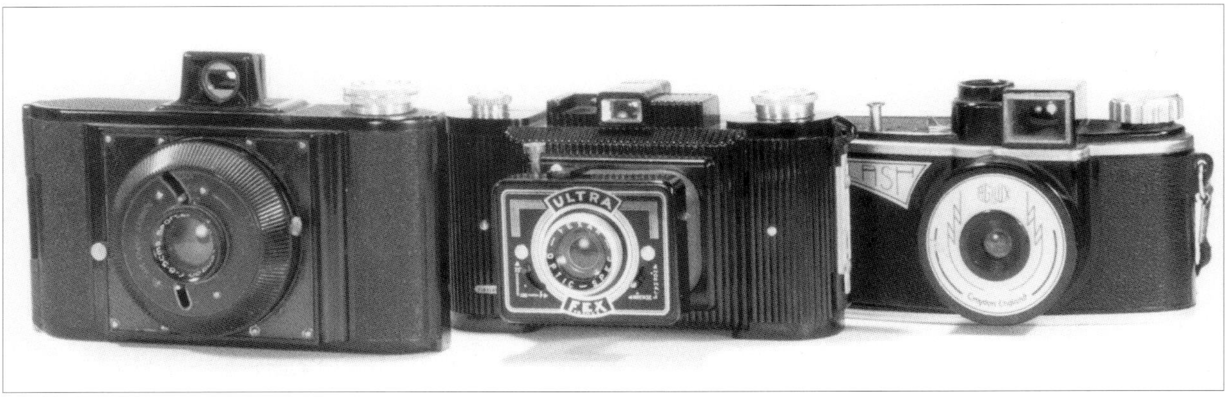

The Wembley Sports, Ultra Fex and Agiflash continue the box camera philosophy in a more streamlined camera shape.

speed and lens, but it adds the luxury of a built-in flashgun, taking large PF-14 bulbs. It was made in England, by Agilux, in 1954 and shoots eight exposures on 127 film. Reflecting the style of the era, it sports a streamlined design that uses leatherette over Bakelite.

These three models show one direction that simple cameras took in the 1940s and 1950s; many other post-1945 box camera derivatives can be broken down into two types: Kodak Brownies and fake TLRs.

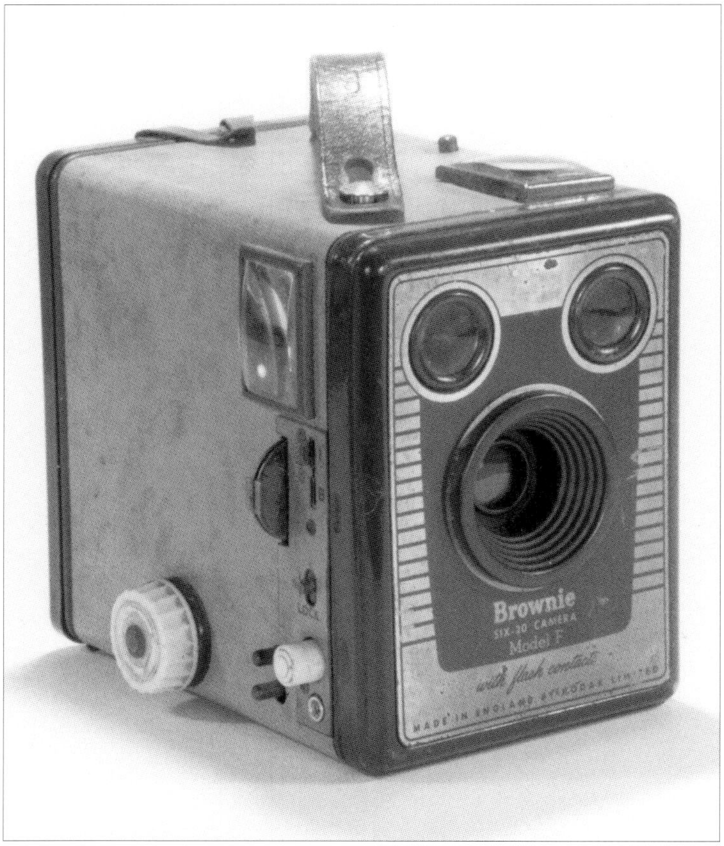

The Kodak Brownie Six-20 Model F, among the last of the Box Brownies.

KODAK BROWNIES

Brownie is a name that has always been associated with box cameras. In fact, the term 'Box Brownie' has entered the language as meaning almost any form of simple camera, in much the same way that ball-point pens have become Biros and vacuum cleaners are known as Hoovers. The first Brownie appeared in 1900, but it was during the era covered by this book that the Brownie really branched out.

Brownie Six-20 cameras

Even as late as the 1957, Kodak still clung to the traditional box camera shape with a series of cameras for 620 film, designated as the Six-20 C, D and E. (The first Six-20, followed by the Model B had been made in the 1930s.) Made of metal, with larger viewfinders than on older box cameras, they can be found with two different face plates; the first cameras arrived in 1946 and the face plates were changed in 1953. In 1957, the camera was relaunched as the Model F along with the very similar Brownie Flash IV in an attractive tan covering with brass trim. And that, really, marked he end of the Box Brownie in its most traditional shape.

Brownie Reflex

Strictly speaking, the Brownie Reflex was made in 1940 but it didn't became popular until the war was over in 1945. It's a camera that could slot into either of the two sections we're considering here because, as well as being a Brownie, it's also a camera that pretends to be a twin lens reflex. Following that style, it has two lenses, the lower one for taking pictures, the upper one to reflect its image onto a large condenser lens viewfinder under a hood at the top. But the lenses aren't linked and can't be focused, and the total control is a shutter that offers 'T' and 'B' settings.

Brownie 127

Coronation Year in the UK, 1953, saw the arrival of the Brownie 127. Made of Bakelite, it takes 127 film and has the Brownie's familiar lack of any controls other than a fixed shutter speed, aperture and focus. The stylish rounded corners are not only very typical of 1950s styling, but also serve a real purpose. In fact, the whole back of the body is curved because the camera has a very simple meniscus lens which isn't good enough to retain focus in the centre and at the edges at the same time. So instead of going to the expense of adding a better lens, Kodak simply curved the camera back and the film plane, so that the edges of each negative were closer to the lens than they would be if the film was held more conventionally flat, thus retaining as much focus as possible right across the image.

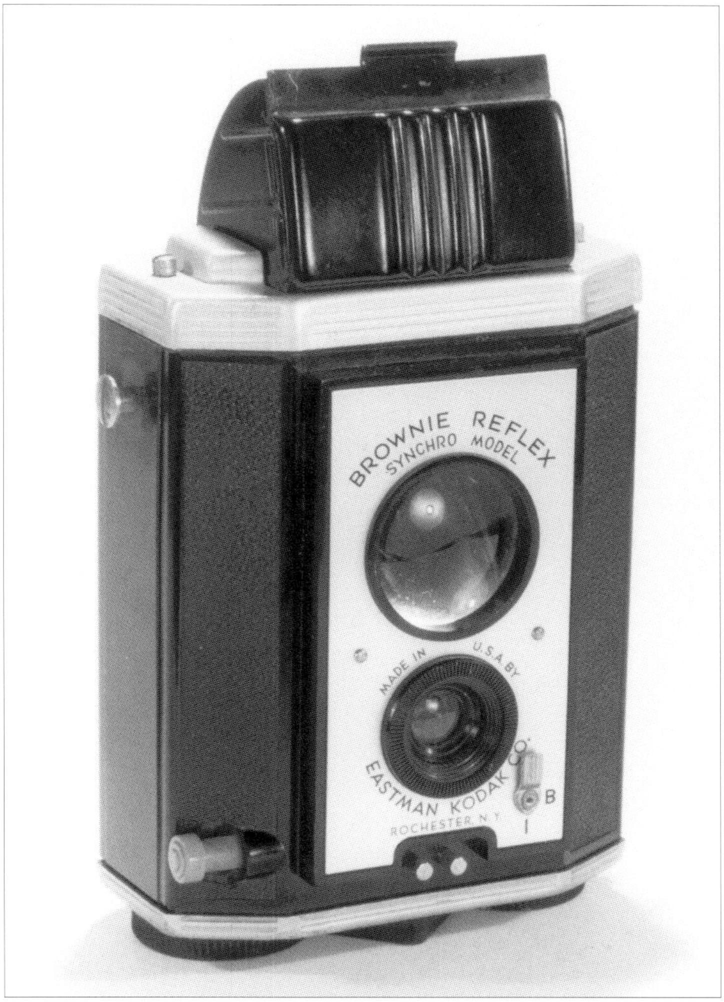

The Brownie Reflex tried hard to be a twin lens reflex.

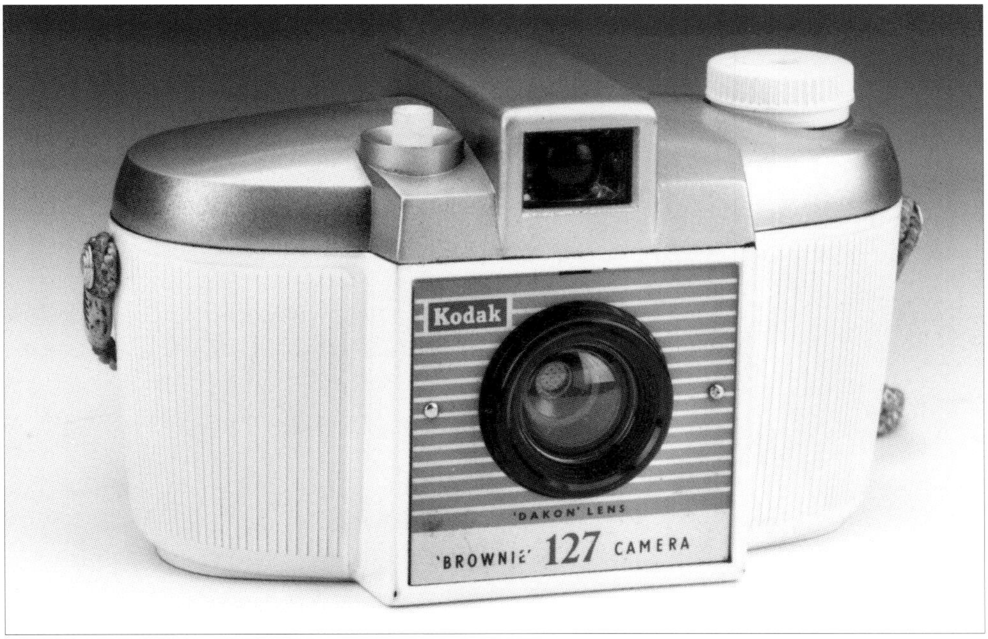

The Brownie 127 in its rare white form.

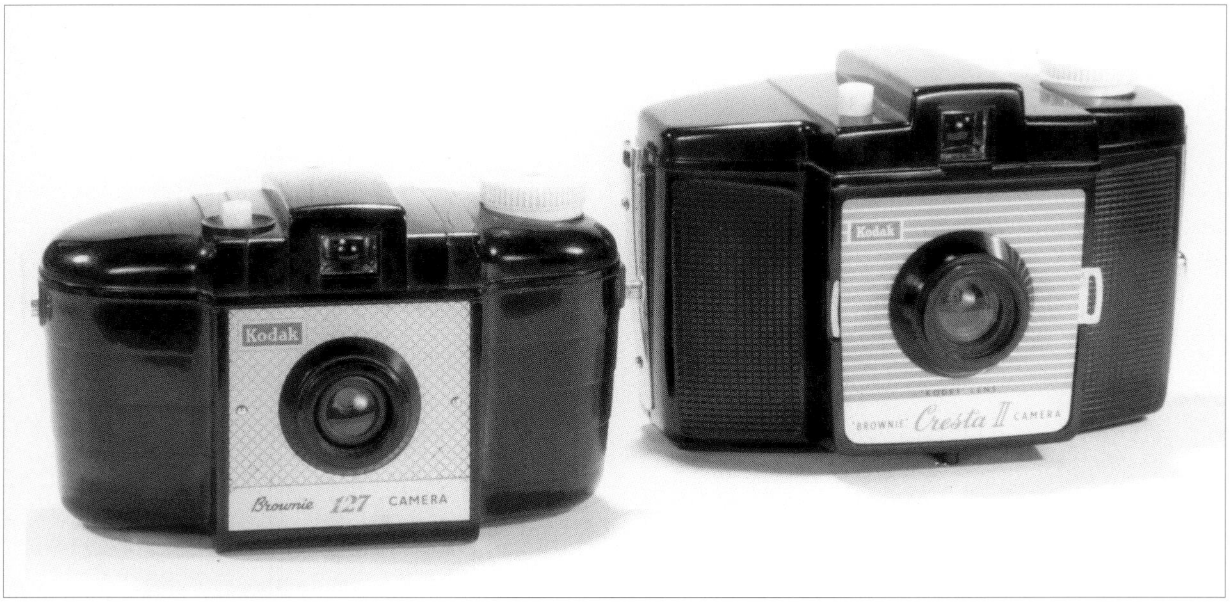

The extremely popular Brownie 127 with its larger cousin the Brownie Cresta.

Watch out for three variations of pattern on the face plate - diamonds, plain cream and horizontal stripes. But look in particular for the white version. Only 5,000 of these were made for test marketing in Jersey, which presumably led Kodak to believe they wouldn't sell. Today, as collector's items, they are worth about thirty or forty times the price of the far more common black versions.

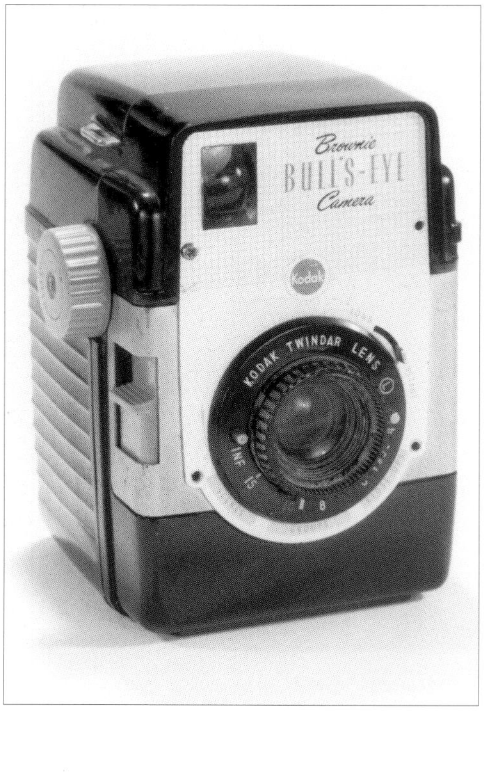

Brownie Bulls-Eye from 1954.

Brownie Cresta

This one is similar in style to the Brownie 127, but less well known. Looking like a larger version of the 127 camera, the Cresta takes 120 film, producing 12 6 x 6 cm images to a roll.

Brownie Bulls-Eye

This one has a bit of a pedigree because Bulls-Eye cameras, back in 1892, were the first to use the little red window through which film frame numbers could be read. The cameras were made by the Boston Camera Company, to whom Kodak's founder George Eastman had to pay a royalty for the use of the same idea in his own cameras, until he eventually bought out the Boston Camera Company and continued to make their cameras under the Kodak name.

So it's nice to see the Bulls-Eye name rearing its head again in 1954 on this simple snapshot camera, made of Bakelite with a metal faceplate, focusing Twindar lens and two shutter speeds marked simply 'Instant' and 'Long'. Another nice touch is a lightning bolt symbol that springs across the viewfinder window as soon as a picture has been taken, warning that another can't be shot until the film has been wound on. It is synchronised for flash and gold versions sell for about half as much again as black.

Brownie 44 A

Restyling the Brownie 127 resulted in the Brownie 44A. The film remains as 127, but a new format gives 12 pictures to a roll, each one 4 x 4 cm. The camera, made in 1959, is recognisable by a hinged cover fitted to the base which folds up to cover the lens. If you find one without the cover, that's a 44B launched a few years later.

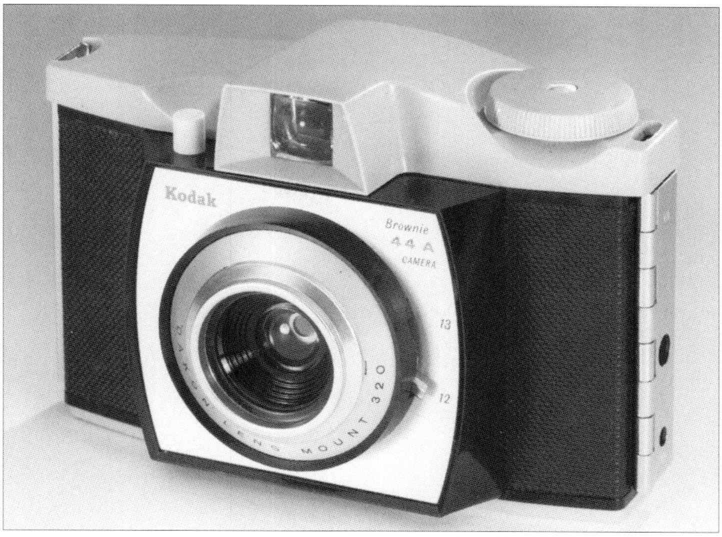

The Kodak Brownie 44A updated the Brownie 127 with a new style and format.

Brownie Twin 20

From the end of the 1950s and into the early 1960s, Kodak came up with a new style of Brownie, epitomised by the Twin-20. It takes 620 film, producing 12 pictures to a roll and is so named because of its twin viewfinders, an eye-level and waste-level, side by side. The lens focuses, the shutter is fixed and there are three apertures, marked '13' for colour, '14' and '15' for black and white.

Brownie Flash 20

Essentially, this is the same camera, but made in blue with the waist-level viewfinder

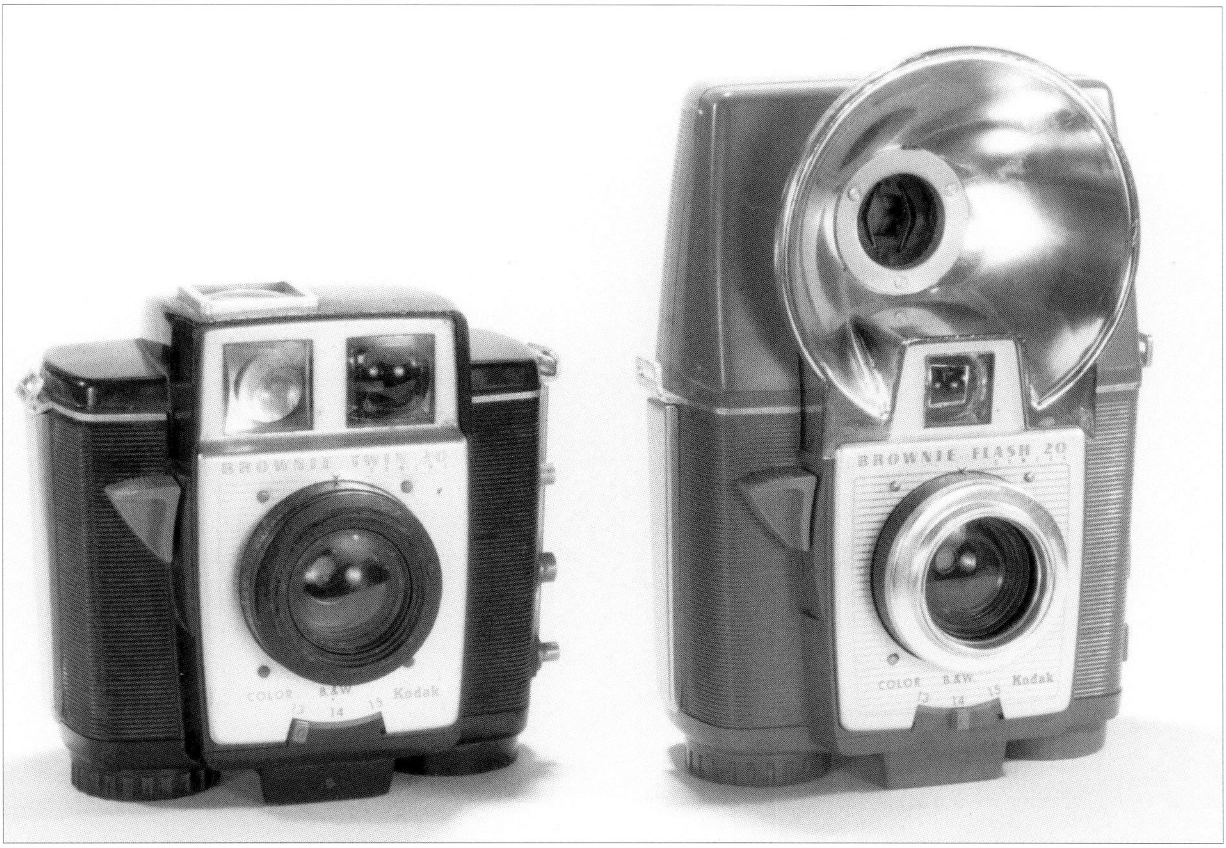

The Brownie Twin-20 and Flash 20.

Brownie Vector, very much a product of the Swinging Sixties.

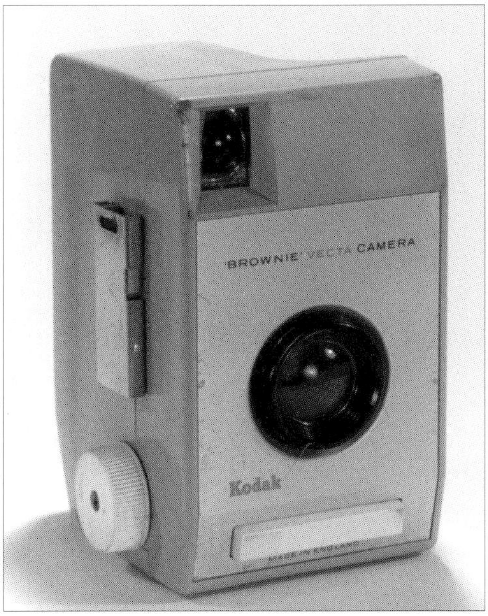

removed and a big, ugly flashgun built on the top to take PF-1 bulbs. The rest of the specification is the same as on the Twin-20.

One interesting feature of both these cameras is the smaller frame etched into the middle of their viewfinders. This was there so that the photographer could compose 4 x 4 cm pictures within the actual 6 x 6 cm format. The resulting slides could then be shown on a normal 35mm projector.

Brownie Vecta

The 1960s began to show some really unusual shapes in Brownies and this one, very much a product of the pop culture that prevailed at the time, won a design award. It's a vertically styled camera for 127 film, all controls are fixed and the shutter release is an unusual long bar that runs along the front.

The last of the Brownies in 1980.

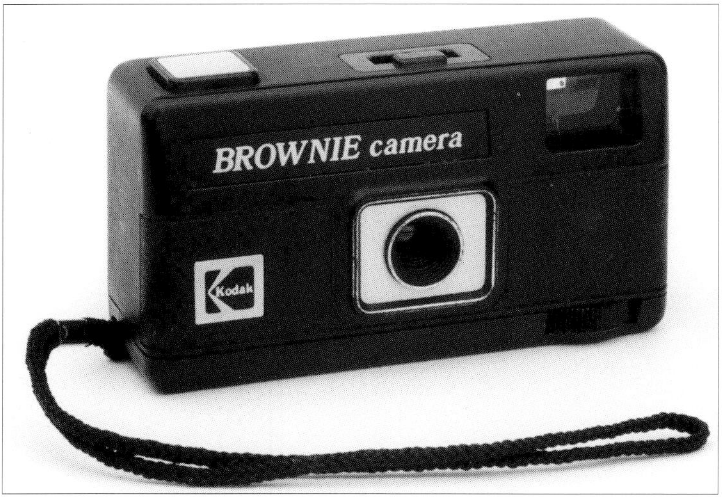

Brownie Camera

Eighty years after the first Brownie was launched, the last camera to bear the name appeared in 1980. It's a small plastic model for 110 film and is almost identical to another camera produced by Kodak a few years before and called the Pocket A1. It is probably the least valuable of all the Brownies, but if you're building a collection based on the name, you can't afford to ignore the fact that it's the last of an extremely illustrious line.

FAKE TLRs

The viewfinder was one major aspect of box camera design that was vastly improved in post-war years. Traditionally small to the point of impracticality on older box cameras, it gradually grew larger as designs changed. The next step was the addition of a large lens above the taking lens to serve the new size of viewfinder which was situated on the top of the camera body and usually took the form of a large condenser lens. It meant that very soon, the cameras began to resemble twin lens reflexes. The difference, of course, lay in the fact that the lenses weren't coupled for focusing the way they would have had to be in a true TLR and, in many cases, the camera lens was a fixed focus design anyway. Nevertheless, these cameras that tried to be TLRs became a style all their own and represent a major leap in the design that started as a box camera.

Coronet Twelve-20

After Kodak, the English company of Coronet was probably one of the most popular makers of box cameras and their derivatives, including a fair few quasi-TLRs.

The 1950 Coronet Twelve-20 is one. It takes

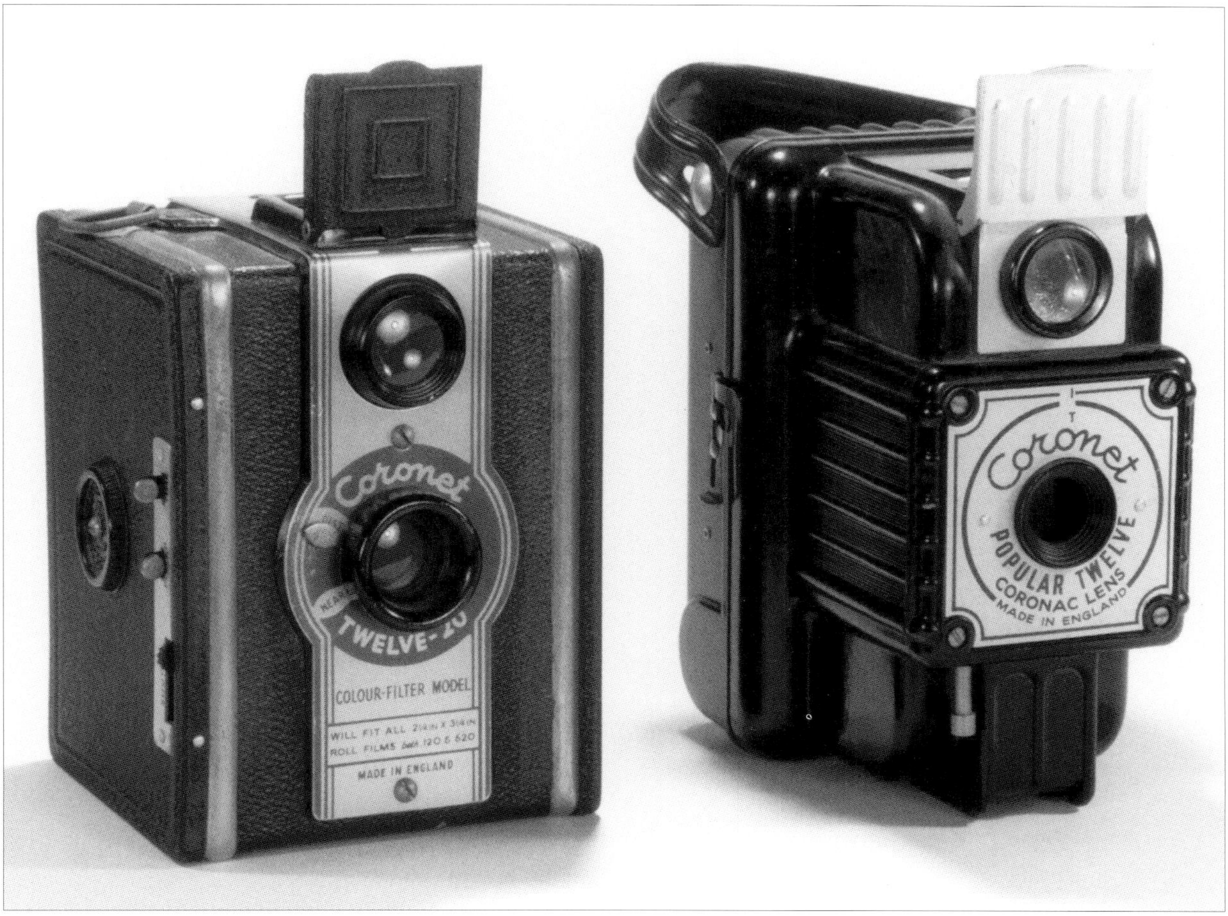

Two Coronets, the Twelve-20 and the Popular 12.

12 square pictures on 120 or 620 film and has a fixed focus meniscus lens which can be focused by a scale on the face plate with settings for 'near' and 'dist'. It also has a built-in filter for enhancing skies in black and white pictures that is brought into place by pulling out a lever on the side of the body. The lens above the taking one reflects its image onto a fairly large viewfinder on the top of the camera, protected by a metal flap. Name variations in the same design include the Coronet F-20 Coro-Flash.

Coronet Popular 12

This one takes much the same idea and turns it out in an unusually shaped Bakelite body. The specification is even less than on Twelve-20, with nothing more than a single shutter speed, a fixed aperture and fixed focus. But the camera still tries to be a twin lens reflex with almost the same viewing system as the Twelve-20.

Kodak Duaflex

The Duaflex looks even more like a twin lens reflex. It was made in 1947 and there are two models. On one the focus is fixed, the other has a focusable lens - though naturally not connected to the large viewfinder. Instantaneous and 'B' settings are the only speeds available on the shutter.

Beacon Reflex

Sporting a design that could only have out of America, the Beacon Reflex was made by Whitehouse Products in 1947. It offers two apertures for black and white or colour and that's all - apart, of course, from a good try at being a twin lens reflex with its large viewing lens reflecting an image to the viewfinder under a flap on the top of he camera. Coloured models are rarer than black ones.

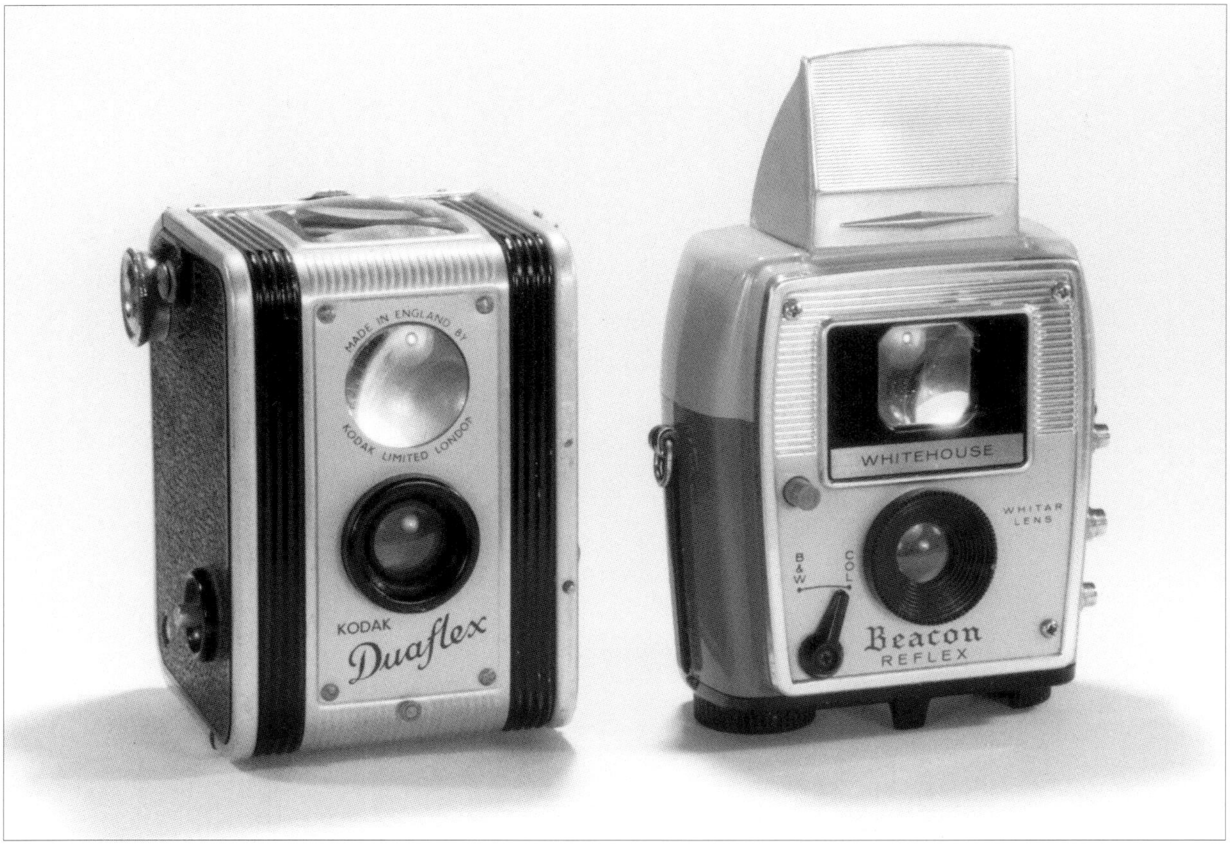

Kodak Duaflex and Beacon Reflex.

Ensign Ful-Vue

The Ensign Ful-Vue started life as a black, metal, box camera with a much larger than normal viewfinder on the top of the body, whose image was supplied by an equally large lens above the real taking lens on the front. That was in 1939, but the camera became most popular when it was relaunched in a new style in 1945.

The post-war design is streamlined with unusual rounded corners on the part of the body that encases the reflex viewing system, but otherwise the Ful-Vue is still a box camera at heart with simple, basic controls: a fixed aperture, a shutter offering 'instantaneous' and 'time' and a lens with three focusing positions: two feet, three to five feet and six feet to infinity. The Ensign Ful-Vue is common in black, but can also be found in red, grey and blue.

A few years later, The Ful-Vue took another turn with the launch of the Ful-Vue Super. This takes the same basic look, but with the rounded corners giving way to a more angular design and with a flip-up hood over the viewfinder. The Ful-Vue Super was made in black and red.

The Ful-Vue saga ended in the 1950s, by which time the Ensign company had been through various name and management changes and was known as Ross Ensign. They took the Ful-Vue Super, adapted it very slightly, made it in plastic instead of metal and called it the Fulvueflex.

Ilfoflex

This is cheekiest of all the cameras shown here because it actually sets out to look like a miniature twin lens reflex and, in fact, measures up size for size with the Baby Rollei. But this one is made of plastic and, as you might expect, all the controls are fixed. The Ilfoflex, which was made in China, is identical, in all but name, to the Bedfordflex. Both cameras taken 12 pictures on 127 film.

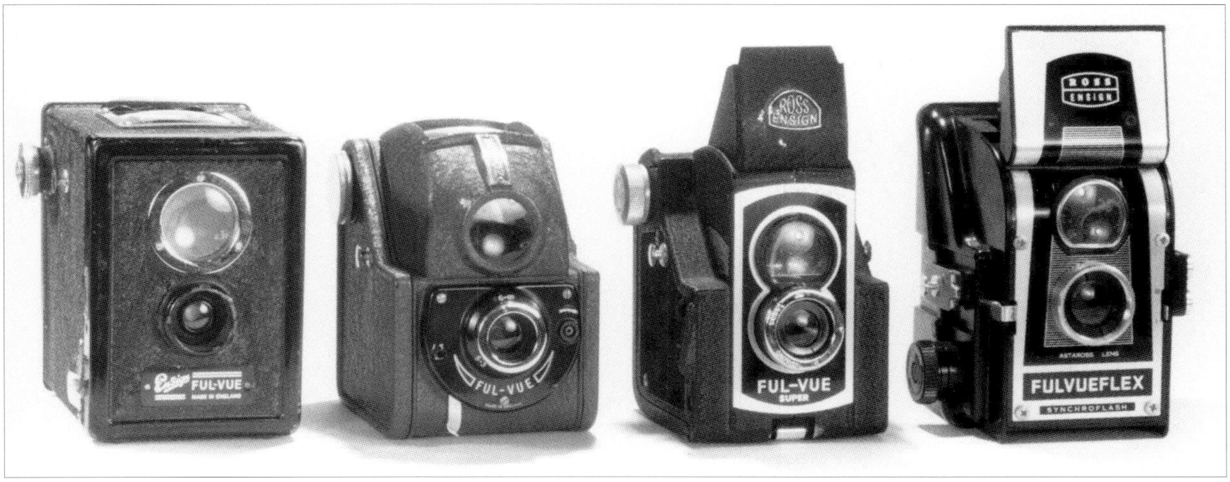

The Ensign Ful-Vue family, from box camera, through the streamlined version of the 1950s, to the Ful-Vue Super and Fulvueflex.

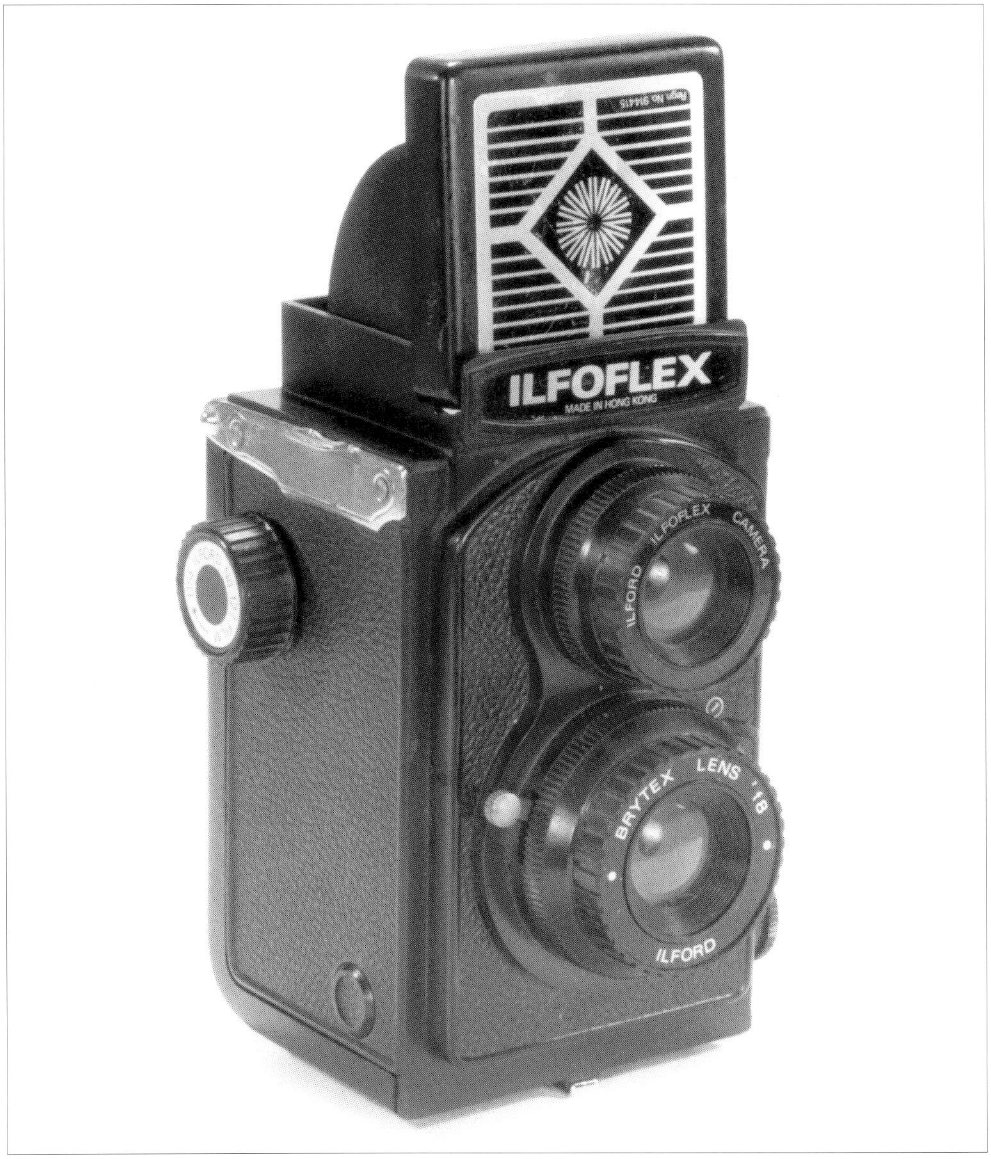

The Ilfoflex looked more like a true twin lens reflex than most cameras of this type.

Yesterday's Compacts

THE 35MM COMPACT is today's most popular camera design, but there's nothing new about it. The genesis of today's compacts - small, 35mm cameras with fixed lenses and rigid bodies - can be found in many models of the past. Here are few that are worth collecting

Ilford Advocate

The Advocate was the camera to which Ilford turned its attention after losing interest in the Witness (see page 83). It isn't in the same league, but it's still an interesting camera in its own right - and a lot easier to find on today's collector's market.

The Advocate was made for Ilford by Kennedy Instruments and launched in 1949. Straight away, the British Journal Photographic Almanac proclaimed it as 'a landmark in British camera construction.'

It's a 35mm camera, but one which is unusual in having a wideangle 35mm lens as standard, rather than the more usual 50mm. Because of this, the manufacturers claimed a depth of field down to 12 feet with the lens set to infinity, even at the widest aperture of f/4.5. Advertisements of the day claimed that this made the use of a rangefinder unnecessary - as good a way as any of getting round the fact that the camera isn't fitted with one.

Its other unusual feature is its colour.

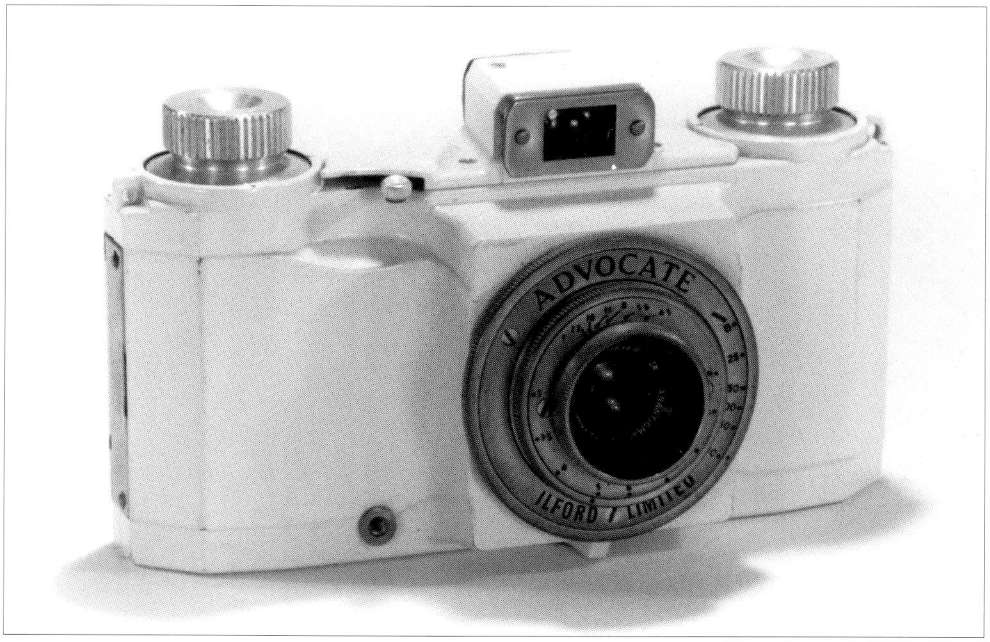

The Ilford Advocate, unusual at the time for its wideangle lens.

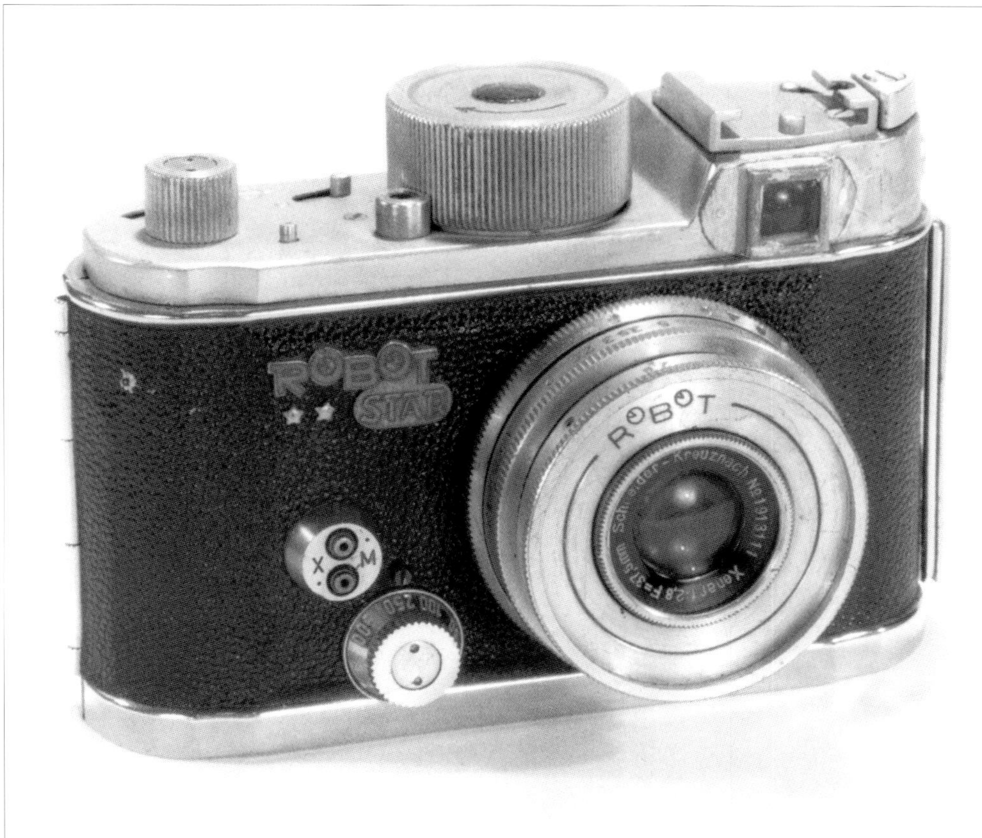

The Robot Star has a built-in clockwork motor drive.

Although camera manufacturers over the years had flirted with colours other than the traditional black - notably red, green, blue, brown and grey - few had ever gone for white as the standard colour. But that's just what Ilford did with the Advocate. The body is a pressure die casting of aluminium silicon alloy, finished in a hard-stoved ivory enamel, making it resistant to scratching, dirt and wear and meaning that the cameras on today's market have usually managed to keep their good looks.

The lens, which is not interchangeable, was originally an f/4.5 Dalmeyer, but later models sport f/3.5 Dalmeyers, whilst a few were made with Wray Lustrar lenses and even fewer with Ross lenses.

The between-lens shutter is speeded from 1/25 second to 1/200 second. It is released by a lever set into the top of the front of the body beside the lens and designed to be pulled sideways. The cable release socket is unusually placed right at the bottom of the front of the body, beside the lens.

Robot Star

It's a prime requirement for today's compact cameras to have built-in motor drives, but there's nothing new in that. A few of those from the past had them too, albeit powered by clockwork rather than batteries. The Robot Star is a good example from the era we are studying.

Robot cameras were made by Berning in Germany and the first model appeared as far back as 1934. There was a second model, called the Robot II, in 1939, then in 1952 the Robot Star appeared, the first Robot to use conventional 35mm cassettes. Before that, Robot cameras used 35mm film, but it had to be preloaded into the camera's own special cassettes.

Considering its need for a fairly heavyweight clockwork motor, the Robot Star is very small, measuring only 10 x 7.5 x 5cm. The model illustrated here sports an interchangeable 37.5mm f/2.8 lens and shutter speeds from 1/2 second to 1/1000 second. It takes square pictures, 24 x 24 mm on standard 35mm film which, unusually, travels right to left across the body. The clockwork motor drive is wound by a large knob on the top plate that needs a very strong wrist indeed to get it turned all the way. It supplies 24 exposures to each wind.

With the motor fully wound, the camera is used in the normal way. The actual exposure is made as the shutter button is pressed down and the film winds automatically as it travels up again. It is also possible to wind the film manually by turning the knob until a slight resistance is felt, at which point one frame has been advanced. Continuing to turn the knob does not move the film any more, but instead tensions the clockwork motor for future automatic winding.

The camera is synchronised for electronic and bulb flash and is also unusual in having a right-angled viewfinder which, coupled with the automatic film advance, would have been very useful for candid photography. It is switched into play by a small stud on the camera's top plate and used by looking into a tiny viewfinder window on the end of the body.

Other post war Robot cameras to collect include several models of the Robot Recorder, including the 24, 24e, 24F and 36, the last of which took a standard 24 x 36 mm frame size; the Robot Royal cameras, which included the 18 with a mask for 18 x 24 mm half frame images, the 24 for the more usual Robot size of 24 x 24 mm and the 36, for a 24 x 36 mm frame; and other Robot Stars including the Star II, Star 25 and Star 50. The rarest and most valuable today is the Robot Luftwaffe model, produced between 1940 and 1945, identified by an extra tall winding knob.

Berning also produced a very wide range of lenses for their Robot cameras that cover focal lengths from 30mm wideangle to 400mm telephoto.

Voigtlander Vito B

Photographers from the 1950s sigh nostalgically at the mention of the Voigtlander Vito B, then go on to tell you that its Color Skopar lens was one of the best of its time. Today, the cameras are still very common, relatively inexpensive and easy to buy on the collector's market.

The Vito name began in 1939 with a folding 35mm camera that was improved on with the Vito II, IIa and III up to the early 1950s. When Voigtlander went on to improve it even more by turning it into a rigid body design, they called it the Vito B.

One of the camera's most attractive features

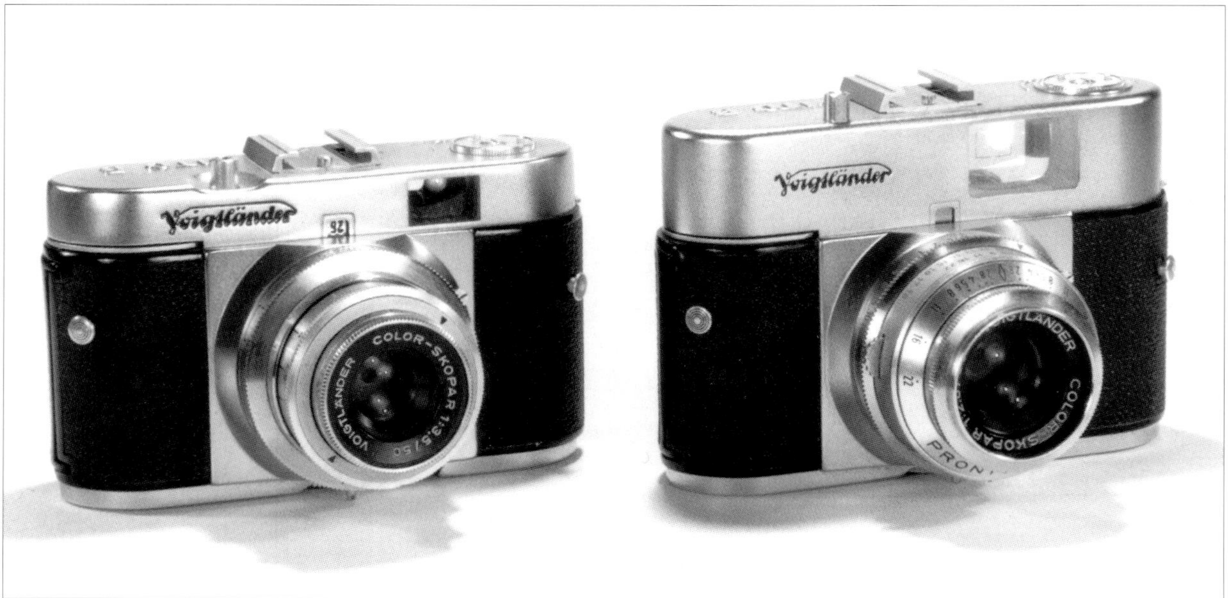

Two models of the Voigtlander Vito B, with f/3.5 and f/2.8 lenses.

is its size, the more common model measuring a mere 11 x 6.5 x 3 cm. But into those trim dimensions Voigtlander packed a full frame 35mm camera with an f/3.5 lens that focuses down to 3.5 ft and with shutter speeds from 1 second to 1/300 second plus 'B'.

That's the basic and most often found model. But there is another rarer version of the Vito B with a slightly different specification.

First of all, it adds an extra 10mm to the height of the body to incorporate a much larger viewfinder which, unlike the smaller model, has a bright frame incorporated. The lens on this model is upped to an f/2.8 Color-Skopar and the aperture and shutter speed dials are linked by an interesting mechanism.

The two controls that circle the lens are locked together with a third scale, marked in red between them. This shows Exposure Value numbers between 2 and 18. In normal use, the aperture and shutter speed ring are locked together: changing one automatically resets the other so that setting a smaller aperture is compensated for by the automatic setting of a slower shutter speed. Pressing in two studs on the exposure value scale then allows you to rotate the aperture ring independently of the shutter speed settings, thus setting a different exposure. With the studs released, the two are again locked so that shutter speeds and apertures, at the new exposure setting, are once again compensated for. Although the second model is better specified than the first, it looks somehow out of proportion in comparison and isn't nearly as attractive in its styling.

One other thing about the Vito cameras. The shutter is cocked by the film running over and turning a sprocket inside the body as it is advanced. So without a film in the camera, the shutter won't cock or fire and it is easy to assume that it is broken. To test the camera before buying, open the back and turn the sprocket with your thumb until it clicks, before you try the shutter.

Other cameras in the Voigtlander Vito series include the Vito C, CD, CL, CLR and Automatic. After that, Voigtlander moved on to Vitomatics, Vitorets and, in the Vitrona of 1964, they produced the first camera with a built-in electronic flash.

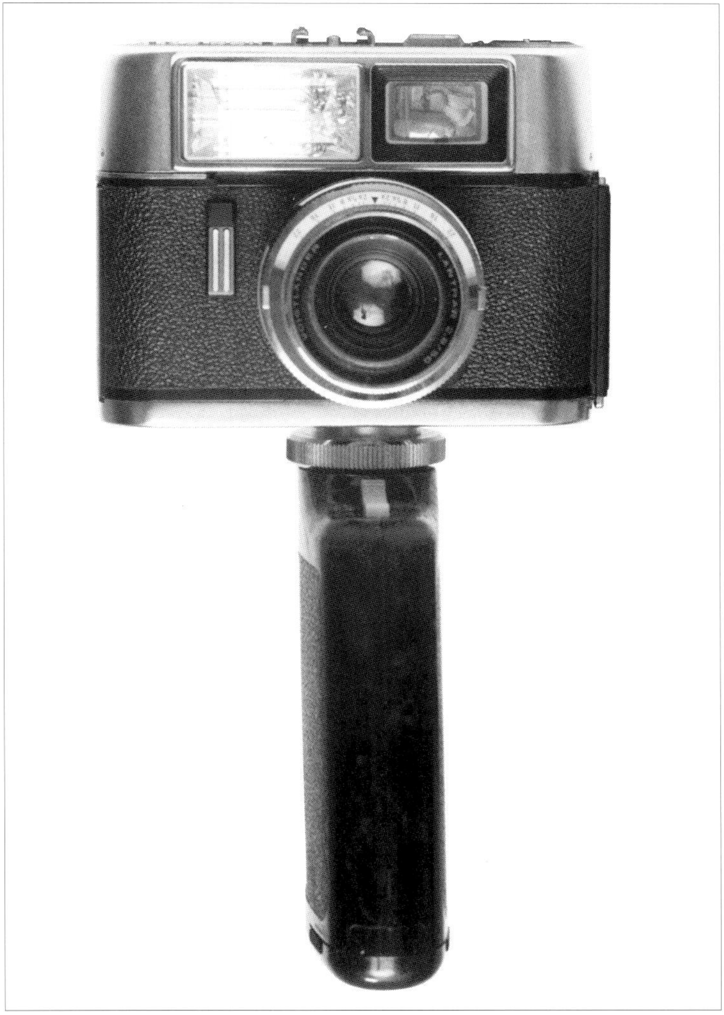

The Voigtlander Vitrona was the first camera with built-in electronic flash.

Braun Paxette and Super Paxette

Here's another delightful little camera, about the same size as the smaller Vito B, but with some additional features packed into its extremely trim dimensions.

The original Paxette I from 1952 has what appear to be two rangefinder windows and yet no sign of a rangefinder. That's because the second window actually houses an extinction meter, which makes it interesting to collectors. Later models added optical meters and non coupled rangefinders. Later again, but still in the 1950s, came the Super Paxettes, which had

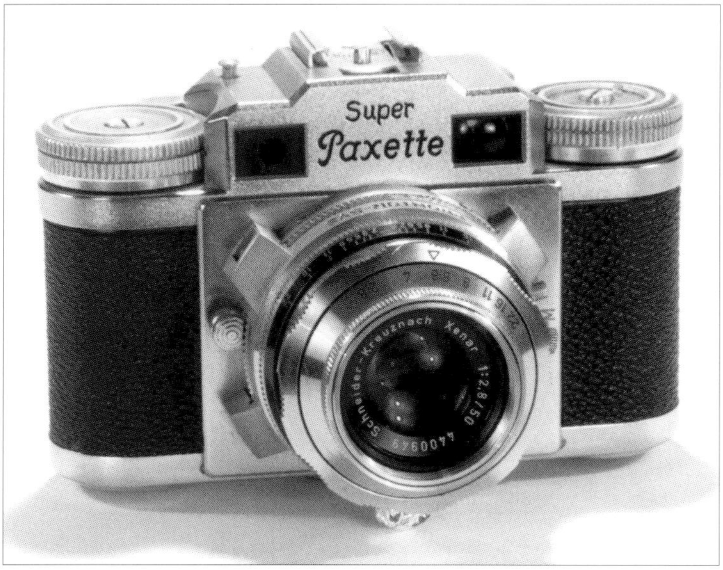

The Braun Super Paxette.

coupled rangefinders and, in 1956, the Paxette II cameras added interchangeable lenses.

When buying, don't be fooled into thinking the shutter is broken after you have wound the film and tried the release because it takes two strokes (actually more like one and three-quarters) to advance the film and cock the shutter on these models.

Halina 35x

When it was launched in 1959, the Halina 35X found itself being compared to the Leica, though more for its looks than its quality. Made by Haking in Hong Kong, it does, in fact, look very much like a scaled down screw lens Leica. The body is metal, finished in black grained leathercloth and the back is completely removable.

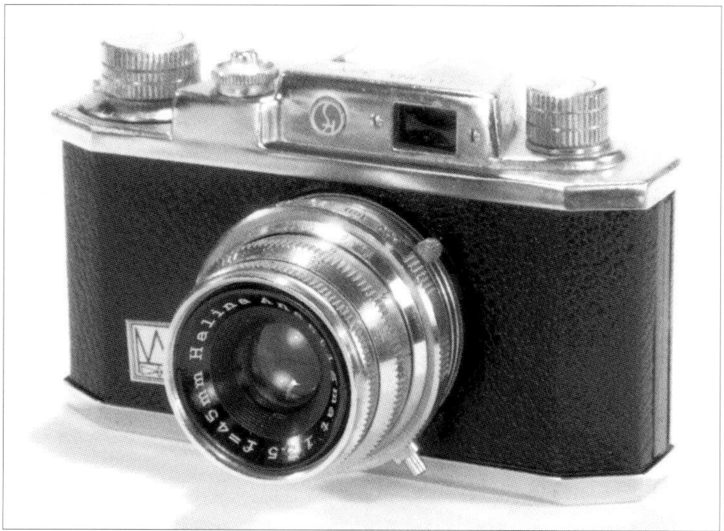

The Halina 35X.

The 45mm f/3.5 Halina Anastigmat lens focuses down to 3.5 ft, but is non-interchangeable. Apertures close down to f/16 and shutter speeds run from 1/25 second to 1/200 second plus 'B'.

The Halina 35X has two design faults. The first lies in the fact that the shutter needs to be independently cocked by means of a small lever on the side of the lens. If the film is wound and the shutter release pressed without first operating the cocking mechanism, then the double exposure prevention mechanism is activated and the next picture cannot be taken until the film is again advanced. Result: one wasted frame.

The second problem concerns the aperture ring around the lens. It is so stiff that attempting to change an aperture inevitably moves the focusing ring at the same time. To set an aperture it is necessary to hold on tight to the focusing control whilst turning the aperture ring and 35X photographers of the past soon found the need to set the aperture first before focusing, rather than the other way around.

The Halina is a fairly basic camera without a hint of a built-in rangefinder that was pretty much a standard on most German rivals of the time. But it is a solidly made little camera and its low price at the time made it a good seller in the late 1950s and early 1960s.

Bolsey B and B2

Despite Bolsey being known as an American company, its origins were in Switzerland with the man from whom the company and its cameras take their name: Jacque Bolsey. In 1923, he built the Cinegraph Bol, a combined still and cine 35mm camera that doubled as a projector. He went on to design and produce the Bolex, one of the most famous of all cine cameras, which he made until 1931, when the manufacturing rights were bought by Paillard, the name more usually associated with Bolex.

He also designed Alpa cameras before emigrating to America in 1939.

Immediately he saw a market for a quality, low-cost 35mm camera, against many of the American models of the time that he considered too expensive. The result was the Bolsey B.

It's a camera that is smaller than most 35mm models of this era, but also a little deeper with rounded corners tapering towards the back. The lens is a 44mm f/3.2 Wollensak set in an Alphax shutter that gives speeds from 1/10 to 1/200 second plus 'B' and 'T'. The lens is focused on a helical mount down to a closer-than-usual 2 ft. On the camera back, there is an adjustable depth of field scale that doubles as a film type reminder, though speeds are not set by ASA or DIN in the usual way. Instead, the reminder refers to film by name: 'Plus-X', 'Supreme', 'Super', 'Ultra Speed Pan', 'Type A Kodachrome', 'Daylight Kodachrome', 'Tungsten Anscocolor', 'Daylight Anscocolor' and 'Pan X'.

One advantage of the Bolsey over its contemporaries lay in its short body width of just 10.5cm. Because the film doesn't have to be wound as far as other cameras at the start or finish, it is possible to get an extra four exposures out of a standard length, although the counter still only goes as far as 36. Film wind, however, is a little unconventional It involves lifting the wind knob slightly before commencing the wind, then releasing it to continue and complete the action.

The camera can be used with flash by the addition of a rather crude external synchroniser which takes the form of an attachment that screws into the cable release socket just below the shutter release lever. As the shutter lever is depressed, it trips a spring that closes a circuit between two prongs and so fires the flash.

The Bolsey B was introduced in 1947 and was followed in 1949 by the B2, which has internal synchronisation. The flash is attached via two contacts in the back of the body just behind the rewind knob.

The B2 also has a novel form of double exposure prevention, not seen on the original camera. As the shutter lever is depressed to make the exposure, a spring loaded piston behind the lever jumps out, blocking the lever's full return and therefore preventing another exposure from being made. The piston withdraws and allows the release lever to travel to the top of its throw and so tension the shutter, as the film is wound on. If intentional double exposures are required, the piston can be pushed in manually.

The Bolsey was an interesting little camera, but it had a couple of shortcomings. The first was that it was rather small for large hands, a fact that made it unpopular with men, but more popular than usual with women photographers of the 1940s. The other was that although Jacque Bolsey was an innovative camera designer, he didn't know too much initially about the American economy. He produced a camera that was cheaper than its rivals, but he didn't take into account the rising economy of the country. Within five years of producing his first American camera, wages had all but doubled. American cameras, with their higher initial prices, weathered the storm. The Bolsey, with prices pitched low to begin with, ran into trouble.

Nevertheless, Bolsey did go on to produce further variations on the same basic theme,

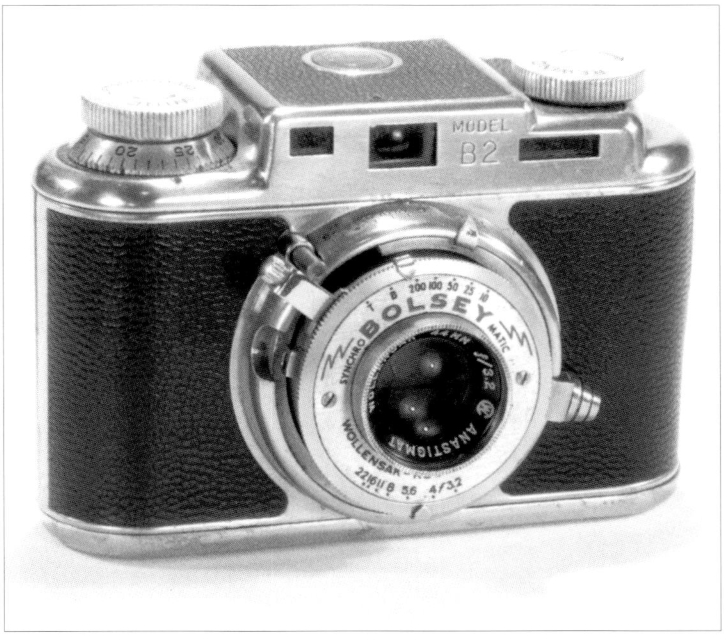

The Bolsey B2.

including an unusual twin lens reflex (see page 54), throughout the 1950s.

Rollei B35

This is one of a series of beautifully crafted 35mm cameras made by Rollei from 1966 through to the 1980s, some in Germany, but many in Singapore. Models include the original Rollei 35, then the B35, 35C, 35LED, 35S, 35SE, 35T and 35TE. Watch out too for special gold-plated editions - very expensive and a little out of reach of the average collector.

The B35 is one of the more common models and more attainable on the collector's market. For a full frame 35mm camera, it is amazingly small, measuring only 9.5 x 6 x 3.5 cm. The lens is a 40mm f/3.5 Triotar that lies flat against the body when not in use and extends on a shiny metal tube for picture taking. The shutter release cannot be fired unless the lens is extended.

The camera has no rangefinder, but it does have a built-in meter that deflects a needle across a scale built into the shutter speed dial With a chosen speed, from 1/30 second to 1/500 second set, the needle indicates the correct aperture, which is then transferred manually to the lens.

Film is advanced by a single stroke lever, unusually placed on the left of the body so that the film runs right to left. To compensate for the lack of space on the tiny top plate, the flash hot-shoe is on the base, next to a slightly raised tripod bush and the film rewind crank.

The camera has one small idiosyncrasy that can lead to damage for the unwary. When the lens is extended, it is locked into position by a small clockwise twist. Once the picture has been taken, the lens can then be retracted by pressing a tiny stud at the seven o'clock position and twisting the lens back the other way. But it won't twist until the film has been wound on. So the camera always has to be stored between use with the shutter tensioned.

Rollei B35, made in Singapore.

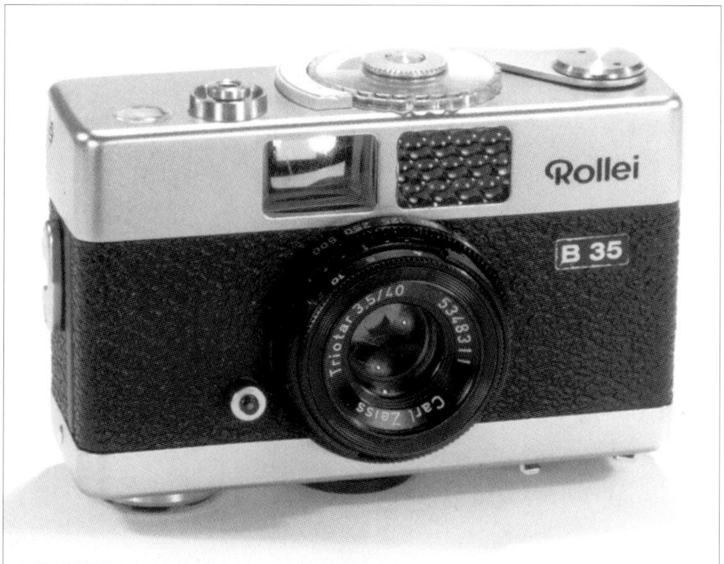

Contessa S310

Made in 1971, right at the end of Zeiss Ikon's lifetime, the Contessa S310 is now something of a rarity. The name has historical connections, dating back to the beginning of the century. In 1919, Contessa merged with Nettel to form Contessa-Nettel and that company, in turn, joined three others (Goerz, Ica and Ernemann) to form Zeiss Ikon in 1926. Zeiss first started to use the name on a series of 35mm folding cameras in the very early 1950s.

The Contessa S310 is an extremely compact full frame 35mm camera that measures only 10 x 7 x 5cm and features a 40mm f/2.8 Tessar lens. Focusing is by a small lever to the side of the lens that rotates the front element, at the same time moving an indicator on the left of the viewfinder up and down a scale that shows symbols for portraits, groups and scenes. It's an automatic camera that requires the user to set the aperture between f/2.8 and f/22. Moving the aperture control also shifts an indicator at the top of the viewfinder to indicate the setting. On the right side of the viewfinder, opposite the focusing scale, a needle then moves to indicate the automatically chosen shutter speed, though only three settings are shown: 1/30 second, 1/125 second and 1/500 second. The actual shutter speeds, however, stretch to a full eight seconds.

A control on the front of the body switches the camera from automatic to a fixed speed for flash photography, used in combination with manually set apertures. Film advance is by a lever wind with the frame numbers shown in a neat little window in the top plate as an indicator moves in a small rear mounted window to show that the film is advancing correctly. Rewind is by a rather over-large crank handle that folds out from the base plate.

An even rarer variation of the S310, called the S312, adds a coupled rangefinder to the specification.

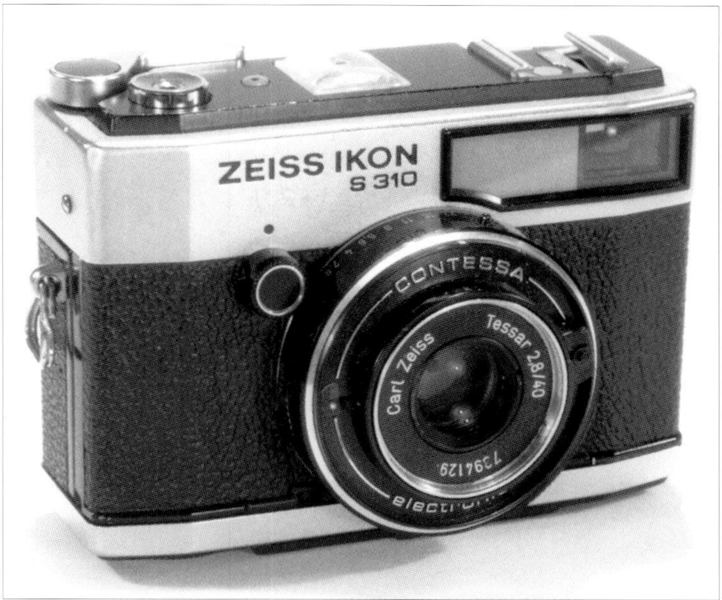

Zeiss Ikon's Contessa S310.

Olympus Trip

From the rare to one of the more common collector's items. This is the camera that put Olympus on the map. They made the Trip continually between 1968 and 1984, during which time it became one of the most popular cameras of its time.

The Trip, of course, is a full frame 35mm camera, but a quick glance shows how it was derived from the Olympus Pen cameras, not least in the incorporation of a large Selenium cell that surrounds the 40mm f/2.8 Zuico lens as it does in the Pen EE series (see pages 145-146). Zone focusing is controlled by a ring around the lens, click-stopping at four positions. Exposure is automatic, but apertures can be set manually from f/2.8 down to f/22 for flash photography, when a flashgun can be attached, either direct to the hot-shoe or via a separate synch socket.

Olympus Trips are not at all rare or expensive. Yet their place in an undoubted position of supremacy among mid-20th Century snapshot cameras makes them a collector's item today.

If you are buying one to use, watch out for sticky shutters and worn out meters.

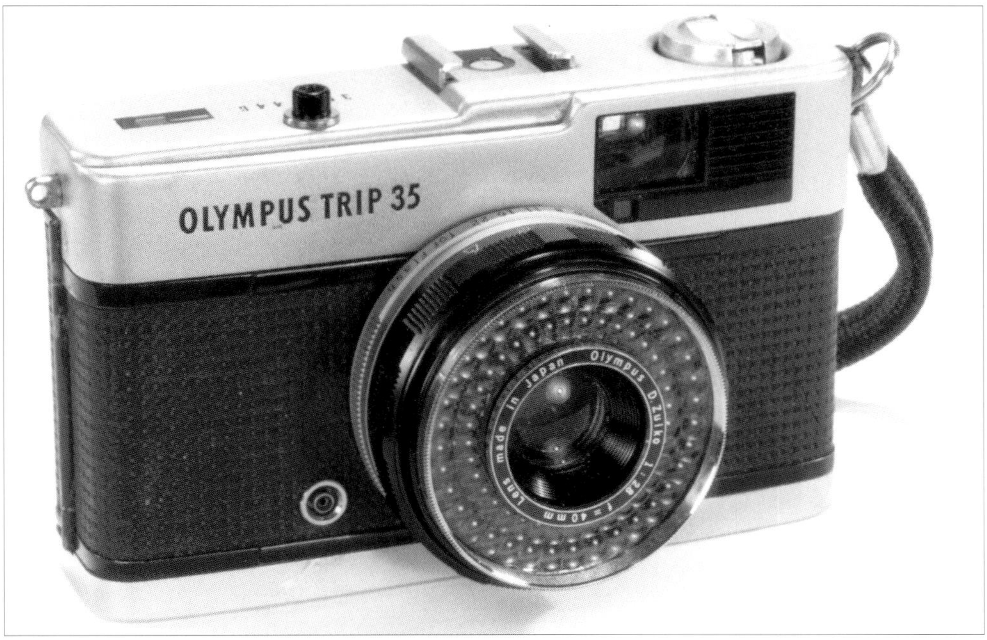

The extremely popular Olympus Trip.

Leica's First M Camera

IT'S A PRETTY safe bet to say that if it's Leica, it's collectable. Whole books have been written on the marque and it is not the intention of this one to deal with the subject in the sort of depth that can be readily found elsewhere. Instead, we're looking at one landmark that no collector can afford to ignore - the Leica M3.

The M3 was launched in 1954. Until then, the design of the Leica cameras, although having gone through many major improvements, still followed a basic body shape that owed a great deal to that first model introduced in 1925. The last screw-fit camera launched before the advent of the M3 was the Leica IIIf; the now legendary IIIg, the very last of the screw-fit models, being launched in 1956, two years after the M3.

The M3, however, represented a total rethink in style and design, offering, among many new features, a bayonet mount for lenses, a rangefinder with a longer base extended from 4cm to 7cm for greater accuracy of focusing and a viewfinder that automatically adjusted to the lens in use.

The idea for a new-look Leica with these three main attributes had actually been lying in a draw of the company's research department since 1936, but the Second World War from 1939 until 1945, followed by post-war reconstruction of Germany and its camera industry, meant that the launch of such a radically new design was delayed until the 1950s.

Around 1953, the Leitz factory at Wetzlar produced a small amount of special cameras with a very new look that were undoubtedly pre-production models of the M3. Film was wound by a lever rather than the knob that had been used on Leicas until then and the rewind knob was unusual in that it turned anti-clockwise. The film frame counter was external and stood slightly proud of the body and, on the camera's back, there was a small button to activate a film marking punch.

The production M3 on the collector's market, differs in several ways. The film marking punch is omitted; the wind lever, slightly curved in the pre-production model, has been straightened; the rewind knob is changed to the more traditional clockwise rotation; and the frame counter is sunk into the top plate.

Replacing the 39mm screw mount on previous models, the Leica M3 has a bayonet-fit lens which locks into position when mounted and turned through 30 degrees. The new rangefinder uses four fixed prisms in conjunction with a swinging lens coupled to the lens barrel via focusing linkages, and precise focusing with lenses of different focal lengths is achieved by the accurate matching of different lens barrel movements. The M3's new viewfinder represented a major achievement by Leitz, consisting of more than 100 individual components, built to a hitherto impossible precision and made to fit in an extremely small area of the camera's top cover. Despite that, it gives a view that, at 90 per cent life size, is large for a camera of this era.

The film is still loaded through the base, as with older screw Leicas, but the addition of a hinged door in the camera back makes it easier to insert.

The shutter speed dial which, on previous Leicas, rotated as the shutter was tensioned and released, remains stationary on the M3. Shutter speeds from 1 - 1/1000 second are set by the same control rather than the original two (one for fast, the other for slow speeds). The automatic frame counter resets automatically and, on the back of the camera, there is an adjustable disc to indicate the film in use: daylight colour, artificial light colour and black and white, together with a film speed reminder marked in ASA and DIN. Flash synchronisation is for electronic and bulb guns, with separate 'X' and 'M' sockets for each type.

The front of the M3 features three windows. The largest, at the far end, is the viewfinder, linked to the small one for the coincident image rangefinder that appears in the viewfinder. In the centre, a third window covered in ground glass is there to illuminate bright line frames in the viewfinder, matching to the lens in use.

With a standard 50mm lens in place, the viewfinder shows a large frame that corresponds to the image that appears on film, with a border round the edges so the photographer can see what is moving into the frame. As a 90mm or 135mm lens is bayoneted onto the body, this bright line frame changes to show smaller areas, once again corresponding to the angle of view of each lens. Whichever frame is displayed, focusing the lens causes it to move diagonally across the viewfinder, thus automatically correcting for parallax. For wideangle photography, Leitz made a special 35mm Summaron-M lens, complete with 'spectacles' - correcting lenses that adapt both the rangefinder and viewfinder windows.

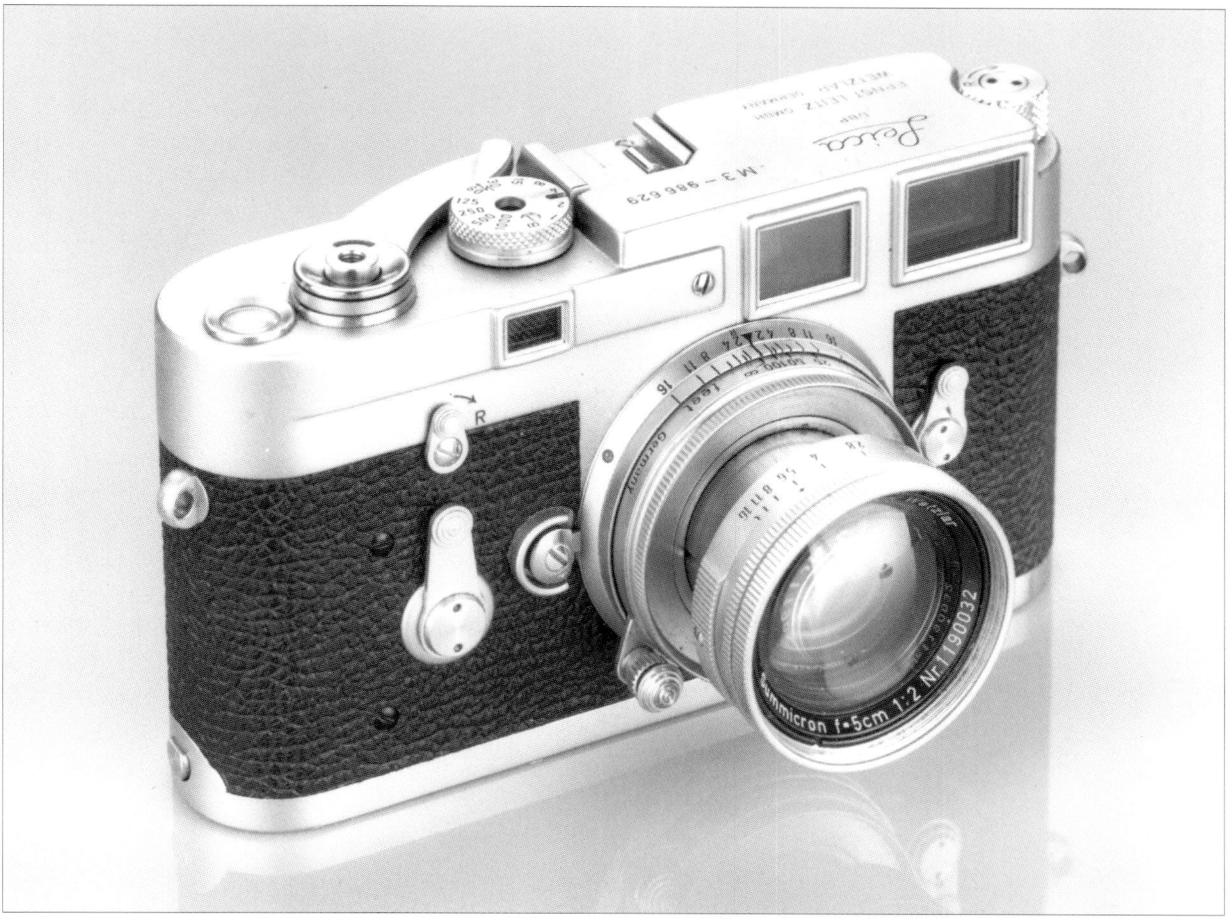

The M3 was the first bayonet-mount Leica.

Although the bright line frames appear and disappear as lenses are interchanged, it is possible to preview the effect of other lenses without removing the 50mm by pressing the release button on the 50mm lens, while twisting it very slightly one way or the other, causing each of the two long focus bright lines to appear in the viewfinder.

Over the years that followed its launch, the M3 was subject to several changes and improvements, and looking at the specification can help you identify which model you have. In 1955, a frame selector was added, allowing viewing frames in the viewfinder to be changed manually without the need for fiddling with the lens. In 1956, the shutter speeds were changed. Until then, the sequence was set at B-1-1/2-1/5-1/10-1/25-1/50-1/100-1/200 -1/500-1/1000. This was changed to the newer configuration appearing on other cameras at that time: B-1-1/2-1/4-1/8-1/15-1/30-1/60-1/125-1/250-1/500-1/1000, the new sequence allowing for one extra speed. In 1957 the pressure plate was changed from glass to metal. Until 1958, the lever wind required two strokes to advance the film one frame; that year, it was changed to one. That's why, on today's collector's market, the cameras are described as double stroke or single stroke. The original M3 was made in chrome but, from 1959 on, batches were made in black, 100 in that year, around 200 in 1960 and 1961, 2,000 in 1962 and then a few more small batches up to the time the camera was discontinued in 1966. Different finishes were also made for military use.

The Leica M3 was a revolution in camera design, influencing not just other manufacturers, but also allowing Leitz to produce different variations on the basic theme.

In 1956 the Leica MP appeared, the 'P' standing for 'Professional'. It was produced following consultations with press photographers and aimed principally at that market.

The Leica M2 followed the M3.

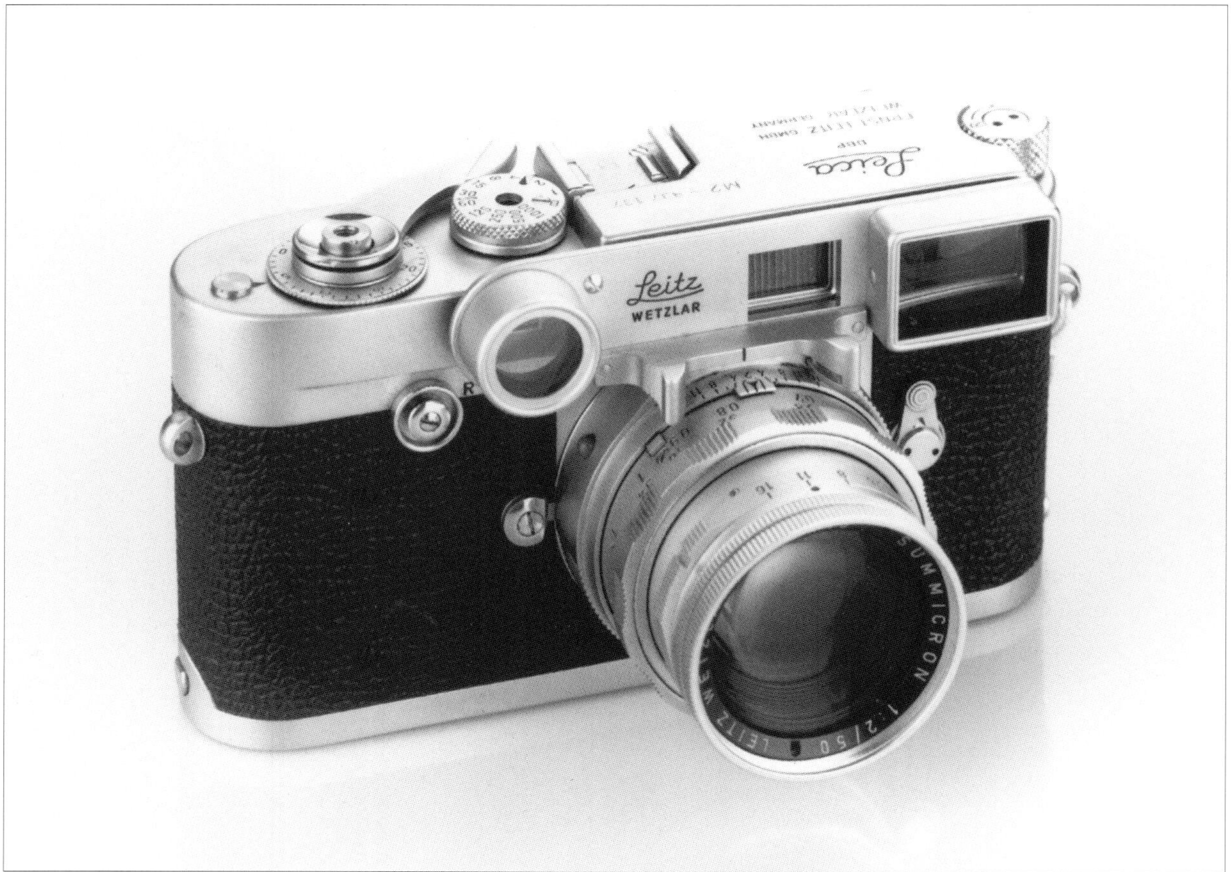

The camera is equipped with the Leicavit MP, a manually operated rapid wind base that means film can be advanced by an extendible, base-mounted trigger. The Leicavit can be adjusted for either single or continuous operation and, in the latter mode, the camera shutter is automatically released by an internal lever when the film advance trigger returns to its start position. Operating the trigger therefore advances the film and fires the shutter in one movement.

In 1958, a simpler version of the M3 was produced and called the M2. It has no self timer or automatic frame counter reset, and the viewfinder system is also different, featuring bright line frames for 35mm, 50mm and 90mm lenses, rather than the 50mm, 90mm and 135mm frames on the M3. The M2 was made in black and chrome versions. The camera also offers one interesting extra feature in the form of depth of field indication in the viewfinder, consisting of two small tabs in the rangefinder's field of view, one wide, the other narrow. When an unfocused subject, shown as a double image by the rangefinder falls within the width of one of these tabs, sharps focus is, nevertheless, indicated at one of two apertures. The narrow tab indicates sharp focus for an aperture of f/5.6, the wider one for an aperture of f/16. The device was subsequently fitted to the M3.

In 1959, the M1 was introduced as a very simplified version of the M2 for use in scientific photography. It has no rangefinder, although the viewfinder does offer parallax compensation with moving bright frames for 50mm and 35mm lenses.

The same year also saw the manufacture of what is now an extremely rare version of the M3, in the shape of the MP2, fitted with a Leitz Wetzlar electric motor on its base for automatic film advance, activated by the shutter release. Power is supplied by batteries in a special hand grip that attaches to the base of the camera. The MP2 was never sold commercially and it's a lucky collector who finds one on today's collector's market.

Even as late as 1994, the M3 was exerting its influence on Leica cameras. By then, the latest of the Leica rangefinder cameras was the M6, and that had been in production for ten years. To mark the 40th anniversary of the M3, however, a special version of the M6 was produced and called the M6J. As far as the body, shutter mechanism and meter are concerned, the camera is an M6, but the brass top plate and controls are almost identical to the M3, complete with 'Leica' engraved in the old style. It has a rangefinder adjuster screw on the front, as with the M3, but the viewfinder shows bright frames for 35mm, 50mm, 90mm and 135mm lenses, as on the M4 (introduced in 1967). The redesigned viewfinder, with its magnification of 0.85x shows nearly the same size of image as that of the M3. It also has the M4-style slanted rewind knob. The standard lens for the M6J is a 50mm f/2.8 collapsible Elmar in a new design recomputed to match existing Leica lenses and comes complete with an old-style chrome front lens cap and hood. Focusing is similar to the old Elmar but, unlike the M3, as the rear focusing ring is adjusted, the front section of the lens remained stationary. The M6J was made, specially for collectors, in a limited edition of 1,640.

The Best of British

In the early days, Britain had a major camera manufacturing industry that included some of the most respected names in photography - names like Sanderson, Thornton Pickard and Houghton, to name but three. Post-war, the products of British manufacturers began to be overlooked by the public in favour of, first German, then Japanese cameras. Many simple and fairly basic cameras continued to be designed and made in Britain but, after the mid-1950s, there were no real classics that could stand comparison with, for example, the likes of Zeiss Ikon. Nevertheless, in that decade that followed the Second World War, there were still a few manufacturers who, for a while at least, strived to keep the British flag flying among the real quality names in camera design.

Reid & Sigrist

Reid & Sigrist made one of the best Leica copies. They weren't alone, because literally hundreds of cameras have been built and copied from the Leica, in countries that include, notably, Japan, but also England, France, Italy, America, Russia and Germany. The English Leica appeared first in 1947. Originally, it was known simply as the Reid, but later, as other models were introduced, it was renamed the Reid III. That first model was followed by the Reid II and the Reid I.

The reason for the seemingly unchronological order of the models is simple. The I, II and III do not refer to the order in which the cameras were produced, but are references to the cameras from which they were copied.

The Reid III is a copy of the Leica IIIb. It is a coupled rangefinder camera with a Taylor Hobson 50mm f/2 lens and a focal plane shutter that offers speeds from 1 second to 1/1000 second. Like the Leica, speeds from 1/20 second down are adjusted by means of a separate control knob on the front of the camera.

The Reid II appeared in 1958, which was the point when the original camera became known as the Reid III. This second model is similar to its predecessor but without the slow speeds.

The Reid I, which also appeared in 1958, is a copy of the Leica Standard which, in turn, is a variation on the Leica I. It is similar to the Reid III, but without slow speeds or a rangefinder and was used mainy by the military.

The fact that Reid & Sigrist could legally build a camera that was so similar to the Leica without infringing patents or copyrights goes back to the end of the Second World War when German patents registered abroad were confiscated by the Allies by means of the Control Council Law of 1945. The following year, each of the Allies' member governments made the German patents available to the public free of charge. Also, British occupying authorities spent time at the Leica factory in Wetzlar and were allowed to remove various designs. As a result of all this, Reid and Sigrist were allowed to legally make their own ver-

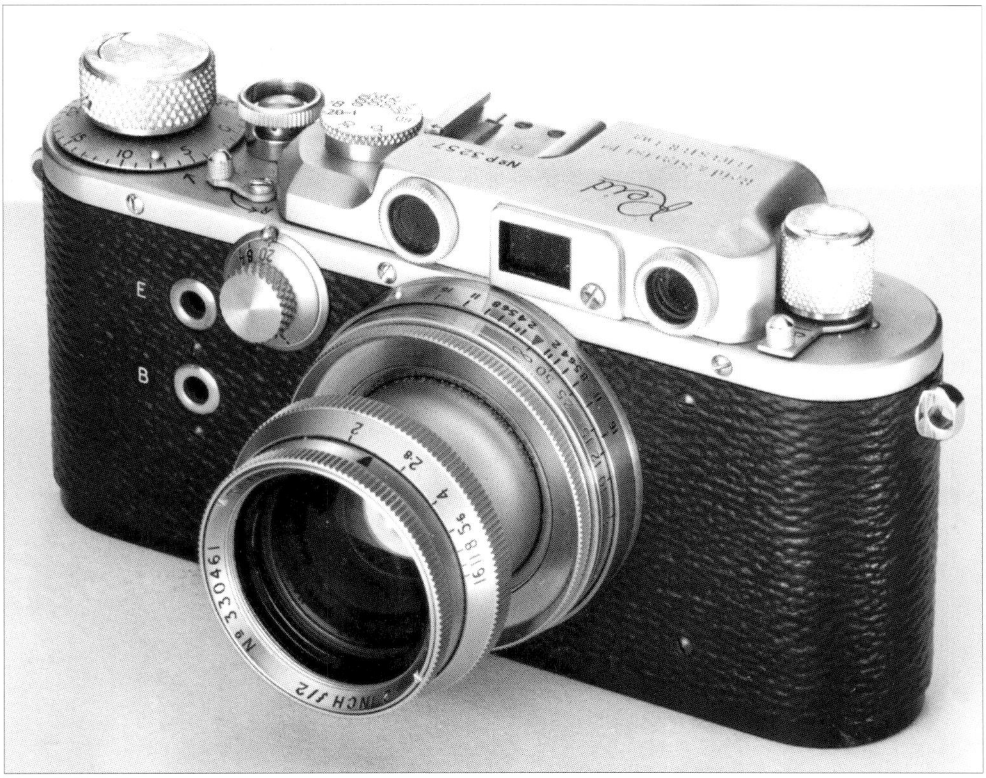

The Reid III, best of Britain's Leica copies.

sions of Leica cameras, and work began for the military in 1946, just one year after the end of the war.

The most common model on the collector's market today is the Reid III, followed by the Reid I. It has been reported that the Reid II has never been officially sold, but this isn't strictly true. Only a very few examples, however, have ever reached the collector's market.

Ilford

Say 'Ilford' to most photographers and they will think, first and foremost, of film. Turn the conversation to cameras and cheap snapshot models like the Craftsman, Envoy, Sportsman, Sporti and Sprite come to mind. But there was, in fact, one top quality camera from the Ilford stable which bears extremely favourable comparison with Leica. The camera in question is the Ilford Witness.

The Witness had an excellent pedigree, its genesis emanating from its two designers who came from Leitz and Zeiss respectively and who approached Ilford with their ideas at the end of the 1940s. After several abortive attempts to make the camera, Ilford placed its manufacture in the hands of a radio manufacturer from Surrey called Peto Scott Electrical Instruments. They too had manufacturing difficulties and, in the end, only about 350 cameras were actually built. It eventually reached the market in 1951.

The Witness is a beautifully streamlined camera whose appearance owes a lot to the influences of both Leica and Contax, hardly surprising when you remember where the original designers came from. It is a rangefinder camera and the rangefinder base is extra long at 65mm. To split and coincide the image, it uses prisms, rather than the mirrors that were being used in most cameras of the time.

Again, the influence can be seen, because shortly after the launch of the first Contax in 1932, the rangefinder design was switched by Zeiss away from mirrors, to a system that used two glass wedges to form a prism to bend the light, a design culled from the Super Ikonta.

The Leica influence, however, is back when

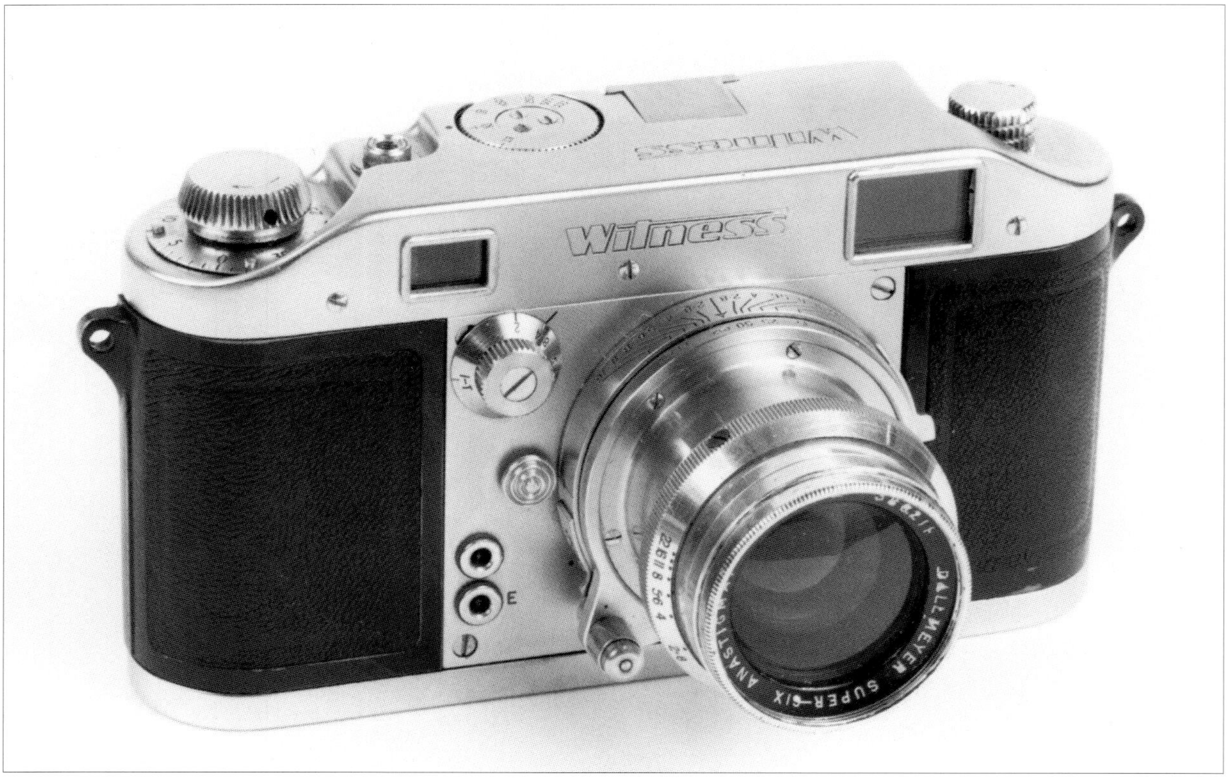

The Ilford Witness, an interesting combination of Leica and Contax, made in England.

it comes to the shutter speeds. Like the Leica, but unlike the Contax, the Witness uses a cloth focal plane shutter. It is speeded from 1 second to 1/1000 second and, like the Leica, the slow speeds, from 1 second to 1/25 second, are set on a separate dial on the front of the body.

One nice little quality touch that neither Leica nor Contax had thought about is a dust cover over the accessory shoe that springs up flush with the top plate when not in use.

Continuing with the Leica and Contax analogy, the lens mount is a clever combination of screw (as in Leica) and bayonet (as in Contax). Basically, it uses a 39mm Leica screw thread, but with three slots cut out of it. The result is that the original Witness lenses can be removed quickly with a bayonet movement, whilst most normal Leica lenses can be screwed into place. The camera is usually found with a 5cm f/2.9 Daron which is collapsible like Leica's Elmar, but you might also find a Witness with a 2 inch f/1.9 Dallmeyer Super-Six lens.

When it comes to removing the camera back, the Witness shows its Contax influence again. It comes off in one piece at the turn of two Contax-like catches on the base.

The Ilford Witness was proof that the English could make precision 35mm rangefinder cameras, but the company never seemed to take the interest in it that it deserved and it died soon after its launch. Today, it's a rare and collectable camera.

Wray Optical Works

The 1950s saw the rise and fall of England's only commercially successful 35mm single lens reflex. Made by the Wray Optical Works of Bromley in Kent, it was called the Wrayflex and there are three models to collect.

The first model was launched in 1950, at a time when SLRs traditionally sported waist-level viewfinders. Wray was the first to patent an SLR with an eye-level viewfinder in 1947. It worked by way of a pentaprism, but one that was unusually mounted on the camera's base, rather than in the more traditional place on the top plate. The proposed camera also had a built-in clockwork motor drive and a form of through the lens metering which wouldn't actually be incorporated into an SLR until the Topcon RE Super in 1963. But the camera was never built and Wray was beaten in the eye-level viewfinder race in 1949 by the Contax S, the first 35mm SLR with a pentaprism. A year later, in 1950, Wray launched its first 35mm SLR.

Today, collectors call this first model the Wrayflex I, but then it was known only as the Wrayflex. The camera is smartly finished in satin chrome and black grained leather. It has an eye-level viewfinder but, surprisingly considering Wray's original patent, it uses mirrors in the viewfinder rather than a pentaprism. A moving mirror in the traditional place at 45 degrees behind the lens reflects its image to a ground-glass focusing screen, where it is viewed via two more appropriately angled mirrors and the viewfinder eyepiece.

The result is a viewfinder image that is the right way up, but laterally reversed, just as is the case with a waist-level finder: subjects moving left to right in front of the camera, move right to left in the viewfinder. With the camera held upright for a vertically composed picture, the viewfinder image turns upside down. It's not an ideal method of viewing the subject, but it's a system that helped keep costs down: reviewing the camera in 1953, Amateur Photographer magazine pointed out that the addition of a pentaprism might have added £20 to the price of the camera which was already selling for more than £94 with an f/2 lens.

By today's standards, the image is rather dim, but to aid focusing there is a small magnifier cemented in the centre of the focusing screen to give an enlarged and brighter portion of the scene.

Unscrewing the lens reveals another surprise for those weaned on traditional SLR designs. The mirror and the focusing screen are joined in a single unit that folds down, as the film is advanced, to put the mirror at the usual 45 degree angle. Then, as the shutter release is pressed, not just the mirror, but this whole unit swings back and up, so that the mirror now lies flat across the top of the inside of the body, its

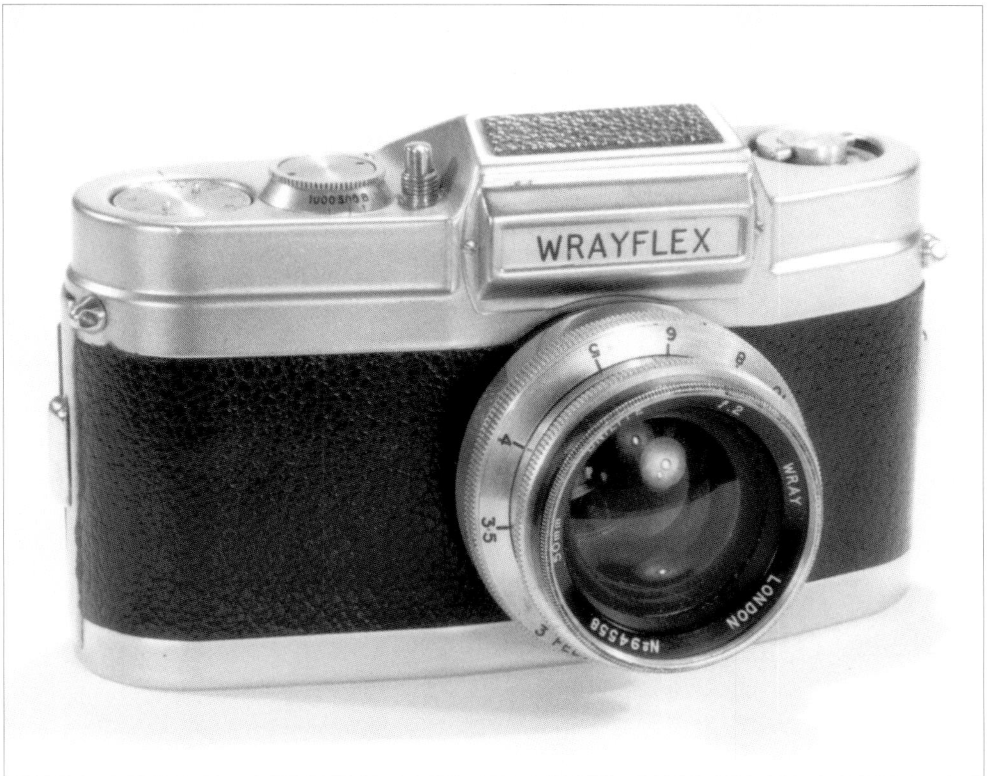

The Wrayflex I, made to take 24 x 32 mm negatives.

reflective surface facing down, while the focusing screen disappears inside the hollow viewfinder space where any other 35mm single lens reflex would have been housing a solid pentaprism.

Using the mirror arrangement rather than a pentaprism gives the Wrayflex smoother lines than most other 35mm SLRs, in which the viewfinder hump is always a predominant feature, leaving a very clean top plate whose only controls are the frame counter, a shutter speed dial and shutter release to one side of the viewfinder; a rewind key (not a knob) on the other.

Film wind is by way of another larger key that recesses into the base of the camera and which works very well in theory. All it takes is a half turn of this key to advance the film, tension the shutter and bring the mirror into place behind the lens. In practice, however, it creates obvious problems when the camera is mounted on a tripod, something that Wray solved in 1955 with the launch of the Wrayflex Tripod Cradle.

This consists of a T-shaped light alloy platform. With the camera held in place by a screw into its tripod bush at one end and a pair of small pins at the other, the whole thing is mounted on a tripod by means of one of two bushes: the first immediately beneath the camera body, the other beneath the lens.

At the same time, the film wind key fits into a deep slot within a disc mounted flush with the top surface of the cradle. Two felt pads at either end hold the camera itself slightly proud of this disc, which protrudes from beneath the camera body and, when turned by its milled edge, winds the key to advance the film.

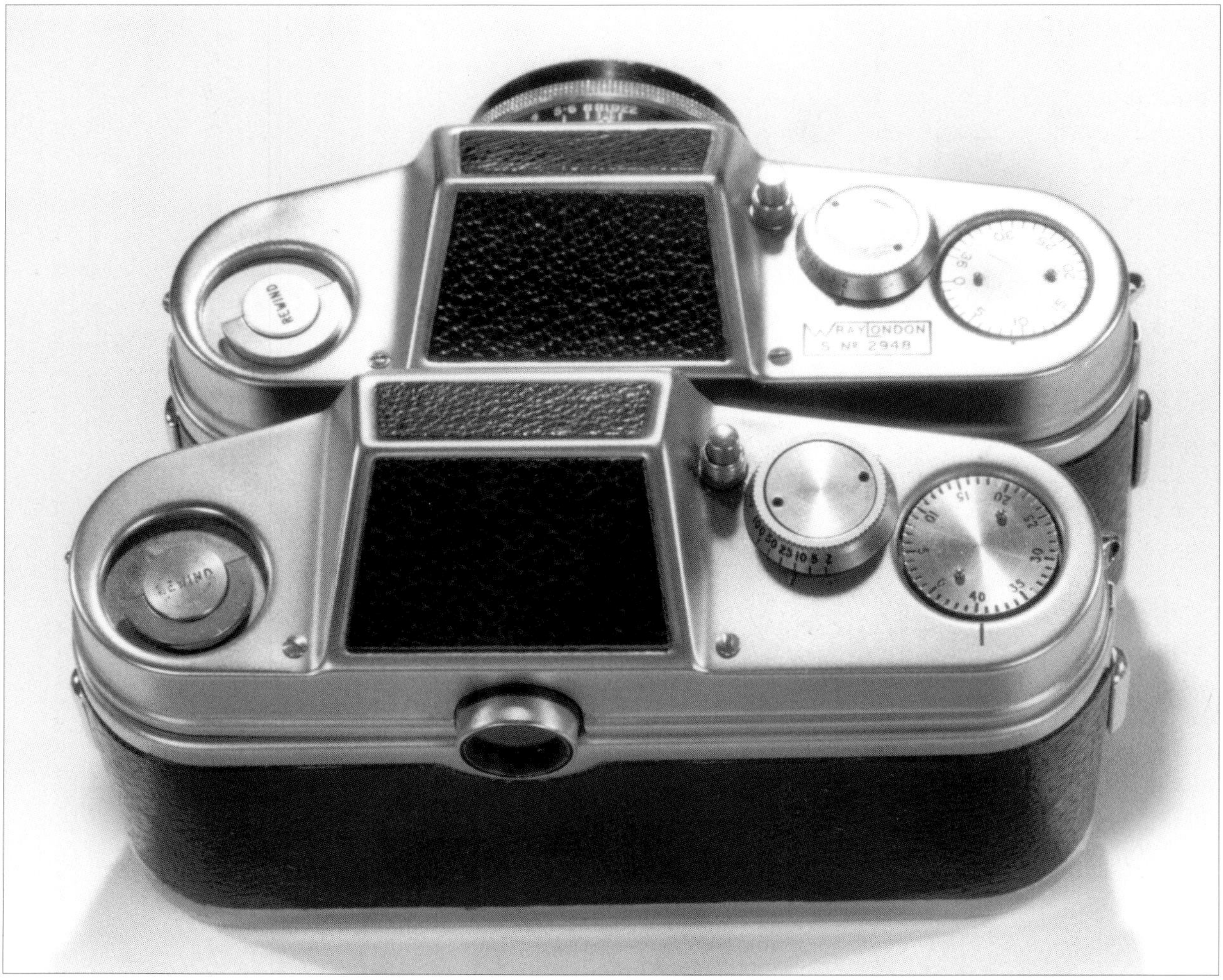

Externally, the Wrayflex I and Ia are identical, apart from the frame counters.

The first cameras have no flash synchronisation, but this was soon remedied by later cameras synchronised for either flash bulbs or electronic flashguns, via three sockets next to the lens: top and centre for electronic, middle and lower for bulbs. A shutter speed of 1/25 second was recommended by the makers for both types, although synchronisation is possible up to 1/50 second.

If you are a collector who likes to use classic cameras, beware of using flash because electrical contact on the Wrayflex is maintained from the time the shutter is released up until it is reset. This means that if a flashbulb is inserted into an attached gun before winding the film and so resetting the shutter, it will fire prematurely - and probably burn your fingers into the bargain!

Another unusual aspect of that first model Wrayflex is its film format of 24 x 32 mm. At the time of its launch, there was a consensus of opinion that thought this was a better format than the traditional 24 x 36 mm. Firstly, it gave more exposures to a film, particularly important at a time when, with the Second World War just ended, film was still scarce and expensive. Secondly, its ratio matched the traditional shape of photographic papers more exactly than a 24 x 36 mm format, which invariably led to the image having to be cropped to fit.

The 24 x 32 mm format was one that the Wrayflex shared with the Nikon I. Unlike the Japanese company, however, who went on to produce the Nikon M and S with a 24 x 34 mm format, Wray soon saw the error of its ways and, in 1954, a new version, now usually referred to as the Wrayflex Ia, was launched with the standard 24 x 36 mm film format. The new camera did not replace the first model, but sold side by side with it, giving buyers a choice of two formats.

To most outward appearances, there is no difference between the Wrayflex I and Ia and, short of opening the back to measure the format, the only way to tell them apart is by looking at the film counters, small graduated discs inset into the top plate. The model I counts up to 44, whereas the Ia goes only as far as 36.

The focal plane shutter on the Wrayflex is speeded from 1/2 - 1/1000 second, lenses are interchangeable on a screw thread and apertures have to be stopped down manually after focusing at full aperture. Standard lenses are the five-element 5cm f/2 Unilite and four-element 5cm f/2.8 Unilux, both internally coated. The Unilite has marked click stops down to f/22, but there is another unmarked stop past the smallest one that gives in the region of f/45. Other lenses listed at the time of its launch include the 3.5cm f/3.5, 9cm f/4 and 13.5cm f/4 Lustrars.

Only about 700 Wrayflex I cameras were produced, followed by a further 1,700 Model Ia cameras.

Then, in 1959, the company produced the Wrayflex II. In style, it was similar to the I and Ia, but incorporated the long-awaited pentaprism, which gave the top plate a new and somewhat ugly top-heavy look, compared to the sleeker designs of its predecessors. Beside the pentaprism, the camera substituted a rewind knob for the key found in both Model I cameras, and all the Model IIs use the standard 24 x 36 mm film format.

Unfortunately, despite everything, it was too late to seriously succeed. By then, previously enforced import restrictions had been lifted, allowing foreign cameras into Britain more freely than ever before. Suddenly, British pho-

The Wraflex II, the first Wrayflex with a pentaprism, but produced too late to be successful.

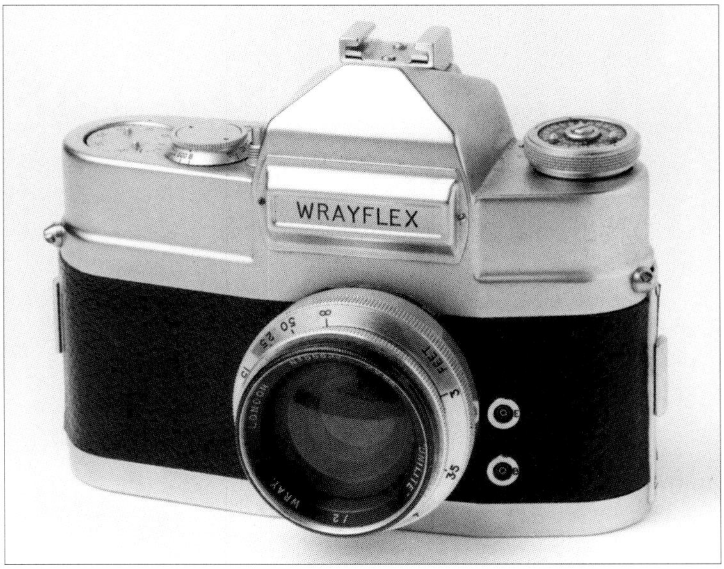

tographers had a choice of top names from Germany and Japan, less costly and with far better specifications. In the end, only around 300 of the Wrayflex II were made, making this third model the rarest - and most collectable - of the three.

Corfield

In 1953, the British Journal Photographic Almanac carried an advertisement for a camera that didn't exist - at least, not in the form that was illustrated. The picture showed an artist's impression of a camera that owed a little to the Leica I. The top plate featured film wind and rewind knobs, shutter speed dial and a square viewfinder with accessory shoe on top. The shutter release was on the front of the body to one side of a lens that might have been slightly influenced by Leica's Elmar, but which actually bore no real resemblance to any lens of the day.

"The new 35mm camera by Corfield for Great Britain and the World," proclaimed the text, which went on to point out that the new camera took all Leica type lenses and had a focal plane shutter. More than that it didn't say.

The reason this advertisement was so vague was because it had been rushed out to meet a tight deadline at the end of 1952 before plans for the new camera were finalised. In the illustration, the lens, like the viewfinder, was a figment of the artist's imagination, attached to a body which existed only as a prototype and, by the time the advertisement actually appeared in 1953, the project had been reworked to produce a rather different camera. The result was the first Periflex, which today is a very collectable English camera.

The Periflex I with its unusual method of focusing.

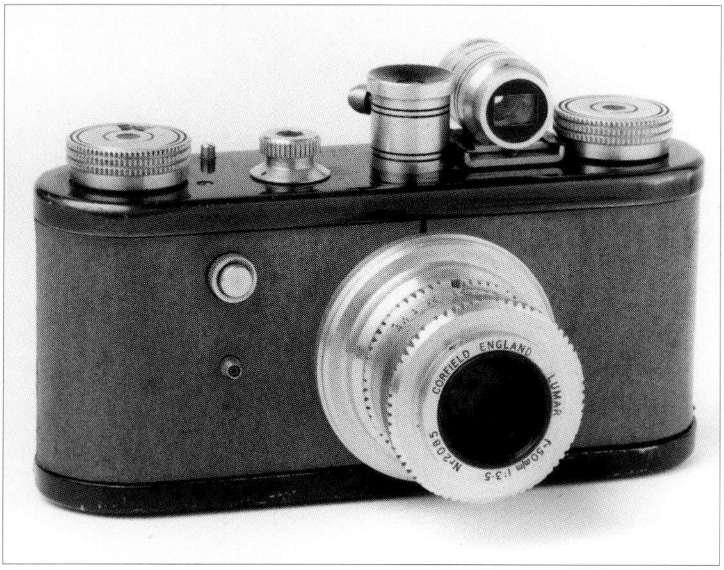

It was the brainchild of Kenneth Corfield, later to become Sir Kenneth for his work in the industrialisation of Northern Ireland to which the factory moved in 1958. A decade before, however, he and his brother John, founded K.G. Corfield Limited, based at Wolverhampton, initially to make photographic accessories. But Corfield had always harboured a longing to make his own camera and soon began work on a highly sophisticated subminiature 16mm camera, modelled around the Mikroma cassette. That plan was abandoned for marketing reasons and research shifted to a new idea for a moderately priced 35mm body for Leica lenses.

At this time, not long after the end of the Second World War, it was all but impossible to buy new Leicas in the UK. Board of Trade restrictions prevented the import of expensive foreign cameras unless justification could be found on medical, industrial, research or technical grounds, and English purchase tax added further restrictions. But secondhand Leica lenses were available. So Corfield turned his attention to making a camera body with a focal plane shutter that would take the German optics, aiming it at Leica photographers who required a second body.

By the middle of 1952, he had a working prototype of a body with a focal plane shutter and Leica thread, but no viewfinder. With the deadline for the BJ advertisement looming, an artist was hired to produce the illustration, based on the existing body, with the addition of an imaginary lens and viewfinder. Corfield was disappointed with the result, but it went off to the printers.

Meanwhile, Corfield had begun to think about designing and adding a lens and persuaded the British Optical Lens Company in

Walsall, not far from his own premises, to build it. The result was the Lumar and, with that, the concept of the camera began to change.

In September 1952, the Corfield brothers came to the decision that some kind of focusing device was needed in their new camera. A rangefinder, such as that featured in Leicas of the time, was beyond the technical skills of the Corfield factory. A single lens reflex design was considered but it would have meant a lot more tooling and capital investment than was available. It would also have meant a redesign of the body which was too slim to take a reflex mirror.

The compromise that followed resulted in one of the more unusual features seen in camera design, and one which became synonymous with Corfield cameras.

A periscope was added that could be manually pushed down into the film plane to pick up one small area at the top of the image (later cameras would take the periscope all the way to the centre). It wasn't meant as a viewfinder, only as a method of focusing and, as such, the camera still featured a separate optical viewfinder on the top plate - though one which was round rather than square as in that original artist's guesswork.

The periscope idea was planned, designed and tested in three months flat and the new camera launched in May 1953, ready for the Queen's Coronation on 2nd June that year. It was called the Periflex, the name taken from the two words that epitomised its design: PERIscope and reFLEX.

The original Periflex 1 is distinctive for having a brown pig-skin covering on an aluminium body, the top and base plate in a black anodised finish. The 50mm f/3.5 Lumar lens was made in an aluminium mount and available in coated and uncoated versions. But the pig-skin version didn't prove as popular as expected and was soon dropped in favour of a second version of the Periflex 1 with a more traditional black leatherette covering. However, what made the Periflex unpopular then makes it extra collectable today because pig-skin Periflexes are much rarer than their black leather cousins.

Early versions of the Periflex 1 used the Lumar lens, later versions featured the Lumar-X. A third version can also be found with either black or silver anodised top and base plates.

The pressure plate on the very early cameras is made of plate glass, chosen not only for its flatness and smoothness but also because it was cheaper than tooling up for a metal plate. All three cameras use the manually operated periscope focusing device, have shutters speeded from 1/30 - 1/1000 second, use M synchronisation for flash and have a range of clip-on optical viewfinders to suit 28mm, 35mm, 45mm, 50mm, 85mm, 90mm, 100mm and 135mm focal length lenses.

In 1957, a very new style of Periflex appeared on the market, starting with the Periflex 3. The periscope focusing system is still in evidence, on these cameras, but is now integrated into the body, wound down automatically as the film is advanced and returning as the shutter is released. A built-in optical viewfinder has interchangeable front elements for different focal lengths of lens and the slowest shutter speed is 1 second. Next to the viewfinder a small window displays the selected film and shutter speeds.

The following year saw the release of the Periflex 2. Following the example of Leica,

The Periflex III.

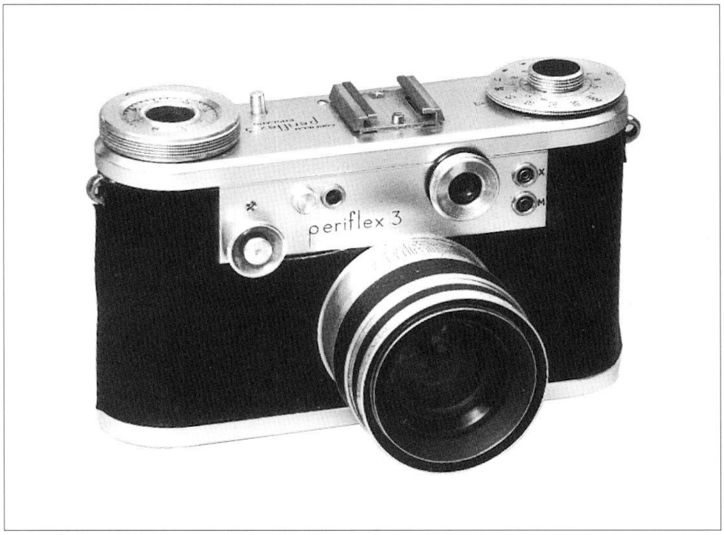

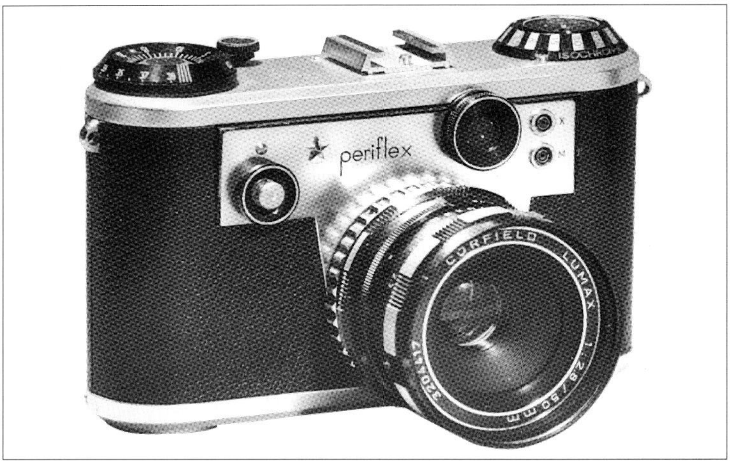

The Periflex Gold Star.

who released the M3, followed by the less expensive M2, the Periflex 2 is a cheaper version of the Periflex 3, with a maximum shutter speed of 1/500 second and an interchangeable optical viewfinder.

The Periflex 3a that followed in 1959 is similar to the Periflex 3, but with the addition of lever film wind. The following year, the 3b arrived, available only in black lacquer.

Then came the Periflex Gold Star in 1961 to replace the Periflex 2. This one features a Prontor focal plane shutter with speeds only from 1 - 1/300 second, which might seem like an unusual move when previous cameras were speeded to 1/1000 second. There was, however, a good reason.

Until then, movement of the first blind on a focal plane shutter was used to trip the second blind. This inevitably meant that the release of the second blind interfered briefly with the movement of the first one, resulting in uneven exposure across the image. In the Gold Star's shutter, the two blinds were released separately, by means of the same mechanism used in Prontor shutters, holding black and then releasing the second blind, independent of the first. Today, the system is commonplace in focal plane shutters; in the 1960s, it was an innovation.

The Periflex Interplan.

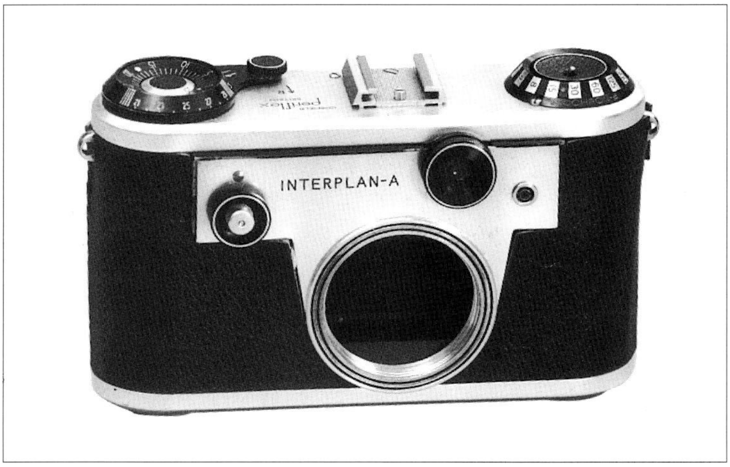

Finally, there is the Interplan range of cameras, produced as simplified versions of the Gold Star, without the now famous periscope but with interchangeable viewfinder lenses. You'll find three versions with three different lens mounts: the Interplan-A with a Leica screw thread, the Interplan-B with an M42 screw thread for Pentax, Edixa and Praktica lenses and the Interplan-C with an Exakta bayonet mount.

Well, not quite finally, because late in 1961, the Periflex Maxim was developed, primarily as a simple amateur camera. It had no periscope, the shutter speeds covered only 1/30 - 1/500 second and the intention was to sell it with the 45mm f/3.5 Lumax. By the early 1960s, however, Corfield was suffering the fate of so many English and not a few German camera manufacturers, as the Japanese began to get a hold on the market with mass produced, cost effective yet sophisticated cameras. Along with the Maxim, Corfield produced a medium format 6 x 6 cm single lens reflex called the Corfield 66, but only 300 or so were made.

As for the Maxim, last of the Corfield 35mm cameras, a mere six prototypes were produced, of which only one is still known to be in existence.

For the collector, the three Periflex 1 cameras are the most interesting and the pigskin version the most attractive of them all.

Small, Smaller, Smallest

EVERY AGE has had its 'miniature' cameras. In the 1930s, photographers called the 6 x 6 cm format produced by Rolleiflexes miniature, which it was when compared to the cut film and plate film cameras of the day. As 35mm became more popular, that too became the new miniature format. But the late 1940s, through to the 1960s saw a spate of cameras that were more than miniature - they were *sub*miniature, designed to take 16mm film.

For a time during the 1950s, 16mm really did look like the format of the future and it was used in some amazingly sophisticated cameras, including the Hapyucc SLR (see pages 47-49) and the Minicord TLR (see page 58). There was even a panoramic camera made for 16mm in the shape of the 1961 Viscawide.

Neither was 16mm the only subminiature format. Here's a selection of small, smaller and the smallest cameras from this era.

Minolta 16

This range of cameras is perhaps the easiest to find and among the least expensive to buy. Their style typifies 16mm cameras of the 1950s, a flat package with a lens on the side whose genesis owes a little to the Minox, albeit a rather fat version of that older and much sleeker design. In fact, the first Minolta 16, made in 1950, even had a push-pull film advance, just like the Minox.

From then, right up until the mid-1970s, many different models were made in Japan, with varying degrees of automation, early models purely manual, later ones with built-in match-needle metering. The cameras produce

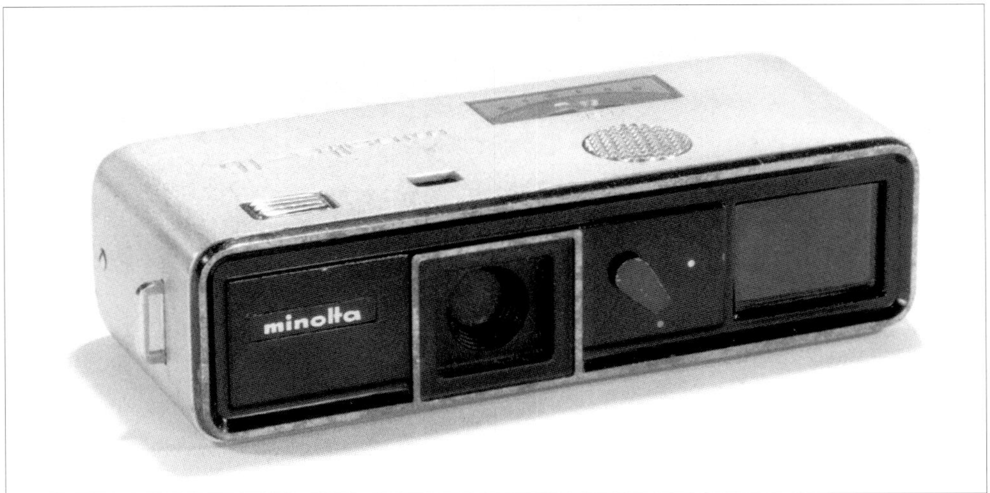

Minolta 16PS, one of the many Minolta 16mm cameras.

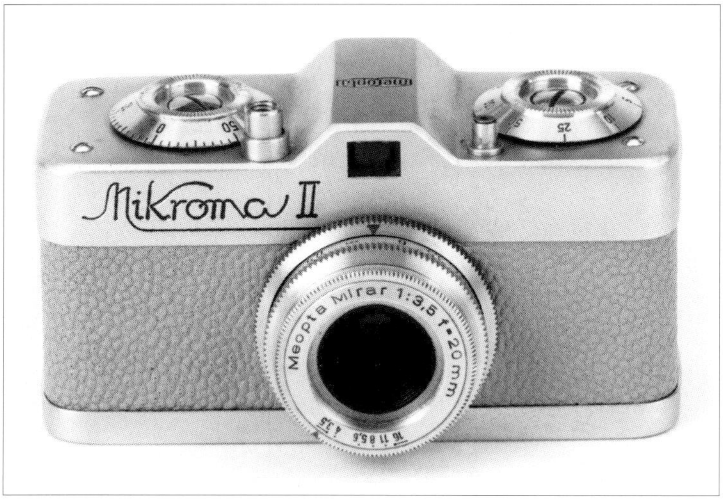

The Mikroma, made in Czechoslovakia by Meopta.

10 x 14 mm images and, with the exception of that first model which had an f/3.5 lens, they usually feature an f/2.8 Rokkor with focal lengths that vary between 20mm and 25mm.

The camera illustrated is a Minolta 16PS, made in 1964. It has a 1/100 second shutter speed for normal daylight photography, which can be shifted to 1/30 second for flash. Apertures are adjusted by a thumb wheel that moves a pointer across a scale with symbols for bright sun, hazy sun, cloudy bright and cloudy dull.

Mikroma

In 1949, Meopta, a Czechoslovakian camera manufacturer, made the Mikroma for 16mm film. It's a fairly sophisticated little camera with a three-speed shutter.

Much rarer is the model made for the Czechoslovakian police in 1960. This one is black and, as well as an eye-level viewfinder, it has a waist level one mounted on the front. The Mikroma II appeared in 1964. It is similar to the first model, but increases the shutter range to seven speeds from 1/5 - 1/400 second. Most models have a green covering, but you might also find a rarer beige version.

In 1961, the design was used as the basis for a subminiature stereo camera (see page 109).

Mamiya 16

The Japanese Mamiya 16 is similar in design to the Minolta 16, but more sophisticated. Early models, first launched in 1949, were manual, but by 1959, when the camera illustrated here was introduced, built-in meters had arrived with match needle exposure control.

This one is the Mamiya 16 Automatic. It

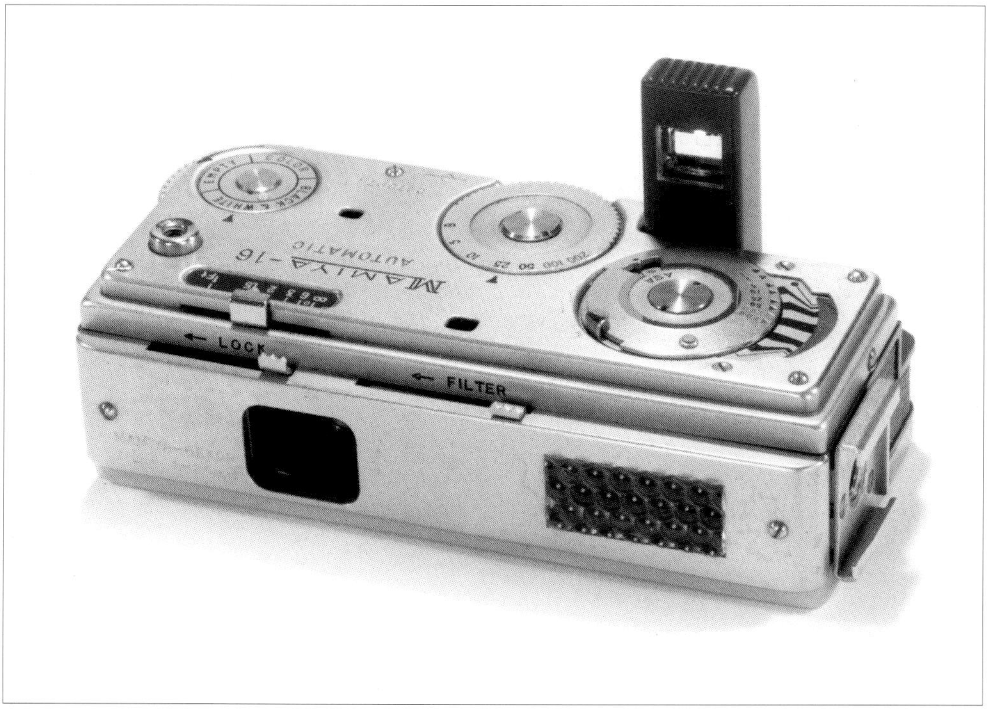

Mamiya 16 Automatic.

takes 10 x 14mm images and features a 25mm f/2.8 Mamiya Sekkor lens, focused by a sliding control on the top of the body. Shutter speeds are from 1/5 second to 1/200 second, a built-in yellow filter slides into place over the lens and an optical viewfinder swings up from the back of the body.

Mamiya 16s are fairly easy to find on the collector's market, but keep an eye open for a special version of the first model, made for the Japanese police. It's black with detachable waist level viewfinder, no filter, fixed focus lens and shutter speeds of 1/25, 1/50 and 1/100 second, plus 'B.'

Mec 16SB

Another of the flat package shaped 16mm cameras, this one was launched in 1960, the third of three similar cameras made by Feinwerk Technik in Germany for 10 x 14 mm exposures.

A slide pulls out from one side, revealing a direct vision viewfinder and unmasking the Rodenstock Heligon lens which is set deep into the body. Unlike some 16mm cameras, however, the slide doesn't advance the film, there's a lever wind on the back of the body for that.

Shutter speeds from 1/30 - 1/1000 second and apertures from f/2 - f/16 are controlled by dials on each side of the body and juggled until a moving needle meets an arrow in a small window to get correct exposure.

But this is not the readout from any ordinary built-in meter. The Mec 16SB is important for being the world's first camera with through the lens metering.

Rollei 16

The Rollei 16 was first sold in 1963 and takes 12x17mm exposures on 16mm film, wound from a cassette by a claw mechanism. The film wind is activated by a sliding section that push-pulls in and out from one end of the body and which also incorporates the viewfinder. At the end of the roll, the film is wound back again into the cassette in the way of a 35mm camera.

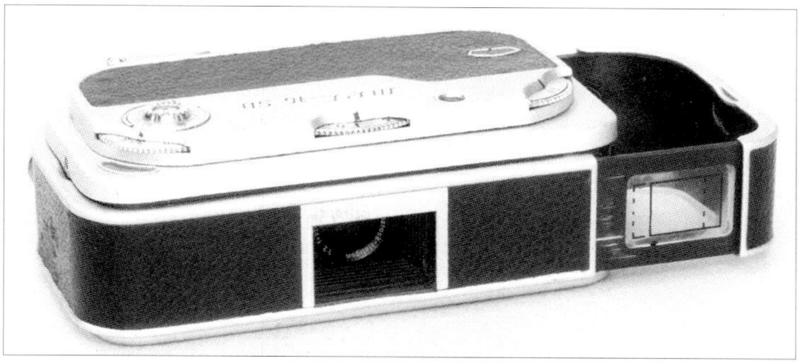

Mec 16SB, the first camera with through the lens metering.

The Rollei 16 incorporates a Selenium cell meter, linked to an automatic exposure system, but apertures can also be set manually, on either of two scales. One is for flash photography, the other automatically sets the shutter speed to its 'B' setting, so time exposures can be made at any aperture. The standard lens is a 25mm f/2.8 Tessar, focused by a thumbwheel on the top plate, from 0.4 metres to infinity. As the lens is focused, a brightframe shifts across the viewfinder to compensate for parallax.

The camera can be adapted with add-on wideangle and telephoto Mutar lenses which bayonet onto the front of the standard to change the focal length to about 15mm and 43mm respectively.

A second version, of the camera, known as the 16S, had an improved film winding mechanism and shutter release.

Look for the cameras in different coloured bodies: cream snakeskin, green and red versions are the rarest, followed by black snakeskin and the standard black version.

Production of Rollei 16 cameras ended in 1972, the year Kodak launched the 110 format. Two years later, Rollei introduced their

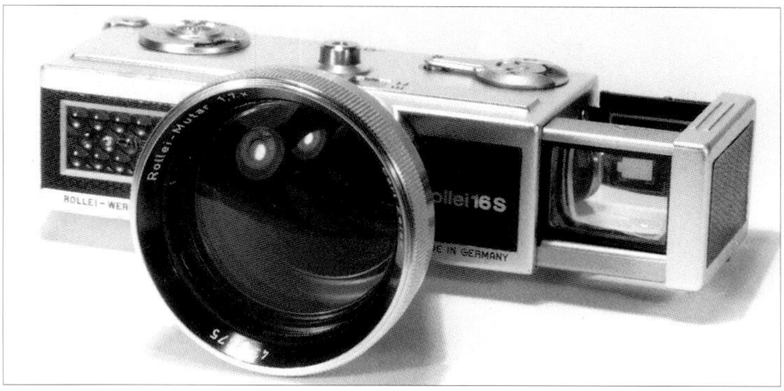

The Rollei 16 with 1.7 x Mutar telephoto lens attached.

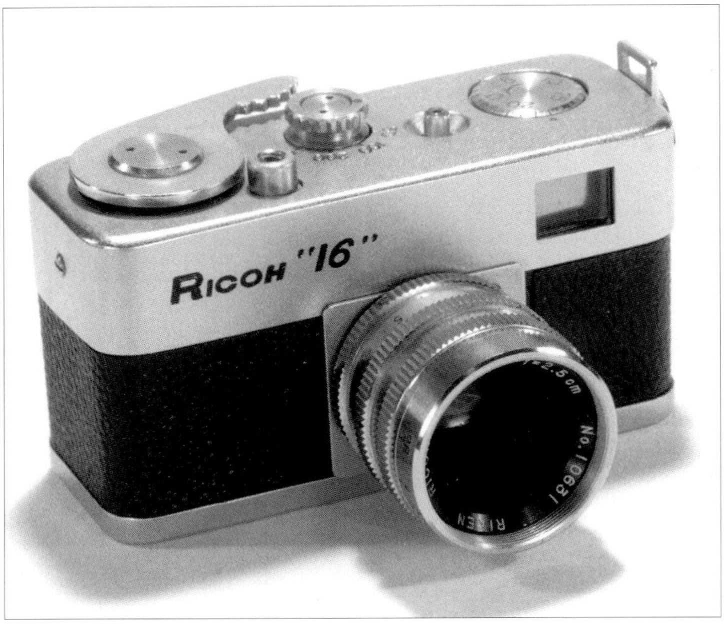

Ricoh 16.

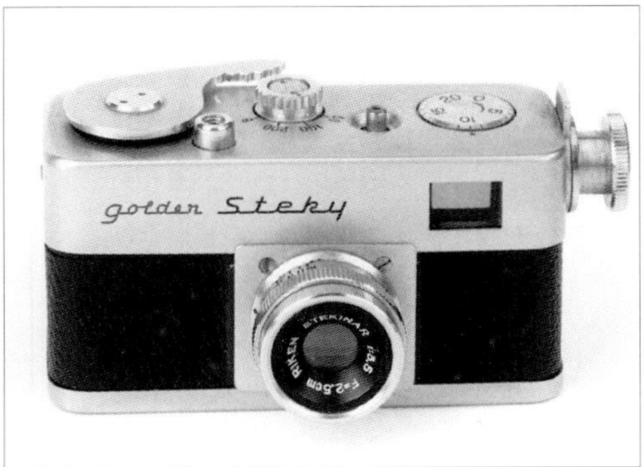

The Golden Steky.

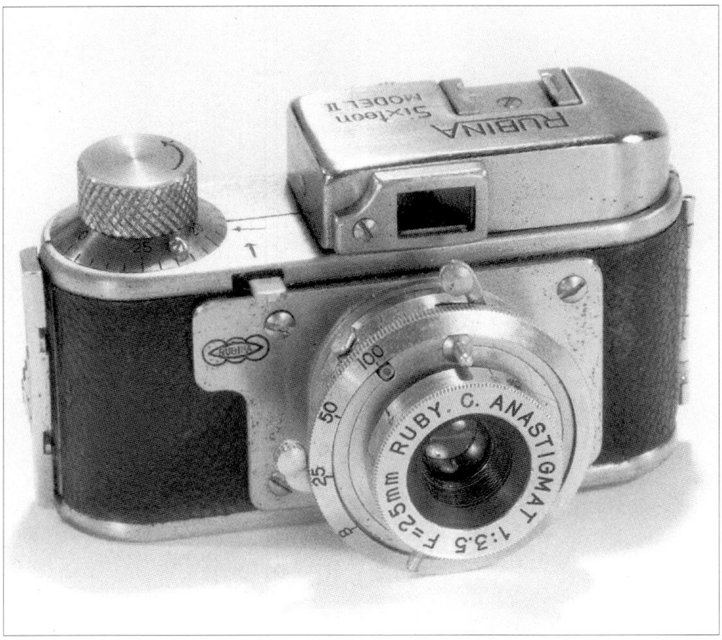

Rubina II.

own 110 camera, also with the push-pull film wind system (see pages 122-123).

Ricoh 16

The Ricoh 16 looks like a very small 35mm rangefinder camera, but its size - just 7cm long - identifies it as a 16mm model. Made by Riken (the original company name for Ricoh) in Japan in 1958, it was a chrome version of an earlier gold-plated camera, called not surprisingly, the Golden Ricoh 16, which in turn was a name variation on the Golden Steky.

The Ricoh 16 has a lever film wind, takes pictures 10 x 14 mm and offers shutter speeds from 1/50 - 1/200 second. Its golden cousin has a 25mm f/3.5 fixed focus lens, but the lens on the chrome version, while the same focal length and aperture, was focusable and interchangeable with a 40mm f/5.6 telephoto.

Rubina II

Here's another 16mm camera that looks like a larger model, but this one is even smaller than the Ricoh. The Rubina measures only 6.5 x 3.5 x 4cm, about the length of the average little finger.

Yet, into these truly miniature dimensions are packed an f/3.5 lens, focusing down to 1 metre, apertures down to f/16 and shutter speeds from 1/25 - 1/100 second. Image format is 10 x 14 mm.

It was made in 1951 by Tokyo Koki in Japan.

Minute 16

The Minute 16 (that's Minute, as in extra small, not as in 60 to the hour), looks like a tiny cine camera, measuring no more than 5.5 x 4.5 x 3.5cm.

It's American, made by the Universal Camera Corporation in 1949 and, to all outward appearances, it's a precision-made camera. Inwardly, however, it's pretty shoddy, with a fixed focus meniscus lens, boasting three stops - f/6.3, f/11 and f/16 - and a single speed shutter.

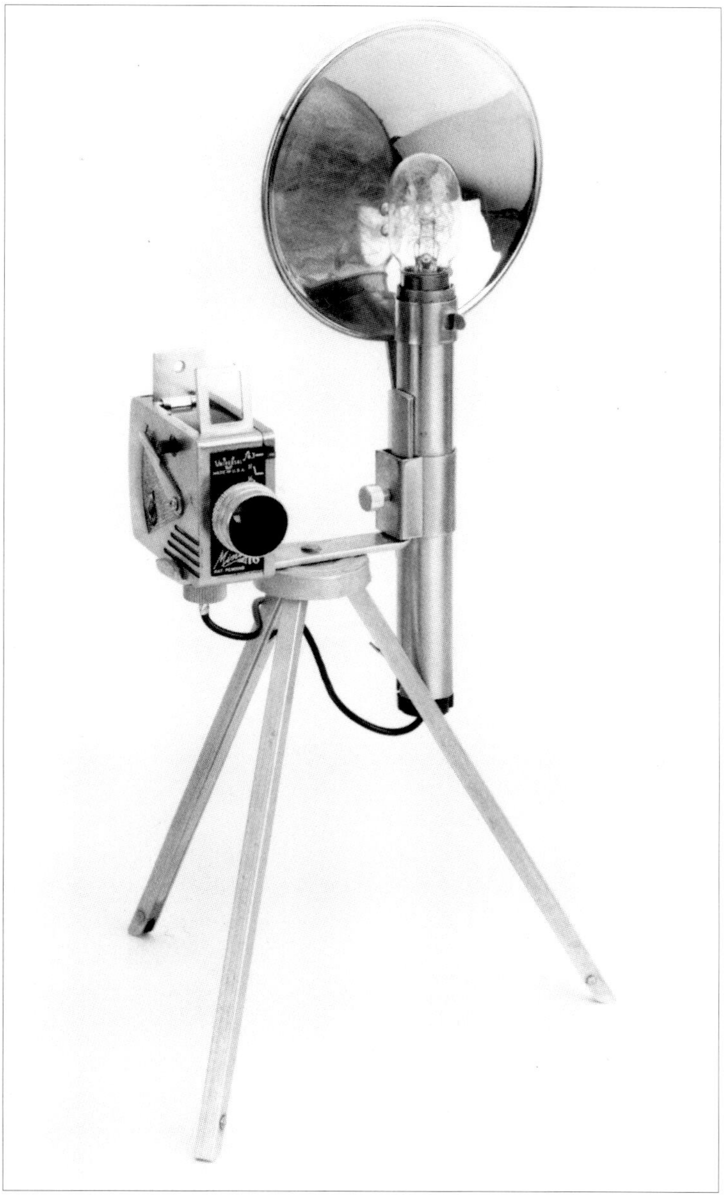

Minute 16 with its slightly impractical flashgun.

Film advance is by a lever on the side that claws the film by its sprocket holes from one cassette to the other, and which was totally unreliable.

Today, the Minute 16 is an interesting collector's item, but when it was made, it was a financial disaster. The Universal Camera Corporation had invested a small fortune in the development of the camera which, because of the mechanical problems and low quality lens, turned out to be a complete failure - a fact that was largely responsible for the manufacturers going bankrupt in the early 1950s.

Look out for a Minute 16 sold complete with its flashgun which is about four times the size of the camera!

Steky

The Japanese Steky was made over the course of ten years, starting in 1947. First made by a company called Asahi Musen, production was soon taken over by Riken.

Several different models were made, but basically, it's a 16mm camera for 10 x 14 mm images, sporting a fixed focus 25mm f/3.5 lens that stops down to f/11 on the first model and f/16 on the second, with shutter speeds from 1/25 - 1/100 second plus 'B'.

The lens is interchangeable and there are wideangle and telephoto lenses, the tele with a viewfinder mask and the wideangle with a separate viewfinder that clips onto the top of the normal one.

On the side of the body, just below the viewfinder, there's a small circular hump the same diameter as the lens, which is a clue to why it's there. It's a place to keep a filter.

Keep an eye open for models with an engraving just below the filter hump that says,

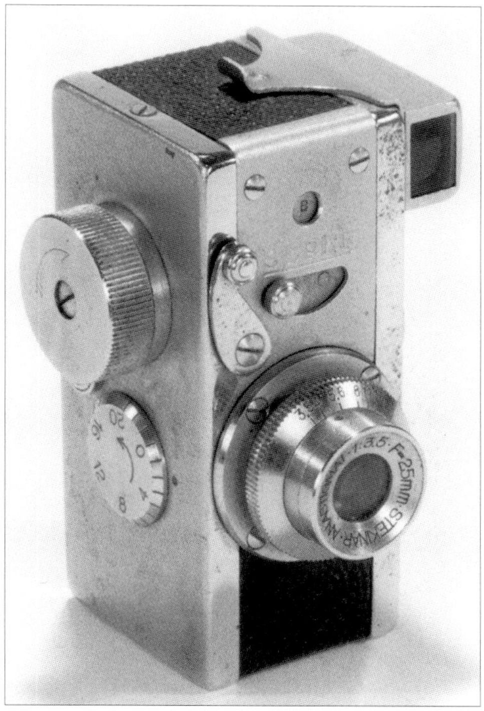

Right: The Steky.

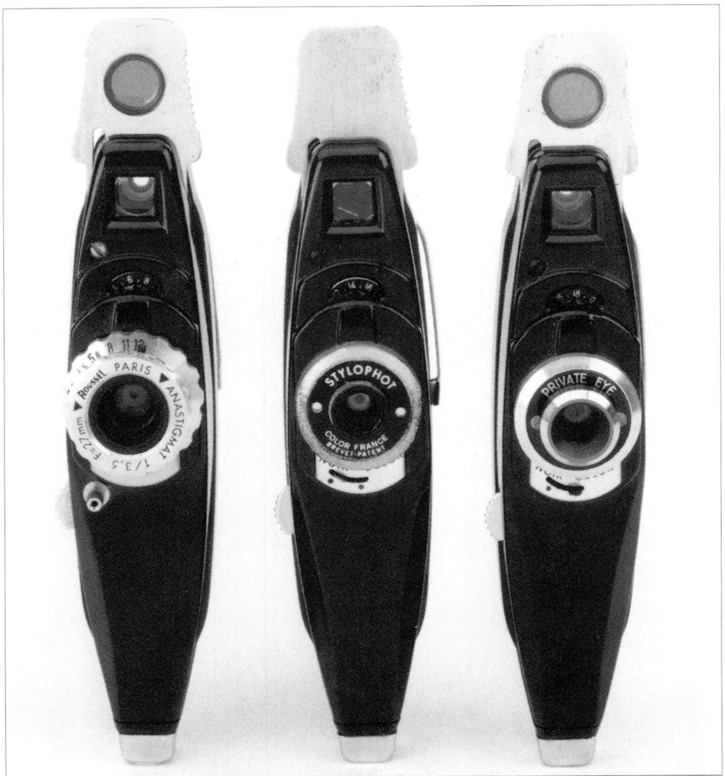

Three cameras from Secam: the Stylophot, another with direct vision and right-angle finders, and a Private Eye version.

'Made in Tokyo Japan'. This version is a rarer than the standard models.

Stylophot

Made first in 1955 by Secam in France, the Stylophot takes pictures 10 x 10mm. It's supposed to look like a pen, but is a little bulky and wouldn't really fool anyone. Nevertheless, it does have a clip on the side, just like a fountain pen, so that it can be carried in the top pocket.

The Stylophot has a fixed focus lens and single 1/50 second shutter speed. The Color model, illustrated here, was made later in 1960 and has two apertures, marked 'Color' and 'Noir' - f/6.3 and f/11 respectively - for colour or black and white exposures. Film advance is interesting. It works when a metal framework is pulled up from the top of the camera, which also unmasks the viewfinder. Pushing it back into place after exposure locks the shutter and puts a red mask in the viewfinder as a warning not to take pictures.

When you are buying, watch out for the pen clip on the side, which is easily broken and devalues the camera dramatically if it is missing.

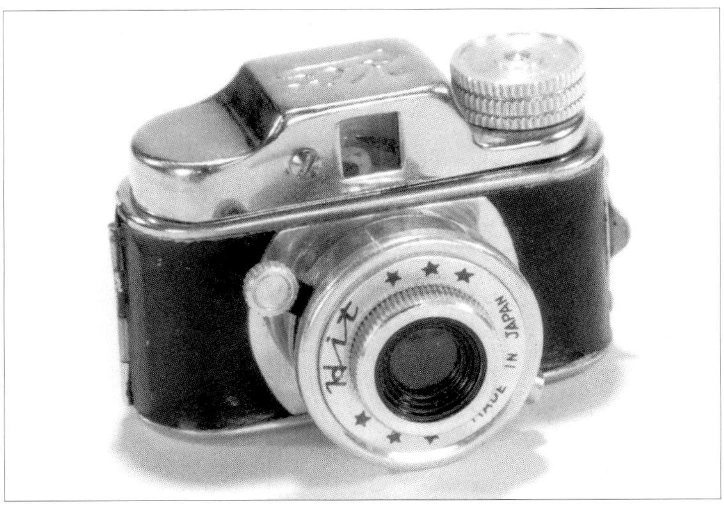

The original Hit camera.

Hit cameras

Whilst many of the major camera manufacturers were turning out serious and sophisticated cameras with top specifications for 16mm film, another branch of the industry was taking more of a snapshot approach to the format. Suddenly there was a plethora of tiny models, made even smaller by the fact that they didn't need the cassette arrangement used by the more serious 16mm cameras. These took a very similarly sized film - not actually 16mm as is often supposed, but 17.5mm in width - and wound it onto spools with backing paper, just like the larger formats. The cameras have red, or sometimes green, windows in the back to read the numbers on the film's backing paper.

There wasn't actually anything new about this film size, because it had been used in several subminiature cameras before the Second World War, including the Coronet Midget and the Merlin, made in England around 1934-36.

The majority of the models from the 1950s, however, have come be known as Hit cameras, since they were nearly all based on a model actually called the Hit, which was one of the first of this type made by the Tougodo Optical Company in Tokyo in the very early 1950s.

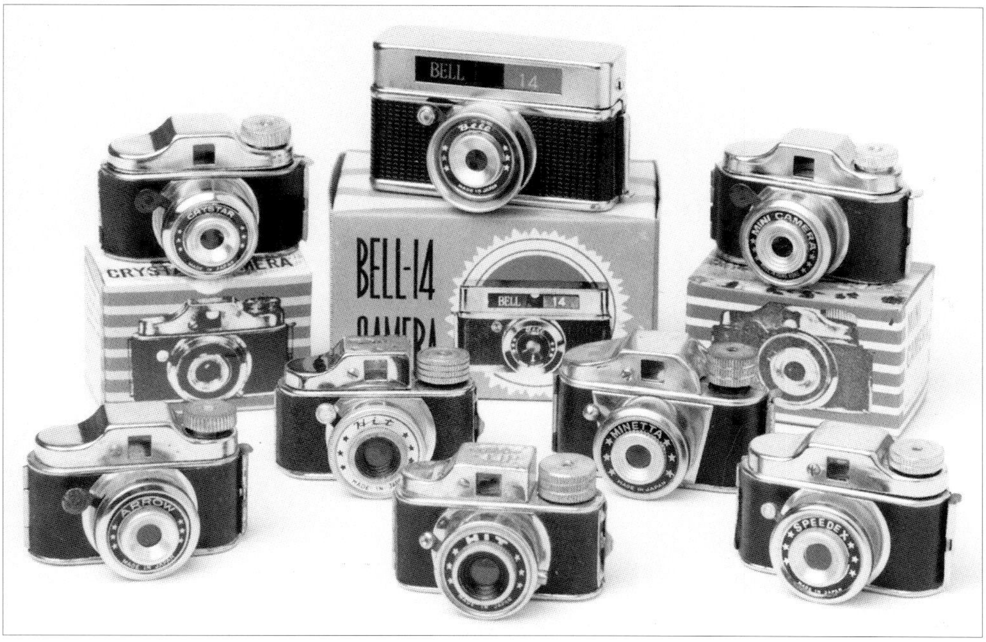

Just a few of the many variations on the Hit camera theme.

This first model measures a mere 45 x 30 x 32 mm. It has a single shutter speed, fixed aperture and fixed focus lens, and takes pictures 14 x 14mm. The quality of the image was poor, but that didn't stop other manufacturers copying the style and adapting it to their own ends.

Here are just some of the names that you'll find on these cameras: AHI, Amerex, Arcoflex, Arrow, Astra, Astropic, Atomy, Babymax, Barco, Beica, Bell 14, CMA, CMC, Colly, Crown, Crystar, Dale, Diplomat, Electronic, Elite, Emson, Enn-Ess TC, Francya, Fuji, Global, Globe, Hadson, Hamco, Happy, Hartex, Homer, Homer 16, IGB, Jay Dee, Kassin, Kent, Lens, Lloyd's, Lucky, Madison, Marvel, Midge, Midget, Mighty Midget, Mineta, Mini Camera, Miracle, Pamex, Peace, Pen, PFCA, Prince, QP, Real, Regent, Rocket, Satellite, Shalko, Shayo, Sil-Bair, Sing 88, Siraton, Speedex, Spesco, Sputnik, Star-Lite, Stellar, Sterling, Swallow, Tee Mee, Tiny, Toyoca, Traveler, Vesta and Walklenz.

Each of these follows the same or a very similar styling with just slightly different approaches to the basic design that make them collectable. They were made mostly in Japan, usually in chrome and black but sometimes in gold with other coloured bodies such as red, green or blue.

But whilst the majority of these tiny rollfilm cameras follow the basic Hit design, a few manufacturers moved slightly away from the style, giving their cameras a different look and even offering some models with a range of apertures and shutter speeds. These are more valuable and more collectable than the standard Hit cameras. Here are a few to watch out for.

Kiku 16

This one is particularly collectable and costs around four times the price of a standard Hit camera. In appearance, it looks like a very tiny

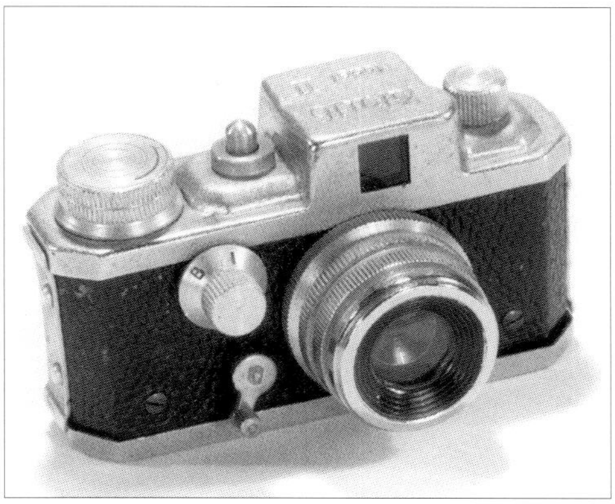

The Kiku 16, sometimes called the Gem 16.

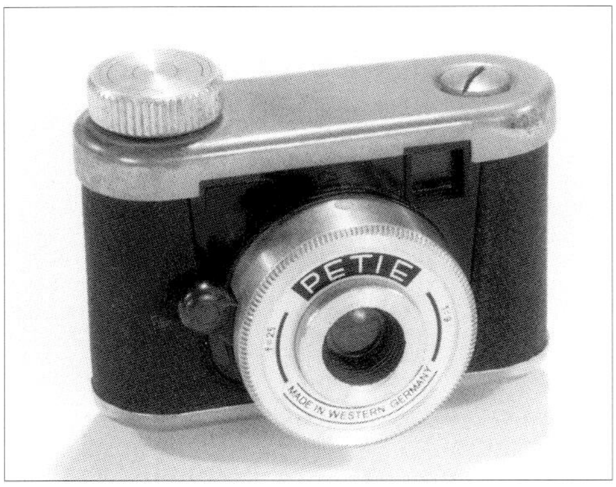

The Petie.

Leica IIIa, complete with a speed setting on a small knob on the front of the camera. Unlike the Leica, however, this one offers only instantaneous and brief time exposures and those are the only two controls it has. The 25mm lens is fixed at an f/8 aperture and the camera cannot be focused. It is unusual, however, in having a shutter cocking lever just below the speed control that has to be clicked across before the shutter fires.

The Kiku 16 was made by the Morita Trading Company and originally sold in souvenir shops as part of a small kit that contained a couple of filters, a lens hood and an ever ready case. The camera's full name is the Kiku 16 Model II, although there is no evidence of a Model I having been made. The same camera is also known as the Gem 16 Model II.

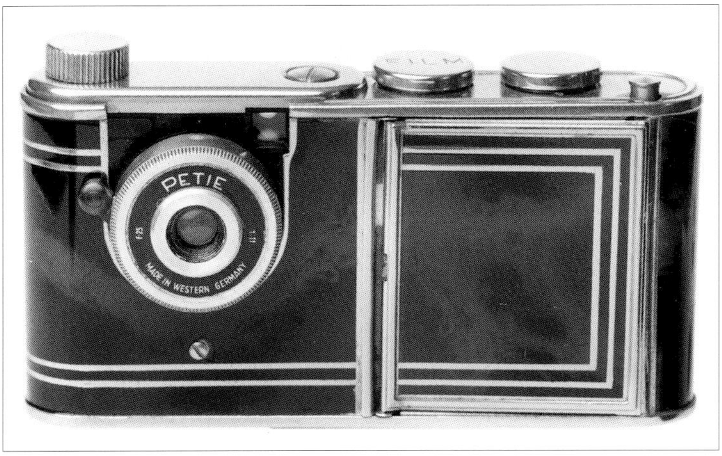

The Petie Vanity, built into a ladies' make-up compact.

Petie

The Petie, unlike most cameras of this type, was made in Germany by Walter Kunic. It follows a different style to the others, with a relatively large circular shutter assembly on the

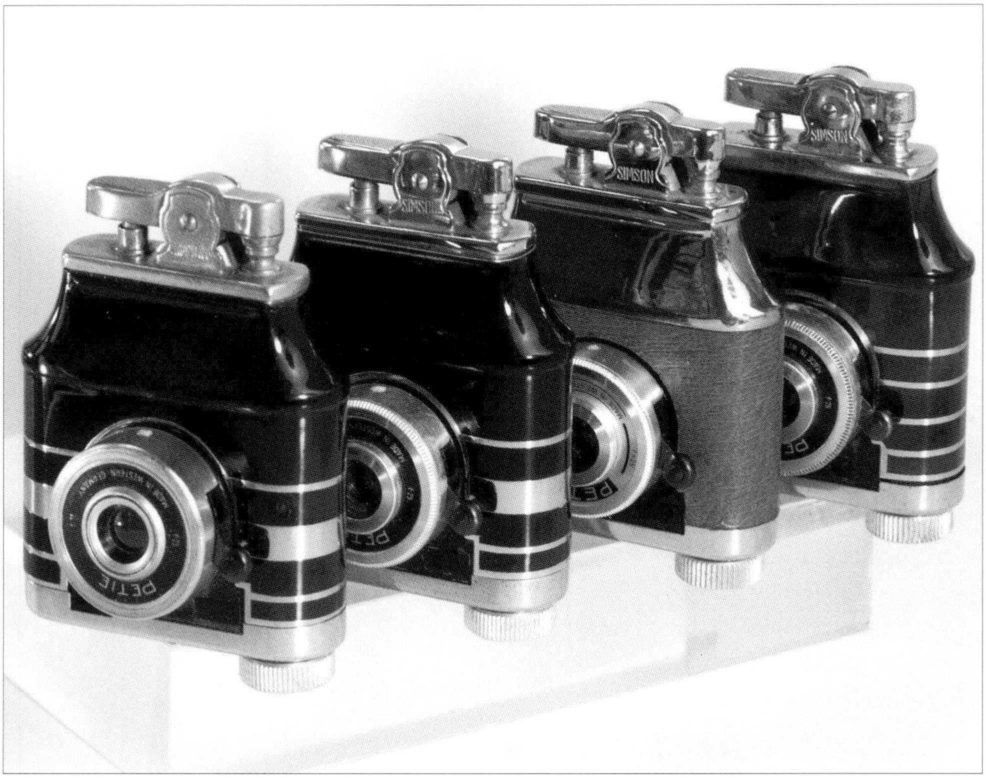

Petie Lighter cameras came in a range of colours.

front, incorporating a 25mm f/9 lens. All functions - aperture, shutter speed and focus - are fixed.

Petie cameras were also built into cigarette lighters and ladies' compacts. The lighter version has the mechanism built into the Petie base so that it is used with the camera upside down. The other version sees the camera built into a make-up compact, complete with mirror, powder, lipstick and a spare roll of film. These are known as Petie Vanity cameras and are beautifully decorated in an art deco design of different colours that include red, green, blue, chrome and gold. They are very collectable - and very pricey.

Mycro IIIA

The Mycro IIIA is about as sophisticated as a Hit camera can get. It features an f/4.5 lens that can be stopped down to f/11 and shutter speeds from 1/25 second to 1/100 second plus B. Made by Sanwa Shokai in Japan, the first model was produced as early as 1938. Slight variations were made again in the 1940s, but most come from the 1950s and were on sale until the middle of the 1960s.

Coronet Cameo

This is not really a Hit Camera and not really of this era either. The reason for including it here is because, first, it takes the same size rollfilm as the other cameras mentioned above and, second, although it was first made before the war, it was revived again in the era we are considering, when it achieved most of its success.

Although it takes the same film as a Hit camera, the Cameo manages to provide a larger image, 13 x 18 mm. It still retains the basic lack of specification, however, with fixed focus, aperture and shutter speed, but it also differs from the standard Hit camera by using a pull-up viewfinder with sites at the front and rear of the body. Pushing the rear site down also covers the red window to keep out extraneous light.

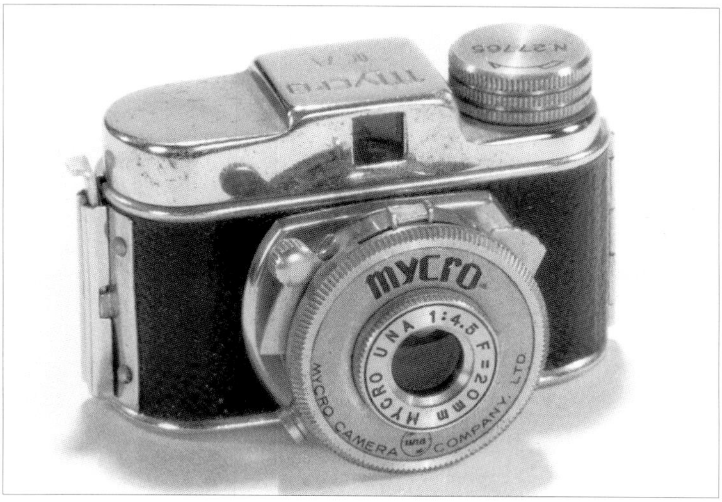

Mycro IIIa, a more sophisticated model with a range of shutter speeds and apertures.

The Cameo was made of black Bakelite by the Coronet Camera Company in England.

The Petal

The Petal has gone down in history as the smallest production camera ever made, measuring no more than 30mm in diameter if you exclude the small optical viewfinder that sits on the top. It features a fixed focus 12mm lens, with a fixed f/5.6 aperture and two shutter speeds, adjusted by a tiny thumbwheel on the front for instantaneous or brief time exposures.

The camera was made in 1947 and there are several different models in two different shapes - one round, the other hexagonal, the

Coronet Cameo.

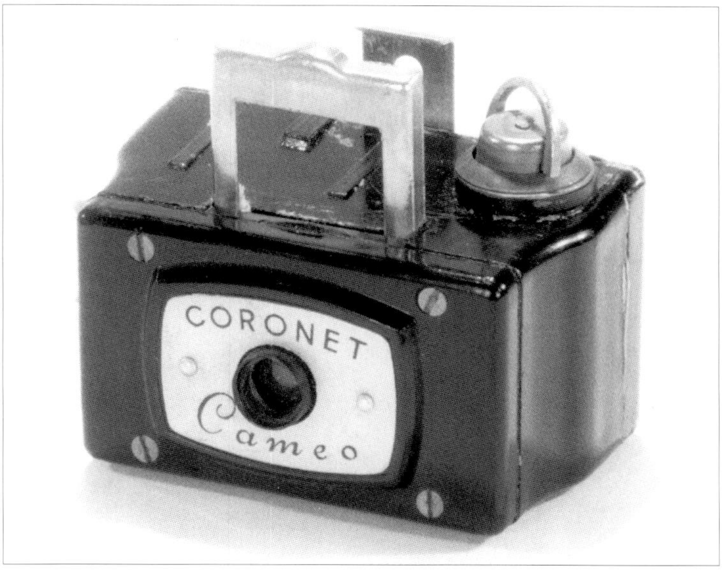

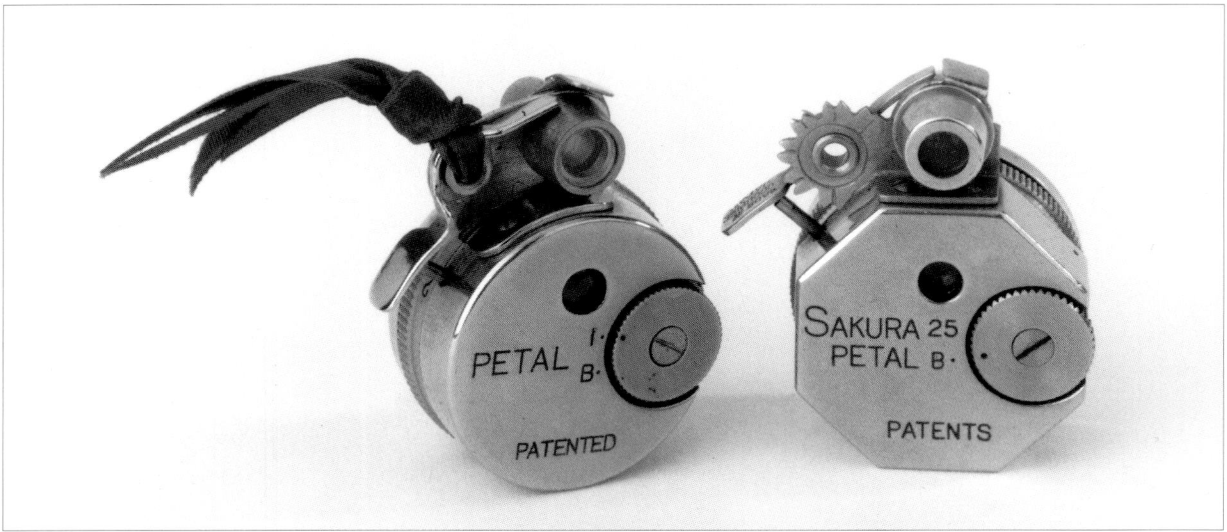

The two basic styles of Petal camera: round and hexagonal.

most common being the round one. The origins of this unusual little camera are a little confusing with much of its history lost in obscurity.

What is pretty much certain is that the first Petal was round in shape and probably made by the St. Peter Optical Company in Japan, which at that time was occupied by the Americans. The shutter speeds are designated as 'I' and 'B'.

About the same time, a very similar camera called the Evarex A was produced by the Petal Optical Company. This one was Hexagonal in shape, engraved with a flower motif and the shutter speeds were shown as 1/25 and 'B'.

This in turn, was very similar to another Hexagonal model called the Sakura Petal, which was made by Sakura Seiki, with the same shutter speed designations but without the engraving.

But the Sakura name also appears on round models. And round models have also turned up bearing the name Petal Kogaku Company.

Petal film is as unusual as the camera. It's circular, held in a disc-shaped cassette that has a circular aperture with a shutter across it that lines up with the lens. The camera back is unscrewed, the disc dropped in and the back replaced. The back is then twisted to open the shutter across the film aperture in the cassette and, thereafter as the back is turned again between each exposure, the aperture stays in its place behind the lens as the film inside the cassette moves around to the next unexposed area.

That's the theory anyway. In fact, the system didn't always work as well as it should and a lot of trouble was experienced by Petal photographers who ended up with overlapping exposures. The discs were also difficult to develop and print.

The other unusual thing about the Petal is its ribbon. Originally, the camera was sold with a red one tied through a hole beside the viewfinder. It's one of the characteristics of the Petal and it enhances the value if you find one with its original ribbon intact. But its origins are one more example of its obscure past.

In 1950, a Petal Lighter Camera appeared on the market, combining a round Petal with a cigarette lighter. One school of thought says these were made by the Petal Optical Company, another says they were more likely adapted by an unknown independent company.

Back in the 1940s, a special punch was also sold that gave photographers the ability to stamp out tiny discs of Petal film from larger roll or 35mm films.

The cameras can often be found in their small leather cases and sometimes in their original miniature wooden boxes, complete with instructions. Petal film is also fairly easy to find on the collector's market, but for some reason, you'll usually find it labelled as 'Patel', rather than 'Petal' film.

Every Spy's Favourite Camera

WHEREVER there's a spy, there's a Minox. At least that's what television and film dramas would have us believe. The Minox is that little cigar shaped camera that the spy usually removes from his top pocket to snap the secret plans lit only by the light of a desk lamp, opening and closing the body between exposures to wind the film.

It's a camera that started life in 1935, as a hand-made prototype taking a 6.5 x 9 mm image, chosen for its relationship to the standard 35mm frame. Its designer was Walter Zapp who was born in Latvia, the son of a German businessman, and educated in England; and it was at Riga in Latvia that the first cameras were made in 1937. Zapp came up with the name. He felt it should contain something of the word 'miniature', whilst being influenced by the fact that the Contax was enjoying a particularly good reputation at the time. Putting the two together, he came up with Minax, which sounded ugly and was changed to Minox.

Those first cameras, known as Riga Minoxes, are the rarest and most valuable today. But the post war cameras, made after production had shifted to Germany, are more accessible to the collector and one of the easiest to buy is the Minox B, which you'll find in chrome, black and gold. Chrome is the most common, black is twice as expensive, gold is very expensive indeed.

In its retracted position, the Minox B is only 95mm long - about the length of the average middle finger. Pulling the two sections of the body slightly apart adds 15mm to the size and reveals the lens and viewfinder. There is also an in-built Selenium cell exposure meter (the main upgrade from the Minox A), which adds slightly to the camera's length.

There is no aperture scale because the lens is

The Minox B, epitomising everything you expect from a spy camera.

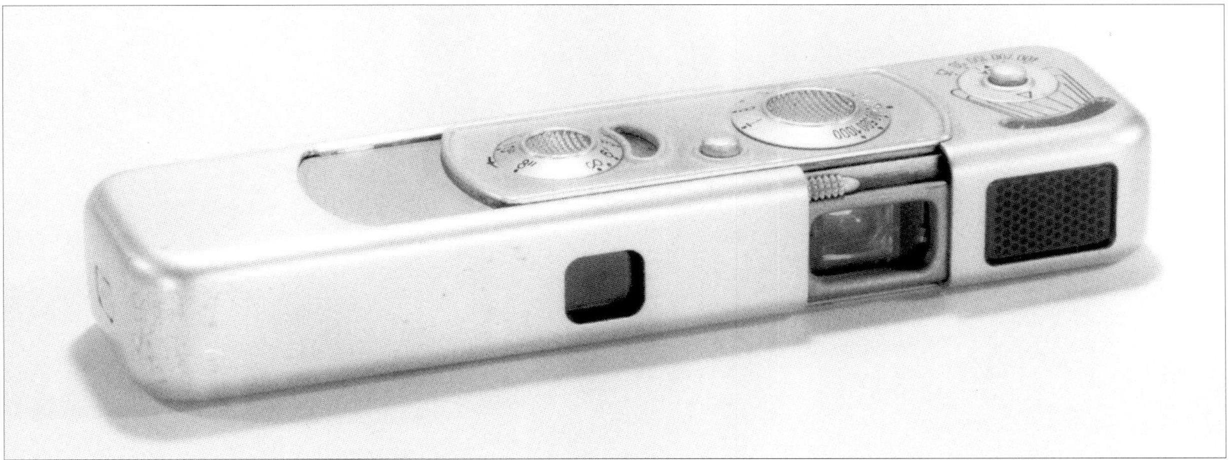

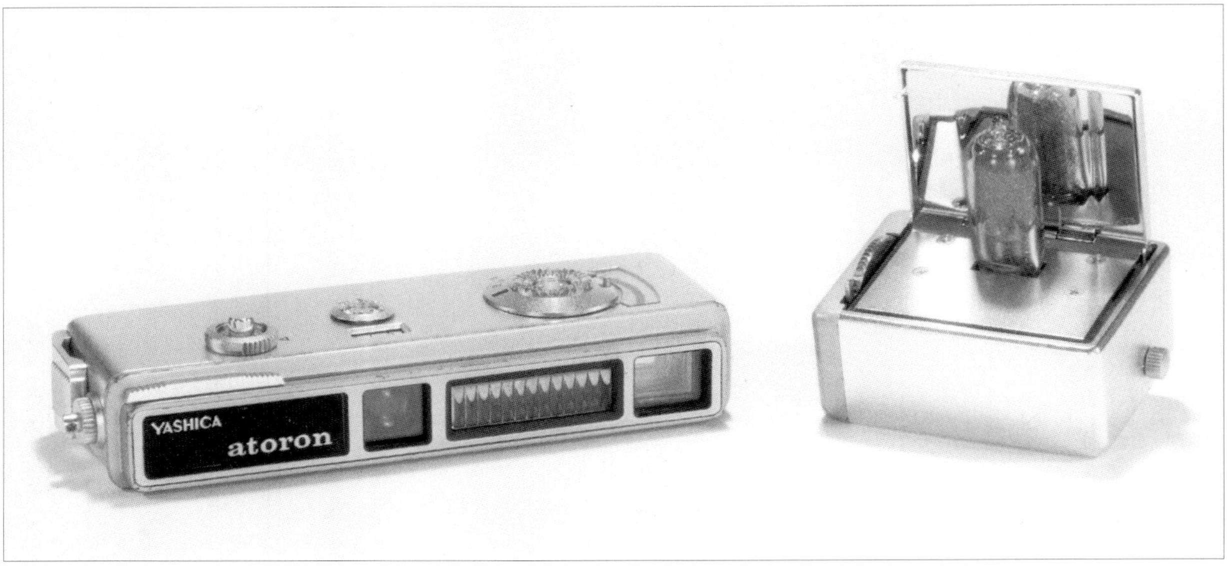

The Yashica Atoron with its accessory flashgun.

fixed at its maximum aperture of f/3.5. Exposures are controlled, then, by shutter speeds alone and, on the Minox B, these range from 1/2 second to 1/1000 second. They are adjusted by a dial on the top of the body, next to another dial that focuses the lens.

The Minox B is still a very usable camera today. The film is 9.5mm in width and comes in a special double cassette that drops into a chamber in the body. Black and white, colour print and even colour side films are all available from specialist dealers but, if you do buy one to use, there is a knack to loading it and setting

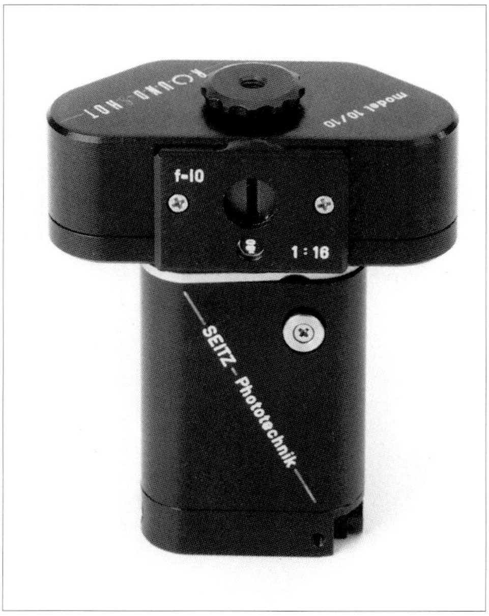

The Roundshot, a panoramic camera that uses Minox film.

the film speed on the meter that's difficult to fathom at first. Here's how it's done.

The camera is first opened to its normal shooting position and then the film speed is set by turning the shutter speed dial which also turns a second dial with a pointer to line up with the appropriate speed setting. Turning the camera over, a small crescent shaped catch is found which is depressed with a thumb nail so that the two halves of the body can then be pulled further apart, revealing the film chamber.

At this point, the shutter speed should be set to 1/100 second, identified by a small red dot on the dial. With the two halves of the camera apart, this shutter speed dial no longer turns the film speed setting as well, so the correct film speed is now set.

The next step is to drop the film into its chamber, but that can't be done until the film gate just behind the lens has been opened. This is effected by slowly pushing the two halves of the body back together again until a slight resistance is felt. That resistance was the film gate opening. The body is then pulled apart again, the cassette dropped in and the two halves pushed all the way home. The Minox B is then ready for photography.

In use, the camera is pointed at the subject and a small stud on the top of the body is depressed, releasing the meter needle to swing across a scale and locking it in position when the finger is removed from the stud.

As the shutter speed dial is turned, an arrow on a small rotating disc, scans the same scale and, when it matches up to the needle's position, the correct shutter speed for an aperture of f/3.5 has been set. If conditions are too bright even for 1/1000 second at f/3.5, there is a built-in neutral density filter which slides across the lens and automatically re-adjusts the meter needle as necessary. There's a built-in green filter too.

The shutter is released and the film is wound on by closing and opening the body again. A glance at the shutter that covers the front of the lens tells you whether the film has been wound or not: when the shutter is tensioned, there is a small black dot in its centre, which disappears as the exposure is made.

At 8 x 11mm, the image size might seem too small to be taken seriously, but this was about the size of disc camera negatives that were very popular in the 1980s and whose film speed was ISO 200. Minox films are available in speeds from ISO 25 to ISO 400 and, with the lower speed emulsions, the Minox produces perfectly acceptable enlargements.

Other cameras for Minox film

If you thought Minox film can be used only in Minox cameras, then think again. Several other manufacturers have made cameras to take the tiny Minox cassettes... and some of the cameras they produced are a little out of the ordinary.

One of the more conventional styles is the Japanese Atoron, made by Yashica in 1965. It's a similar shape to the Minox, but has a fixed body which is a little deeper than its German cousin, but only fractionally longer than the closed Minox. Film wind is by a metal tab that is pulled out from the end of the body to spring back as the film is advanced. Unlike the Minox, the lens is a fixed focus type, an f/2.8 Yashinon, and shutter speeds run from 1/45 second to 1/250 second plus B. Like the Minox, they are set by turning a dial that rotates a pointer against a scale across which a needle from a Selenium meter swings.

The Atoron has its own flashgun which takes AG1 bulbs and screws to the end of the body, adding about half as much again to the length and turning this sleek little camera into a rather ugly design. The camera can often be found in a presentation box that contains the flashgun, a case and filters.

A later model with automatic shutter and CdS meter can also be found for about the same price as the original. That one was produced in 1970.

The Roundshot is a little more unusual. It's the smallest panoramic camera ever made, produced by the Swiss Seitz company that specialises in larger format cameras of a similar type. This one, made to take Minox film, has a 10mm f/10 lens and takes pictures from 100 degrees to a full 360 degrees, producing up to 10 exposures on a single length of film. As the exposure is made, an electric motor rotates the camera on its base with the film moving in the opposite direction, similar to the style used in the Globuscope (see page 117).

Then there was the Lanack M1, made in Germany and worn on the wrist like a watch. That too takes Minox film and has a 14.3mm f/4 lens.

Even as late as the 1990s, new cameras were appearing for use with Minox film. The Slimax is a Japanese example that combines a camera with a cigarette lighter. It has a 15mm f/5.6 fixed focus lens and a set shutter speed of 1/150 second. Film advance is by a thumb wheel that is stroked through 120 degrees and which should not be confused with the lighter control which could result in a lot of photographers with burnt noses!

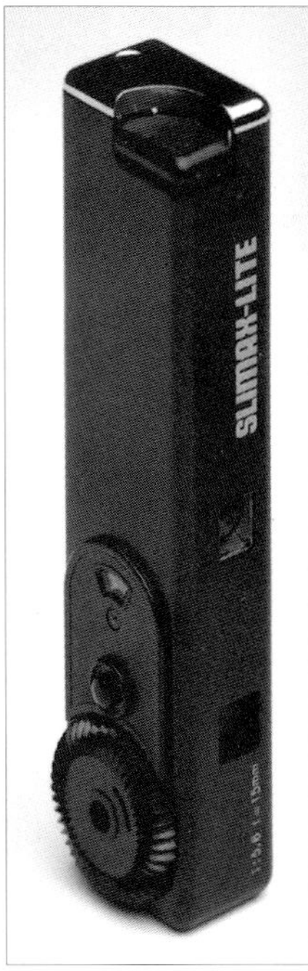

The Slimax combines a Minox-style camera with a cigarette lighter.

Stereo Cameras

STEREO CAMERAS are as old as photography itself - older even. Way back in 1832 Sir Charles Wheatstone was making stereo drawings in the form of two views of the same subject seen from slightly different viewpoints, the way human eyes see them. So when photography camera along, it wasn't long before he approached Richard Beard, a well known portrait photographer of the day, asking him to take two pictures of the same subject from different angles and thus producing some of the first stereo photographs.

Let's look at the theory. The reason we perceive depth and so see the world in three dimensions is because we have two eyes. Because they are spaced a little way apart, each one sees a slightly different viewpoint of the same scene. The information is passed to the brain which combines the two images and interprets the information from the individual viewpoints to provide the illusion of depth.

In the vast majority of stereo cameras, two different pictures are taken simultaneously by two different lenses. They are then viewed in such a way that the left eye sees only the image taken with the left lens and the right eye the image taken by the right lens. The brain, once again, gets the two different viewpoints on the same scene and combines them in a way that allows the viewer to see a three-dimensional image.

The most common method of separating the two images for separate eyes is with a hand viewer, held to the eye so that each one sees only the appropriate image. When stereo images are projected, different methods of separation are used. The two images might be projected through two different filters - usually red and green, but sometimes red and blue - then viewed through spectacles with the same two colours used, one for each eye. A better method is to use polarising filters over the projection lenses with their equivalents in spectacles worn by the viewer.

Although there have been stereo cameras in every age of photography, the last big craze came within the period covered by this book: slightly before, during and for a little while after the 1950s. Here are some of the cameras that were popular during that period, plus one that popped up again in the 1980s.

Stereo Realist

Whilst most stereo cameras have two lenses, the Stereo Realist - launched by the American David White Company in the late 1940s and popular through much of the 1950s - at first sight, seems to have three. The outside lenses take the pictures, while the one in the middle, which has the shutter speed dial around it, is actually for the viewfinder. Light from this lens is led through a kind of periscope to the viewfinder window situated, not on the top of the camera in the usually position, but on the bottom.

In use, then, the camera is held to the eye in what feels like an upside down position, the body resting against the forehead. Beside the viewfinder there is a second window for a split

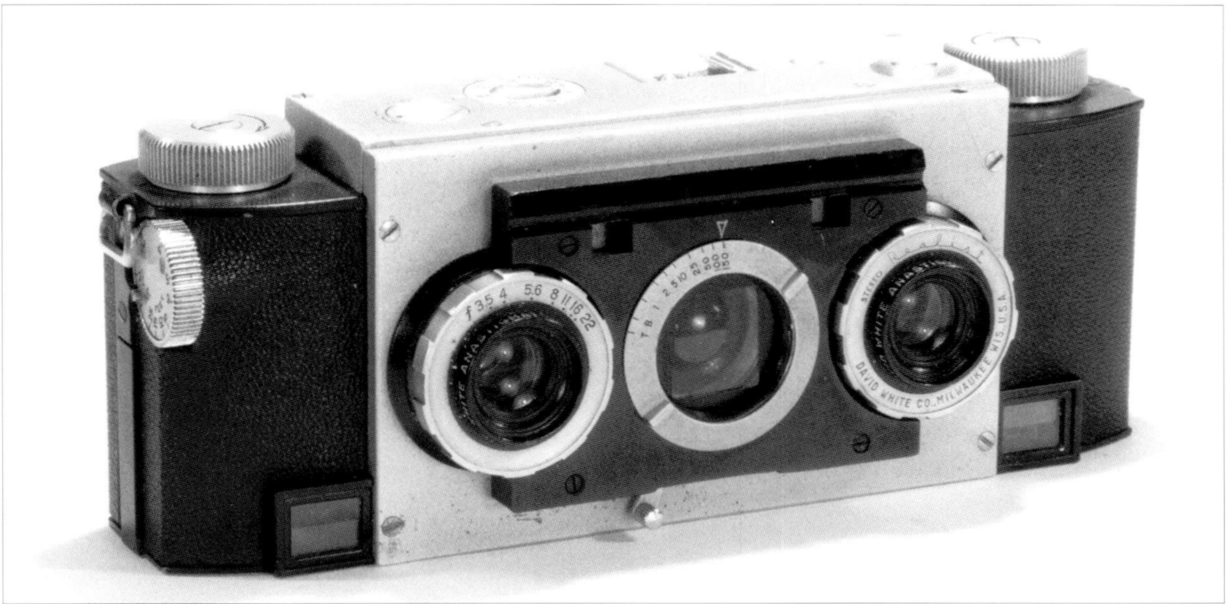

The Stereo Realist, unusual in being seemingly used upside down with the camera body pressed against the forehead.

image rangefinder that divides the view into two halves. It too has its windows on the bottom of the camera rather than the top and is coupled to a focusing mechanism, which is also a little out of the ordinary.

Focusing is controlled by a milled wheel that protrudes from the right of the body, falling conveniently under a joint of the first finger of the right hand that would normally be used for releasing the shutter. No problem there, though, because the shutter is released with the left hand.

As the focusing wheel is turned, the lenses remain stationary with focusing achieved by moving the film plane backwards and forwards inside the body. Apertures are adjusted by a ring around one of the lenses, the control automatically coupled to the second lens so that both irises open and close together.

The Realist takes 35mm in standard cassettes, producing 24mm square images and the way those images are placed on the film is a real artform. The space between the stereo pair is the width of two images and, each time the film is wound, it moves the equivalent of three frames. In this way, the film gradually builds up a complete set of evenly spaced images, each of which has its pair three frames away, separated by two other images.

The only drawback is that it means one blank frame near the start of the film, but even this doesn't go to waste. The Realist Film Identifier clips onto the left hand lens. It has a built-in close-up lens and a place to slip a card with any information on it. This can then be exposed onto the blank frame right at the start, to record written information about the film, location, date, or whatever - a sort of early, do-it-yourself data back!

Iso Duplex

The 24 x 24 mm format was one of the most common among stereo cameras of this era, as the maximum size possible for a square picture on 35mm film.

So it was also the format used by the Italian ISO company when they made their Duplex stereo cameras in 1950. The Italians, however, got round the awkward film winding system by the very simple expedient of using 120 rollfilm, rather than 35mm, running it through the camera vertically and placing the twin images side by side. Using two windows to wind each film number to two different positions, the cameras takes 16 stereo pairs to a roll. There is also a control that allows a choice between single or stereo pictures.

Look out for two Duplex models, but take care if you find one. They are prone to sticking

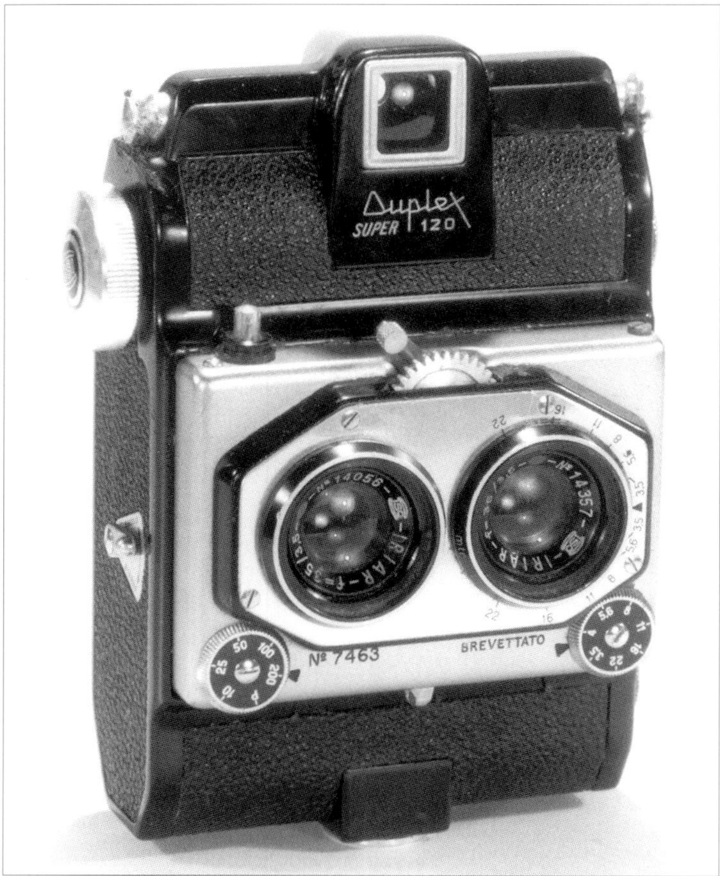

The Iso Duplex Super 120 takes twin 24 x 24 cm images on 120 film.

shutters, so examine cameras carefully before buying.

The Duplex 120 has fixed focus 35mm f/6.3 Iperang lenses and a three-speed shutter. The Duplex Super 120 has 35mm f/3.5 Iriar lenses, focused together by means of a knurled wheel between and above them, and a six-speed shutter from 1/10 second to 1/200 second.

Stereo Graphic

"The camera bringing 3-D to everyone!" said an advertisement for the Stereo Graphic when it was launched. The camera originally came from Graflex in America but was made by the Wray Optical Works in England under licence in 1959. The Graflex version uses Graflar lenses, whereas the Wray version sports Wray optics and takes 28 stereo pairs, each one 24 x 26 mm.

The shutter offers only instantaneous and brief time with the instantaneous speed fixed at 1/50 second. Exposures are adjusted by changing the apertures, based on the assumption that you are using Kodachrome film. Settings are designated in a small window between the lenses as Cloudy f/4, Hazy f/5.6, Bright f/8, Brilliant f/11 and f/16 without a weather description. Obviously they never thought the sun could get to f/16 brilliance in the UK.

Focus on the lenses is fixed - but at two different distances which, between them, give a depth of field from 4ft to infinity, the theory being that, the sharpest aspects of each image should combine in the stereo effect to produce a universally sharp focus throughout. An interesting idea, guarantied to give the viewer a nasty headache.

Another drawback for the collector who wants to get into stereo photography concerns the way the sprockets used to transport the film actually touch the pressure plate on the inside of the camera back. The result is that the plate tends to get scratched as the camera back is slid off which, in turn, can lead to scratches on the film as it is advanced.

Launched at the same time as the camera was a small hand stereo viewer, also made by Wray under licence to Graflex.

View-Master Personal Stereo

View-Master is probably best known in connection with cheap little plastic stereo viewers and cardboard reels of 3-D pictures that seem to cover every subject under the sun from 'Life In New York City' to 'The Coronation of Queen Elizabeth II'. They have been part of most childhoods since the 1950s right up until now. But if you think of View-Master stuff as little more than toys, then think again. In 1952, there was a View-Master camera designed to shoot your own stereo reels taking 138 images - or 69 stereo pairs - to a roll of 35mm film, and the way it does that is rather interesting.

Like other stereo cameras, the View-Master Personal Stereo sports two lenses spaced

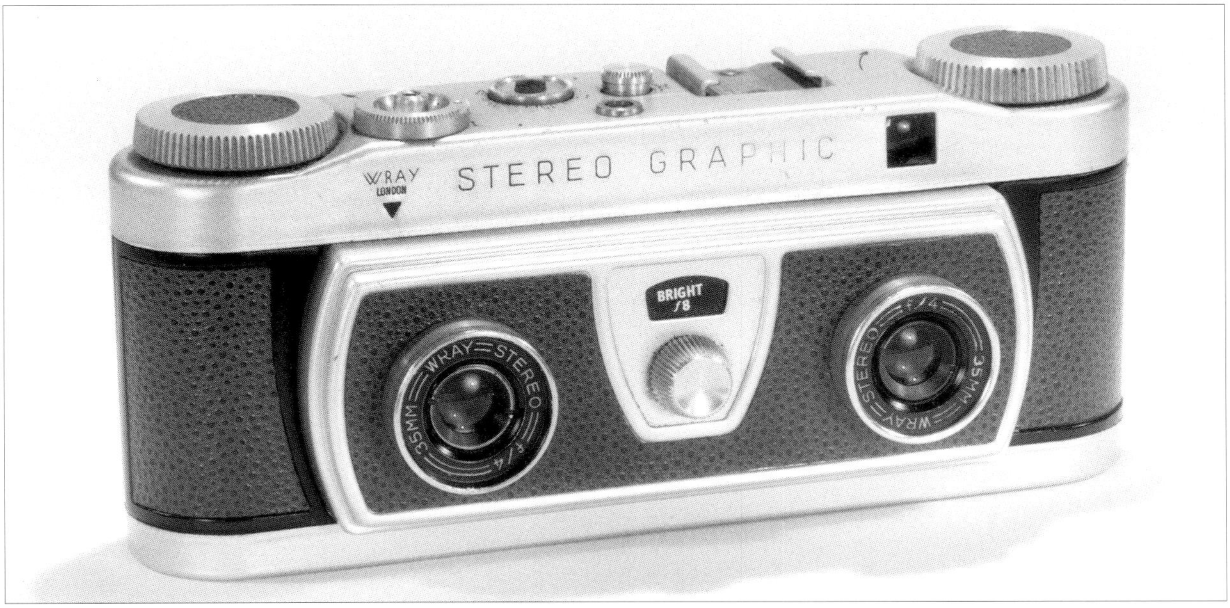

60mm apart to provide two images. Shutter speeds and apertures are controlled by thumbwheels on the camera's top plate, which also incorporates an exposure calculator.

Unlike other 35mm stereo cameras, however, the images are subminiature - 12 x 13 mm to be precise, because that's the size demanded by the View-Master reels, a size which very conveniently allowed the manufacturers to fit two frames, one on top of the other, within the width of a strip of 35mm film, by running it through the camera twice. Here's how it works.

Opening the back of the camera reveals twin shutters and apertures at the end of a couple of small boxes that allow the image to be recorded at the bottom half of the film, whilst masking an equivalent space at the top.

The film is loaded in the normal way, the back closed and the film counter set to '20X' or '36X', according to the length of film. The shutter button and film wind are then operated three times, bringing the counter to '19' or '35'. Pictures are taken and the film advanced as usual until counter reads back to '1'.

At that point, a knob on the front of the camera is rotated and, inside, those two boxes move up to the top of the film, now masking the bottom half where the first set of exposures have been made. At the same time, a gear is engaged which means that, when the film wind knob is rotated, it now operates the rewind mechanism and the film is gradually wound back into the cassette until the counter reads up to '19' or '35' again. The shutter button is then pressed and the film wound five more times before the back is opened to reveal the film back in its cassette.

The View-Master Personal Stereo was made in America and, a decade later, another model was produced in Germany, which ran the film diagonally through the camera to maximise on the number of stereo pairs that could be obtained from one roll of film. That one was called the View-Master Stereo Color, or the Mark II.

The Stereo Graphic has two lenses, focused at different distances.

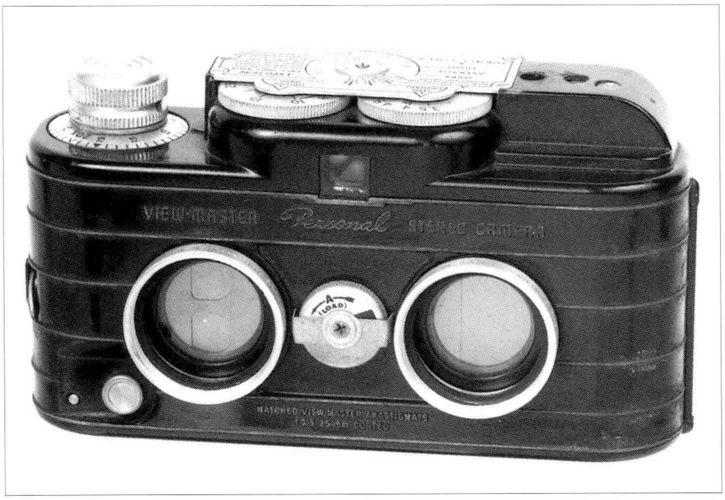

The View-Master Personal Stereo runs 35mm film through the camera twice.

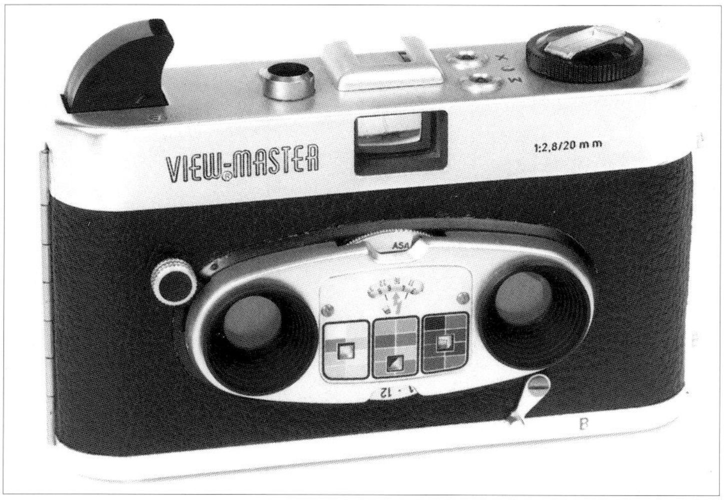

View-Master Stereo Color runs film through the camera diagonally.

screens against which the pictures are viewed forming his eyes.

View-Master also made projectors for their reels. The one illustrated here is the View-Master Junior model, made in plastic and using a 30-watt bulb to project an image from the subminiature images about 45mm wide. The View-Master discs slot in and are advanced in much the same way as in the hand viewers, but with only one lens, the projector produces a non-stereo image.

There was also a View-Master Senior projector that used a 75-watt bulb to produce a non-stereo image twice the size as that from the Junior, and others that used higher wattage bulbs for even larger screen images, although by this time, the quality from the tiny 12 x 13 mm slides must have been pretty poor.

View-Master also sold a picture punch that stamped out the stereo pairs to the exact size for mounting into empty cardboard reels, but the job was very fiddly and, whilst the stereo reels and viewers have continued to sell over the years, the do-it-yourself side died out in the 1960s.

View-Master viewers and projectors

There are many different View-Master viewers to collect too. Apart from the standard type in several different colours that can be picked up cheaply at any flea market or bric-a-brac fair, there are others with battery operated torch bulb illumination and even models made to resemble Mickey Mouse's face, the twin

Meopta

Whilst on the subject of View-Master, it's worth taking a look at a couple of cameras made by the Czechoslovakian company Meopta in the 1960s.

The first is the Stereo 35 that takes 35mm film which, like the second View-Master camera, is run once through the body diagonally. The result is 80 stereo pairs in two diagonal rows. The camera is fairly simple, made of metal and plastic, with a 25mm f/3.5 fixed focus lens and a shutter that gives only 1/60 second and B.

View-Master viewers in different styles and the View-Master Junior projector.

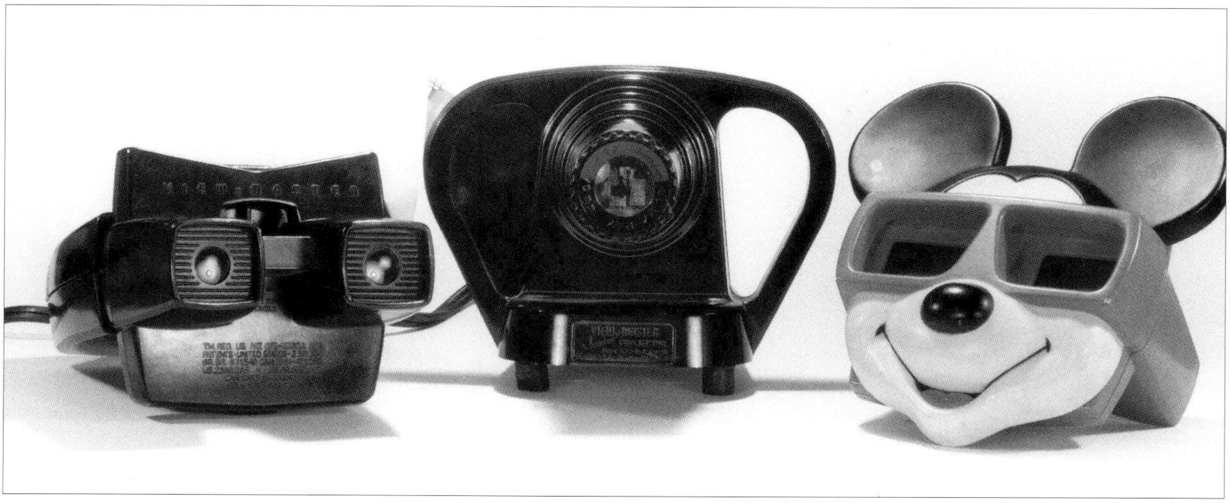

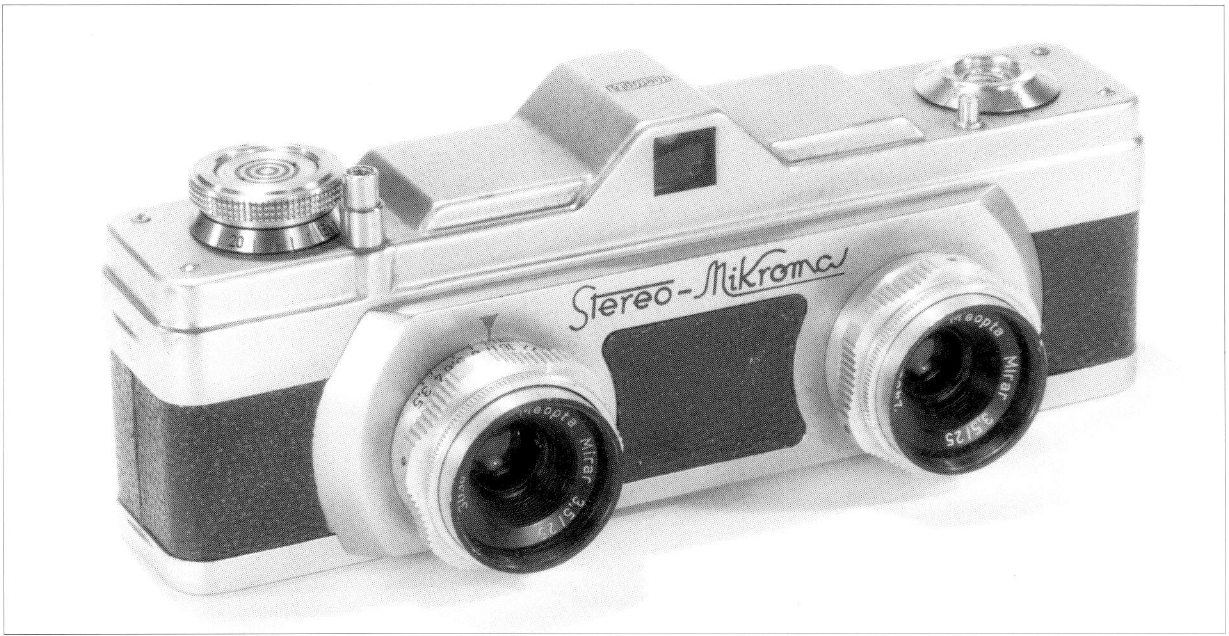

The Stereo Mikroma, first model.

The second camera is the Stereo Mikroma which takes 16mm film to produce 12 x 13 mm images that can be used in View-Master reels.

The Sputnik

Sometimes Russian camera manufacturers copied Western styles to produce their own versions; at other times, they came up with some pretty original ideas. The Sputnik was sort of original in its thinking, but had a few important influences. The camera started life as the Lubitel, a twin lens reflex, first made by GOMZ in 1949 and a fairly blatant imitation of the Voigtlander Brillant, first made in Germany in 1933.

Now, if you go back to 1928, you come to Franke and Heidecke, another German company that was producing a stereo camera called the Rolleidoscop which had two lenses for taking the pictures and a third one in the centre to reflect its image up to a ground glass screen on the top of the camera. Franke and Heidecke took this idea, turned the camera on its end and removed one of the lenses to produce the Rolleiflex, the first truly compact rollfilm twin lens reflex.

So was it this that influenced the Russians to move in the opposite direction? Maybe, because what they did was to take the Lubitel, turn it on its side and add another lens. The result was the Sputnik, whose name in the Cyrillic alphabet on the front of the hood resembles the word 'CNYTHNK'. It was launched in 1960, by which time the company had changed its name to Leningrad.

Like the Rolleidoscop all those years before, the central of the three lenses reflects its image up to the viewfinder, but it doesn't use a ground-glass screen. In its place is a large convex lens - just like the one on the Lubitel, and the Brillant from which it was copied.

The three lenses on the Sputnik are linked by cogs around the rims, so that they all focus together, but the focusing scale, set around the edge of the middle focusing lens, is a bit weird. It's marked in metres, but the distances are not measured in the usual increments. Instead, the scale reads: 1.4m, 2m, 2.8m, 4m, 5.6m, 8m, 11mm and infinity - numbers which are more usually associated with aperture scales.

Beneath the taking lenses, the two aperture scales are connected by a bar that adjusts each simultaneously and adjusting shutter speeds between 1/15 second and 1/125 second on one lens changes speeds on the other at the same time.

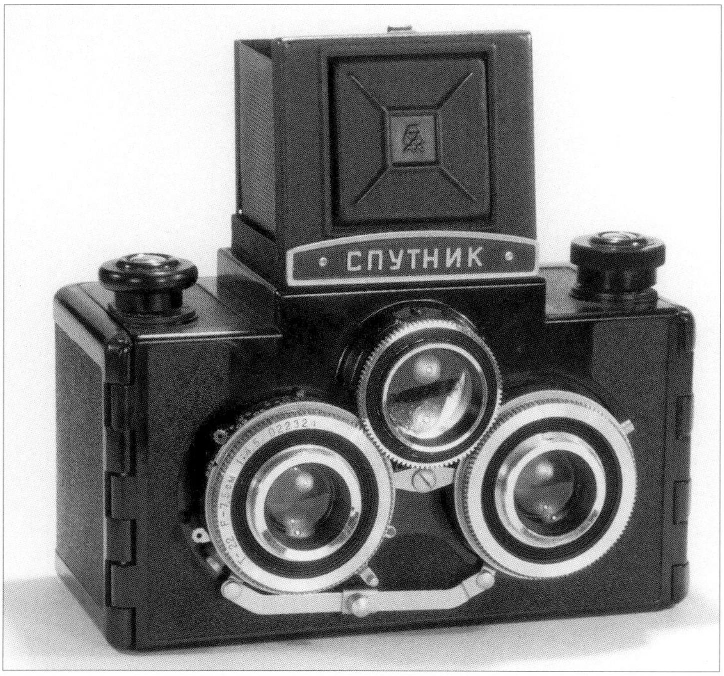

The Sputnik stereo camera from Russia was adapted from the Lubitel twin lens reflex.

The Sputnik takes 120 film, producing twin square images, not 6 x 6 cm as might be expected, but 55 x 55 mm. In use, the film is loaded and wound until the figure '1' appears in the red window in the back and, thereafter, the film is wound to '3', '5', '7', '9' and 11' to give six stereo pairs to a roll of film.

When it was originally sold, the Sputnik was packaged with its own contact printing frame, that allowed either single or double pictures to be exposed, and a collapsible stereo viewer. The cameras are most valuable today when you can find them with these original accessories.

Coronet 3-D Stereo Camera

The English Coronet company, who had a way of producing unusual cameras in plastic or Bakelite based on popular styles of the day, turned their attention to stereo in 1953 and came up with a small series of very similar stereo cameras, some in black, others in an unusual speckled finish. The cameras, which have simple snapshot controls, take four stereo pairs, 5 x 4.5 cm on 127 film.

They are unusual in having twin viewfinders which can be held to both eyes like a pair of binoculars. It's an obvious advantage for the stereo photographer because closing one eye to look through a more conventional viewfinder prevents the photographer from seeing the scene in three dimensions. This way, he can see the scene the way it will appear in a viewer.

Nimslo

In the 1980s, the Americans had one last stab at producing a 3-D camera for the masses. It came from Nimslo and was first seen at

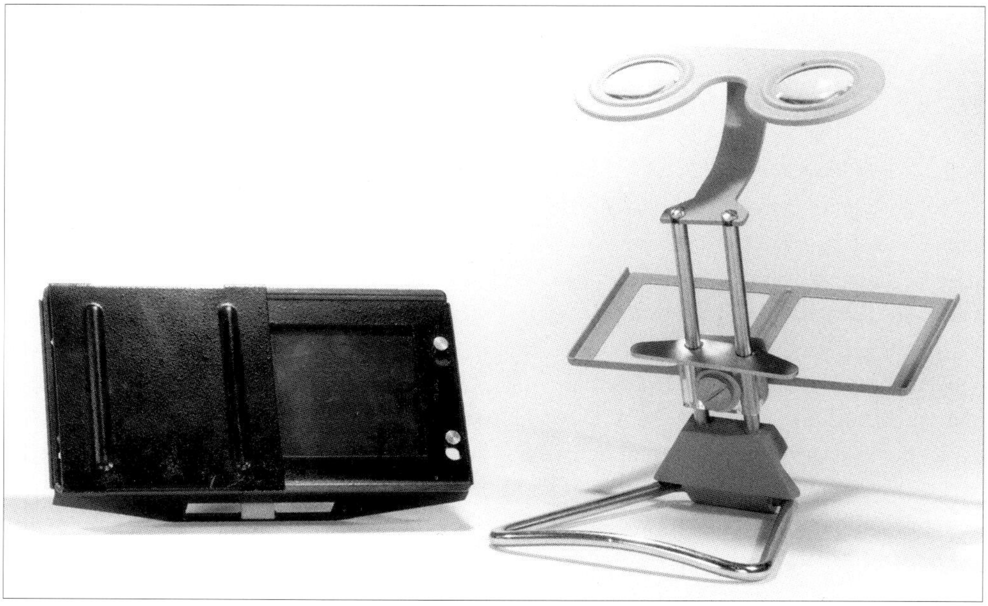

Accessories originally sold with the Sputnik: a contact printing frame and metal viewer.

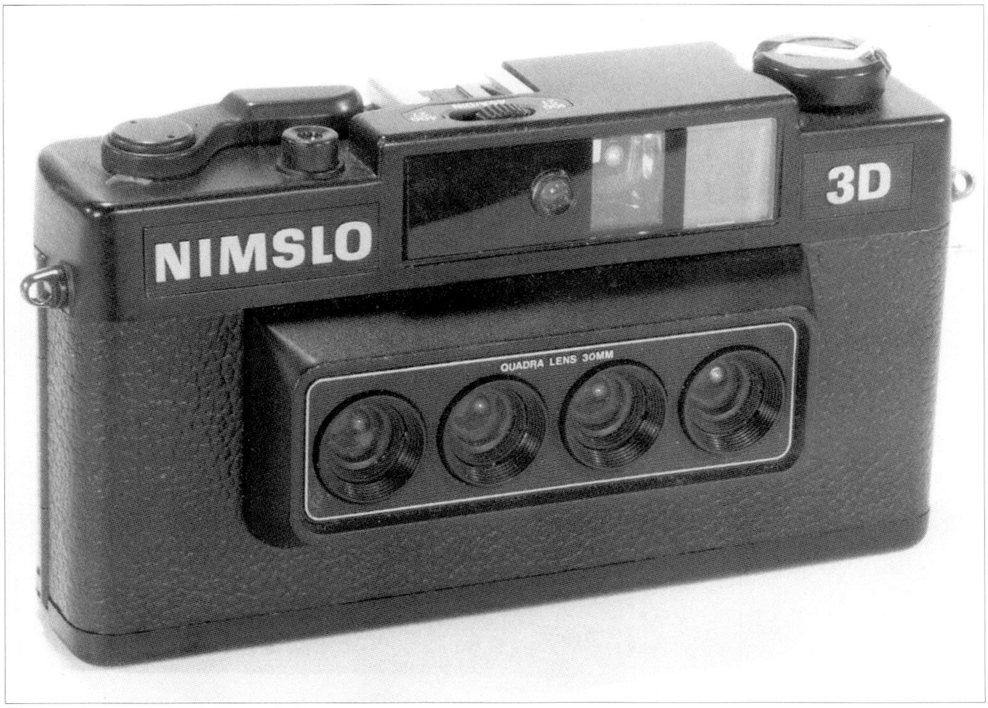

The Nimslo camera that briefly revived stereo photography in the 1980s.

Photokina in 1980, then disappeared for two years, not to be seen again until the next Photokina in 1982. The camera eventually arrived on the market in 1983 - and died very soon after.

The Nimslo system - named after its inventors Jerry Nims and Allen Lo - relied on taking four pictures side by side, each from a slightly different viewpoint. In the very special processing that could be carried out only by Nimslo, these were then split into a series of vertical strips, each one no more than the width of a human hair. Strips from similar sections of each picture were printed side by side and then overlaid with a corrugated plastic screen whose sides acted like lenses so that, when looked at in the normal way, the left eye saw only the left viewpoints and the right eye saw only the right viewpoints. The result: a fairly effective 3-D picture, seen without the aid of any viewer or special spectacles.

Nimslo's first target was the professional market for whom they produced something called the Computrack. This was a metal plate that screwed to a tripod and onto which a conventional camera could be mounted in a cradle which slid laterally, to click-stop in four different positions. The Computrack had six scales which spaced the camera in different positions. To discover which spacing to use, the photographer had to resort to the Compudisc, a circular calculator onto which were set the focal length of lens in use with the distances of important foreground objects, the main subject and the background. For obvious reasons, the Computrack was only really suitable for static subjects. It didn't take off.

Next came the Nimslo camera, which used similar technology, but produced the four pictures by means of four lenses. The Nimslo is a plastic camera not unlike a normal 35mm compact of the 1980s, although slightly longer to accommodate the four 30mm f/5.6 lenses, which have fixed focus from 6ft to infinity. Programmed auto exposure offers settings from 1/30 second at f/5.6 to 1/500 second at f/22 and there's a flashgun called the Optilite which is dedicated to the camera when slipped into the hot-shoe.

The Nimslo takes ordinary 35mm film and was aimed straight at amateur photographers, who ignored it in their thousands. The Nimslo system died soon after it was launched, but the camera lives on as an interesting collector's item.

Panoramic and Wideangle Cameras

The Hologon Ultrawide, made by Zeiss.

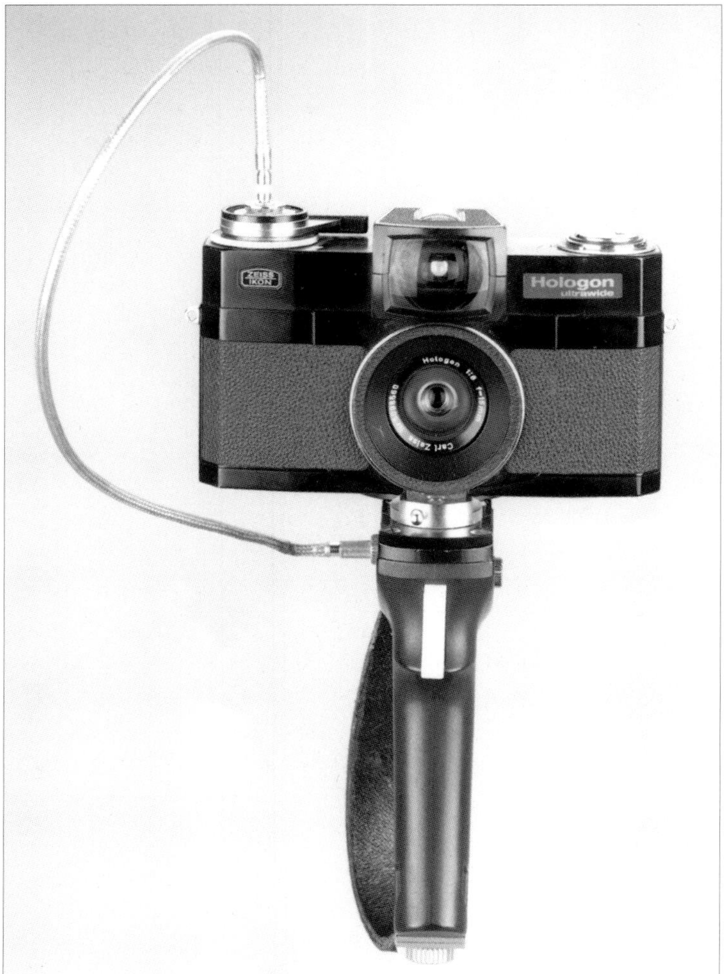

THERE ARE three types of panoramic or wideangle camera. The first uses a standard film format, but shoots it with a wider than normal focal length of lens; the second uses a swing lens that rotates across the field of view as the picture is taken to produce a wider than usual format on normal film; in the third type, the whole camera revolves as the film moves across the film plane to produce an ultra wide view that can take in a full 360 degree circle. Here are some of the more collectable examples.

Wideangle cameras

The first of this type was probably the Sutton Panoramic of 1860, designed by Thomas Sutton and using a spherical lens filled with water to give an extra wideangle effect. But if we are to stick to our chosen period of 1945-1985, let's look first at the Hologon Ultrawide, made by Zeiss in 1970.

The body is similar to the Contarex SLRs of the time, but where you'd expect a pentaprism, there's a large wideangle viewfinder. The lens is a Carl Zeiss Hologon with a fixed aperture of f/8 so exposures are governed only by the shutter which runs from 1 second to 1/500 second. The focal length of the lens is 15mm, which gives a field of view of 110 degrees on a normal 35mm 24 x 36 mm frame. Focus is fixed, but the depth of field is from 10 inches to infinity

The camera is equipped with a pistol grip for holding it steady and it's there for one very good reason: the photographer that holds the camera in the normal way will find his fingers included in the edges of the super wideangle frame.

A similar idea was used on the Veriwide 100, made by Plaubel in 1960, but this one uses 120 rollfilm with a 47mm f/8 Super Angulon lens that gives a field of view of 100 degrees.

Both of these cameras are extremely specialised pieces of equipment and their price reflects that. The collector on a more sensible budget, however, can find a similar, though slightly less ambitious, idea used in the Envoy Wideangle, made in 1950.

It's an English camera, made by Photo Developments Limited of Birmingham, taking eight pictures, 8 x 5.5cm to a roll of 120 film and using a 64mm lens. The result isn't as impressive as those from the likes of the Ultrawide or Veriwide, but it still offers an 82 degree angle of view that's wide compared to that more usually associated with standard, fixed lens medium format cameras that would normally use a focal length of around 80mm. The camera itself is a little smaller than a modern 35mm single lens reflex and is just as easy to handle. Shutter speeds from 1 to 1/150 second are set on a ring above the lens, which opens to f/6.5 at its widest setting, despite the fact that the aperture scale runs only from f/32 to f/11. Maybe the manufacturers felt that, since the focus is fixed, it should be used no wider than f/11 to retain a good depth of field.

The viewfinder comprises a large wire frame that folds up from around the lens, together with a smaller metal frame that hinges up behind it. It's not the most accurate method of focusing, but some attempt at parallax compensation is made by making the aperture in the back site of the viewfinder adjustable up and down to give the correct view at three feet, six feet and infinity.

The camera is made for use either with 120 film or with cut film, pre-loaded into dark slides and slid into the camera in place of its normal back that can be removed for the purpose.

A few camera manufacturers have applied similar thinking to the 35mm format, in which the usual standard lens is a 50mm focal length. When Ilford released the Advocate in 1949, however, they took the unusual step of offering it with a 35mm standard, non-interchangeable lens. (See page 70.)

A few years later, in 1958, Minolta came up with their version, the Minolta Autowide. The specification is similar to that of the Minolta Super A released the year before, but in place of that camera's interchangeable 50mm Rokkor lens, the Autowide offered a fixed 35mm f/2.8 Rokkor. The camera also has a built-in CdS meter and is slightly unconventional in placing both the film advance and rewind controls on the base of the body.

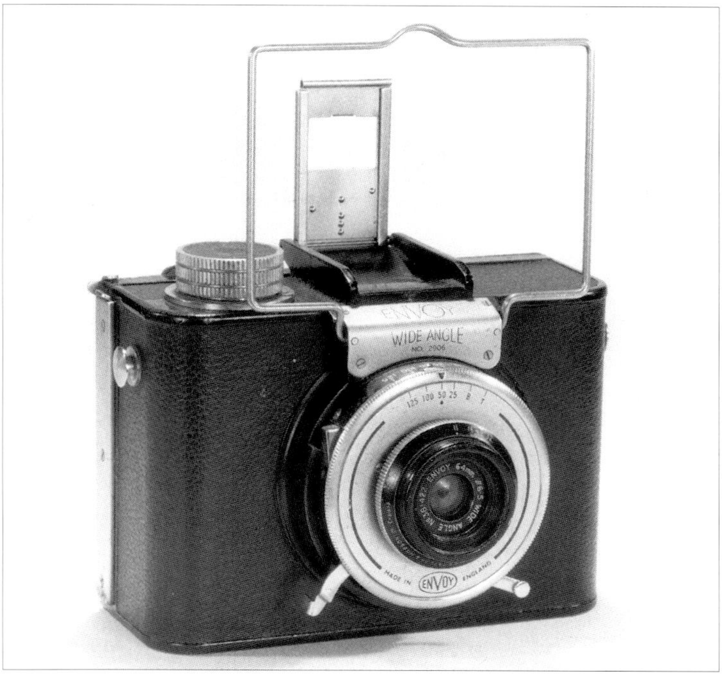

The Envoy Wideangle, made in England.

Swing lens cameras

With swing lens cameras we move into true panoramic photography. They work by bending the film around a curved plane and, during exposure, the lens turns through an arc. The lens is fixed in a short tube and, as it swings, its image is projected onto the film through a slit at the opposite end of the tube, progressively exposing the film from one side to the other.

It's the method that was used in the Megaskop, the first panoramic camera, made by Freidrich von Martens in 1844. The same theory is still being used today and, among those on the collector's market, there are three worth watching out for. In descending order of value, they are the Widelux, the Horizont and the FT-2. All three take 35mm film.

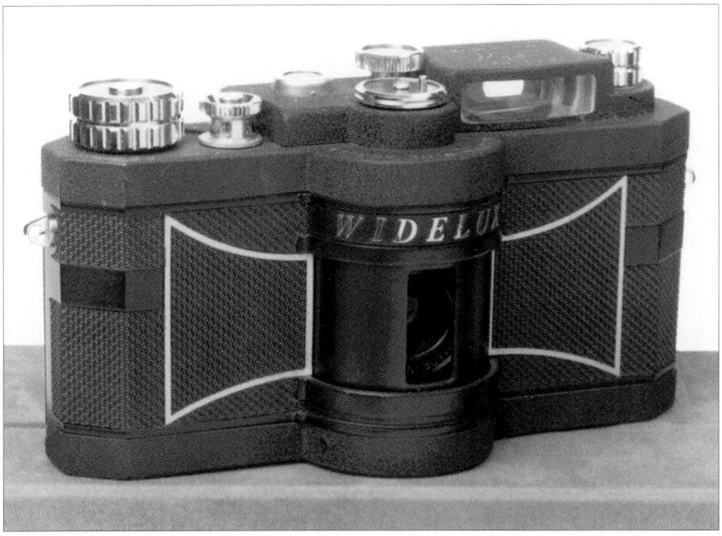

The Japanese Widelux produces images 24 x 59 mm.

The Widelux is Japanese, made by the Panon Camera Company and was first seen in 1959. It takes a 24 x 59 mm image on normal 35mm film, covering a 140 degree angle of view, using a Lux f/2.8 fixed focus lens that stops down to f/11. The speed of the swing determines the shutter speed and is controlled by a dial on the top plate that designates speeds at 1/15 second, 1/125 second and 1/250 second.

If you buy one of these cameras to use, take care to set the speed exactly on the dial. If the setting is slightly off, the intricate shutter mechanism can be easily damaged.

The Russian Horizont, which was made by the Krasnogorsk Mechanical Factory in 1968, works on a similar principle, but gives a slightly less wide angle of view at 120 degrees, resulting in an image of 24 x 58 mm on 35mm film. It uses a 28mm f/2.8 lens and shutter speeds are designated as 1/25 second, 1/60 second and 1/125 second. Unlike the Widelux, setting them adjusts the width of the slit through which the image is projected, rather than controlling the speed of the lens's swing.

The Horizont is usually found with its separate clip-on viewfinder that incorporates a spirit level and the value of the camera decreases a little if this isn't available.

The FT-2 is another Russian-made panoramic camera that came from the same factory as the Horizont a decade earlier in 1958. This one also takes 35mm film, but in its own special cassettes, winding it from one to the other. So if you buy an FT-2 with the thought of using it, make sure it has both its cassettes intact.

The style is unlike any of the other cameras mentioned here, taking the shape of a box, rather like a small black brick. The lens swings through 120 degrees to give an image size of 24 x 110mm, which is actually more than the width of the camera itself and is achieved by the curving film plane which curls around the

Panoramic picture taken with a Widelux.

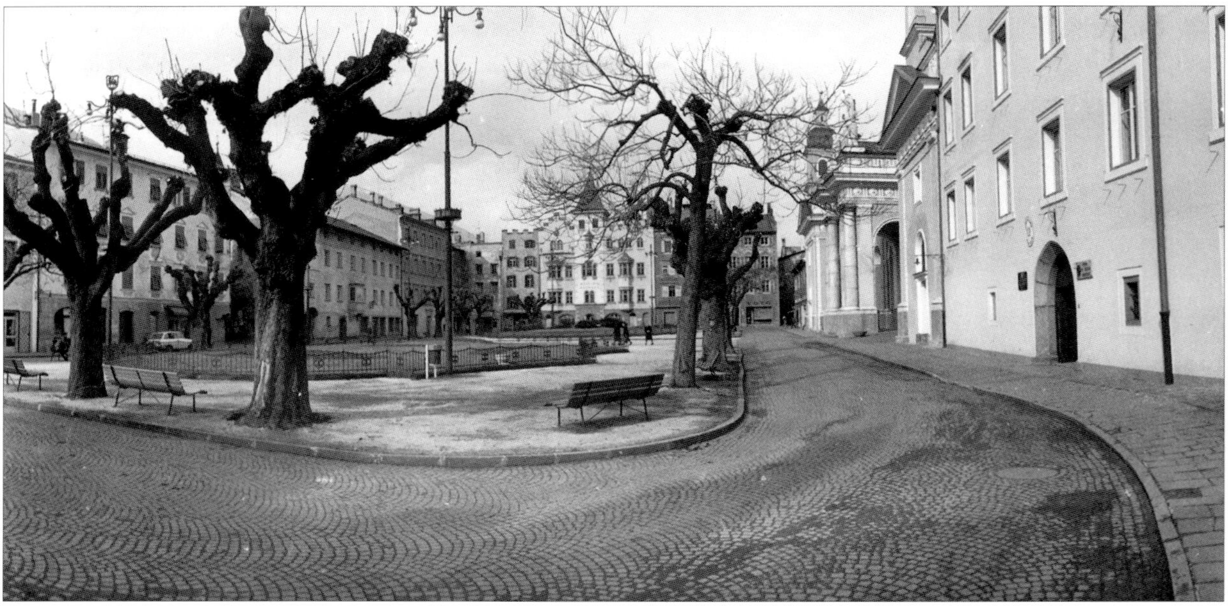

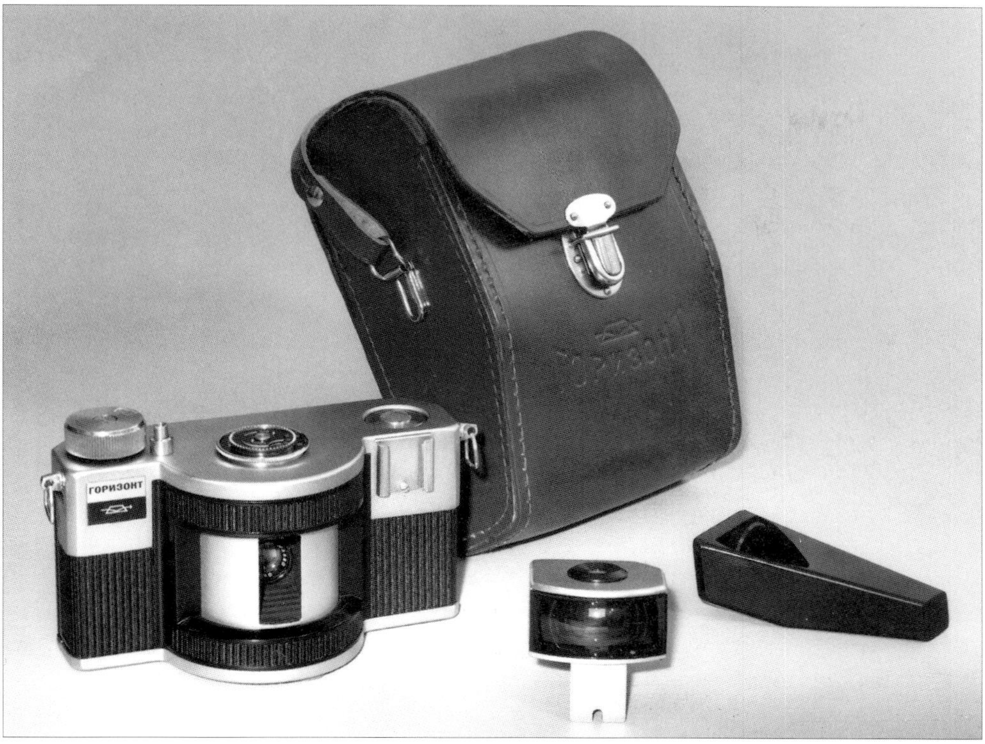

The Russian-made Horizont takes images 24 x 58 mm.

The unusually styled Russian FT-2 that takes images 24 x 110 mm.

Below: A panoramic picture taken by the FT-2.

inside of the camera in a semi-circle.

The controls are simple, but a little confusing at first glance. There's no aperture or focusing to adjust because the camera has a fixed focus 50mm Industar lens with a fixed aperture of f/5. Exposure control is by use of the shutter speeds and there are three, adjusted by juggling two small levers on the top plate, each of which swings through 90 degrees. With both levers pointing down, the speed is 1/400 second; with the left lever pointing down and the right one pointing right, the speed changes to 1/200 second; with the left lever pointing left and the right lever pointing down the resulting speed is 1/100 second.

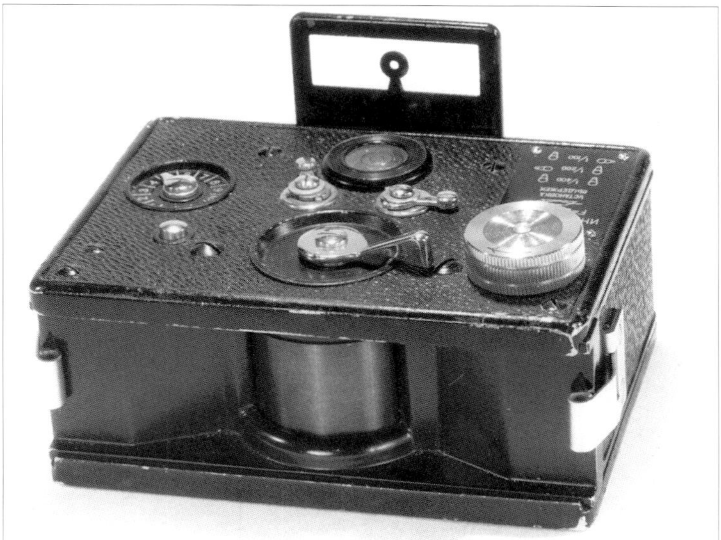

Like the Widelux, but unlike the Horizont,

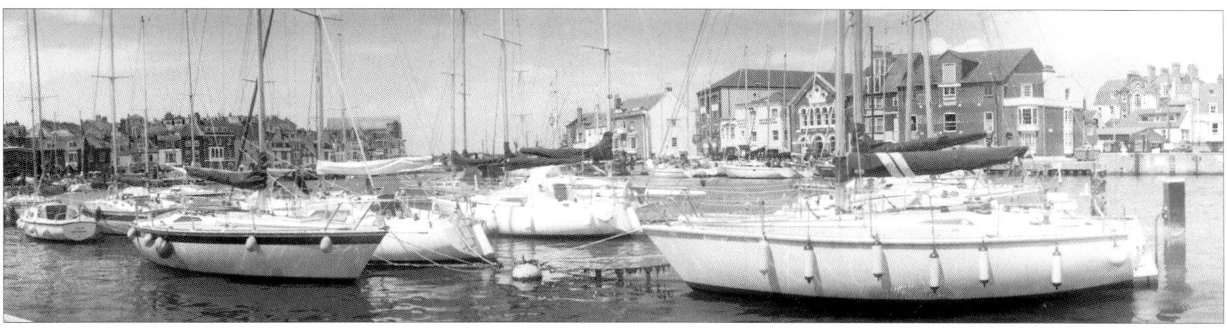

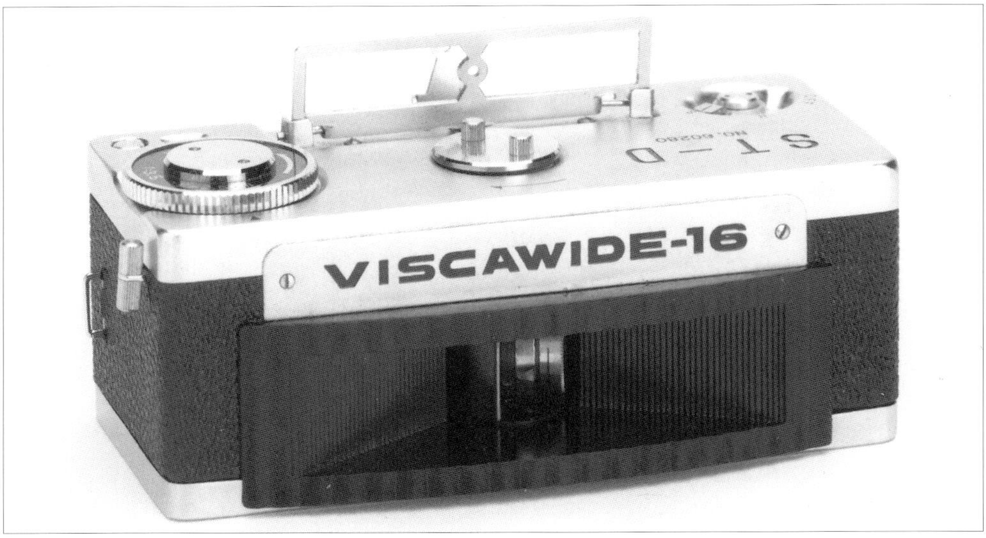

Swing lens panoramic cameras even made it to the 16mm format with the Viscawide-16.

the speeds are achieved by the speed of the lens's swing, which is released by a button on the top plate after first turning a tensioning lever through 180 degrees.

In use, film must first be pre-loaded into one of the special cassettes, and of course that needs to be done in a darkroom or a changing bag. With the loaded cassette in place on one side of the body, the film is pulled across the curved film plane and attached to a take-up spool inside the second cassette beneath the wind knob. The frame counter is like a clock, numbered from '1' to '12' with an empty space just before the '1', which is where the 'hand' of the clock starts. With the back in place, the film wind knob is wound so that the 'clock hand' makes three complete revolutions before coming to rest on the '1'.

There's a panoramic frame that flips up from the back of the camera to serve as a viewfinder and a spirit level just in front of it to help keep everything straight, but the viewfinder isn't very accurate and the resulting pictures always contain a lot more on each side than seemed to be in the finder's framework. After each exposure, winding to the next panoramic frame means turning the film wind knob until that counter has again made three complete revolutions, to stop on the '2', and so on through the film. Because each frame is three times the width of a standard 35mm image, the camera is supposed to give 12 exposures on a 36-exposure roll of film. However, the first frame tends to be lost in the loading, so unless the camera is loaded in pitch darkness it's more likely to produce only 11 pictures.

One unusual aspect of the pictures produced by any swing lens camera is the way the image

A more than 360 degree picture taken with the Globuscope.

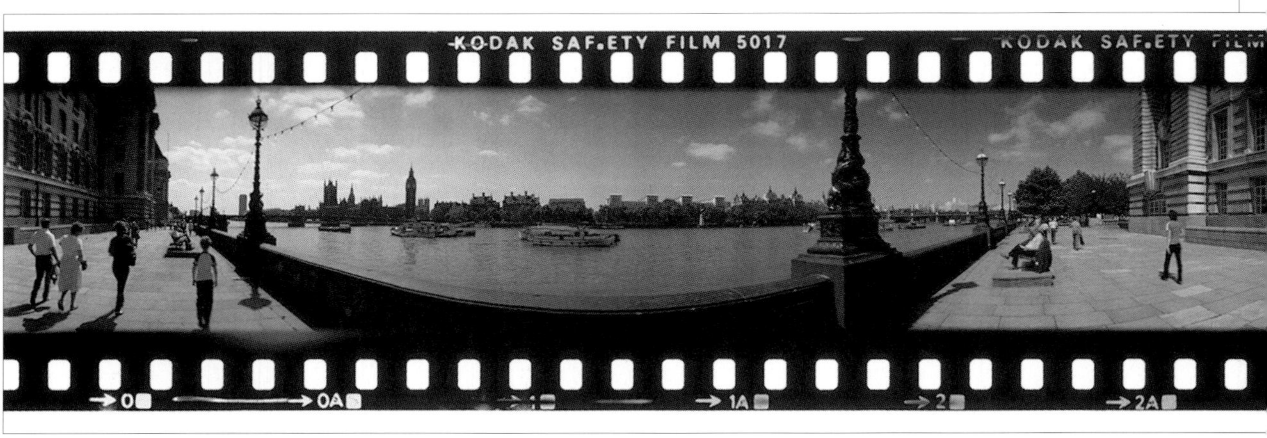

appears to bulge forward in the centre. That's because, with such a wide format, subjects at the centre of the frame are closer to the camera than those at the edges, but careful composition can often disguise the effect.

Revolving cameras

Remember those school pictures when the photographer arrived with a camera on a tripod and arranged everyone in a huge semi-circle around it? As the shutter was pressed, the camera revolved and captured the whole school on a long, narrow panoramic print. If you had your picture taken with one of those, it's a fair bet that the photographer was using a Kodak Cirkut that was first made in 1907 and continued to be manufactured in different sizes right up until 1949.

The same theory is used in another, much smaller, camera from the 1980s, called the Globuscope which produces images 24 x 160 mm on normal 35mm film.

The Globuscope is oval in shape, with a sturdy handle fixed to the base. The shutter release is in this handle and apertures are adjusted by a small pointer on the camera base which opens and closes a V-shaped aperture. They run from f/3.5 to f/22, plus an extra setting marked 'closed' - of which more in a moment.

To use the Globuscope, the handle is first turned until it stops. This tensions a clockwork motor inside. The top of the body is removed and, before the film is loaded, the photographer has to decide what shutter speed he is going to be shooting at because, once set, there's no changing it until the next film is loaded. That's because the 'shutter speeds' are actually controlled by the width of a vertical

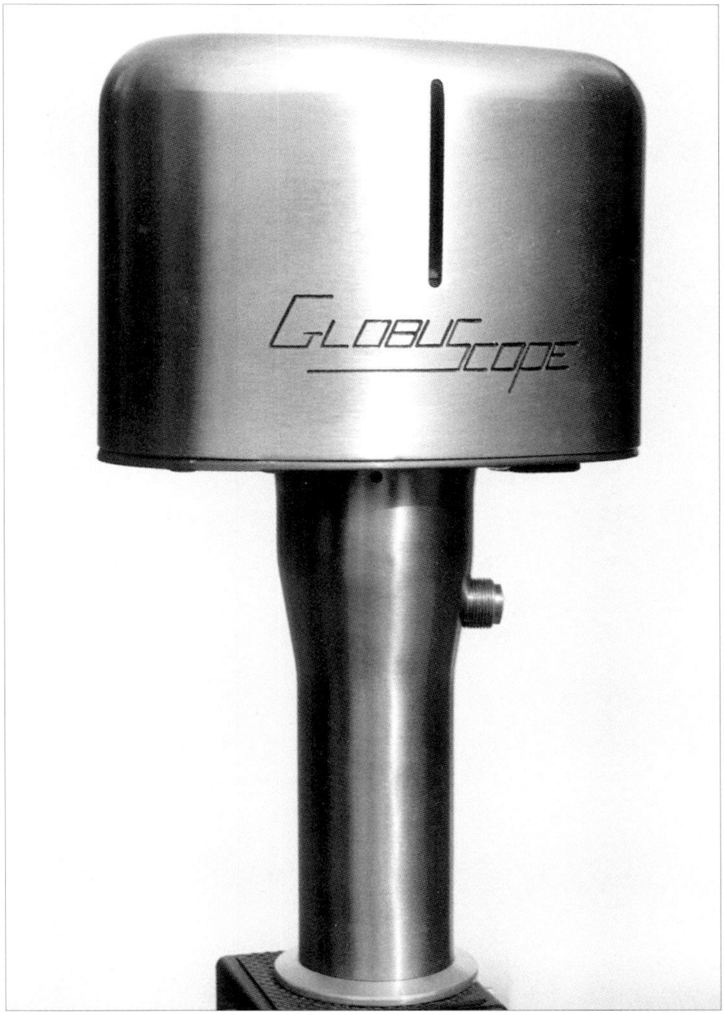

The American Globuscope revolves through 360 degrees to produce images 24 x 160 mm

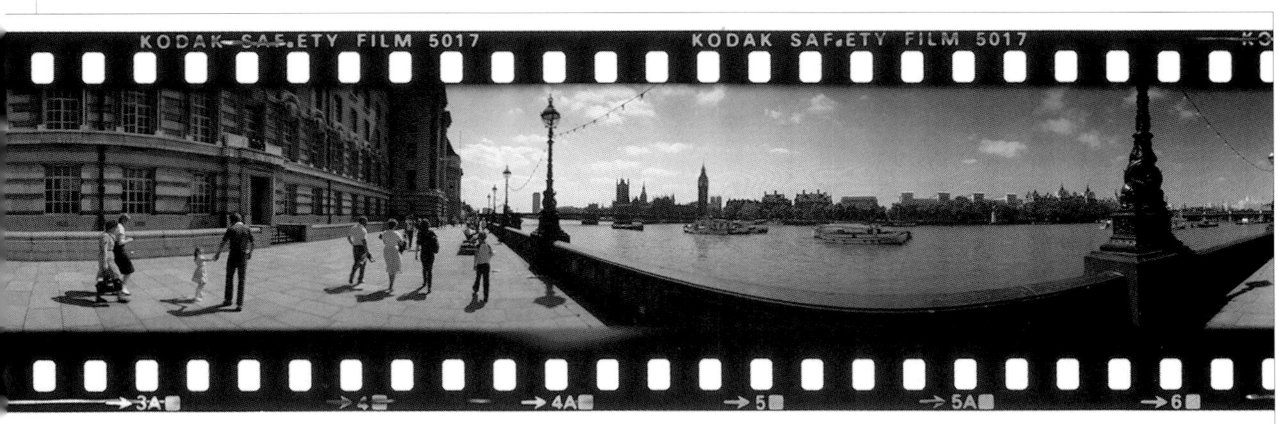

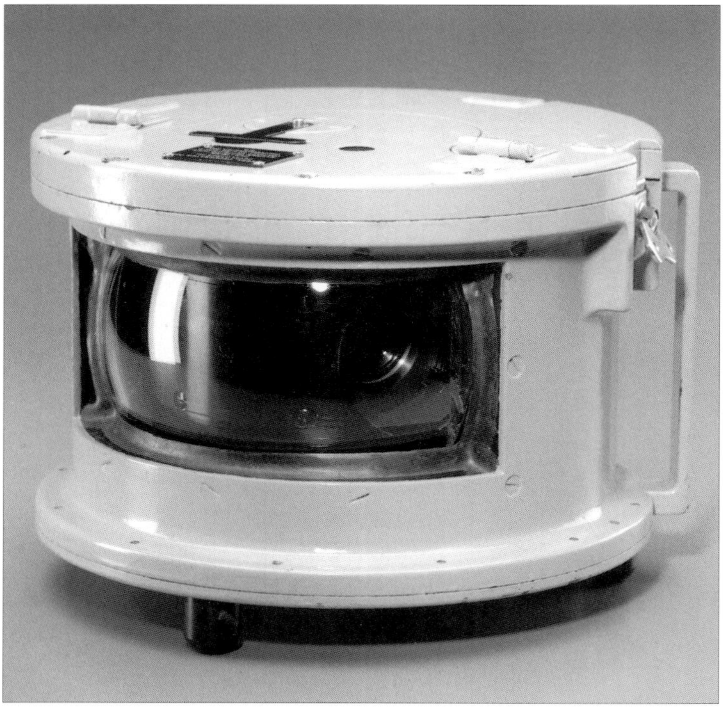

The underwater panoramic camera made by Photogrammetry.

slit running up and down the film plane and there's a choice of three in curved plates that screw into position.

The next task is to set the aperture to the 'closed' position so no light is allowed through. A normal cassette of 35mm film is slotted into a chamber on one side of the body, pulled out across that slit and threaded onto a take-up spool on the opposite side. The top of the camera body can then be replaced.

To take a picture, the camera needs to be on a tripod and the photographer has to sit or crouch underneath. The only alternative is to hold the camera above the head, which would inevitably result in it being held crooked - and it is important to keep this camera level. To make an exposure, the aperture is opened to its appropriate setting, the shutter button pressed and the aperture closed down again.

As the shutter button is pressed, the whole camera rotates in a complete circle, which is why the photographer can't be behind it unless he wants to end up as part of the picture.

As the camera rotates, the film is wound past the slit at the same speed and the picture is exposed onto a length of emulsion. The recommended way to use it is to set the camera to revolve twice so that the best part of the panoramic frame can be selected to give the final composition. The only problem using it that way is that the Globuscope takes only four frames to a 36-exposure cassette of 35mm film.

Underwater panoramic!

Surely the most unusual panoramic camera must be one made by the American Photogrammetry company sometime in the 1950s. It's made to shoot panoramic pictures underwater.

The camera weighs a massive 12.4 kilos, although it would feel lighter underwater. It's the shape of a drum with about one-third of its circumference taken up by an expanse of convex glass which, once underwater, acts as part of the optical system. Behind the glass is the main lens whose apertures, between f/2.4 and f/16, are set by a watertight T-shaped control that lifts up from the top of the body.

The camera takes sprocketed 70mm film which is loaded into special cassettes and, as the lens swings past the inside of the glass panel during exposure, it produces an image size of 60 x 190mm. The shutter release takes the form of a large lever on the side of the body and, as it is depressed, the lens swings from one side to the other, then back again. The exposure is made on the first swing, the second caps the shutter as the lens returns to its original position, ready for the next exposure.

Probably made for the military, it's not the sort of thing you see in too many camera fairs, but it's an interesting item nonetheless.

It Started with a Snap

SNAPSHOT CAMERAS are often thought of as the by-products of more sophisticated models, as the introduction of new ideas in camera design have a knock-on effect that ends in simplified versions for non-specialist photographers. You have only to look at how many snapshot cameras have tried to emulate the style of far more sophisticated twin lens reflexes to see how that has happened in the past. (See pages 66-69.)

But sometimes the reverse is true. Occasionally, the introduction of a snapshot camera has resulted in new thoughts about more serious cameras. Between 1963 and 1982, Kodak launched three new film formats that, for a while, revolutionised camera design in everything from the simple snapshot cameras that came with each new format, up to and including unusual designs of single lens reflex.

126 format

Some collectors frown on Instamatic cameras because they are so simple, so common and extremely cheap to buy at any flea market. But the true collector acknowledges that the first Instamatic, introduced in 1963, was a true landmark in camera design - and what is that if it isn't the definition of a collectable camera?

Kodak introduced the format at a time when most snapshot photographers were put off more serious cameras because they thought of them as difficult to load. The new Kodapak cartridge was given the identification number 126, a number originally used for a rollfilm in 1906. It contained a roll of 35mm wide film

Three early Kodak Instamatics: The 50 and 100 models, with the 154 that has a built-in clockwork motor drive.

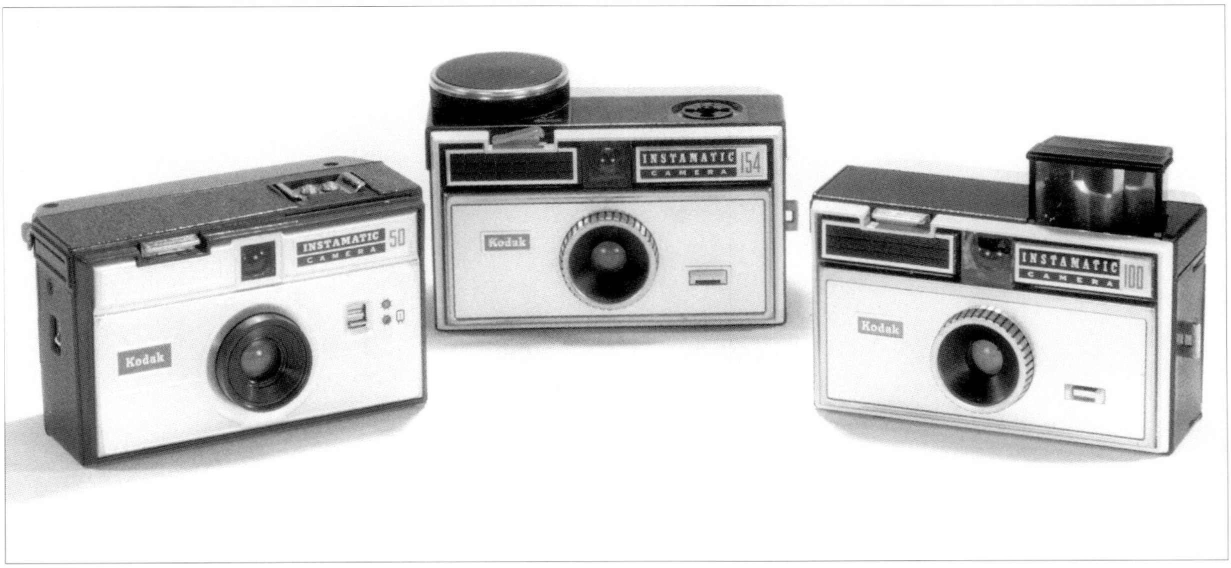

with a single perforation, on numbered backing paper and pre-threaded onto a take-up spool. The whole thing was simply dropped into the back of the camera, ready to shoot 28mm square images. The idea took off immediately it was launched and the Instamatic has become one of Kodak's biggest success stories.

There are hundreds of different Instamatics and Instamatic-type cameras, from Kodak and other manufacturers, although strictly speaking, the word 'Instamatic' should only be applied to Kodak models. The collector should look for the very early cameras, or any that showed an unusual design concept.

The first cameras range from the Model 50, which is little more than a restyled box camera, up to the Model 400, which features auto exposure and a built-in clock work motor drive. The Model 50 has a hot-shoe with contacts for a bulb flashgun or flashcubes via a special accessory, but the others all have built-in pop-up flashguns that take AG-1 bulbs.

Three years after the first cameras were launched, a new range of Instamatics arrived, similar in style, but made to take flashcubes. Their identification numbers end in '4', to give models like the Instamatic 104, 204 and 304. The 'X' range of Instamatics arrived in 1970, made to take the new magicubes.

Some Instamatics, however, were a lot more sophisticated than the basic snapshot cameras that launched the format. The Kodak Instamatic 500 was made in 1963, the year the first snapshot models arrived, but it's a far more streamlined model that was made in Germany for the more serious photographer who wanted the kind of specification more usually associated with 35mm cameras of the day.

A metal body replaces the plastic of the basic models and the camera has a 38mm f/2.8 Schneider lens that focuses from 2.5 feet to infinity on one scale, or which click stops to three settings indicated by symbols on another scale for portraits, groups and landscapes. The lens stops down to f/22 and shutter speeds are available from 1/30 second to 1/500 second. Exposure is set according to a needle that swings across the viewfinder to line up with a central indicator, as apertures and/or shutter speeds are adjusted against each other. Film wind is by a lever.

In 1968, Kodak produced a single lens reflex for the format and called it the Instamatic

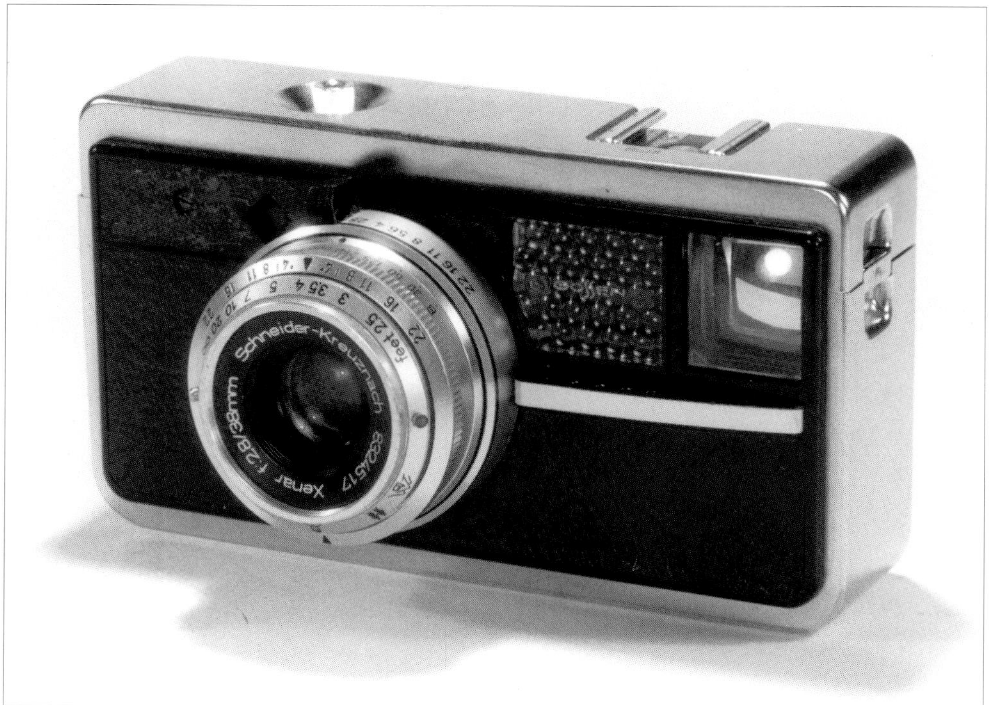

The Instamatic 500, a rather more sophisticated camera for 126 film.

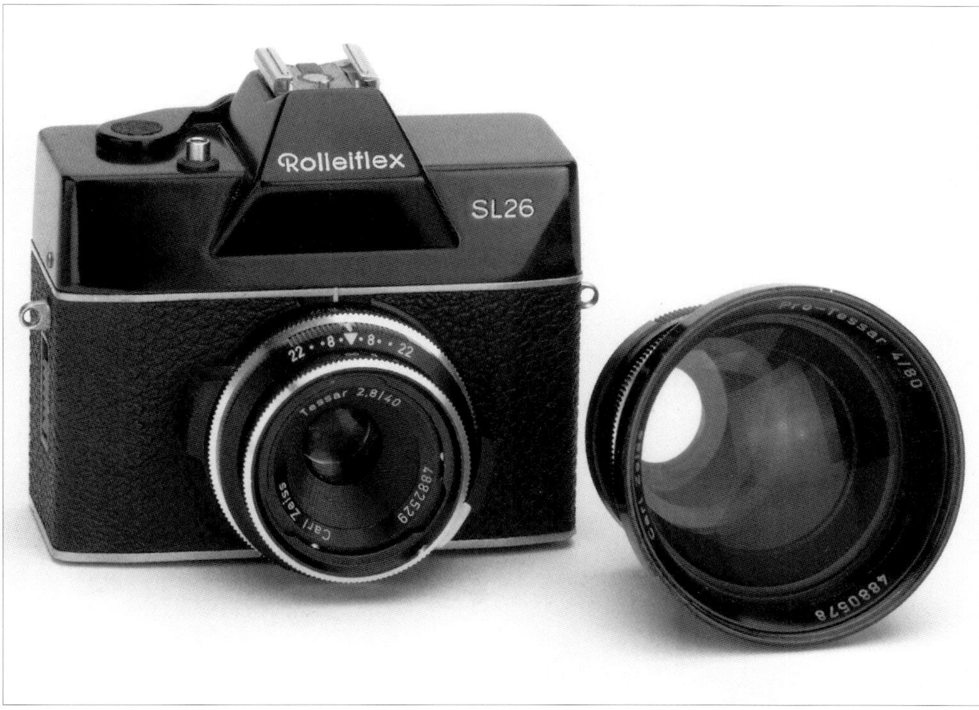

The Rollei SL26 used the Instamatic cartridge in an SLR.

Reflex. It's smaller than 35mm SLRs of the time and has smooth lines that make it a very attractive camera to the collector and the user. Lenses are interchangeable with Kodak's Retina series, it has a built-in CdS meter and one of the first electronic shutters. Watch for black and chrome models.

Rollei was another company that took 126 seriously enough to produce a single lens reflex for the format, also in 1968. This one has an interchangeable 40mm f/2.8 Tessar lens and TTL metering. The camera is called the Rollei SL26 and there are two accessory lenses made for it: a 28mm f/3.2 wideangle and an 80mm f/4 medium tele. They are both Pro-Tessars.

But 126 was primarily a snapshot film and just about every snapshot camera manufacturer tried their hand at making a 126 camera. Even the great names in camera manufacture, like Zeiss Ikon, tried their hands at the format, and this was another area where Rollei also came to the fore with a non-reflex camera. The Rollei A26 became is one of the better 126 cameras of 1973, with a 40mm f/3.5 Sonnar lens and a programmed shutter that offers speeds from 1/30 second to 1/250 second.

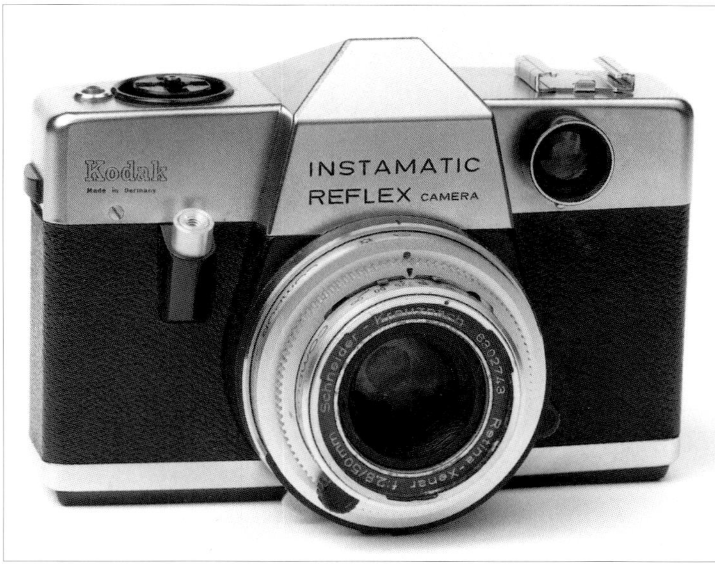

Kodak's own Instamatic Reflex.

But perhaps the most attractive and one of the more unusual 126 cartridge cameras is the Mick-a-Matic, made in 1971 in the shape of Mickey Mouse's head. The lens looks out through Mickey's nose and a flashcube clips into the top of his head. On the early models, the shutter is released by moving the right ear, but later models have a shutter release button between the eye and ear. 126 cameras were also been made in the shape of Charlie Tuna in 1971 and Snoopy, the famous Peanuts dog sit-

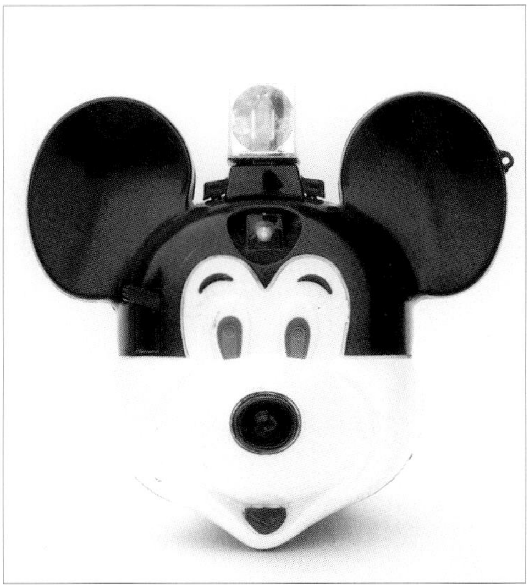

The Mick-a-Matic looks more like a mask than a camera.

ting on top of his kennel. That one is called the Snoopy-Matic.

110 format

Having launched 126 cartridges and led the world's snapshot camera manufacturers along one path, Kodak changed direction and showed them another in 1972 with the launch of 110. A decade on, the result was much the same. Manufacturers immediately started tooling up for 110 cameras, resulting in straightforward snapshot models, three very sophisticated SLRs and a multitude of other unusual designs.

The 110 cartridge took the 126 concept and made it much smaller, producing a mini-cartridge that dropped into a series of long, slim cameras that looked not unlike overgrown Minoxes. The film is 16mm wide, wound onto numbered backing paper inside the cartridge and produces an image size of 13 x 17 mm.

The cameras that started the 110 trend were called Kodak Pocket Instamatics. As representatives of the first of the style, it's worth adding one to any collection and it's equally worth looking out for them in their original packing that contained a film, wrist chain and a special column that extended the flashcube's position to several inches above the height of the camera, in an effort to kill the red eye effect that happens when a flash is positioned too close to the lens.

In the wake of the Pocket Instamatics, other camera manufacturers began turning out similar simple snapshot cameras for the 110 format. Few are worth considering unless you find one that is that little bit more sophisticated than the others. The Agfamatic 2008 Tele Pocket is a prime example.

Made in the mid-1970s, it has 26mm f/11 Color-Agnar lens which, at the press of a switch on the top, is converted into a 43mm telephoto as an accessory lens slides in front of the standard. At the same time, another lens slides into place in the viewfinder to convert its view as well. The other thing that sets the Agfa camera aside from many of its simpler contemporaries is the film wind that is effected by sliding the two halves of the body in and out, similar to the way film is advanced in a Minox.

Rollei, who had embraced the 126 culture in 1973, went on to do the same the following year with 110, producing the Rollei A110, a delightful little camera that measures no more than 8 x 4 x 3 cm in its folded position and which, being made of metal, is pleasantly

The Snoopy-Matic 126 camera.

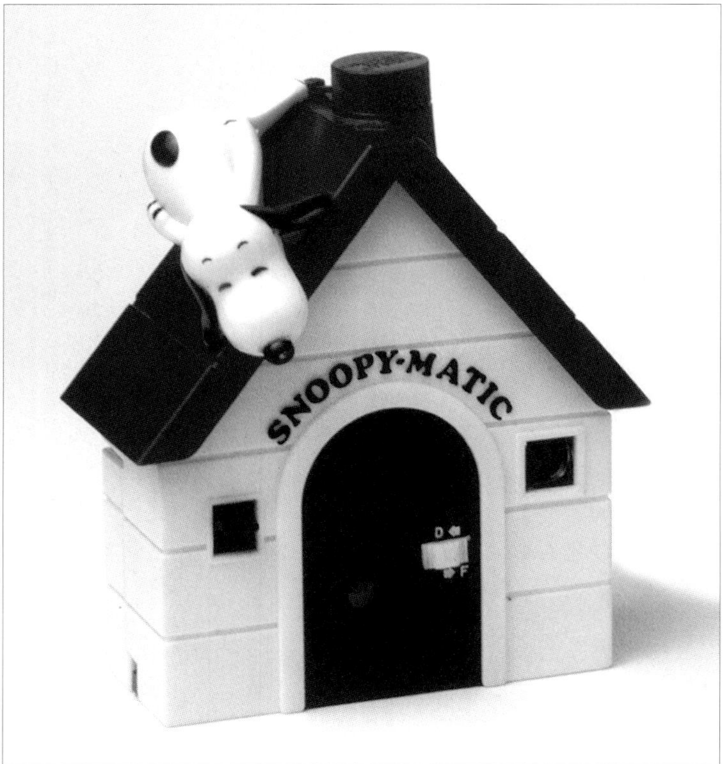

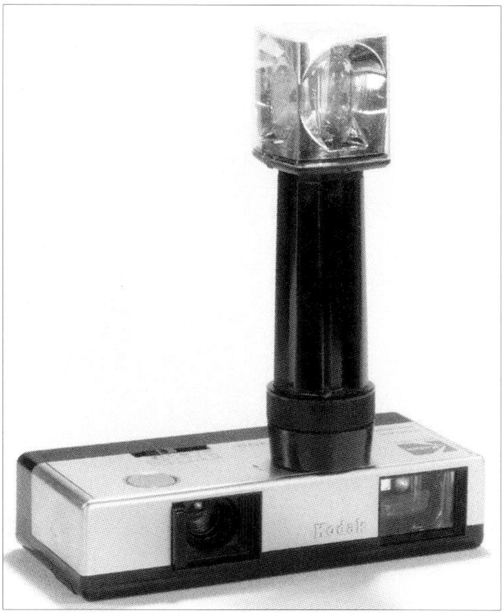

The Kodak Pocket Instamatic with its special flash extension.

weighty compared to most 110 models. The A110 slides open to reveal a 23mm f/2.8 Tessar lens, focused by a sliding control beneath. As the lens revolves, distances are indicated in the viewfinder by a green band that moves behind a feet and metres scale, alongside the traditional symbols for close-ups, groups and landscapes. The camera has automatic programmed exposure control and is usually seen in a matt black finish. Watch out for rarer models too in brushed chrome or gold.

The idea of throwaway cameras didn't begin with the Fuji Quicksnap (first of the modern disposable cameras) in 1988, because there was a 110 version called the Rank Throwaway camera in 1975, made in America where it was called the Lure. The camera has a single speed

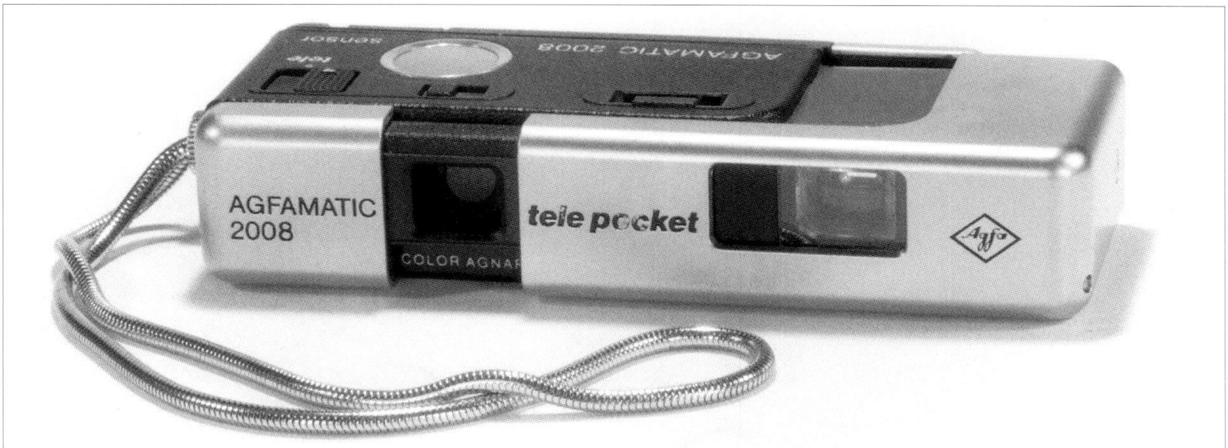

The Agfamatic 2008 Tele Pocket is a well made 110 camera from Agfa.

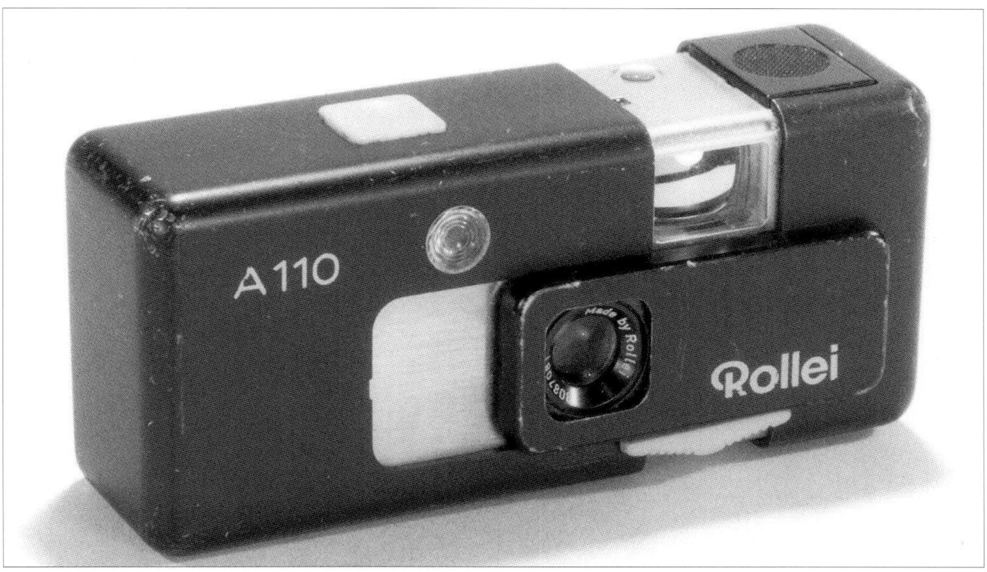

The Rollei A110 also took the 110 format seriously.

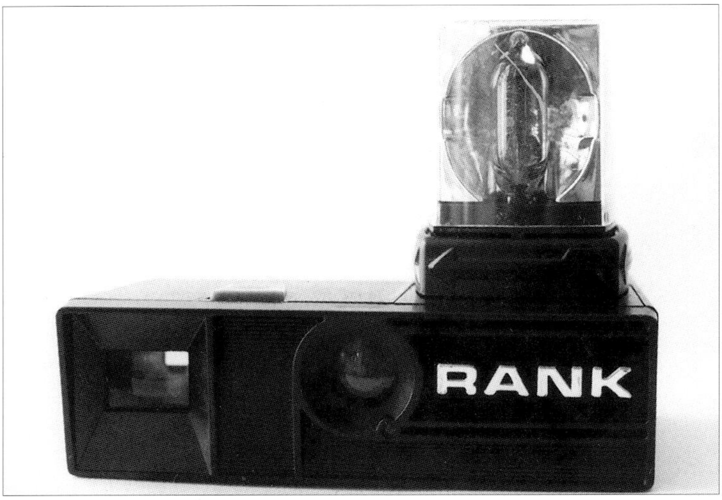

The Rank Throwaway camera was an early disposable model.

1/80 second shutter and fixed focus f/11 lens, but it is synchronised for flashcubes which push into the big film advance knob. After exposure, the whole camera was returned to Rankolor laboratories, where it was broken open and the film processed. Back in the 1970s, for the price of the processing, the photographer received a set of prints and a new camera, loaded with film.

110 cameras have also been prime targets for the premium market, where simple models have been given away for promotional purposes. Some, like the Micro 110, are little more than hollow shells containing a lens and shutter which clip onto the film, so that the cartridge becomes a part of the body. Others can often be found in a series of similar styles, but overprinted with the names of different companies.

Disguised cameras that were popular in the late 1800s and early 1900s, got a new lease of life with 110 cameras in the late 1970s until the early 1980s. Drinks cans were favourites and the camera you see most is the one disguised as a can of Coca-Cola, but beware because there are a couple of different models, made by different manufacturers.

The original Coca-Cola can camera was made in Japan by a company called Tizer. The camera has a fixed focus, fixed aperture f/5.6 lens and single speed shutter. Some versions have hot shoes synchronised for flash. Later can cameras are more likely to have been made by Eiko in Taiwan, including a copy of the Japanese Coca-Cola model. As well as Coke, look out for them disguised as cans of Miller Lite, Budweiser, Orangina, Pepsi-Cola and 7-Up, among others.

Other 110 cameras can be found disguised as Websters Dictionary and small car tyres and this later style was copied by a company called Kiddie Camera in Taiwan, who then used the basic round shape to produce a series of cameras styled to resemble various faces that include bears, pandas and clowns. The cameras

110 cameras printed with trade names make them more collectable.

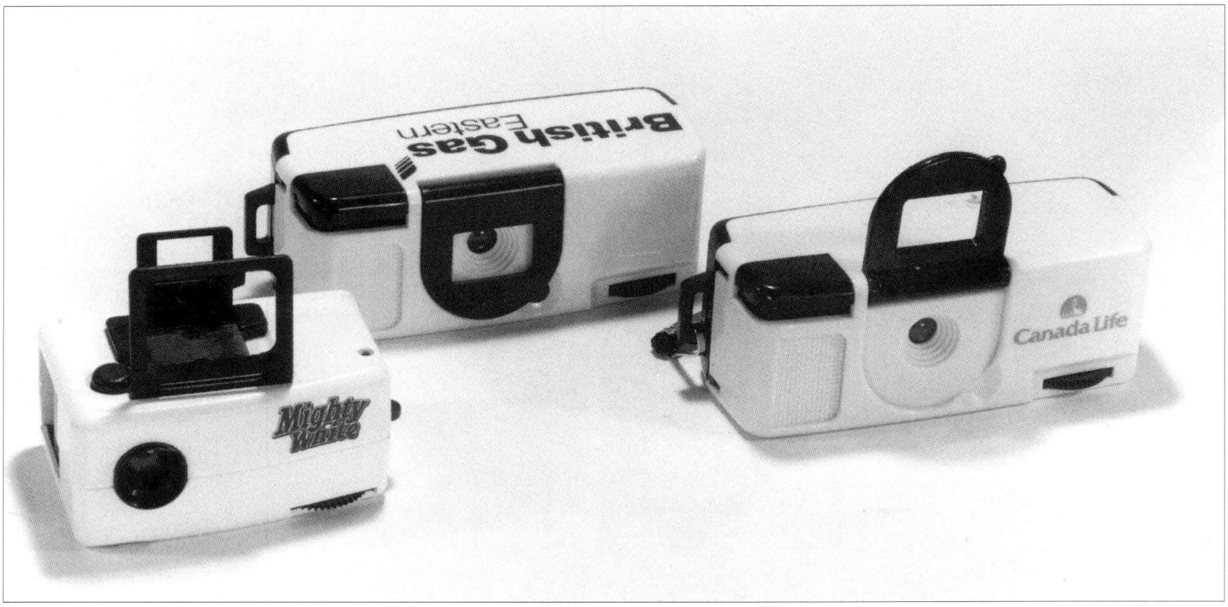

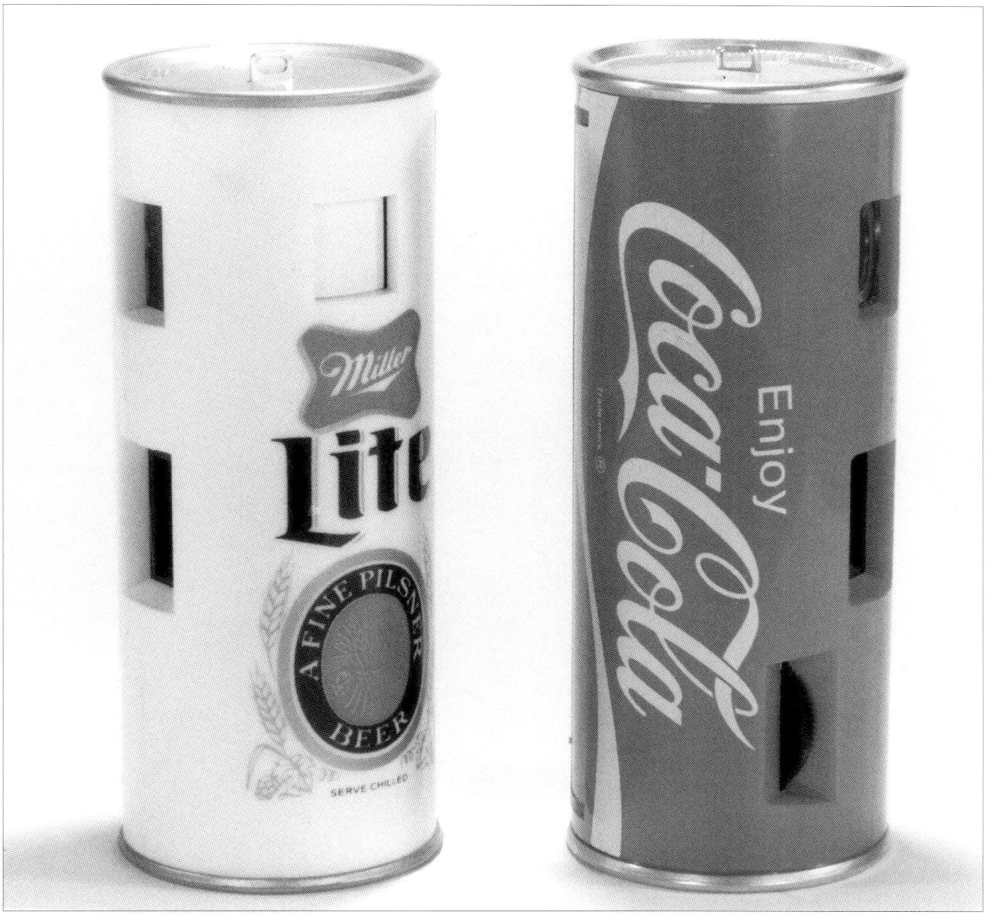

Can cameras: the popular Coca-Cola model and the Miller Lite version.

Last of a line, the Clown Girl camera was made in the 1990s.

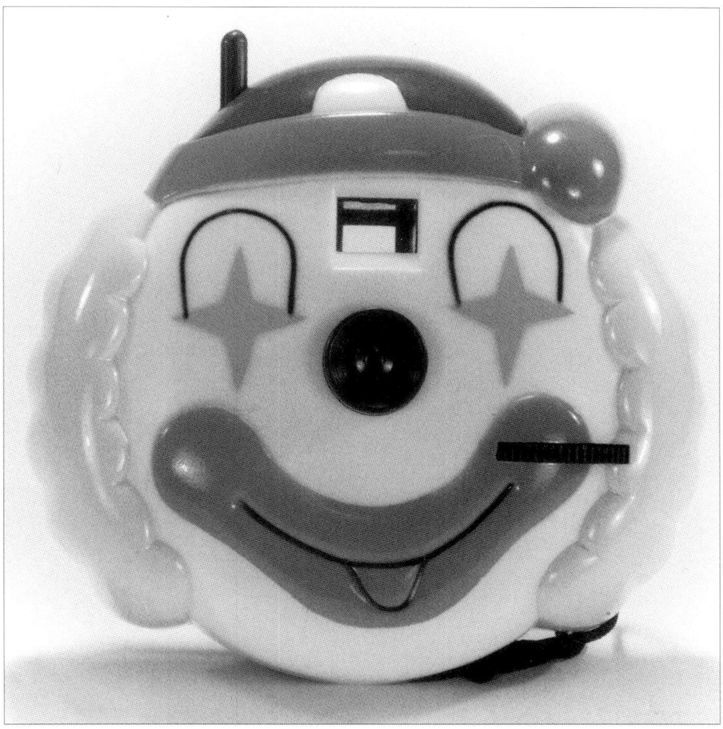

have single speed shutters with fixed aperture, fixed focus lenses. The lenses are usually in the 'nose' of the face, the film wind to one side in a 'cheek' and the shutter release on top of the head. The Clown Girl was the last of the series, made later than the others in 1990.

In the last years of 110, some of the cameras made for the format became as sophisticated as their 35mm counterparts. The Helios 110A, for example, was made in Russia in the early 1980s and, like 35mm compacts of the time, it has not only a built-in electronic flash, but also a built-in battery-driven motor drive.

But the zenith of 110 camera production must surely be the three single lens reflexes made for the format by Minolta and Pentax.

Minolta had always had a strong interest in subminiature cameras, having produced many variations on their Minolta 16 design during the 1950s and 1960s. Maybe it was that which led the company to producing the first 110 sin-

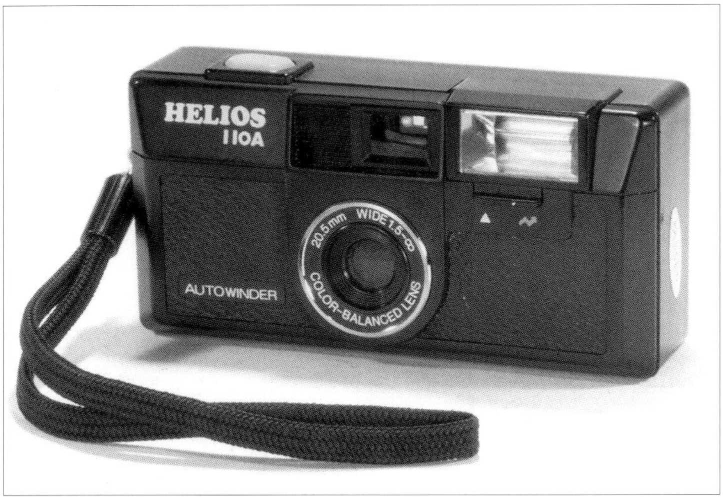

The Russian made Helios has a built-in battery driven motor drive.

gle lens reflex in 1976. It was called the Minolta 110 Zoom SLR.

The design of the camera is influenced more by traditional 110 cameras of the day than by the usual concept of a single lens reflex. It looks, in fact, like a traditional 110 camera with a large lens and metering cell fitted to the front and a pentaprism added to the top - which, really, is exactly what it is. The lens is an f/4.5 25-50mm zoom and exposure is by aperture priority. As the aperture is adjusted on a control beside the lens, a disc is also rotated in front of the metering cell, controlling the light reaching it with a pepper-pot style series of holes that grow larger as the aperture gets wider. Film wind is by a lever and the camera's only other control is a dial that offers settings for automatic, flash (via a hotshoe mounted on top of the pentaprism) and 'B'.

Three years later, Minolta introduced a Mark II version, completely restyled to look more like a traditional SLR, albeit one that is much smaller than a 35mm model and which has an extra large handgrip on the side. The range of the zoom lens on the new camera was increased to 25-67mm, a macro facility added and the maximum aperture increased to f/3.5. Exposure control was still by aperture priority, the aperture adjusted by a dial on the top plate and exposure compensation was available up to plus or minus two stops.

Between these two models from Minolta, Pentax introduced their own 110 single lens reflex in 1978 and this one is a little gem. It looks exactly like a normal 35mm SLR, but measures a mere 9.5 x 5.5 x 3 cm. There are two models to collect.

The first is the Pentax Auto 110 that was originally sold as a kit with 24mm standard lens, 18mm wideangle, 50mm telephoto, dedicated flash, close-up lenses and autowinder. Exposure is programmed with an electronic shutter and apertures adjusted by twin L-shaped masks that slide together within the camera body rather than in the lens. Despite

The two 110 SLR designs produced by Minolta.

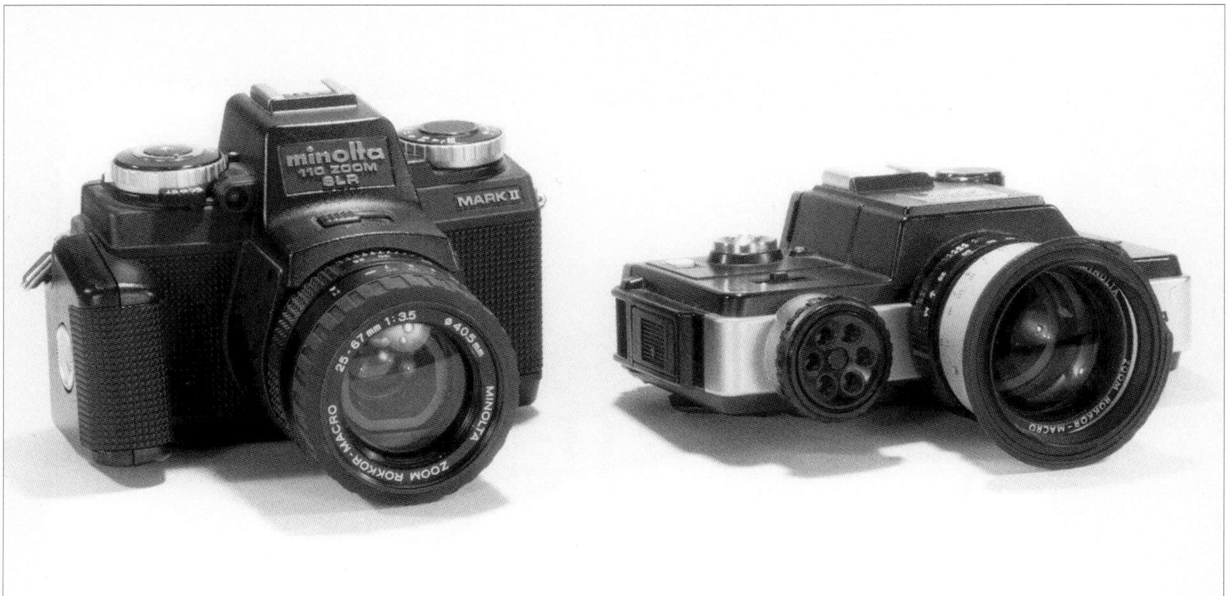

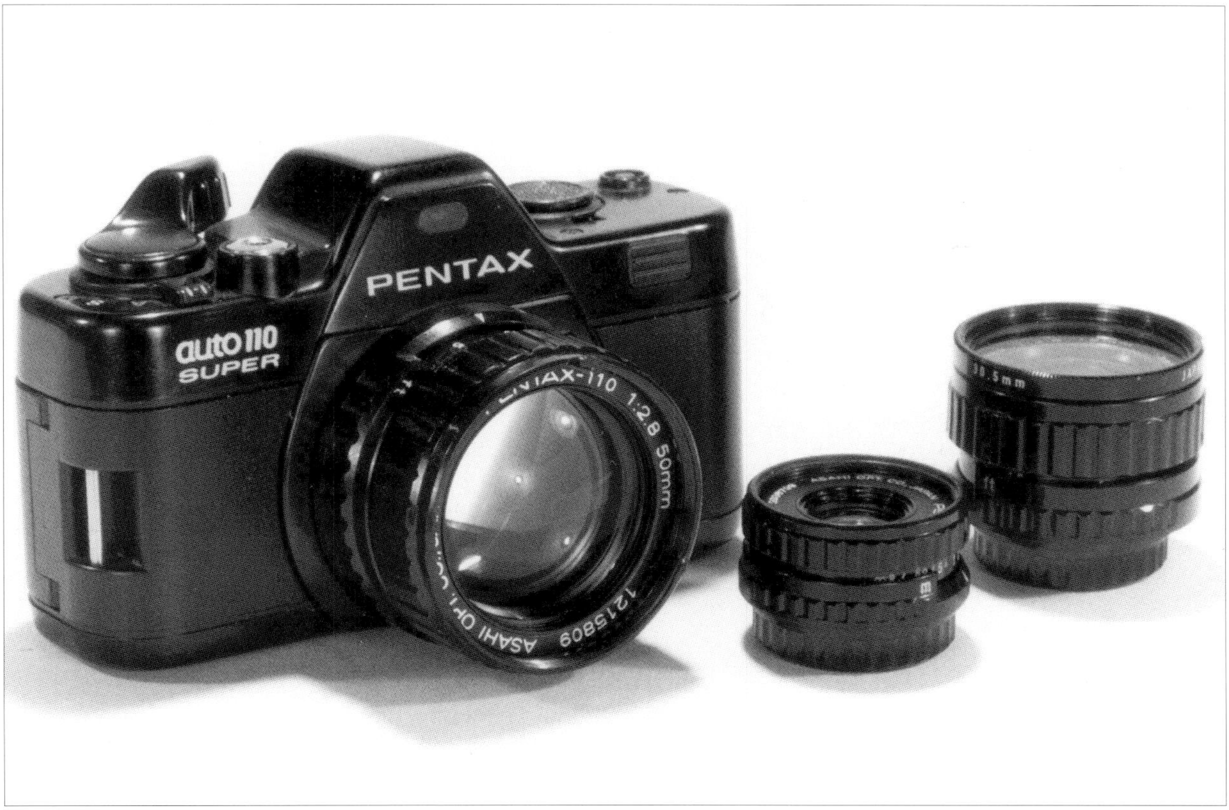

The Pentax Auto 110 Super with 50mm telephoto fitted, plus 24mm standard and 18mm wideangle.

being so small, the camera has a large, bright viewfinder and is a delight to use.

A few years after its launch, Pentax upgraded the camera with a new version called the Pentax Auto 110 Super. Apart from the name on the front, the camera looks identical to the first model. The difference is a brighter viewing screen, the double-stroke wind of the first model replaced with a single stroke and the addition of an electronic self timer. Other lenses were also introduced: a 70mm telephoto and a 20-40mm zoom. Today, these are the rarest of all accessories for the Pentax 110 SLR.

Disc cameras

In 1982, Kodak did it again. This time, they introduced disc film. Once again, snapshot camera manufacturers switched to making disc cameras by the million; and, once again, some produced more sophisticated models than others.

The Disc system was launched amidst the utmost secrecy. Unlike other camera launches, there wasn't the merest hint of a suggestion of what the new cameras were going to look like. Journalists who went to the press conference weren't even told that this was to be the launch of the Disc, and the press conference itself was held at six o'clock in the evening in the UK, to coincide with a noon launch in New York and the middle of the night in Japan and places further west. The idea was that the cameras would be unveiled at precisely the same moment around the world.

The first models were the Disc 2,000, 4,000, 6,000 and 8,000, of which the Disc 4000 was the flagship. The rigid disc which gives the camera its name produces 15 exposures around its circumference, each one 10.6 x 8mm. The camera has a fixed focus 25mm lens with a maximum aperture of f/2.8, auto exposure, auto film wind and a flash that switches itself on automatically when light levels drop.

Because disc cameras are so common, very few are worth collecting. The Disc 4000 is worthy of consideration simply because it was

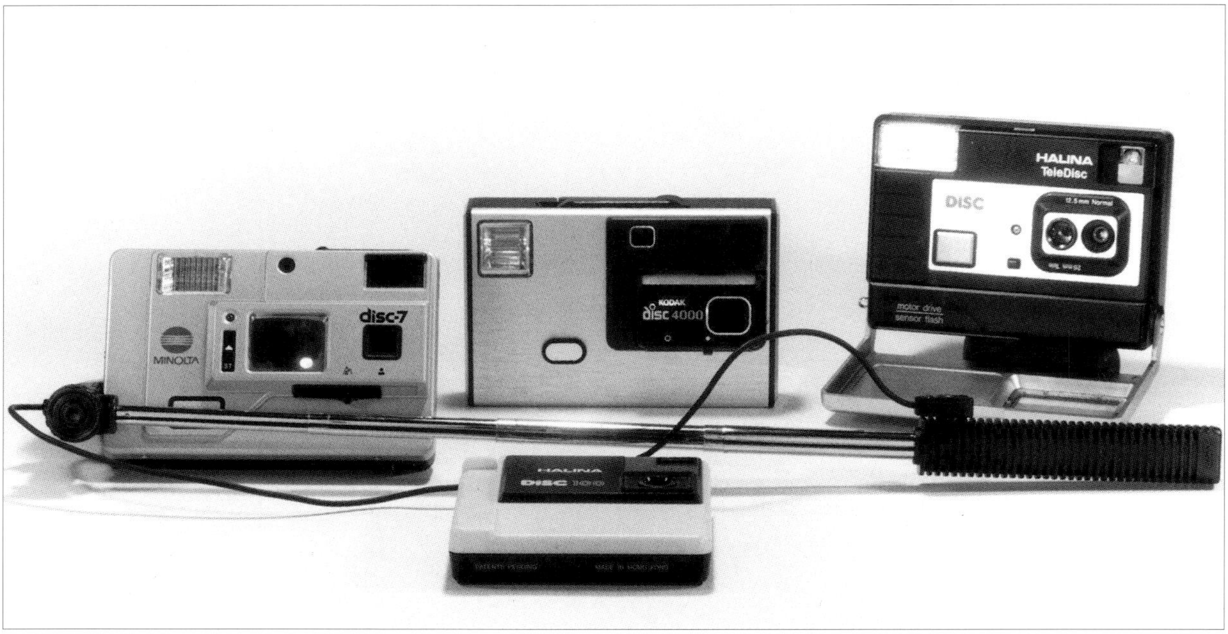

Disc cameras in different guises: The Disc 4000 was one of the first; the Minolta Disc-7 was one of the more sophisticated; the Halina Disc 100 is mechanical and completely manual with a hot shoe for a separate flashgun; the Halina TeleDisc has standard and a telephoto lenses mounted on a miniature turret that can be revolved to move either into place.

the best of the first, and it's also worth looking out for unusual models such as those which add telephoto lenses or which work mechanically rather than electronically. In this field, to find a camera without a built-in flash is the rarity!

Perhaps the most sophisticated disc camera was made by Minolta. Called the Disc-7, it has an unusual accessory in the shape of an extendible rod that screws into the side of the body so that the camera can be held over the heads of a crowd. The rod has its own shutter release in the handle, linked electronically to the camera's shutter. The Disc-7 also has a mirror next to the lens, so the photographer can pose for self-portraits, using the electronic self timer activated by a switch to the side.

Disc cameras were extremely popular among snapshooters for a few years, then died rapidly away when easy-load 35mm compact cameras started arriving on the market, giving the snapshot brigade quality pictures coupled with the easy loading which had always been a stumbling block to them in the past.

The shame is that the disc died before anyone attempted to launch a single lens reflex for the format.

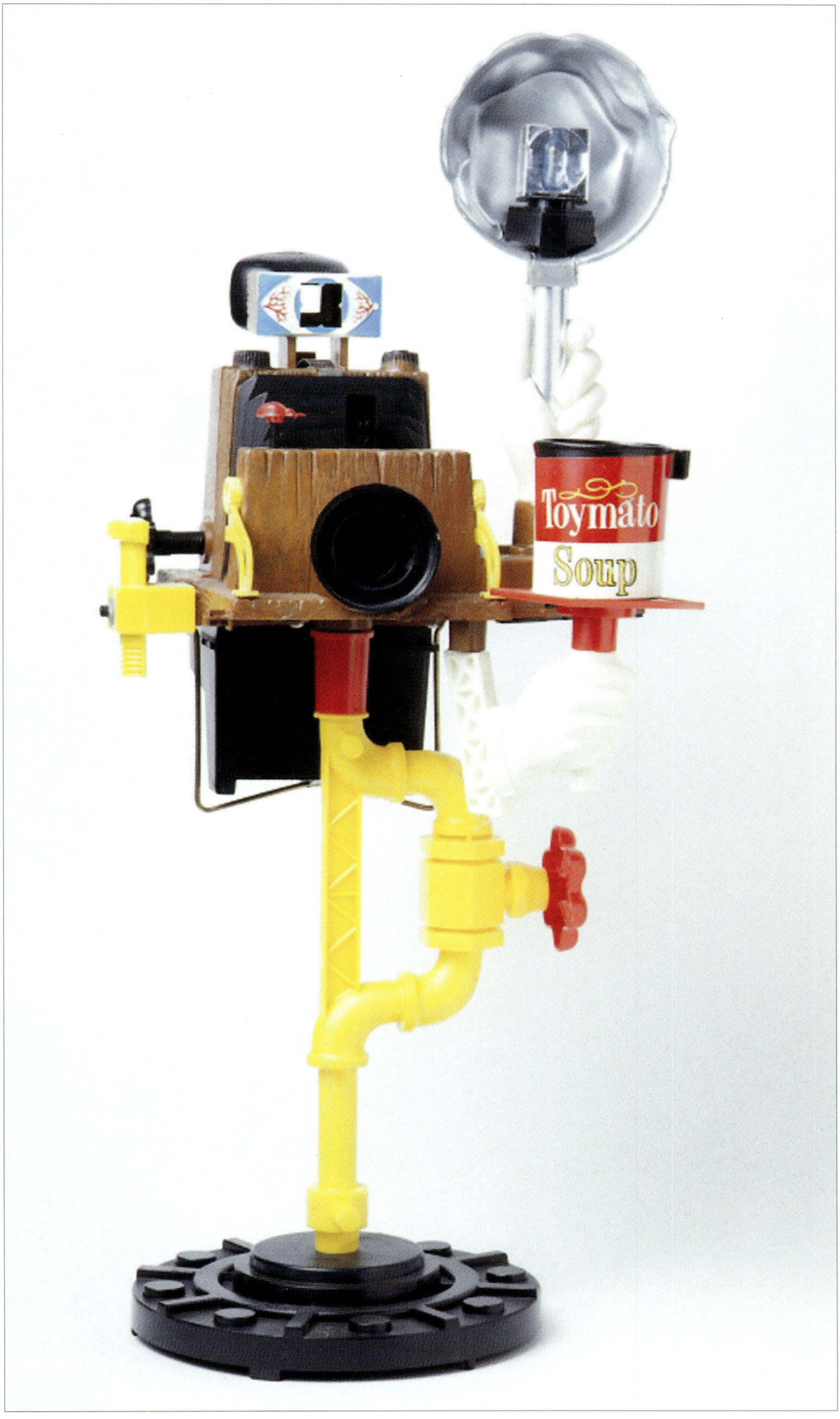

Yes it is a camera, and an instant picture camera at that – it's the American Kookie from 1968.

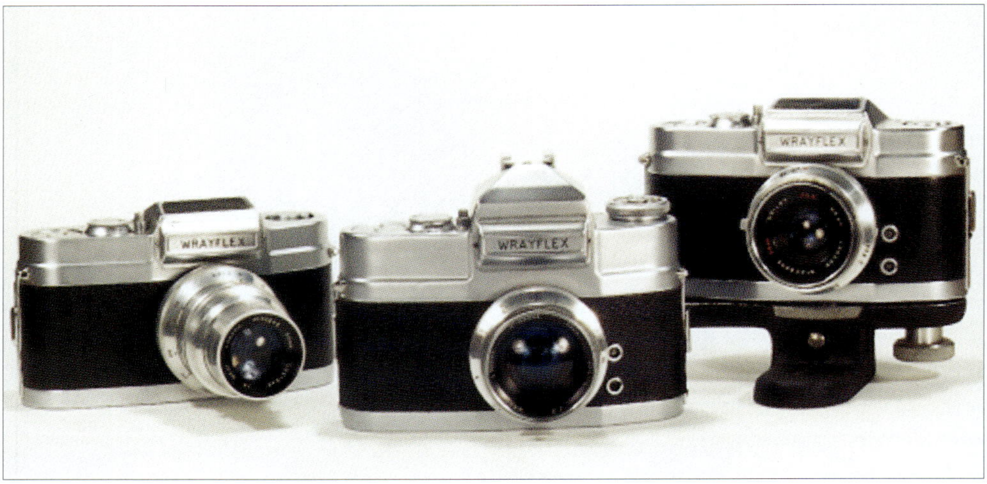

TOP: *The Wrayflex family: the Wrayflex I with 90mm f/4 Lustrar, the Ia, mounted on a Wrayflex Tripod Cradle and fitted with a 50mm f/2.8 Unilux and the Wrayflex II with 50mm f/2 Unilite.*

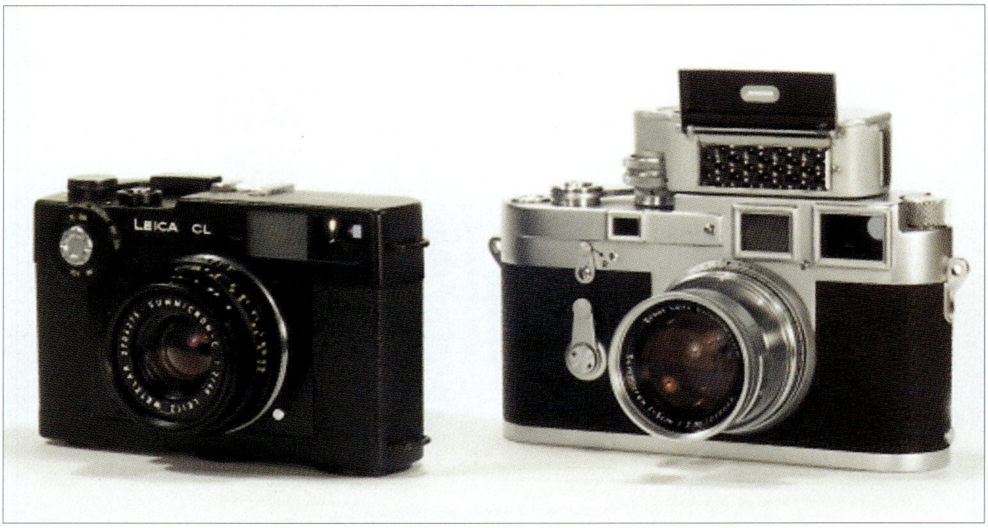

CENTRE: *Two landmark Leicas: The M3, first of the bayonet-mount cameras launched in 1954, and the CL, launched in 1973, whose body was made in Japan by Minolta.*

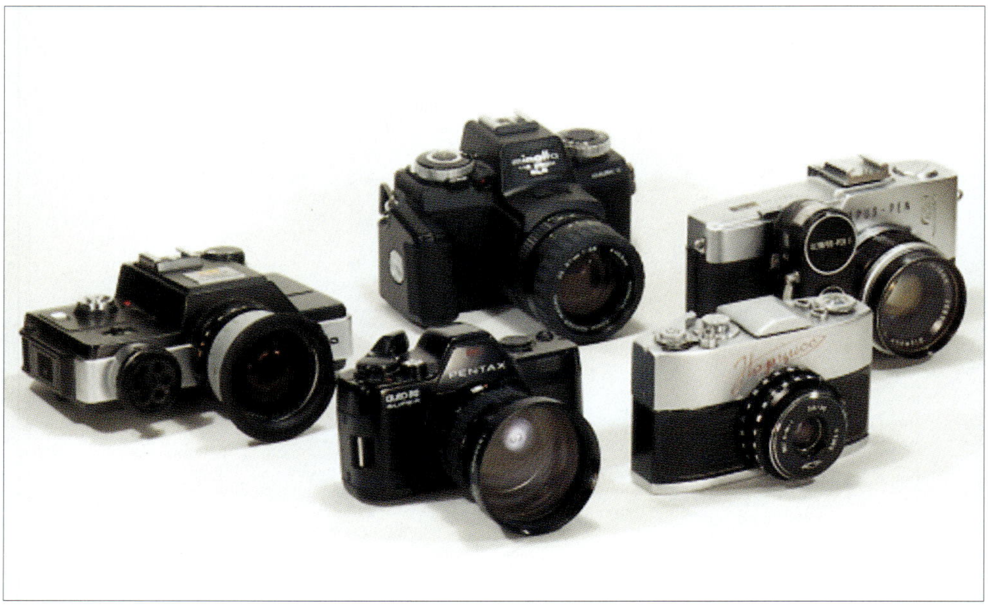

BOTTOM: *Small format SLRs: The Olympus Pen F for half-frame images on 35mm film, the Hapyucc for 16mm film and three 110 cameras - the Minolta 110 Zoom SLR Mark I and Mark II, and the Pentax Auto 110 Super with its 70mm f2/8 telephoto lens fitted.*

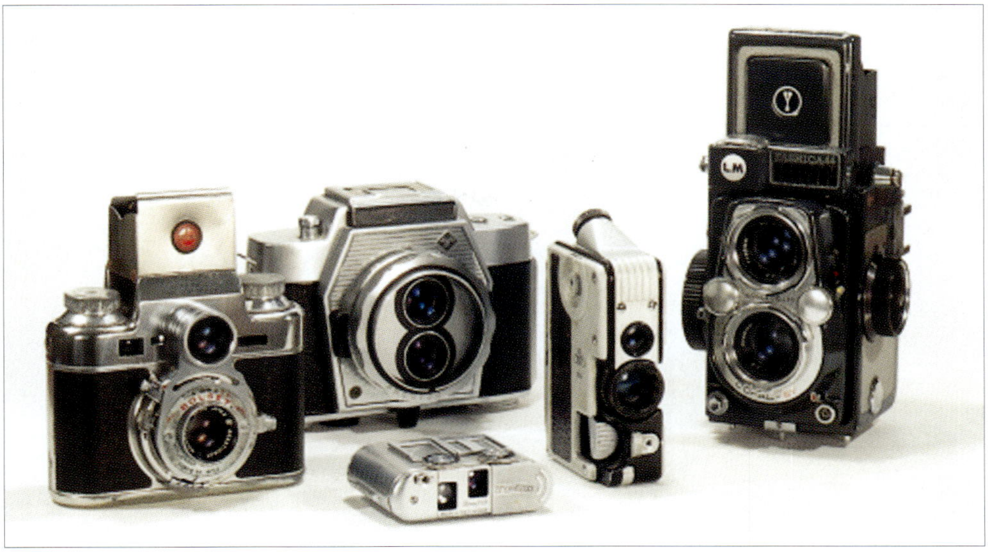

TOP: *Variations on the twin lens reflex theme: Bolsey C22, Agfa Flexilette, Minicord, Yashica 44LM and Tessina.*

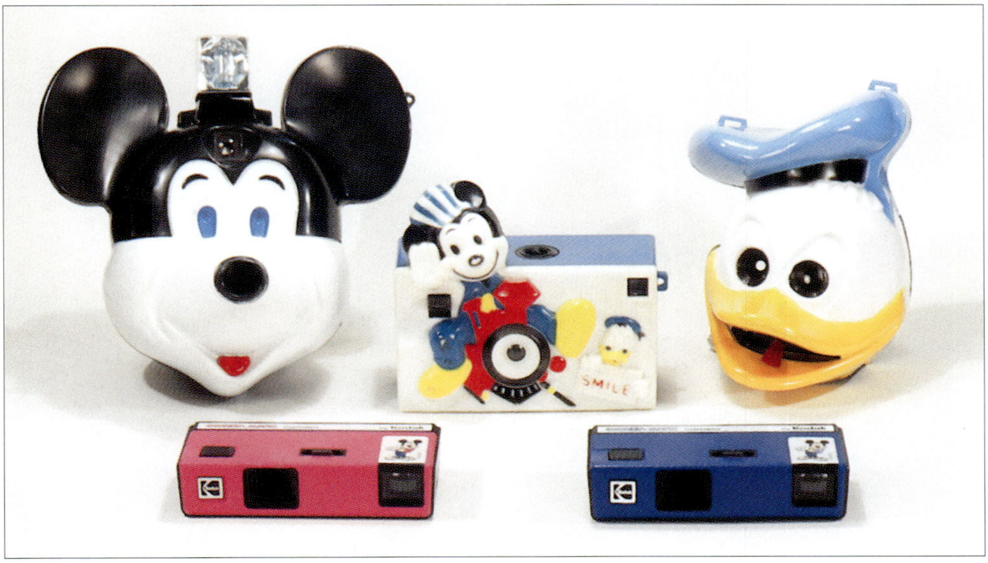

CENTRE: *For camera collectors and Disney fans alike: The Mick-a-Matic and Helm Mickey Mouse Camera, both for 126 film; the Donald Duck 127 camera; and two 110 Mickey-Matics in blue and magenta. (The last two date from 1988, a little later than this book's actual cut-off date.)*

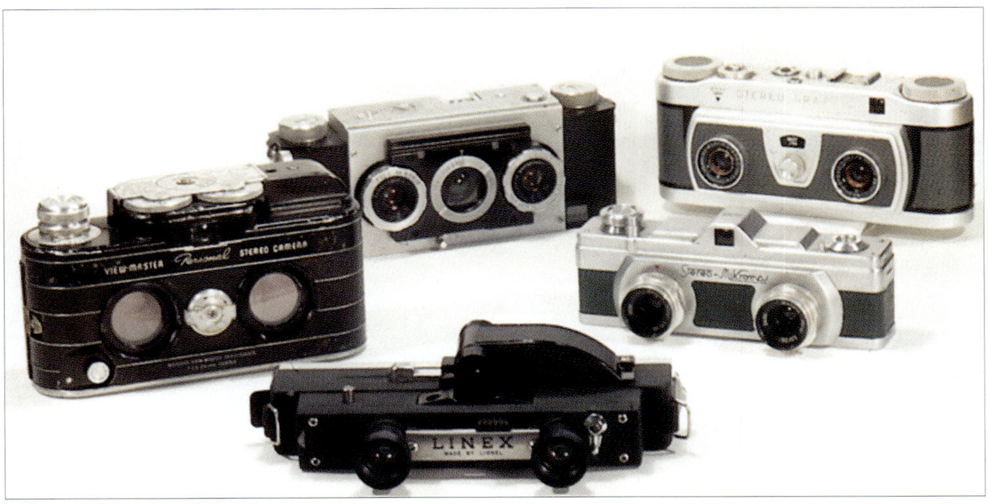

BOTTOM: *A selection of stereo cameras: For 35mm, the View-Master Personal Stereo, Stereo Realist and Stereo Graphic; and for 16mm, the Stereo Mikroma and Linex.*

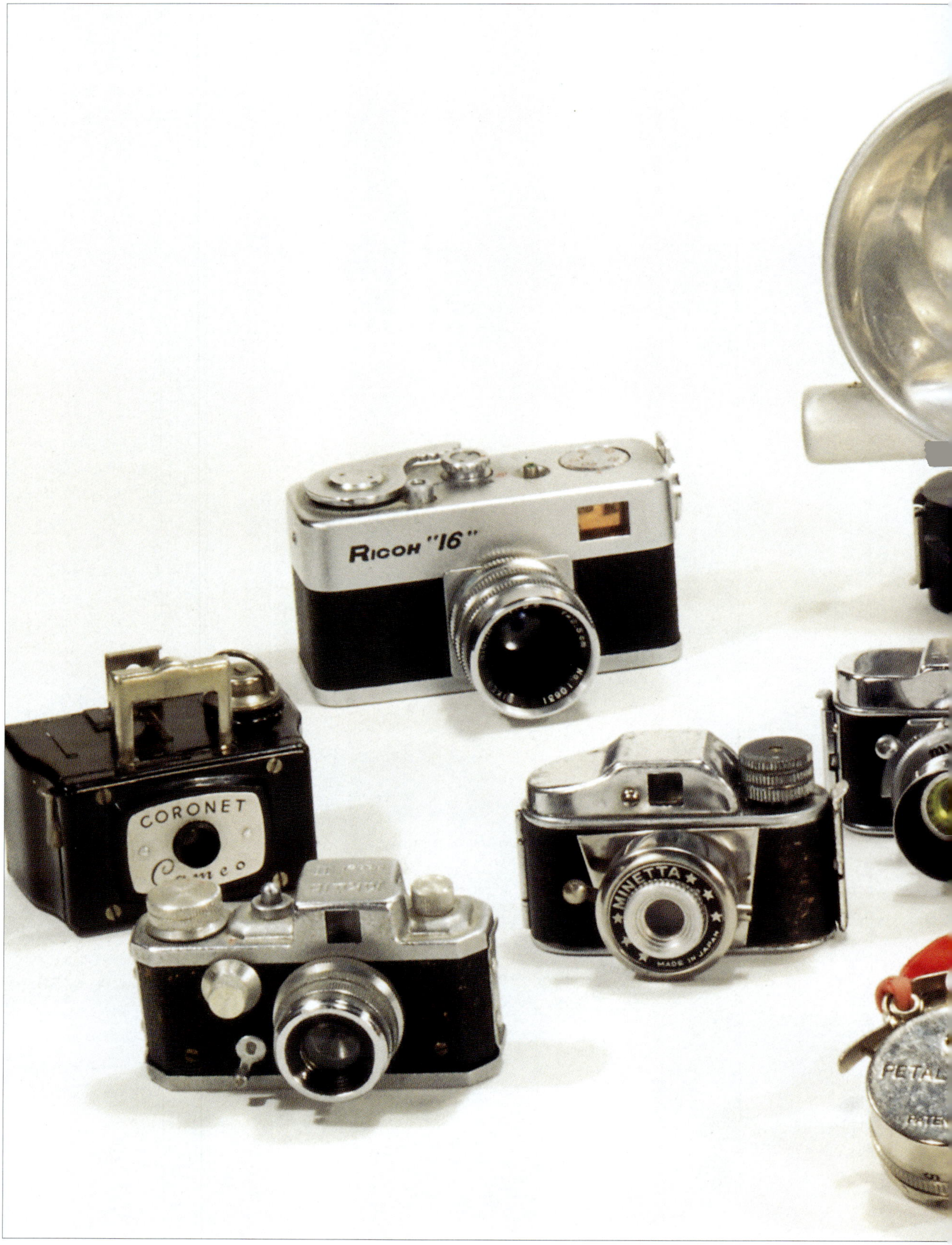
RICOH "16"
CORONET
Cameo
MINETTA
MADE IN JAPAN

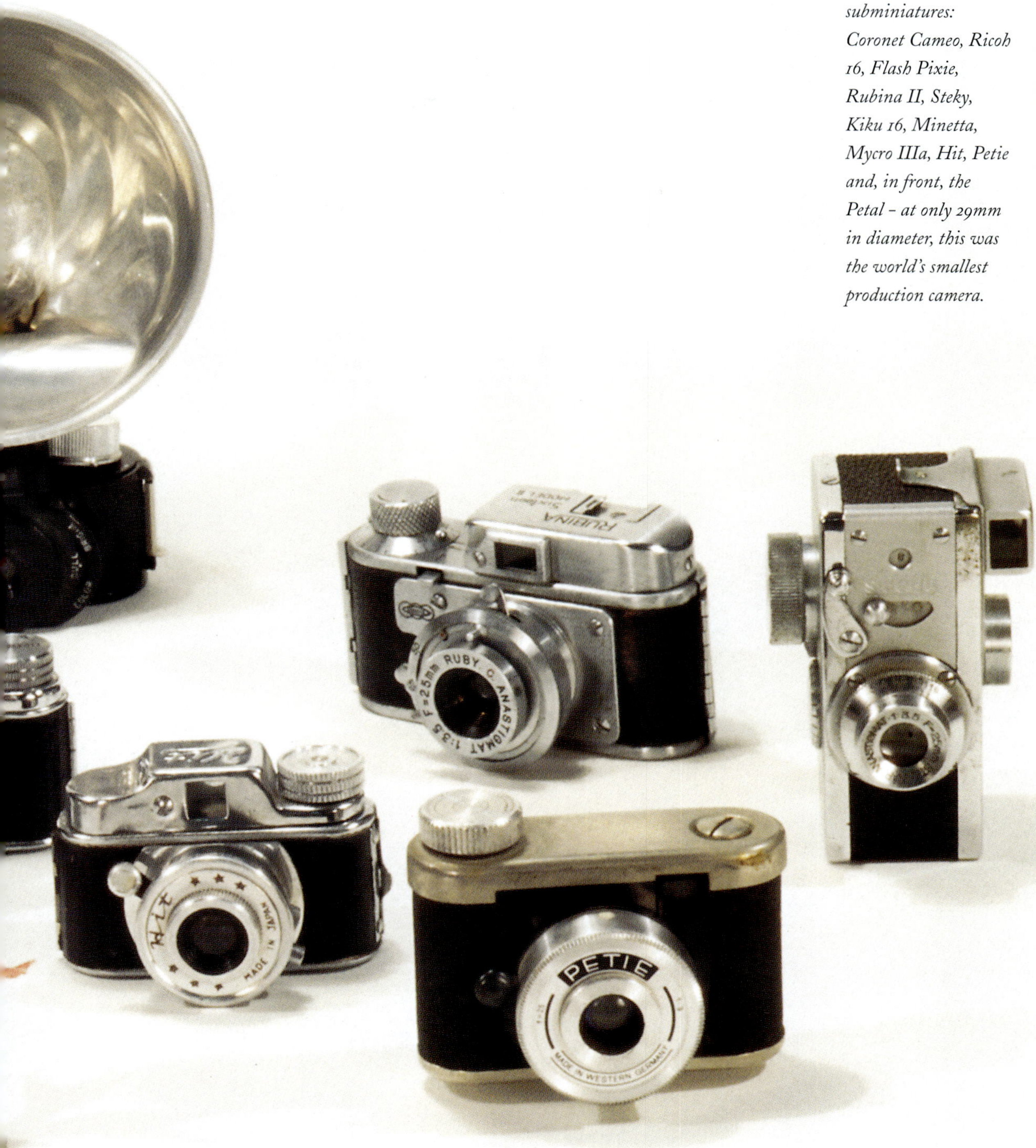

A small set of subminiatures: Coronet Cameo, Ricoh 16, Flash Pixie, Rubina II, Steky, Kiku 16, Minetta, Mycro IIIa, Hit, Petie and, in front, the Petal – at only 29mm in diameter, this was the world's smallest production camera.

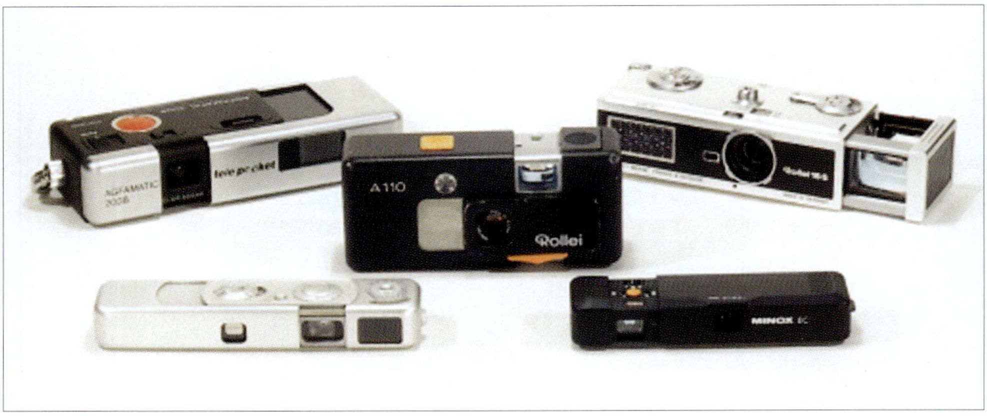

TOP: *Open and shut cases: A style, popularised by Minox, in which the film is wound as two halves of the camera body are slid shut and open again, shows up in several other models too. With the Minox B and Minox EC are the Rollei 16, Rollei A110 and the Agfamatic 2008 Tele Pocket.*

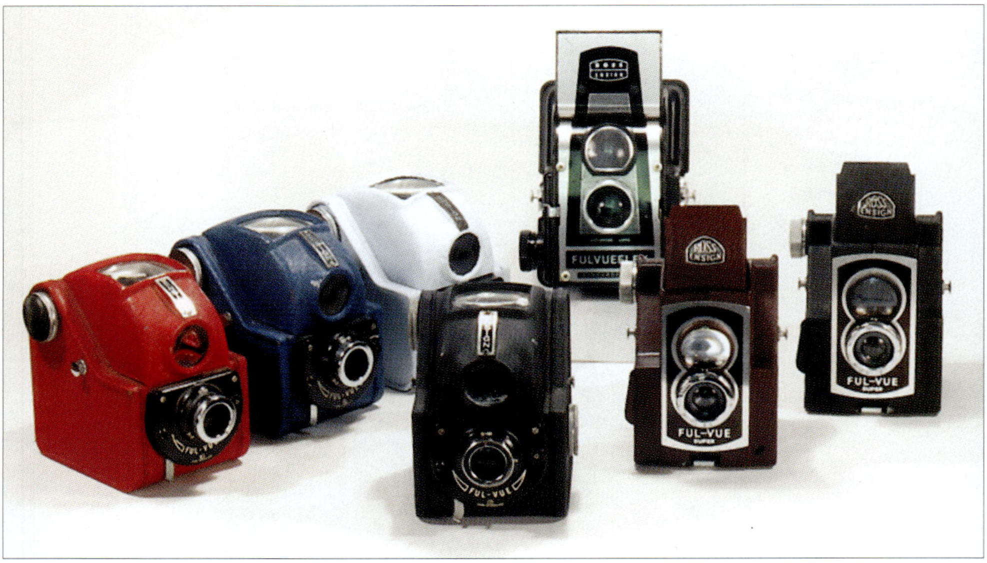

CENTRE: *Sometimes a camera that is particularly common in black will be rarer - and more collectable - in its model variations and colours. The extremely common black Ensign Ful-Vue is seen here with several other incarnations, including red, blue and grey versions, the Ful-Vue Super in black and red and the Fulvueflex, last of the line.*

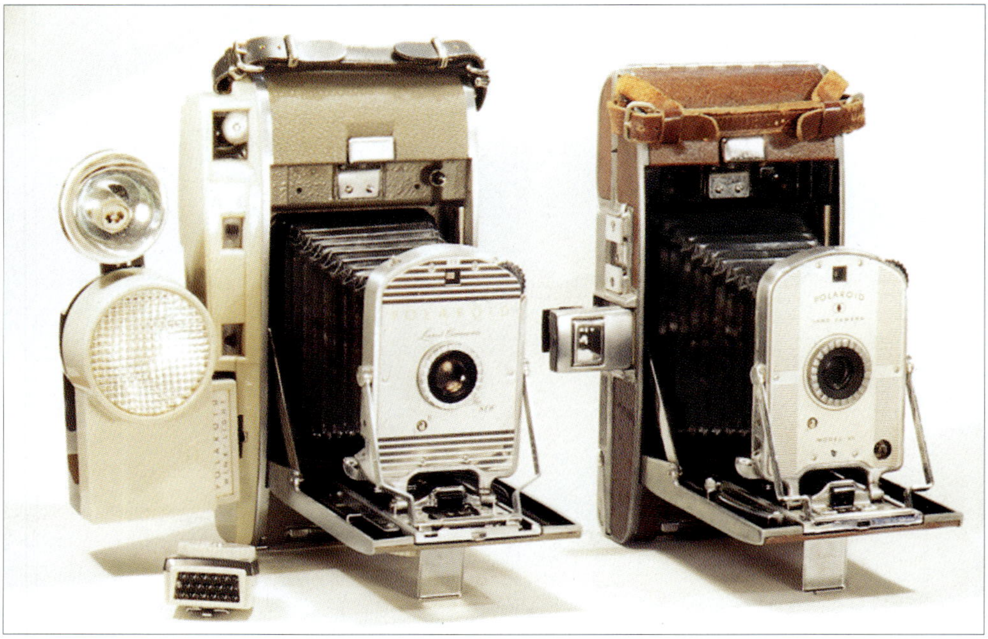

BOTTOM: *Two early Polaroid cameras: The Model 800 with Winklite and AG1 bulb flashguns attached, and the original Model 95.*

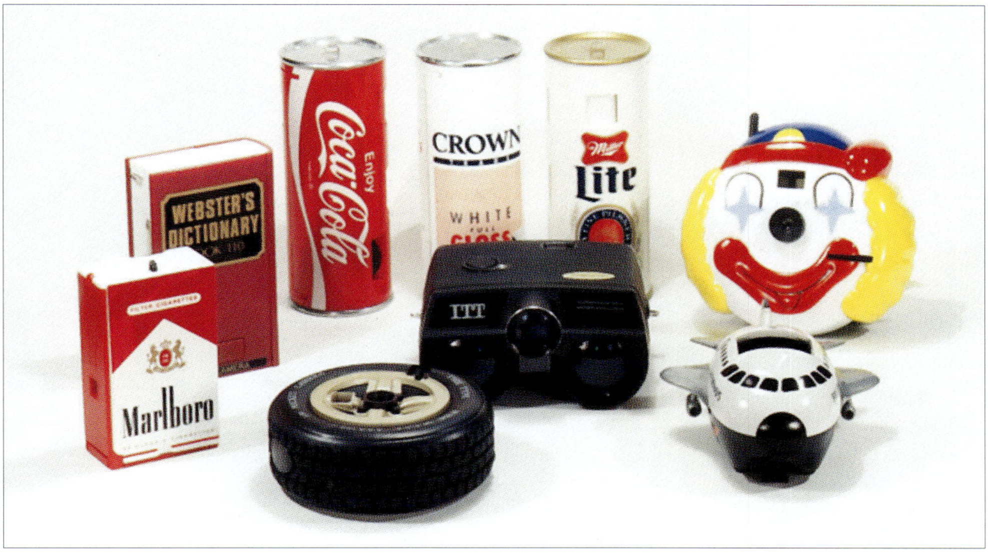

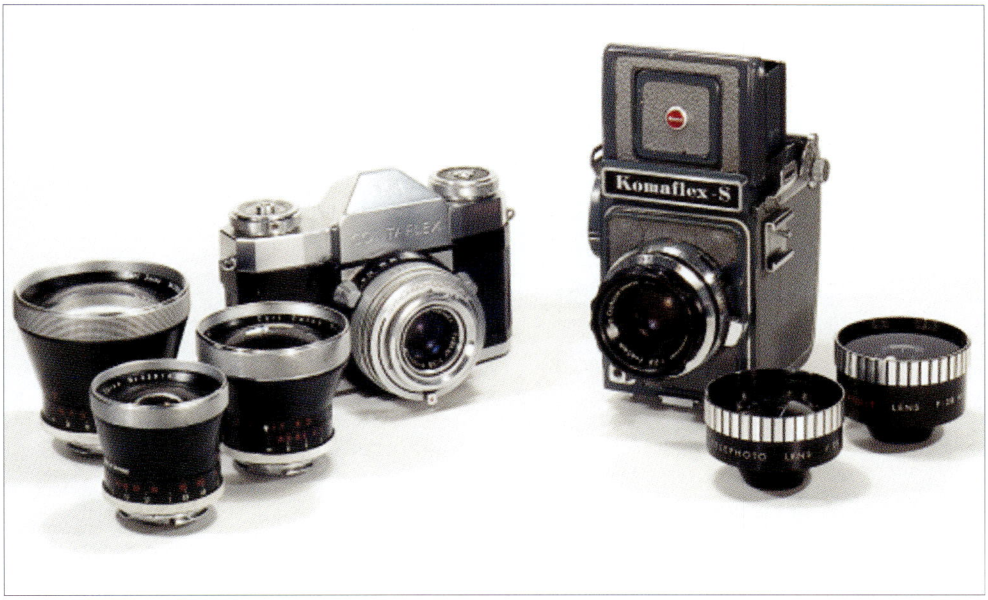

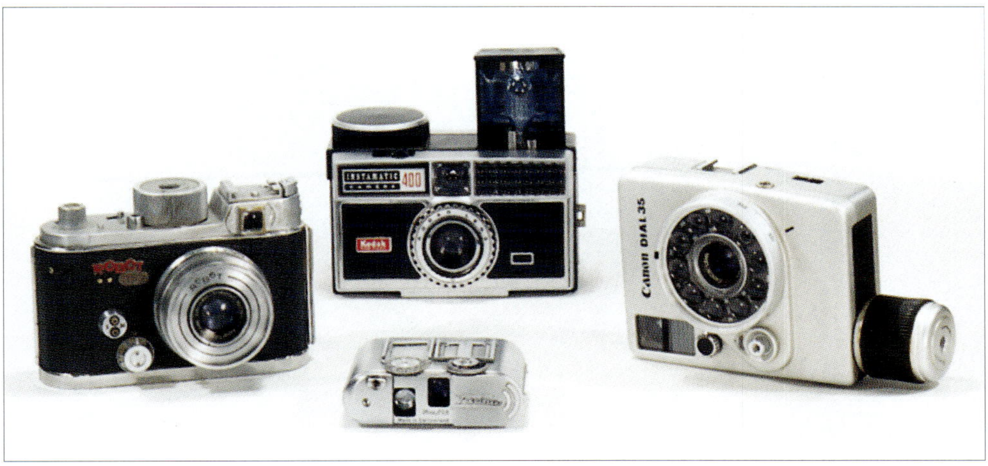

TOP: *Towards the end of this book's era and for a few years more, the 110 format enjoyed a new lease of life in a number of novelty cameras, in various guises. Here are the Marlboro cigarette packet and Webster's Dictionary cameras, three models in the shape of Coca-Cola, Crown Paint and Miller Lite cans, a Clown Girl Camera, ITT Binoculars camera, a Tire Camera [sic] and a British Airways camera in the shape of a miniature jumbo jet.*

CENTRE: *Many classic cameras use add-on optics to convert the standard to telephoto or wideangle. Here is a Contaflex III with 35mm wideangle plus 85mm and 115mm telephoto Pro-Tessars, made to replace the front element of the standard lens, together with the Komaflex-S, Koma Auxiliary Wideangle and Telephoto converters.*

BOTTOM: *Four very different cameras, all with clockwork motor drives: The Robot Star, Instamatic 400, Canon Dial and Tessina.*

RIGHT: *Three cameras and a projector, all specifically designed for still and moving images on the same film. The Pathescope Prince camera and Princess Projector, with the Bolsey 8 and Agfa Family.*

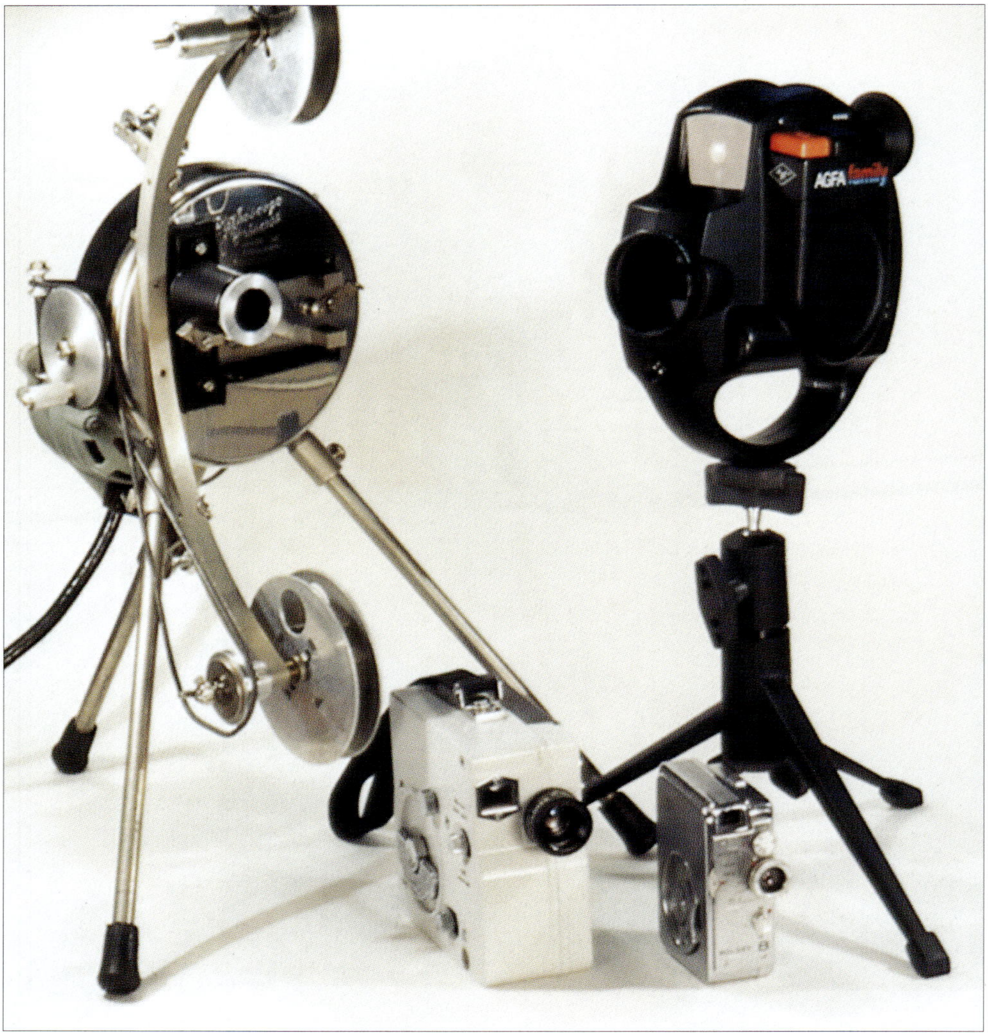

BELOW: *A lot of snapshot cameras try to be what they're not. Here are three that tried hard to be twin lens reflexes: the Brownie Reflex, Brownie Reflex 20 and Beacon Reflex.*

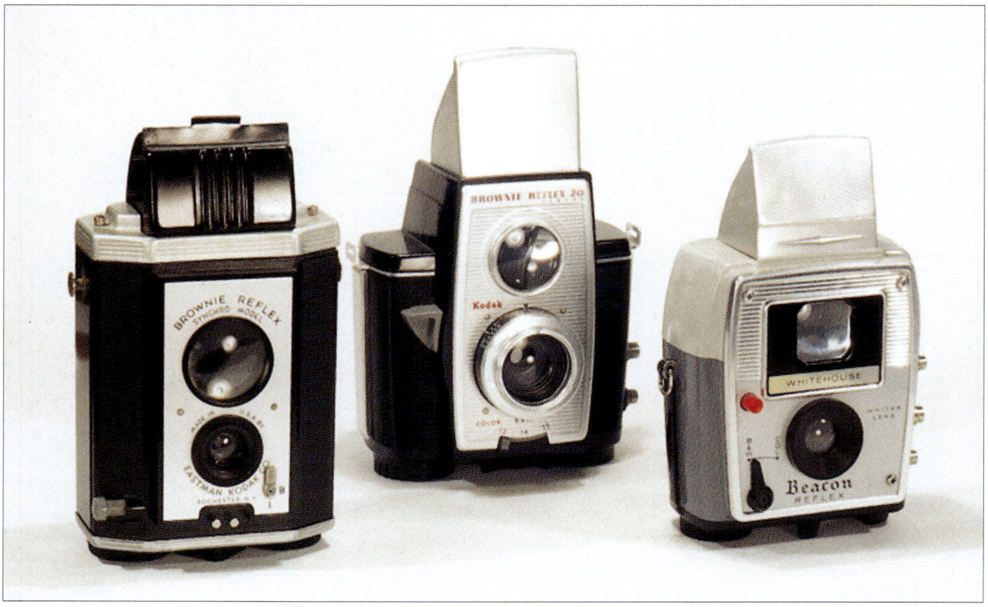

Instant Picture Cameras

The Polaroid Model 95 was the first truly viable instant picture camera.

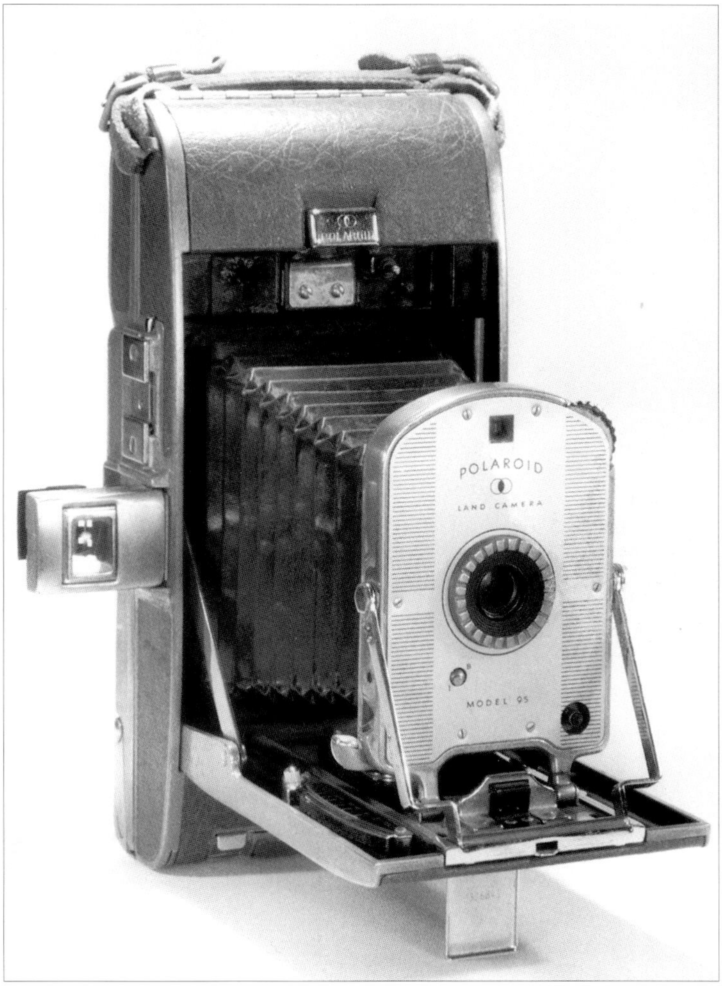

INSTANT PICTURE cameras provide a relatively inexpensive route into camera collecting, since the cameras were made in abundance, there are still a lot of the older models around and they can be bought cheaply.

Don't allow those facts to put you off, however. Polaroid, the principal manufacturer of this type of camera, has played an important role in the history of photography with many notable landmarks along the way. They were, quite obviously, the first people to produce a truly viable method of instant photography. But they also produced the first camera with a fully automatic electronic shutter, the first autofocus single lens reflex and have been outstanding in their innovative approach to automatic exposure control.

Here are a few of the more interesting Polaroid cameras to collect.

Model 95

This, the first Polaroid instant picture camera, was launched in 1948. It's a bulky beast that follows the folding design that was so popular at the time. Folded, it measures 24 x 11.5 x 6cm and, in use, a bed folds down on hinges with the lens panel extending along it on bellows. A lever to one side racks the bellows in and out, moving the whole lens panel backwards and forwards for focusing.

When it comes to exposure control, you begin to see how Polaroid designers thought differently to most others. The Model 95 has apertures from f/11 - f/45 and shutter speeds from 1/8 -1/60 second, but they are all controlled by a single thumbwheel set into the lens panel.

As this is turned, numbers from one to eight are displayed in a small window above the lens.

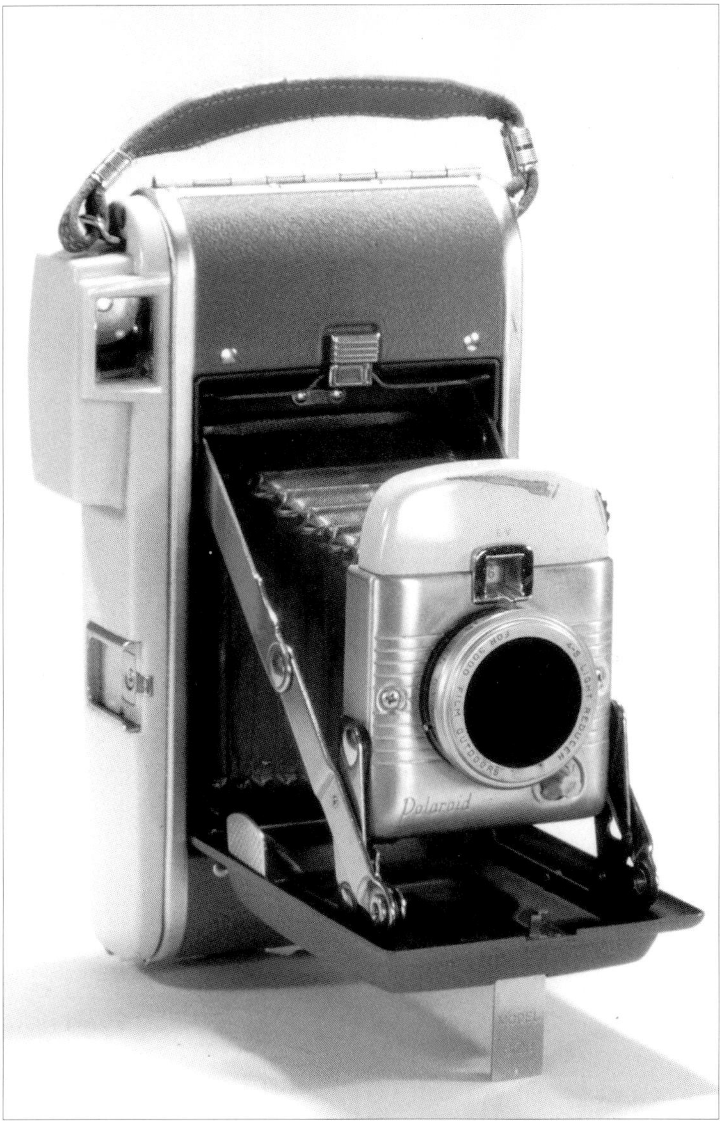

The Highlander was one of the smaller Polaroid cameras made for instant rollfilm.

As the numbers change, a series of apertures cut into a circular disc rotate behind the front element of the lens, but what isn't immediately evident is that the shutter speeds are changing at the same time, rather like a manual version today's programmed automation. The lower the number displayed in the window above the lens, the longer the exposure and the numbers relate to aperture and shutter speed combinations as follows.

1 = 1/8 second at f/11
2 = 1/15 second at f/11
3 = 1/30 second at f/11
4 = 1/60 second at f/11
5 = 1/60 second at f/16
6 = 1/60 second at f/22
7 = 1/60 second at f/32
8 = 1/60 second at f/45

The Model 95 takes an instant rollfilm that actually came on two rolls. To load it, the back of the camera is opened to find a second, subsidiary back inside. Opening this reveals two film chambers, one at each end of the body. Of the two film rolls, the larger one consists of specially treated paper, the smaller one holds a negative paper, and the two are connected by a paper leader.

The larger roll is dropped into its film chamber and the smaller one clipped into a spool holder on the rear of the camera's second, internal back, closing it so that the spool falls into the second film chamber.

Next, the paper leader is threaded between two rollers on the second back so that, when closed, the film, faces the lens. The leader is then pulled across this back and out through a slot in the bottom of the camera body. The main back is then closed and secured. The leader is pulled from the slot until it stops and, at that point, the first frame is ready for exposure, by means of a shutter release at the base of the lens panel.

To develop the film, a small button is first pressed on the back of the body to release the mechanism inside. A cutter, which swivels from the base of the body, is swung up and the protruding leader of film pulled smartly until it stops. The cutter is then swung back and the leader torn off along its edge.

Inside the camera, this action has pulled the exposed paper negative from one spool and the sensitised printing paper from the other into contact, sandwiching them together through a set of rollers. Pods of chemical, consisting of a special developer and fixer in one solution and situated on the film strip, burst under pressure from the rollers, spreading the solution evenly between the two layers of paper.

The negative image develops first. Then the unused silver salts are converted to a soluble solution by the chemistry from the pods and diffused through to the print paper, where they are reduced to silver. The result is a positive image.

All this takes about a minute. After that, yet another catch is depressed on the camera's back to open a large trapdoor, revealing the two strips of paper stuck together. The top layer is peeled away to reveal the instant print which, originally, was a sepia, brown and white image. Two years after the launch of the Model 95, however, Polaroid introduced a new film, which produced black and white pictures.

Highlander

In 1954, Polaroid introduced this new, smaller size camera. There are three models of the Highlander: the Model 80, 80A and 80B. The Model 80 is the first, basic model, with exposures indicated by the number method found in the Model 90; the 80A changes the shutter indicator to EV numbers and introduces a new cutter bar; the 80B incorporates parallax correction marks in the viewfinder.

The body of each model is manufactured from pressed steel, made in grey and, unlike the original Model 95, the lens panel is self erecting to the shooting position.

Model 800

The Polaroid Model 800 appeared in 1957. It's a big camera similar to, and about the same size as the original Model 95, still taking the double roll film but adding new refinements to the original theme. This one has a coupled rangefinder. It also features an unusual flashgun that rejoices under the name of the Winklite.

Like electronic flash, as opposed to flashbulbs of the day, it can be used over and over again. Unlike electronic flash, it uses a torch bulb, powered by a battery-driven capacitor. The recommendation was to use the Winklite only with Polaroid's super-fast ISO 3000 speed film and then only to fill shadows, in conjunction with normal room lighting.

For a more traditional form of flash photography, there was another, much smaller, flashgun which Polaroid called the Flasher and which slots onto the top of the Winklite from where it draws its power from the Winklite's battery and capacitor. It takes AG1 bulbs.

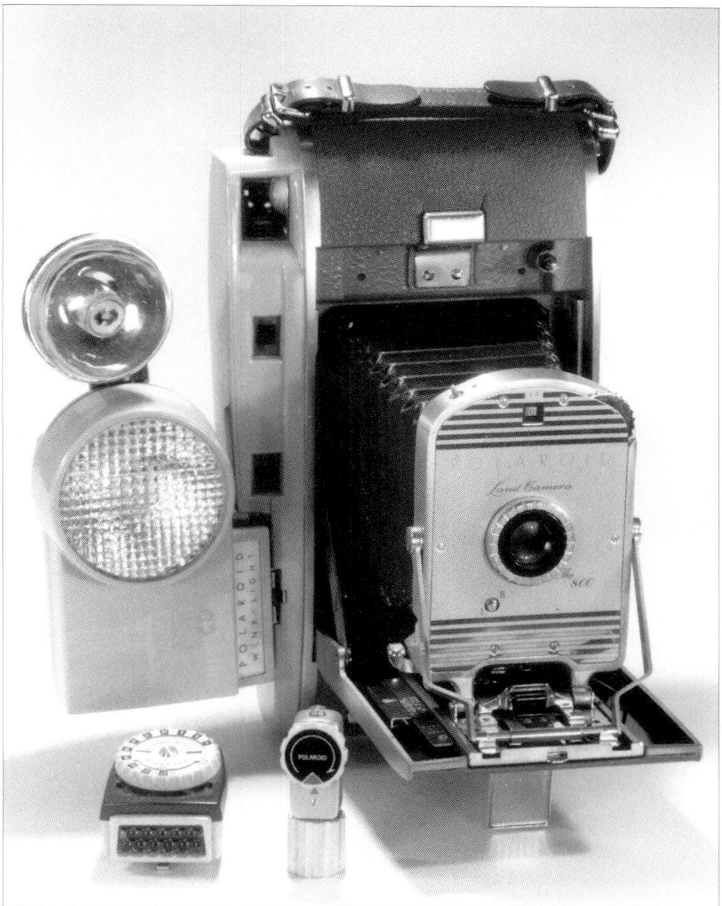

The Model 800 with Winklite and flasher fitted, shown with the camera's own meter and delayed action device.

Electric eye cameras

These were the first Polaroid cameras to offer automatic exposure control by way of a cadmium sulphide photo resistor cell which automatically selects and combines appropriate shutter speeds and apertures. The range runs from 1/2 second at f/8.8 up to 1/600 second at f/82. Manual override is also possible in the form of a sliding bar for lightening or darkening the picture.

Made first in 1960, the body is die cast aluminium, covered in leather-grained vinyl in an attractive two tone grey and there are two models: the 900 and the 850. The 900 came

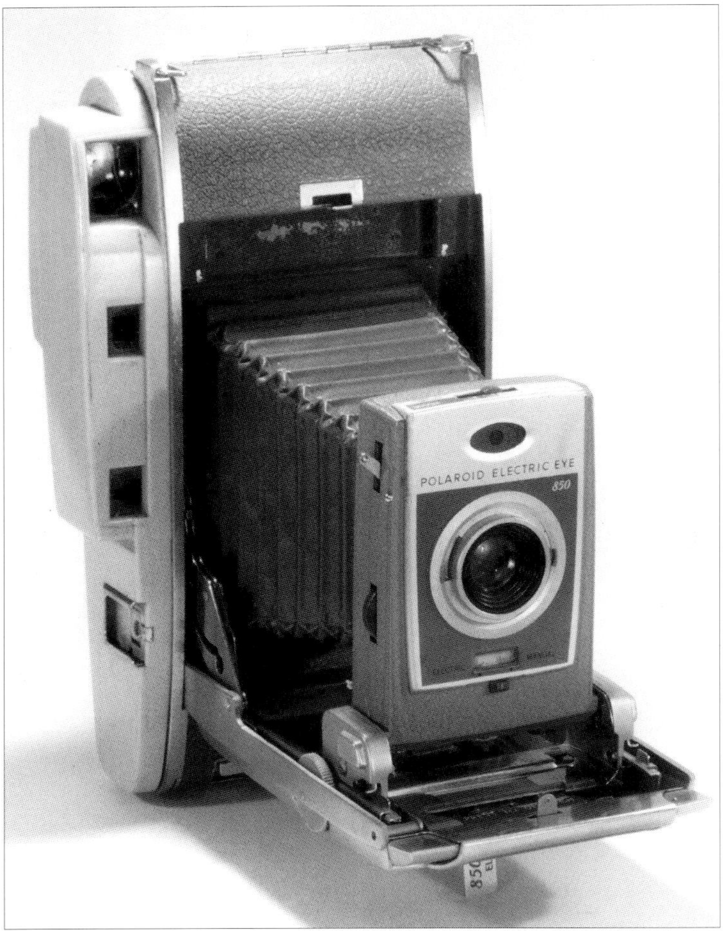

first and you can tell them apart by the viewfinders. The Model 900 has a single eyepiece for viewfinder and rangefinder, the Model 850 separates them in two separate eyepieces.

Polaroid J33

No camera today is complete without a built-in flashgun, but the J33 had one for AG1 bulbs back in 1961, cunningly hidden behind a trapdoor at the side of the lens. Despite being launched in the 1960s, the camera takes the old two roll method of film loading, but produces smaller images than the first films for the early Polaroid cameras.

The J33 has a Selenium cell meter that controls the shutter from 1/15 - 1/1000 second, with an f/19 lens that closes down to f/64 - small apertures but perfectly adequate when the camera is designed exclusively for Polaroid's ISO 3000 speed instant film.

Automatic 100

The Polaroid Automatic 100, launched in 1963, was the first camera to use Polaroid's flat

Electric Eye cameras were the first Polaroid models to offer automatic exposure.

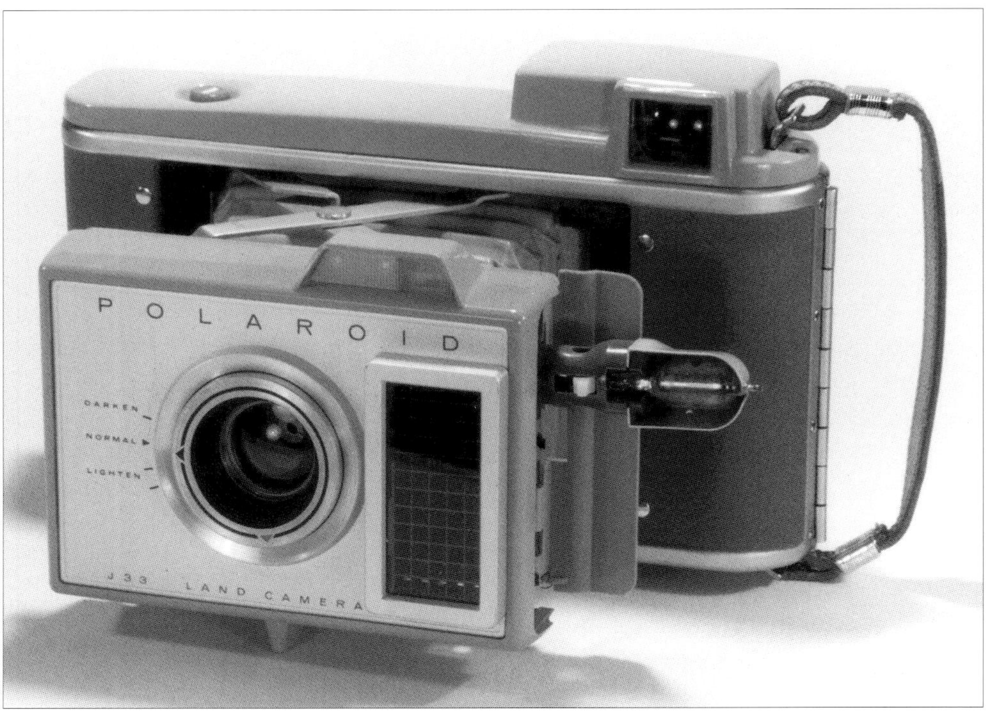

The Polaroid J33 has its own built-in flashgun for AG-1 bulbs.

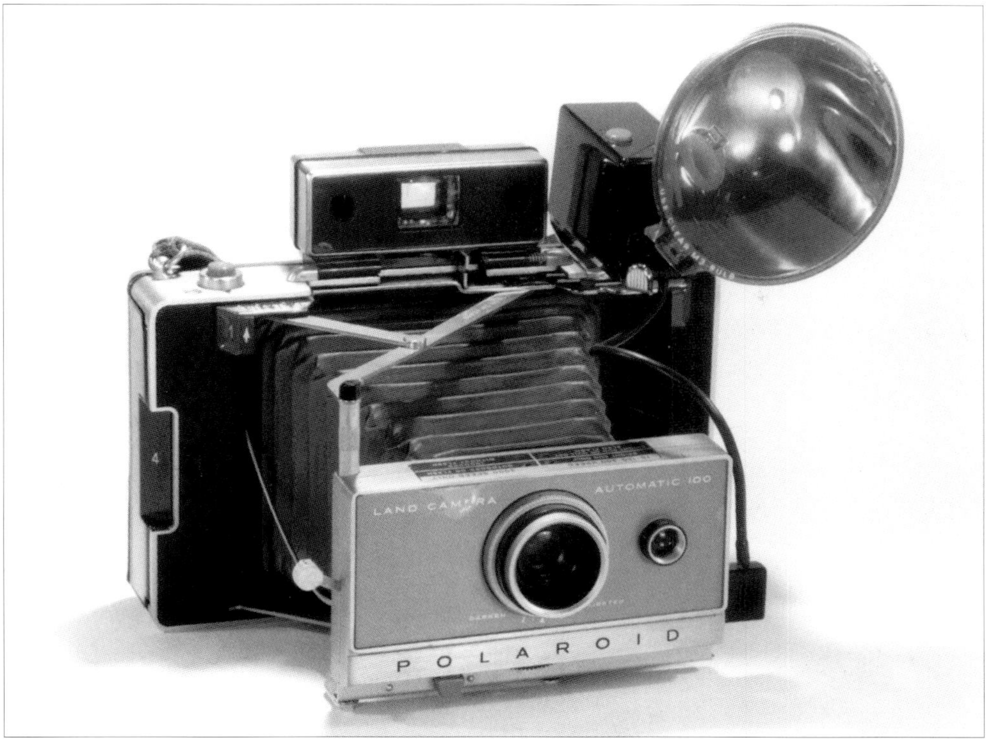

The Polaroid Automatic 100 was the world's first camera with an electronic shutter coupled to an auto exposure system.

pack film that simply drops into the camera back for easy loading - a system still used for Polaroid professional peel-apart films. It was also the world's first camera with a fully automatic electronic shutter.

As the shutter release is pressed, a circuit is activated by a 4.5 volt battery and one shutter blade is moved quickly from behind the lens, allowing light to reach the film. A second shutter blade is held back by an electro magnet while a transistorised auto exposure system begins to measure the light. When enough light has reached the film, the system cuts the current to the magnet and the second shutter blade closes.

The Automatic 100 has a 'lighten/darken' control under the lens for a little manual manipulation. Changing film speed settings from IS0 75 to ISO 3000 changes a series of apertures behind the lens. Focusing is by two sliding levers, one each side of the viewfinder, operated by the index fingers to rack the bellows in and out, focusing the lens and indicating distances by symbols. As the lens is focused, a bright line in the viewfinder moves up and down to compensate for parallax.

The Swinger

There's every chance that the Polaroid Singer, which appeared in 1965, could be the most common camera in the world. But it's a camera whose styling is so typical of what was known in England as the Swinging Sixties, that it deserves a place in any collection.

The Swinger with its supplementary lenses and viewfinder.

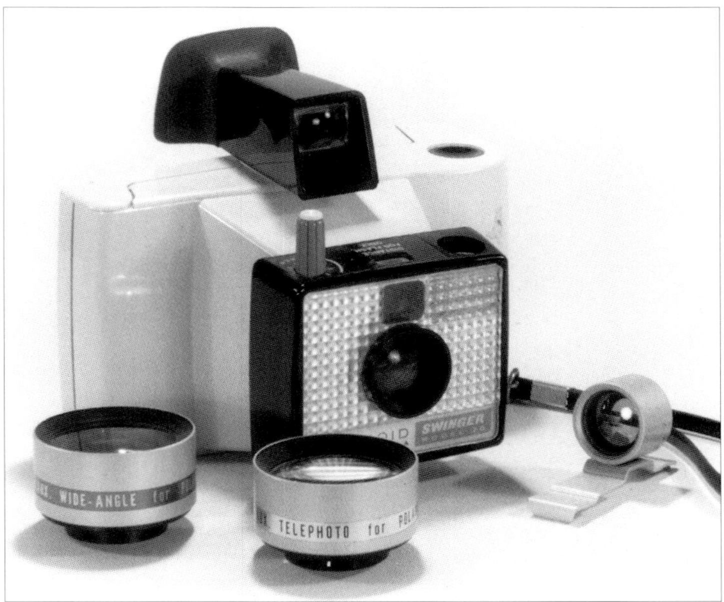

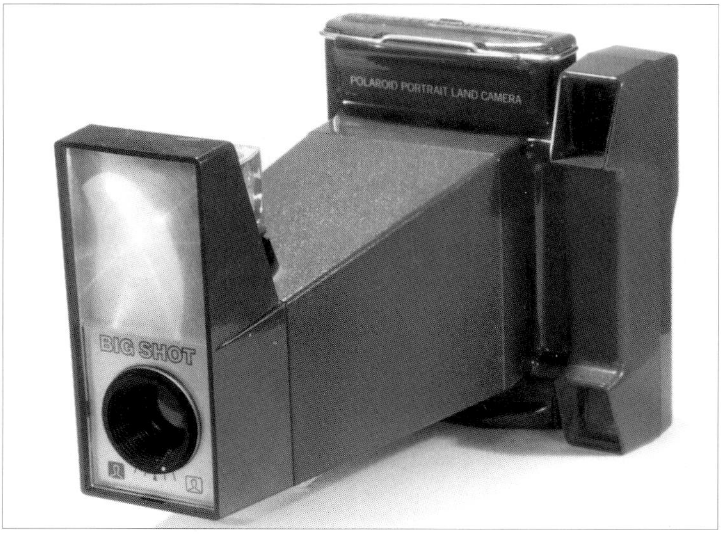

The Big Shot was made specifically for instant portraiture.

The Swinger takes Polaroid's pack film and the cameras can be bought very cheaply indeed. Rarer, however, are the auxiliary wideangle and telephoto lenses pictured here with the camera. Made by Kaligar, they push onto the front of the Swinger's normal lens. Look out for them in their own custom made case, complete with a clip-on viewfinder.

Big Shot

Here's a really unusual Polaroid camera. The Big Shot, from 1971, is specially designed for instant portraits on pack film, using a lens with fixed focus at 1 metre. Despite which, there's a built-in rangefinder. But it's not adjustable, it's only there to tell the photographer when he is the correct distance from the subject. A flashcube drops into its holder behind a large diffuser above the lens, designed to give a softer light for portraiture.

SX-70

In 1972, Polaroid took a very new look at instant photography with the launch of the SX-70 camera. It's a folding single lens reflex that, for the first time, ejected a print from the camera on exposure, to self-develop in normal room lighting.

But, for the collector, equally interesting is the camera's unusual design. Folded, it makes a flat package 17.5 x 10.5 x 3 cm in size, and there's a knack to unfolding it. On the top of the body there is a folded down viewfinder panel and the only way to unfold the camera is to place a finger and thumb on either side of the rear of this and tug upwards. The camera immediately unfolds, roughly into a triangular shape.

Inside, the way light reaches the film and viewfinder are equally unique. Before expo-

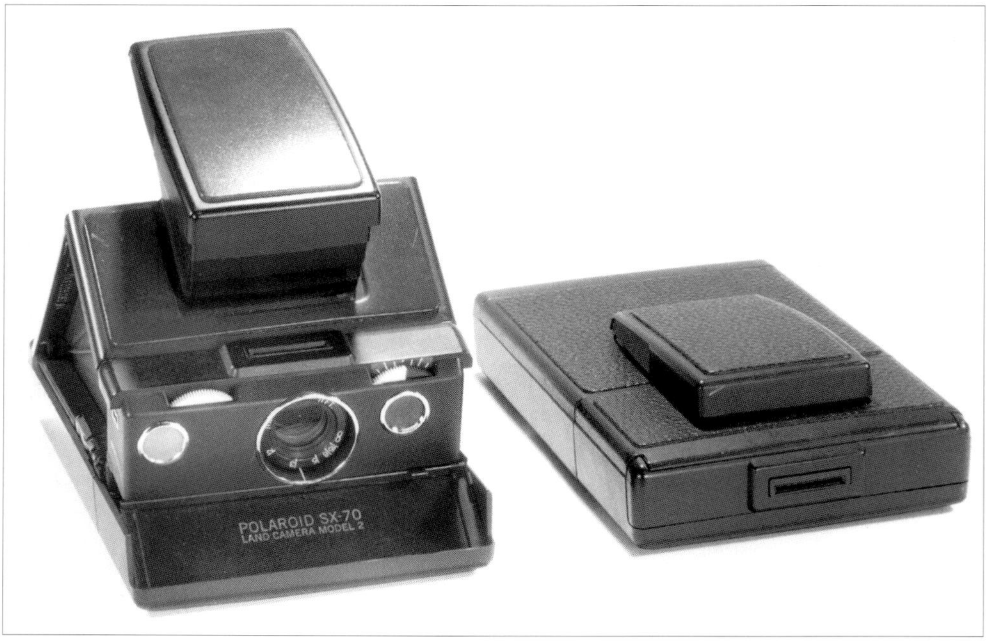

The SX-70, shown here folded and unfolded, was the first Polaroid camera to automatically eject a self-developing picture as the exposure was made.

sure, light travels through the lens to a mirror on the sloping back of the camera, down to another mirror on top of the film pack that lies horizontally flat in the camera base, back onto the first mirror in the camera's back, then to a curved mirror in the back of the viewfinder and so on to the front of the viewfinder and through its eyepiece. As the exposure is made, the mirror in the base of the camera - the one covering the film pack - swings up to cover the mirror in the camera's sloping back. Yet another mirror on the back of this first one then reflects light down to the film in the base of the camera. The mechanics of that alone make it an interesting collector's item.

The SX-70 was later adapted to become the world's first autofocus single lens reflex (see pages 164-165).

The Button

Following the success of the extremely sophisticated SX-70 camera, Polaroid introduced several, much simpler, non-folding, non-reflex models for SX-70 film. The Button was one of the more common. It has a fixed focus lens and the only adjustment that can be made by the photographer is by way of a lighten/darken control.

600 Series

In 1981, Polaroid launched the 600 Series of cameras, which took the SX-70 idea and introduced new technology to both films and cameras. The best camera in the range is the SLR 680.

It features automatic exposure, autofocus by means of the sonic method used in the SX-70, a picture that automatically ejects and self-develops as the exposure is made and an in-built electronic flashgun that fires with every shot to ensure the picture is always correctly exposed and perfectly lit.

The only manual control is a thumbwheel to lighten or darken the picture and, like the SX-70 before it, all functions in the camera are driven by a battery actually incorporated in the film pack so there is never a danger of the power running out.

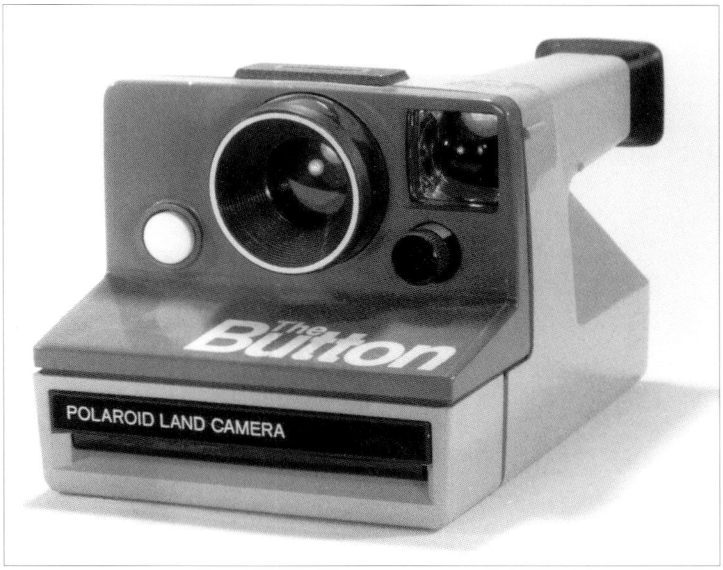

The Button is a snapshot camera for SX-70 film.

And so on...

After the 600 series of cameras, Polaroid went on to introduce further innovations and styles, including the Image System, Impulse and the Vision camera that marked a return to folding SLRs, though in a different style to the previous models. These, however, are all, still on the market at the time of writing and not really considered as collectables... yet.

The Polaroid SLR 680 used the new 600 Series film in a single lens reflex.

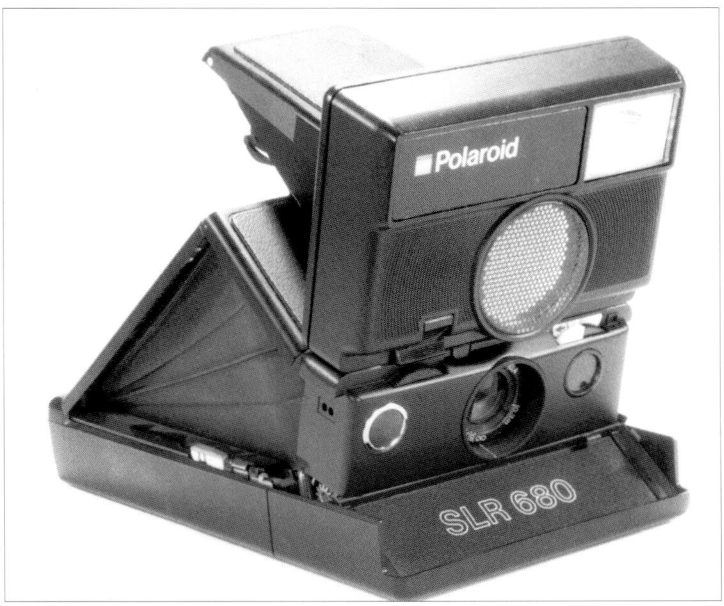

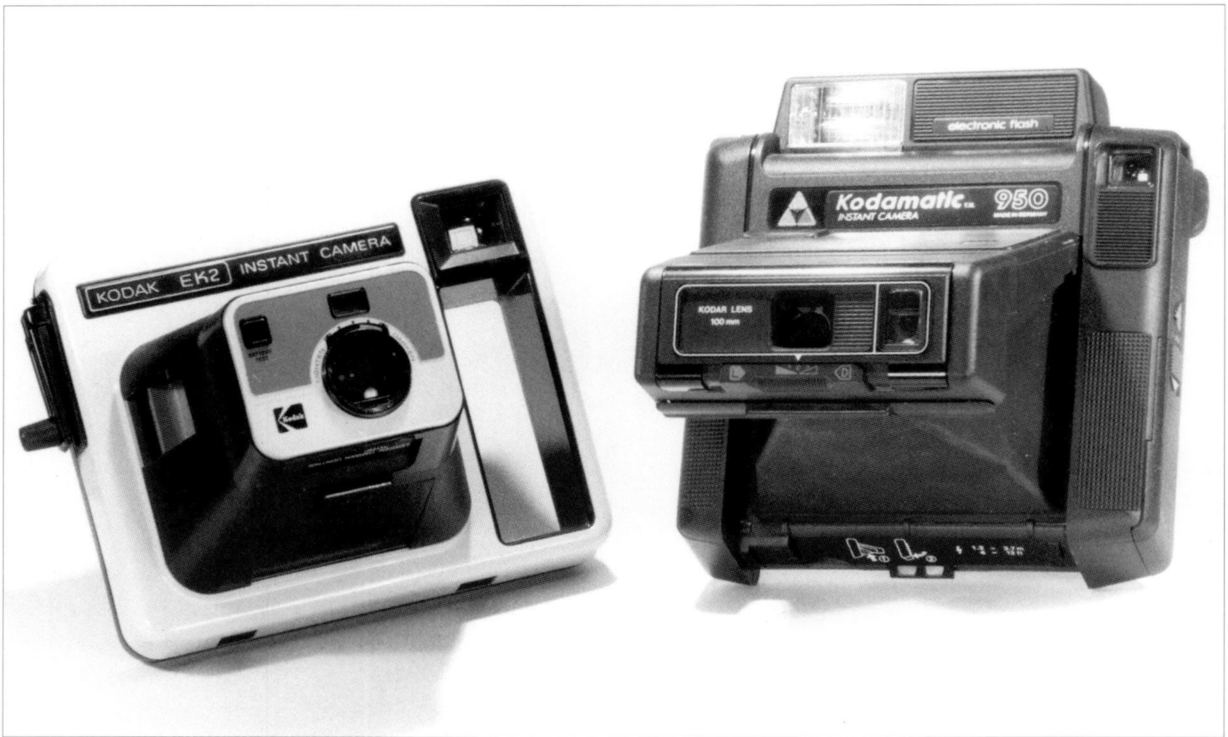

Two from the Kodak range of instant picture cameras: The EK2 with a handle for manual film ejection and the folding Kodamatic 950.

Kodak instant picture cameras

In 1976, Kodak introduced their PR-10 instant photography system at a time when Polaroid already had SX-70 film on the market and, naturally, Kodak's system went straight to self-developing prints.

The company claimed the system to be very different from Polaroid's and in many ways it was. Polaroid, however, didn't agree and sued for infringement of patents in a court battle that raged for a dozen years or so and resulted in Kodak withdrawing completely from the instant picture market.

That has left a lot of cheap Kodak instant cameras on the collector's market and, whilst few of them are really as interesting as their Polaroid counterparts, it's worth adding a few to any instant camera collection.

The very early models do not have automated print ejection like the Polaroid cameras. Once the picture was taken the film had to be wound out with a handle.

Later cameras have motorised print ejection, built-in flash, automatic exposure and most of the features seen on Polaroids of the same era. You can find them in a range of weird and wonderful designs that seem to have been purposely removed as far as possible from the well known Polaroid look.

Early Stirrings from Japan

You might be forgiven for believing the Japanese camera industry began in the 1960s, because that was when cameras from Japan first started appearing in the West in any significant number. In fact, Japanese cameras are as old as photography itself, with models dating right back to the 19th Century and the daguerreotype age. But Japan was, for many years, a closed country and, initially, few of its products were ever seen outside its shores. Right up until 1958, the Japanese were not allowed to exhibit their goods at Photokina, the famous German photographic fair held every two years in Cologne. In that year, however, they rebelled and opened their own exhibition in a separate hall close to the German show. It attracted a lot of interest and, two years later, at the next Photokina in 1960, they were allowed in for the first time. By the end of the 1960s the Japanese camera industry had begun to dominate the rest of the world. So it's interesting to step back from that point, to see how Japan's introduction to the West began and how many of today's household names started out. Which is why Japanese cameras from the 1950s and early 1960s make such interesting collector's items.

The Nikon I, showing a strong resemblance to the Contax II.

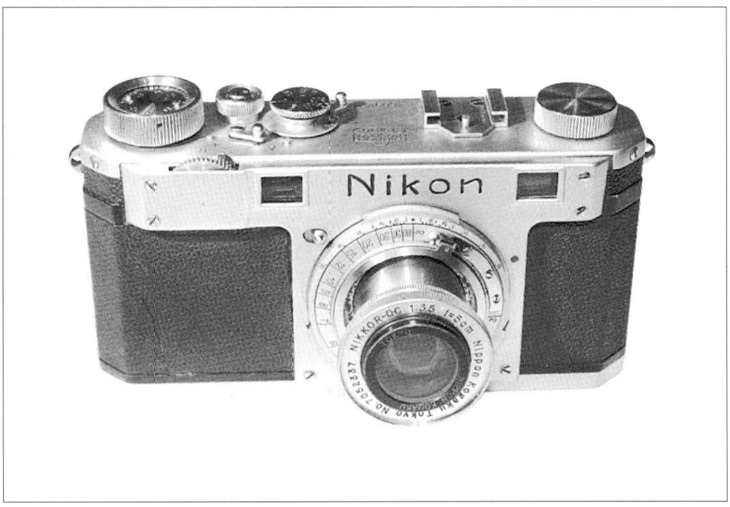

Nikon

Nikon today is known for its SLRs and the first of those was the Nikon F launched in 1959. But before that, Nikon made 35mm rangefinder cameras.

The Nikon I was launched in 1948 and only a little over 700 were made. So today it is an extremely rare and valuable item, a long way out of reach of the average collector. Nevertheless, it's worth a mention if only for its historical interest.

The camera looks like, and was obviously designed under the strong influence of, the Contax II, with which it shares a lens mount. That fact was a strong factor in its early success. As foreign press photographers began arriving in the East to cover the Korean War in the early 1950s, they used Tokyo as a stepping off point, where they discovered Japanese Nikkor lenses that they could use on their German Contax bodies. Since Nippon Kogaku, the company that built the Nikon, were originally specialists in lens manufacture, the quality was high and a lot photographers from outside Japan began to take an interest in Nikon cameras.

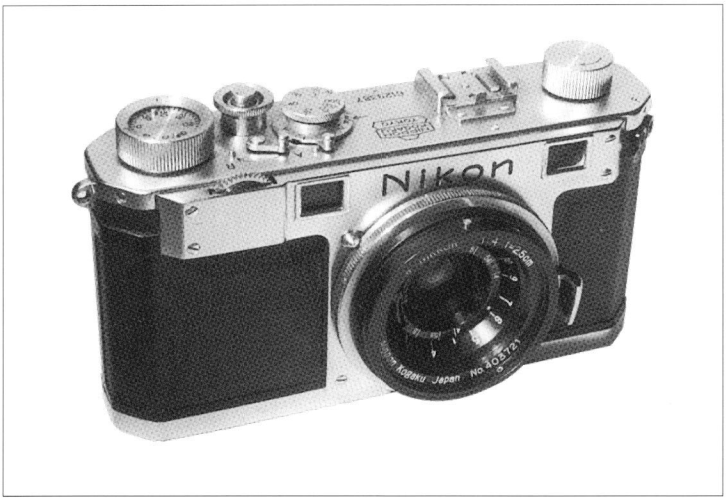

The Nikon S, first with flash synchronisation.

But back to the Nikon I. It might look like a Contax II, but it's actually quite different inside. For one thing, the film format is 24 x 32 mm, rather than the 24 x 36 mm format that had already become a standard for 35mm cameras outside Japan at that time. The lens is either an f/2 or an f/3.5 Nikkor, coupled to a rangefinder that is situated in the viewfinder, rather than in a separate window.

The Nikon I was followed, in 1949, by the Nikon M, which was very similar in its features. More than 3,000 of these were made, so they are more easily found on today's collector's market. The camera still bears a strong resemblance to the Contax and the 'M' stands for 'Medium' - a reference to the film format which, at 24 x 34 mm, is lager than that of the Nikon I, but still not as large as the traditional size.

The Nikon S was the first Nikon with flash synchronisation and the first to be exported from Japan. Other than the synchronisation - the reason for the 'S' in its name - features were similar to the Nikon M, even down to the unconventional film format. That eventually changed to the better known 24 x 36 mm format with the introduction of the Nikon S2 in 1954. This camera is the first with a lever wind for film, as well as a crank for rewind, replacing knobs for both functions on previous cameras. It was also the first Nikon to accept a motor drive.

In 1957, the Nikon SP arrived, the 'P' prob-

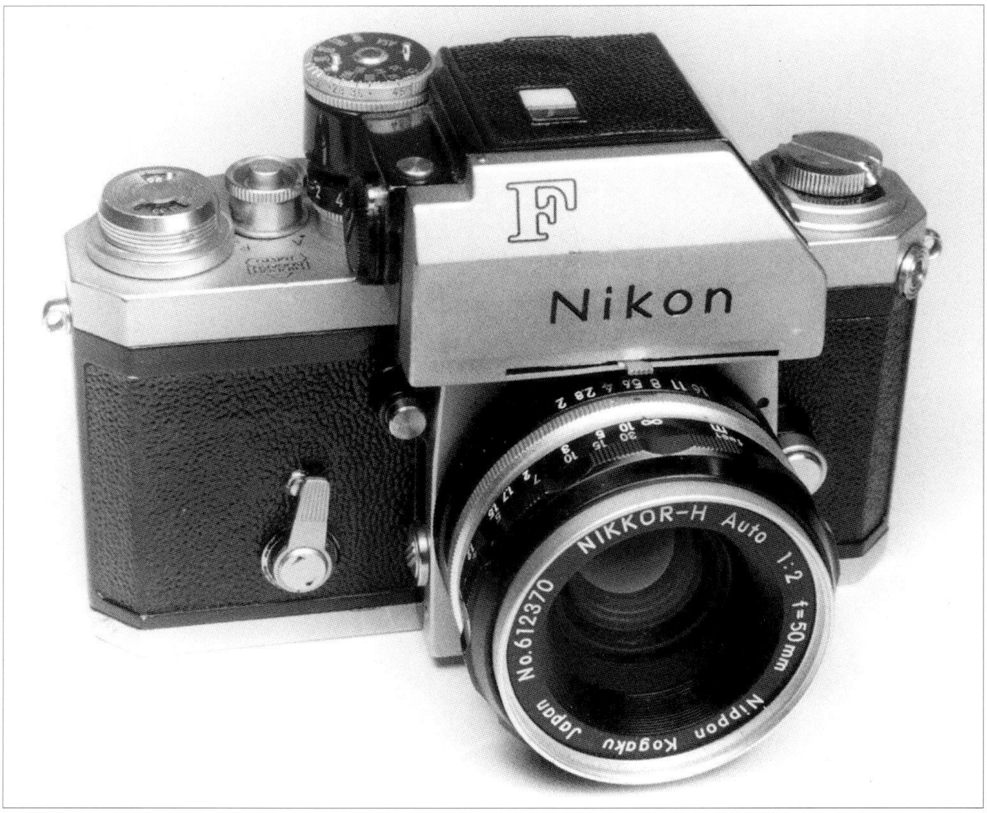

The Nikon F with its Photomic Head.

ably standing for 'professional'. This was the first Nikon to use titanium foil in the shutter blinds and it was capable of taking a battery driven motor drive that offered shooting up to three frames per second. It also had an accessory meter with a Selenium cell that connected with the shutter speed dial.

All of this led inevitably to the launch of the Nikon F, also in 1959. Today, it is more accessible to the collector than the earlier rangefinder cameras and, as the first true system SLR, launched with a full range of accessories, it is certainly worth collecting.

The Nikon F shares many its features with the Nikon SP, including the titanium shutter blinds. Also influenced by the rangefinder cameras it had a bayonet lens mount, at a time when most other manufacturers were producing SLRs with screw mounts. The Nikon F was also the first SLR to show a full 100 per cent view in the viewfinder. A few years after its launch, a new model was produced in 1962 with the now famous Photomic Head. This is a meter built into the interchangeable pentaprism, but it doesn't actually take its readings through the lens. Instead, light is measured via a small circular cell on the front of the viewfinder and the whole thing links with the camera's shutter speed control once mounted on the camera.

Canon

Just as Nikon was influenced by Contax, so the first Canons, produced before the Second World War, were made under the strong influence of Leica. But as we move into the 1950s and 1960s, so Canon cameras take on a style of their own and the Canon P, made in 1959 was the world's first quality camera to be made on an assembly line.

Two of the more interesting and collectable cameras from this era are the Canon 7 and the Canon Pellix.

The Canon 7 was launched in 1961 to become one of the last great rangefinder cameras and the one with which Canon had their greatest success, not least because of its

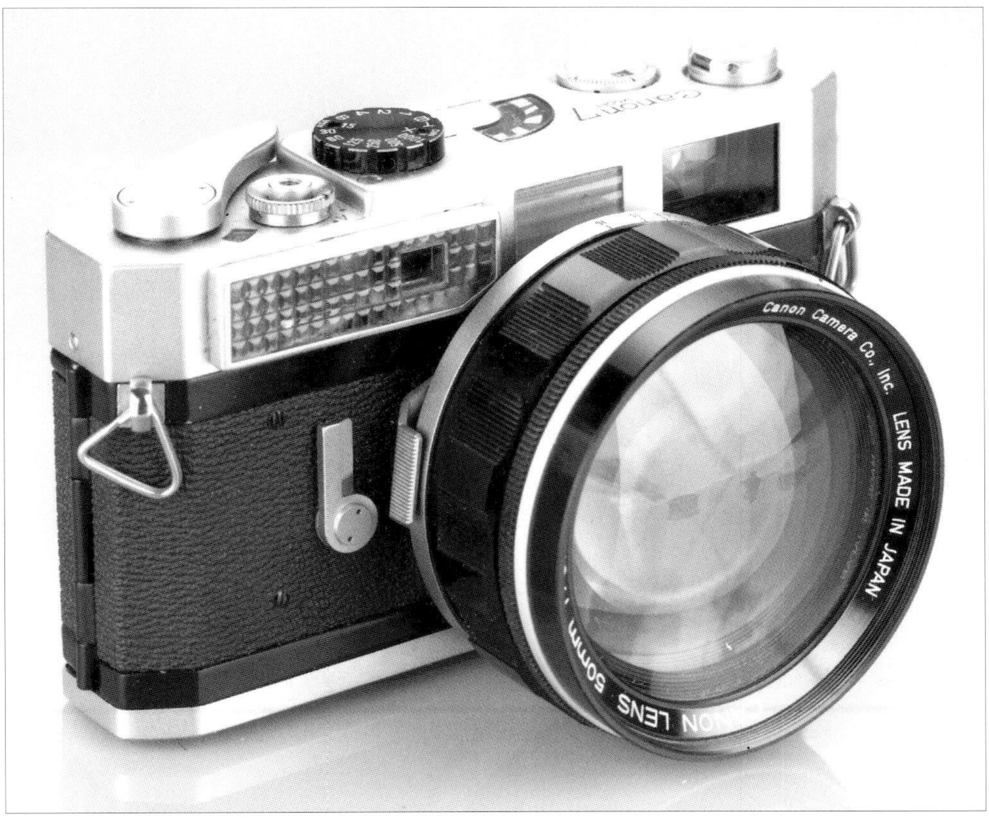

The Canon 7 with its f/0.95 Dream Lens.

unusual lens. The lens in question had a standard 50mm focal length, but an amazingly wide maximum aperture of f/0.95 - which Canon advertised as being four times brighter than the human eye!

The camera was the first made by Canon with a built-in meter, coupled to the shutter speed dial. It's a selenium meter which is read from a needle that swings across a scale on the top plate of the camera to indicate the appropriate aperture, according to the set shutter speed and there are two colour coded scales: orange for high sensitivity, white for low. Sensitivity is changed by a knob and, once read off the appropriate scale, the aperture setting is then transferred manually to the lens.

Looking through the viewfinder shows parallax corrected suspended frames for different focal lengths of lens and that too was a first for Canon with this camera.

Depth of field from the Dream Lens at its larger apertures is obviously shallower than usual, and that has been compensated for by lengthening the rangefinder base by about half as much again as that on previous Canon rangefinder cameras, which in turn led to a problem. The meter cell on the Canon 7 is also much larger than usual, taking up almost half the front and bumping into the rangefinder. Canon overcame this problem by cutting a small square aperture out of the meter cell to accommodate the second rangefinder window.

The Canon 7 also has a different lens mount to other Canons of the time. Like those, it has an internal screw thread that allows the use of more traditional Canon lenses. But that small screw mount simply isn't enough to accommodate the huge diameter of the Dream Lens. So, as well as the internal screw thread, the Canon 7 has an external, three-lug bayonet. It takes both the Dream Lens and a Canon Mirror Box which effectively converts the camera to an SLR.

The Canon 7 has a metal focal plane shutter,

The Canon Pellix was unusual in using a stationary pellicle mirror.

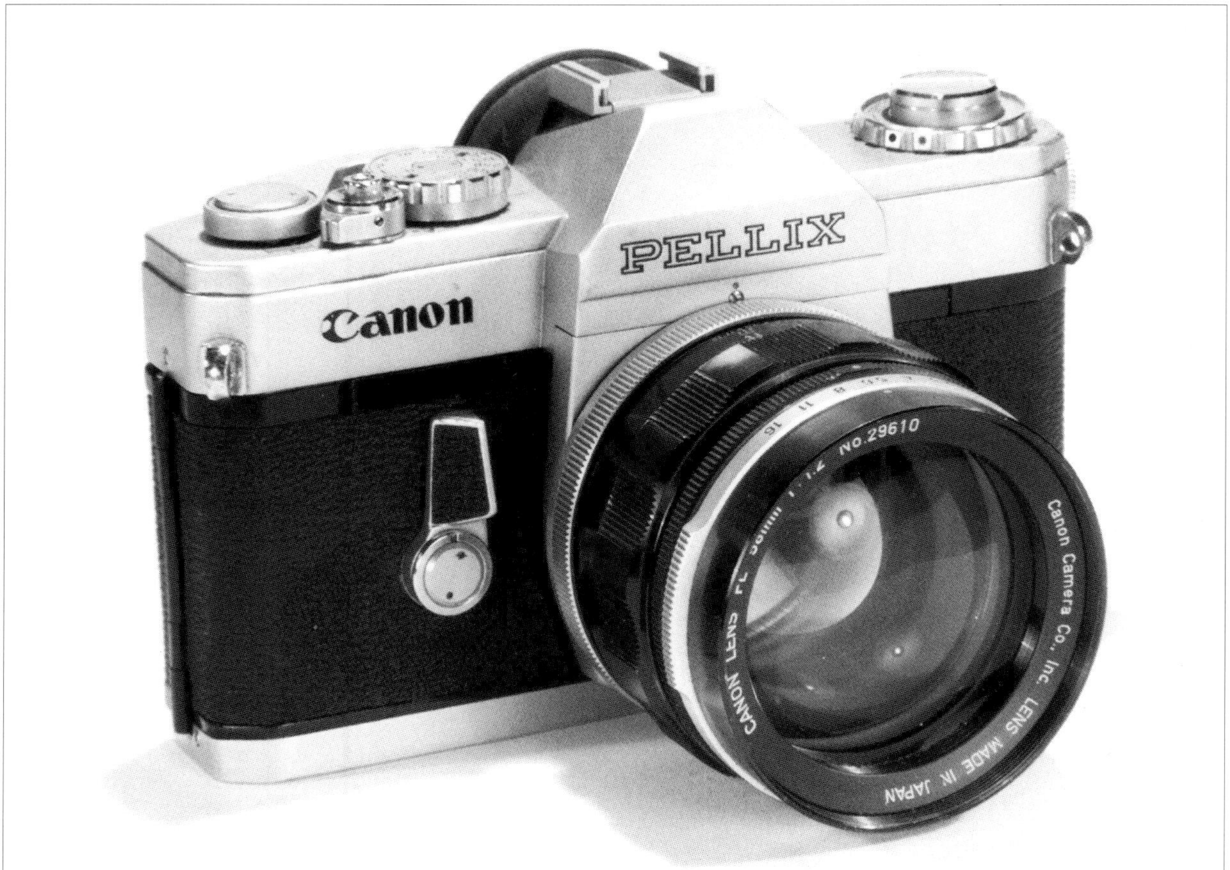

similar to that used in the Canonflex SLRs of the time, and with the unusual addition of a 'T' setting for time exposures as well as the more traditional 'B' setting. The curtains are made of stainless steel sheet 18/1000mm thick, with a black plastic coating. Top speed is 1/1000 second and the shutter can be locked when the camera is not in use or when fitting a cable release - an action that can inadvertently trip the shutter.

The amazing f/0.95 lens has seven elements in a five group combination that aim to kill flare and give perfect edge to edge sharpness. In practice, photographers soon found that the lens wasn't as sharp as it might be at the wider apertures, but was reckoned to be outstanding when stopped down a little.

In 1965, the Canon 7 was upgraded, replacing the huge Selenium cell meter with a smaller, neater CdS version and adding an accessory shoe that had been missing from the original model. The new camera was called the Canon 7s, but by the time of its launch, SLRs were killing the sales of rangefinder cameras for good and it never enjoyed the popularity of its predecessor.

Because the original Canon 7 was made in such great numbers, there are still quite a few around today. Because of its association with the Dream Lens, however, they are often unrealistically priced even when sold as bodies only or with any other lens. The collector shouldn't be tempted to pay big money for one of these cameras unless it has its very special lens with it.

To most outward appearances, the Canon Pellix doesn't look very different from any other SLR of the 1960s. What sets it apart from all the others is what goes on inside.

To get the image from the lens to the viewfinder, a single lens reflex uses a mirror, inside the body, at 45 degrees, which reflects the image to the pentaprism above. Naturally, when the exposure needs to be made, the mirror is in the way, so any other 1960s SLR is designed so that, as the shutter is released, the mirror flips up, allowing the lens's image to reach the film, dropping down again after exposure. Not so the Canon Pellix, made in 1965. The Pellix was the first production SLR in which the mirror did not move.

The reason is in the name. The Pellix is named after the pellicle mirror that is installed in the usual place behind the lens. The difference between this and any other mirror is that it only reflects part of the light; the rest passes straight through it. So the mirror reflects light to the pentaprism to allow viewfinding and focusing, but passes light as well to the film for the actual picture... all without moving.

This led to another first for Canon: the use of a viewfinder blind that can be slid across the viewfinder when not in use, to prevent stray light from the finder fogging the film. It is operated by turning a ring around the rewind knob.

The Pellix is also a landmark for Canon in featuring the first use of through the lens metering in one of the company's cameras. It comes courtesy of a cell that swings up from the base of the camera on an arm as a lever is pushed on the front of the camera. The same lever, which also acts as the self timer when turned in the opposite direction, stops the lens down to the taking aperture, so the metering can only be used in stop-down mode. Positioned in front of the shutter blind, the cell reads the light being transmitted through the pellicle mirror, then drops back again as the lever is released and the exposure is made.

The first model of the Pellix was made until 1966, after which a new version was launched, incorporating Canon's special Quick Load system that makes film loading easier than normal. With this, the cassette is dropped into its normal position and the film pulled out to a red line indicator. The back is closed and the lever wind operated, resulting in the camera's special take-up spool grabbing the film and holding on tight as it wraps around the spindle. The new model was called the Pellix-QL and is identified by a small 'QL' badge on the front of the body. Its only other difference is in the lever that is operated for metering. Unlike on the original model, this one can be locked into the stop down position.

One of the drawbacks of the Pellix system was the fact that it reflected only around one-third of the light to the viewfinder, allowing only two-thirds to reach the film. The viewfinder image, therefore, was darker than most contemporary SLRs and was made worse when the stopped down metering was used. The drop in light to the film was counteracted by Canon to a certain extent by producing the camera with a faster than normal standard lens: an f/1.2, against the more usual f/1.8 or f/1.4 of the day, but it wasn't enough to win the camera too many fans, and the Pellix died soon after the release of the second model.

Collectors buying a Canon Pellix are advised to always remove the lens and examine the mirror before parting with hard cash. (The lens is removed by turning a collar at the rear until a red dot is positioned at the top.) The problem is that the pellicle mirror is actually made up of a partially silvered thin skin stretched taught across a frame, making it extremely fragile and easily damaged by even the softest touch. So make sure the mirror is undamaged before you buy - and when you have bought it, don't touch it!

Put all these factors together and you begin to see why the Canon Pellix failed in the 1960s, but the idea lived on and pellicle mirrors were used again by Canon in the F1 High Speed Motor Camera that was introduced for the 1984 Olympics and the EOS RT of the 1990s.

Pentax

The first Pentax SLR was launched in 1957, but before that came the Asahiflex, a single lens reflex, with a waist-level viewfinder.

The Asahiflex I was the first camera made by the Asahi Optical Company and Japan's first SLR. It appeared in 1952, with a small range of accessories and using a 37mm interchangeable screw lens mount. This first camera is usually seen with a 50mm f/3.5 Takumar

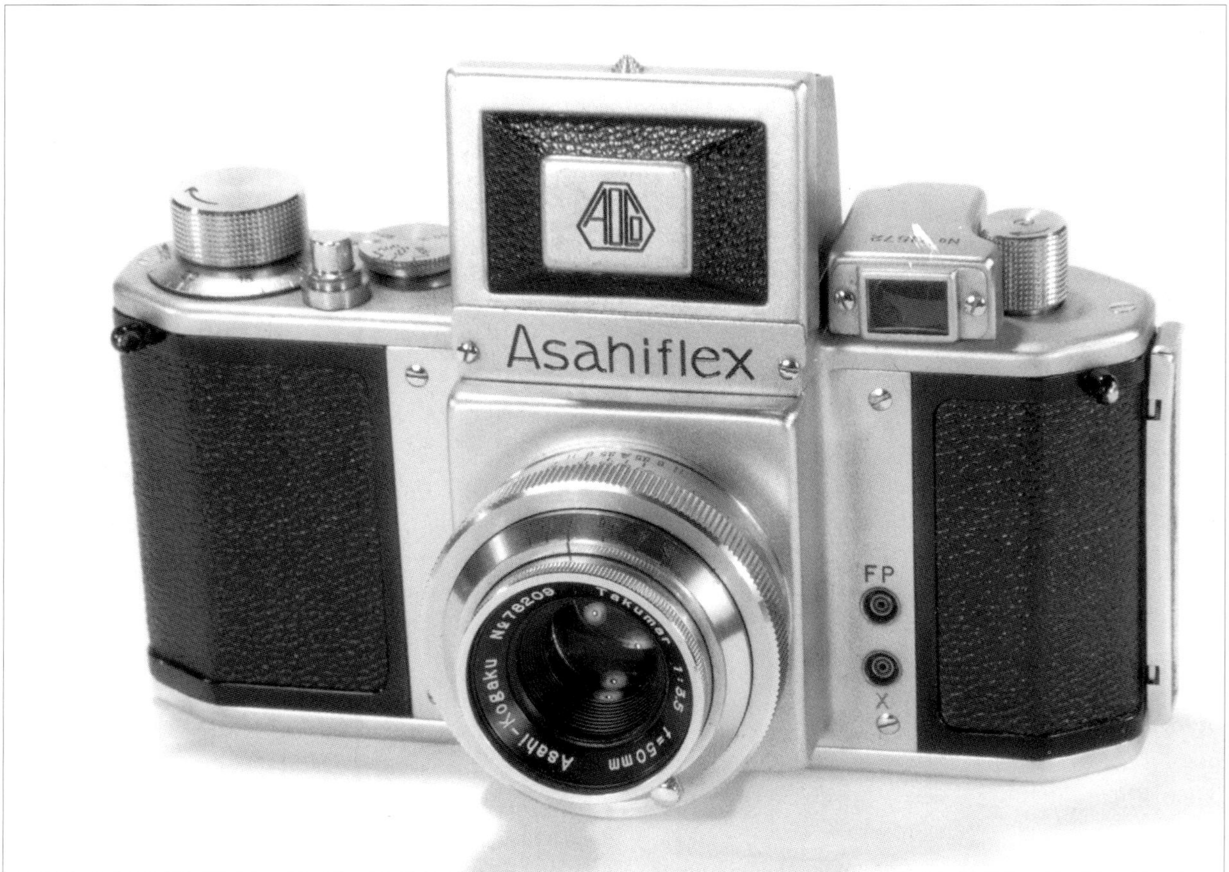

The Asahiflex IIb was the first Japanese SLR with an instant return mirror.

standard lens. A quick way to identify it is by the shutter speeds which run in the following increments: 1/20, 1/30, 1/40, 1/60, 1/100, 1/200 and 1/500 second. It has only X-synchronisation. The Asahiflex Ia appeared in 1953. It can be distinguished from the first model by the addition of FP bulb synchronisation and the re-ordering of the shutter speeds in the more traditional increments of 1/25, 1/50, 1/100, 1/200 and 1/500 second.

The landmark camera was the Asahiflex IIb, first seen in 1954. This was the first Japanese SLR with an instant return mirror and is sometimes credited with being the world's first camera with the feature. In fact, it was predated by the Hungarian made Duflex in 1947 and, if we're being really picky, there was even a form of instant return mirror on the Vanneck, way back in 1890. Both of these, however, are rarities and it's true to say that the Asahiflex IIb is the camera that's best known for introducing the feature to the camera world. The IIb can also be identified by its use, for the first time, of two sync sockets, utilised according to the type of flashgun in place.

The Asahiflex IIa was actually launched after the IIb, in 1955 and is the best of the series. It of course uses the instant return mirror feature and can be identified by the addition, for the first time, of three extra slow shutter speeds: 1/2, 1/5 and 1/10 second.

In 1957, Asahi improved on the design even more, with the addition of a pentaprism eye level viewfinder. The result was the first Pentax, starting a line of cameras that would remain popular for many years to come. Another improvement was the film wind that was changed from knob to lever and the lens mount was also increased in size, from 37mm to the 42mm thread that became the standard for screw lenses for years. The lens was a 55mm f/2 Takumar.

Minolta

Minolta is another name that is best known today for single lens reflexes, but which started life with everything but. The company actually goes back to 1928, when it was founded under the name Nichi-Doku Shashinki Shokai, which means Japan German Camera Company. They made many cameras which were copies of, and slightly restyled versions of, German originals, but their first 35mm camera was the Minolta 35, made in 1947.

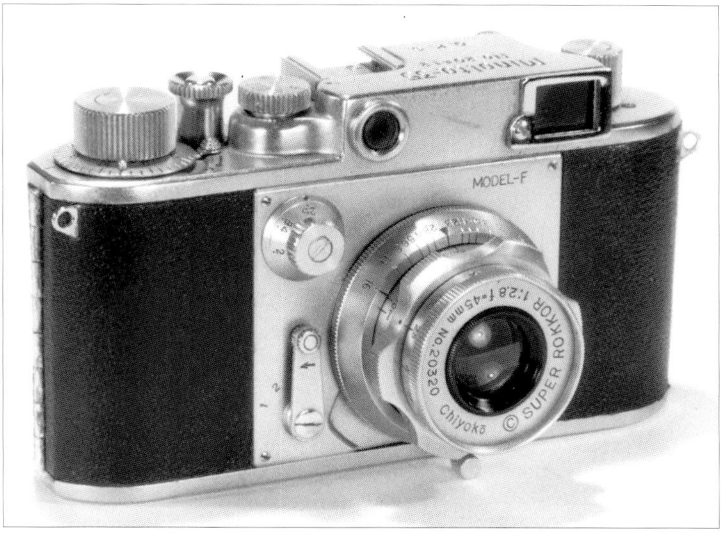

The Minolta 35, the company's first 35mm camera.

The camera is heavily influenced by Leica, but with the 24 x 32 mm format that is associated with early Nikon. Since the Minolta predates the Nikon I by a year, it could be assumed that Nikon followed Minolta in this format, but in fact the size was one that the Japanese camera manufacturers in general

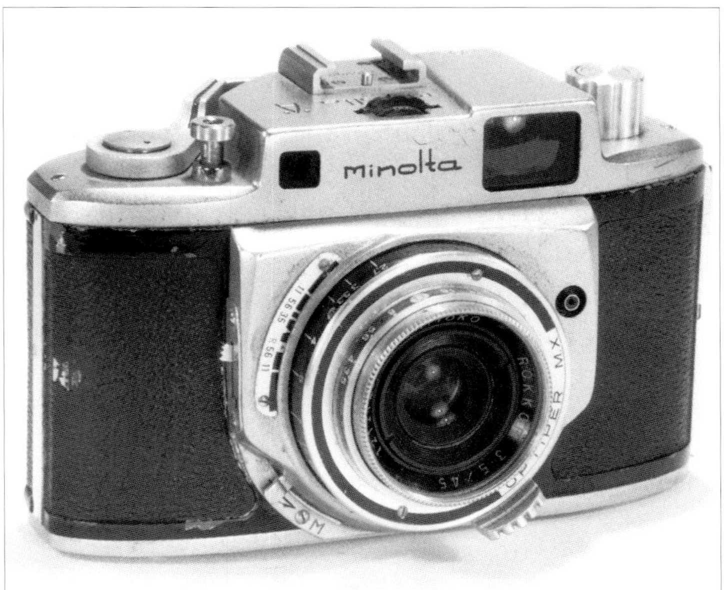

The Minolta A was the first Minolta to be officially exported from Japan.

thought to be more suitable because of its ratio to printing paper sizes and it was Minolta that developed the format first. The lens, made in a Leica mount, is a 45mm f/2.8 Super Rokkor.

There are a number of different models and variations on this first 35mm Minolta camera with frame sizes ranging from that first 24 x 32 mm, through 24 x 33.5 mm and 24 x 34 mm before the company finally rationalised on the now traditional 24 x 36 mm.

These cameras were never originally exported from Japan, which makes them rare and not easily found on the collector's market. The first Minolta to be officially exported, and which is therefore easier to collect today, was the Minolta A, which arrived in 1955.

This is a 35mm rangefinder camera, using a coincident image rangefinder in the viewfinder window. The film format is the traditional 24 x 36 mm and film wind is by lever. Apertures are set in the conventional way by a ring in the usual place and there is a neat little depth of field scale that wraps around a segment of the lens. The shutter speed control, however, is a little out of the ordinary. It takes the form of a wheel set vertically into the camera, with a small segment protruding from the top plate. Rotating it sets shutter speeds, on a between-lens shutter, from 1 second to 1/300 second plus 'B'. In this way, both shutter speeds and apertures can be read from the top of the camera. The non-interchangeable lens is a 45mm f/3.5 Chiyoko Rokkor.

Olympus

Like Minolta, Olympus cameras go back a long way; the company was actually formed in 1919 as Takachiho Seisakusho to make microscopes. Early camera production mostly copied German styles, typified by the Olympus Six cameras that appeared first in 1939. After the Second World War, the camera was updated and restyled with a chrome top plate and became known as the Olympus Chrome Six, although the markings on the camera omit the word 'chrome'.

They are all twin format models, taking 6 x 6 cm or 6 x 4.5 cm pictures on 120 film by use of a flexible mask that clicks into the camera back and twin red windows: a central one for the square format and another above for use when the mask is in place. The cameras follow a folding design, the lens panel self erecting as

Early cameras from Olympus: The Olympus Chrome Six that takes two different formats on 120 film and the 35mm Olympus 35.

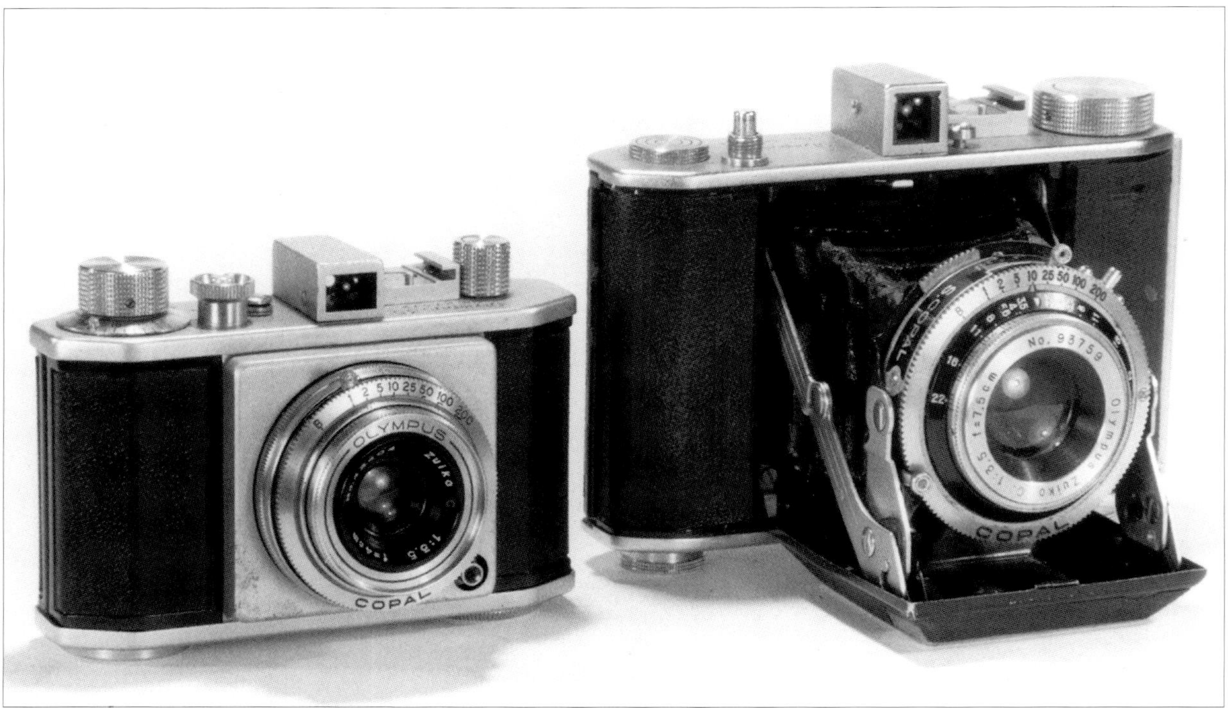

a bed is dropped down from the front. Early models have a tubular viewfinder above the lens, later models have the viewfinder built into the top plate housing. The camera illustrated is the third model, made in 1950. Improvements on previous models include a tensioned supply spool for better film flatness and a synchronised shutter. The lens is a 75mm f/3.5 Zuiko and the Copal shutter offers speeds from 1 second to 1/200 second.

Olympus first began to make 35mm cameras in 1948 with the launch of the Olympus 35, a neat little camera that originally produced 24 x 32 mm negatives. The following year, a second model reverted to the more popular 24 x 36 mm format, which was used in many different versions through until the late 1950s.

The model illustrated here is the Olympus 35 IV, produced in 1949 with a Copal between-the-lens shutter, speeded from 1 second to 1/200 second and 40mm f/3.5 Zuiko lens.

In the era we are considering, however, probably the most interesting Olympus cameras are the Pen range.

The first Olympus Pen was launched in 1959 and the style continued into and through the 1960s and 1970s. The name was inspired by the fact that the cameras were small and, allegedly, as convenient to carry as a pen. One reason why they could be made so small was because they were half frame cameras, taking standard 35mm film in its usual cassette, but producing pictures half the normal size at 18 x 24 mm. The camera began a craze for half frame that continued throughout the 1960s.

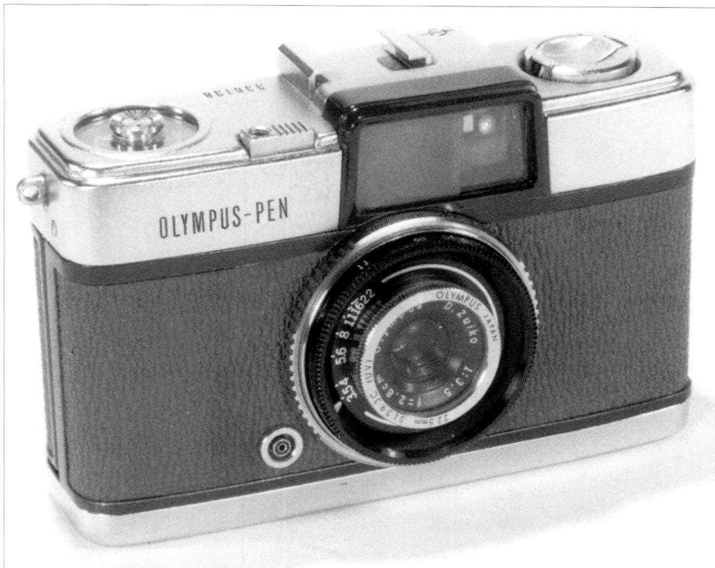

The Olympus Pen that started the half frame craze in the 1960s.

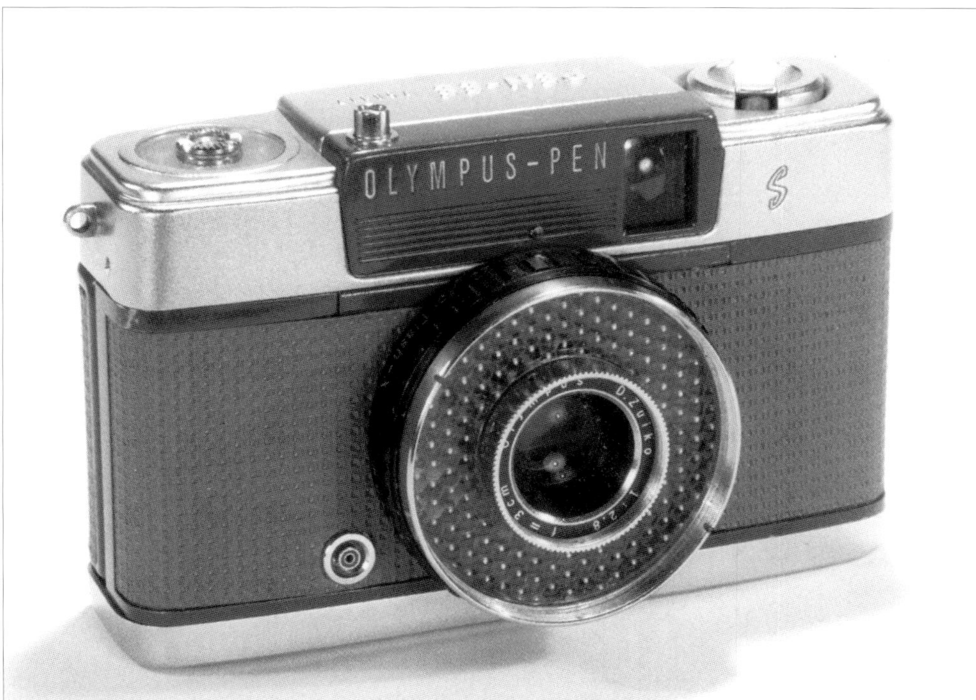

The half frame Olympus Pen EES with its large metering cell around the lens, a style later adopted by the full frame Olympus Trip.

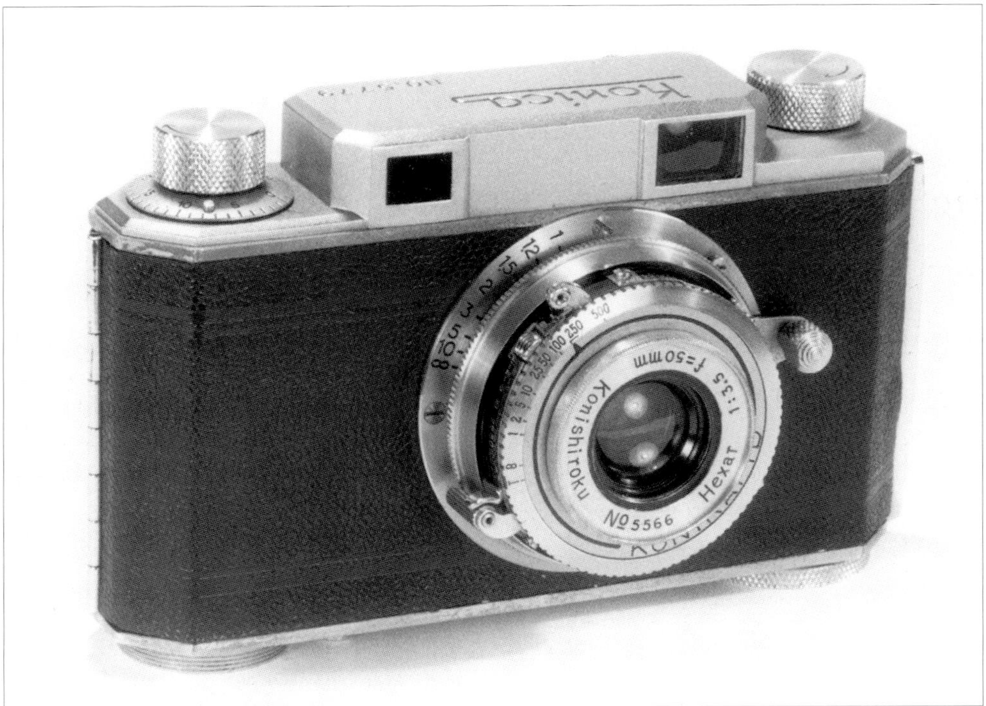

The Konica, made by Konishiroku.

The early models, of which there are four, are the most attractive for the collector.

The first Pen wasn't actually made by Olympus. The company sub-contracted the manufacture, but tested the camera before distributing it. Made in die-cast alloy, the Pen has a 28mm f/3.5 D-Zuico lens which focuses down to 2 ft, using zone symbols. Shutter speeds run: 1/25, 1/50, 1/100, 1/200 second

The Samoca 35 Super, a compact rangefinder camera from Japan.

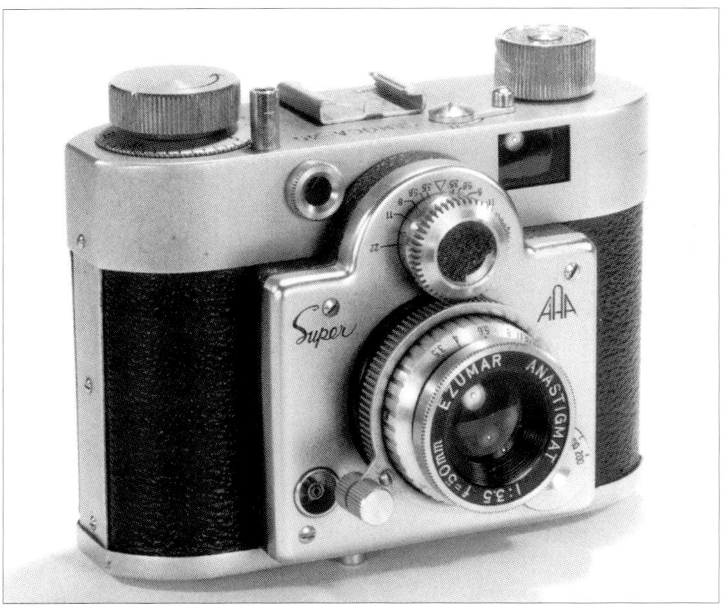

Olympus began construction of the cameras themselves with the Pen S, launched in 1960. It is similar to the original model, but with an f/2.8 lens and the shutter speed range extended in each direction and changed to the more conventional increments: 1/8, 1/15, 1/30, 1/60, 1/125 and 1/250 second.

The Pen cameras that are seen most often are the next two: the Pen EE and EES. The 'EE' in the name stands for Electric Eye and it's not hard to see why, since the small camera is dominated by a large metering cell that surrounds the lens. With the film speed set on a ring around the lens, the correct aperture is selected and set automatically. Alternatively, the film speed setting ring can be rotated further, when a series aperture settings appear for manual setting.

On the EE, the f/3.5 lens is fixed focus and the shutter speed is fixed at 1/60 second. The EES has an f/2.8 lens that can be focused on zone symbols.

After these first four models, the Olympus Pen series changed shape and specification over the course of many different models right through until the 1970s, by which time the Pen F, first of the half-frame single lens reflexes had been launched (see page 43) Other non-reflex Pen models include the D, D2, D3, W, EM, Rapid EES, Rapid EED, EE-EL, EES-EL, EED, EES2, EE-2 and EE-3.

Konishiroku

Not every Japanese camera of the 1950s came from big name companies like Canon, Nikon, Pentax, Minolta or Olympus. Konishiroku was one of the oldest Japanese manufacturers, whose history goes right back to the 1870s. In 1948 they made a 35mm camera whose name was destined to appear on a multitude of different models over the following years. The camera was called simply the Konica.

It's a 35mm rangefinder camera, whose earliest models were made in occupied Japan. The lens, a Hexar or Hexanon f/2.8 or f/3.5, pulls out on a short tube when in use, similar to the early Leicas, and like them, is focused by a lever to the side that rotates around the lens mount. Shutter speeds are from 1 second to 1/500 second.

Samoca

Other Japanese names of the time might not be so well known today, but are still very collectable. Samoca cameras, made by Sanei Sangyo, are among those worth considering.

The Samoca 35 Super was made in 1956, a neat little 35mm rangefinder camera that measures no more than 10.5 x 8 x 7 cm with an interesting way of focusing. The lens is rotated by a stubby lever attached to a collar around the lens barrel. As the collar is rotated, the lens moves in and out, whilst the collar itself is linked to a small wheel above by cogs, so that too turns to indicate focusing distances on a rotating scale. The shutter speed setting is in an unconventional position too, on a small wheel below and to one side of the lens at the 5 o'clock position. Speeds run from 1/10 second to 1/200 second plus 'B'. Equally unusual is the film rewind control, which takes the form of a lever on the top plate, rather than the usual button on the base plate.

Watch out to for a similar model with built-

The Samoca LE-II with its two converter lenses for wideangle and telephoto photography.

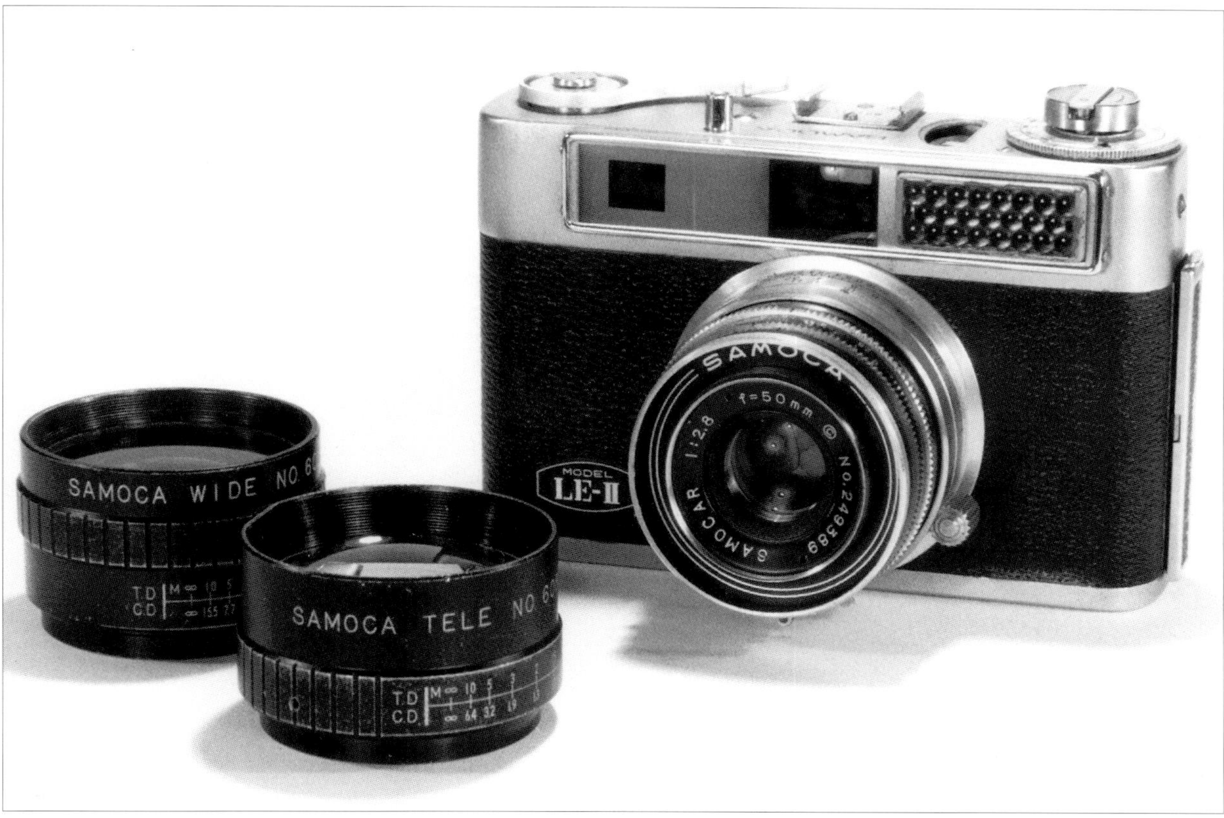

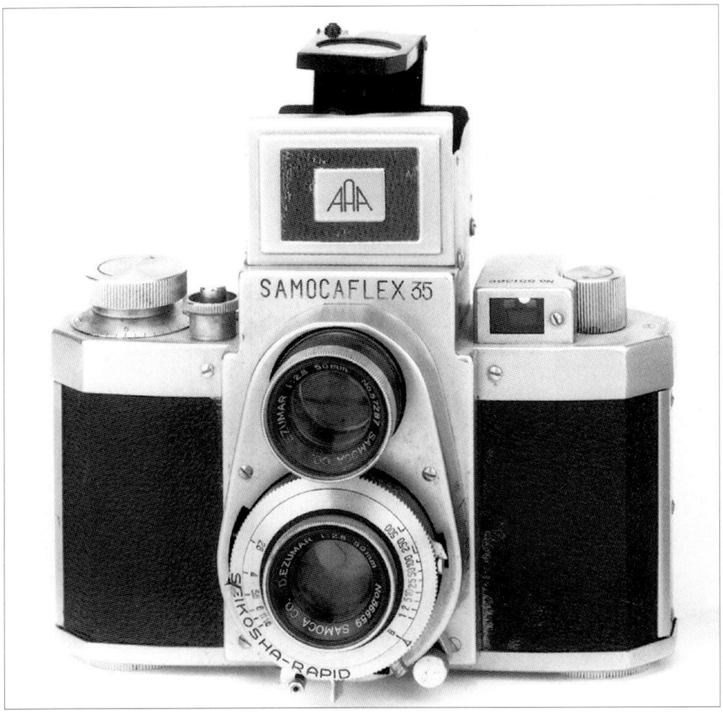

The Samocaflex 35 twin lens reflex.

on exposure meter, and for the Samoca 35V, launched in 1955, similar in appearance to the 35 Super but without a rangefinder.

The Samoca LE-II is another interesting camera from this manufacturer. It's a pretty much standard 35mm rangefinder model with a built in meter that deflects a needle across a window on the top plate. Turning a ring around the rewind knob also moves a pointer and when this coincides with the needle, shutter speeds can be read off against apertures on an engraved scale. These are then set manually on scales around the lens.

The LE-II has a 50mm f/2.8 lens attached, which can't be interchanged, but which can be adapted by two auxiliary lenses that are screwed to the front. One converts the standard lens to a wideangle view, the other to a short telephoto, but without indications in the viewfinder or focal length designations on the adapter lenses, framing the subject is a rather hit and miss affair.

The most unusual of the Samoca range must be the Samocaflex 35, made in 1955. This one is a 35mm twin lens reflex with a waist level finder, incorporating a split image rangefinder, as well as a direct vision viewfinder. In 1956, a second, very similar model was introduced. The only real difference between them is that the first model uses a Seikosha Rapid shutter, while the second model has a Seikosha MX shutter, each with the same rage of speeds. Both cameras look a lot like Asahiflexes with extra lenses added to serve the reflex viewfinders.

Who Made That?

It's accepted and well documented that many cameras weren't made by the manufacturer whose name appears on the body. It's a practice that applies in particular to many of the mass produced snapshot cameras, made by one manufacturer and badged by others in different ways in various countries. But it might come as a shock to find some of the bigger manufacturers playing the same game. Here is a Leica that was made by Minolta and a Praktica that thought it was an Exakta.

Leica CL

Leica is so well known as a German camera manufacturer that it might come as a surprise to find one of its top class models made in Japan by a Japanese camera manufacturer. But that's just what happened with the Leica CL. The design is German, from the Leitz designers at Wetzlar, but the camera body was built for them by Minolta.

The initials 'CL' stand for 'Compact Leica' and the camera lives up to its name, being somewhat smaller than other Leicas of the day. It's a rangefinder camera, influenced by the M series of Leicas which, by the time of the CL launch in 1973, had got as far as the M5. That camera was a little larger than previous and subsequent Leica rangefinder models, mainly to incorporate through the lens metering for the first time. But the Leica CL uses the same

The Leica CL with 40mm f/2 Summicron-C fitted and its own 90mm f/4 Elmar-C.

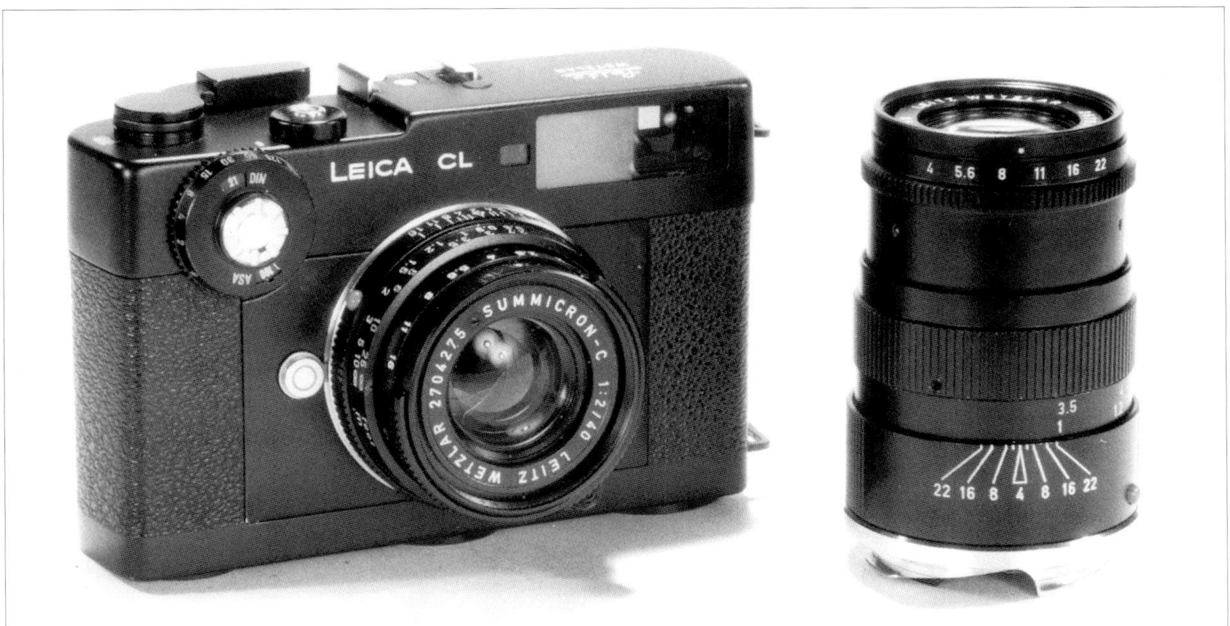

metering system and packs it into a body that measures only 12 x 7.5 x 3 cm.

One way in which the body was made smaller was by changing the position of the shutter mechanism, resulting in a focal plane shutter that runs vertically, rather horizontally, as is the case with previous Leica cameras.

The meter is a CdS type with the cell on a pivoting arm that swings up in front of the film plane as the film is wound and drops back again immediately before the shutter fires. Readings can be taken only when the film is wound and the meter is activated only when the wind lever is in its stand off position.

In this way, the reading is taken directly through the lens, the correct exposure set by adjusting shutter speeds and apertures until a needle in the viewfinder settles in a central spot, indicated by a cut-out in the bright frame around its edge. Shutter speeds, which are set on a large dial on the front of the camera, are also indicated in the viewfinder by a needle that moves behind a scale across the top of the viewfinder. They run from 1/2 second to 1/1000 second plus 'B'.

Two lenses were designed and made specially for this model. The standard lens is a 40mm f/2 Summicron-C; the second special is a 90mm f/4 Elmar-C, each of which has its own collapsible rubber lens hood. Bright frames in the viewfinder indicate fields of view for the lenses. With the standard lens in place, two frames are evident, for 40mm and 50mm focal lengths. With the standard exchanged for the 90mm medium tele lens, the viewfinder frames change to 40mm and 90mm.

Although the camera body was made in Japan, the lenses were made in Germany using special optical glass newly developed to give quality comparable with other M series lenses, but in a much more compact size. Since it uses the standard M-mount, the camera can also take almost every other Leica M-fit lens. The exceptions are some of the extra wide angle lenses from 21mm down and certain 28mm Elmarit lenses (those with serial numbers below 2,314,920). The design of these lenses involves optics that protrude back into the camera body and will fowl the metering arm on the CL. The lenses are coupled to a rangefinder built into the viewfinder.

Since the camera body is so small, the base of the coincident image rangefinder is only 32mm, smaller than that on a normal size M camera, but perfectly adequate for accurate focusing.

The result is a camera that is not only smaller than any other Leica, but one which, in its time, was considerably less expensive as well. It made an ideal introduction to Leica M cameras for the photographer on a budget, whilst serving as an ideal second body for those already within the fold. When Leitz decided to withdraw the camera in 1977, just four years after its introduction, there was a lot of disappointment among Leica photographers. But its withdrawal by the Germans wasn't the end of the story.

During its life as the CL, the camera had also been marketed in Japan under the name of the Leica Minolta CL, and this continued to be sold for a while after the demise of the German version. This camera too had its own lenses of similar focal lengths to those made for the original CL. The 40mm, however, was made by Minolta with their trade name Rokkor on it. There was also a 90mm Rokkor, but this was actually a German lens, supplied by Leica to Minolta, who put their own branding on it.

It seems there was talk of producing a Mark II version of the CL after the withdrawal of the original model, but in the end Leica decided against it, turning its energies towards producing a new M-series camera. The rather bulky M5 had never won the admiration of Leica fans the way previous M cameras had and it was clear that a new version needed to be worked out. The M6, sporting again the trimmer dimensions of previous M cameras despite the inclusion of TTL metering, finally appeared in 1984 and was a huge success.

Meanwhile, back in 1980, Minolta carried on the CL tradition and introduced their own version, which they called the Minolta CLE.

The Minolta CLE is quite probably every-

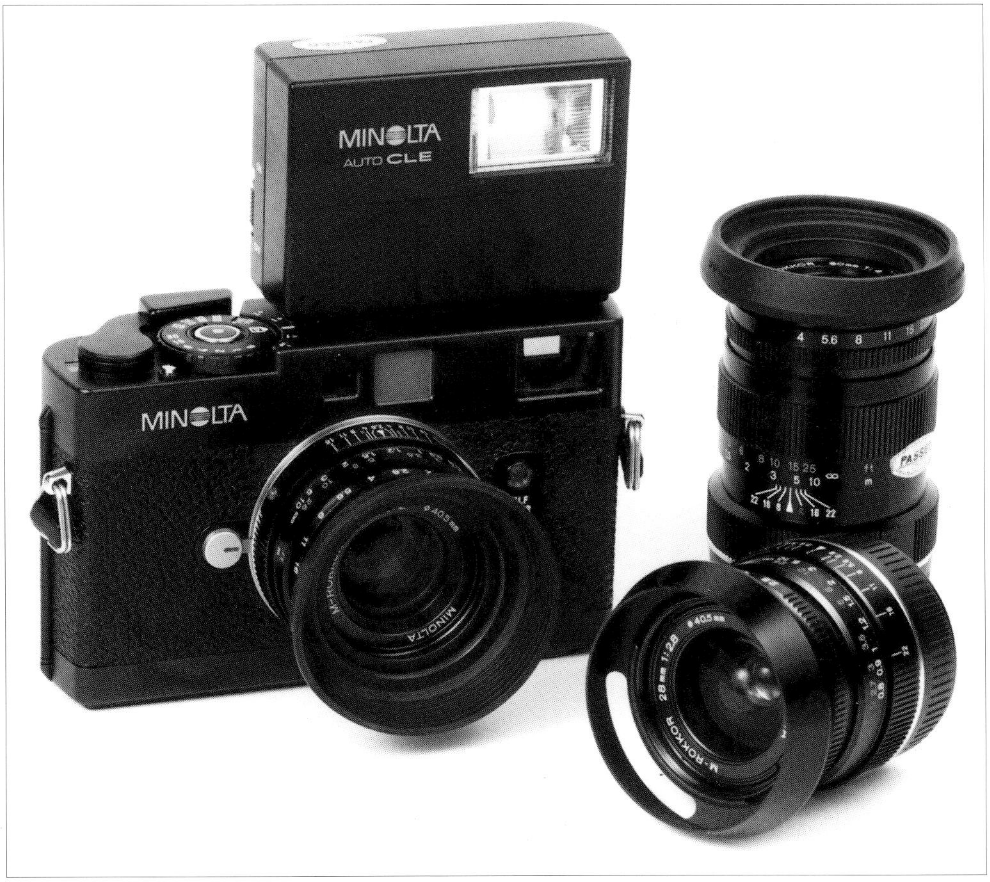

The Minolta CLE that continued the Leica CL tradition.

thing that a Leica CL Mark II would have been. It's the same shape and size, but has a few important differences.

First, there are the lenses. These are now real Rokkors, made by Minolta, though in the 40mm and 90mm focal lengths and very similar optically to their German cousins. At the same time, Minolta added a 28mm f/2.8 Rokkor, made to the same high standards. The mount is still the Leica M type, so most Leica lenses can be fitted to the Minolta CLE, though anyone who tries should take care. The problem with protruding rear elements of super-wide lenses can still cause problems and, in some cases, the rangefinder coupling isn't exactly right; the CLE uses a slightly modified version of the original CL rangefinder.

The other big difference between the CL and the CLE is the metering. The CLE can be used manually like the CL, but adds the advantage of aperture priority automation. The metering system is different too. In place of the pivoting arm that raises to measure exposure, there is a cell in the base of the camera that measures light reflected from a pattern on the shutter curtains or from the film itself.

In the 1970s and 1980s, the Leica CL and the Minolta CLE were revolutionary cameras. Today, they are still lovely cameras to use, as well as being extremely interesting collectors' items.

Exakta RTL1000

The Exakta RTL 1000 is an interesting collector's item because it is something of a hybrid. It was made in 1970, by which time Ihagee, the original manufacturers of Exakta, had been absorbed into VEB Pentacon in Dresden, the company that made Praktica cameras and, in truth, the camera is more Praktica than Exakta. Consequently, the collector who is a purist as far as the Exakta name is concerned can be forgiven for dismissing the RTL 1000

The Exakta RTL 1000, looking more like a 1960s Praktica.

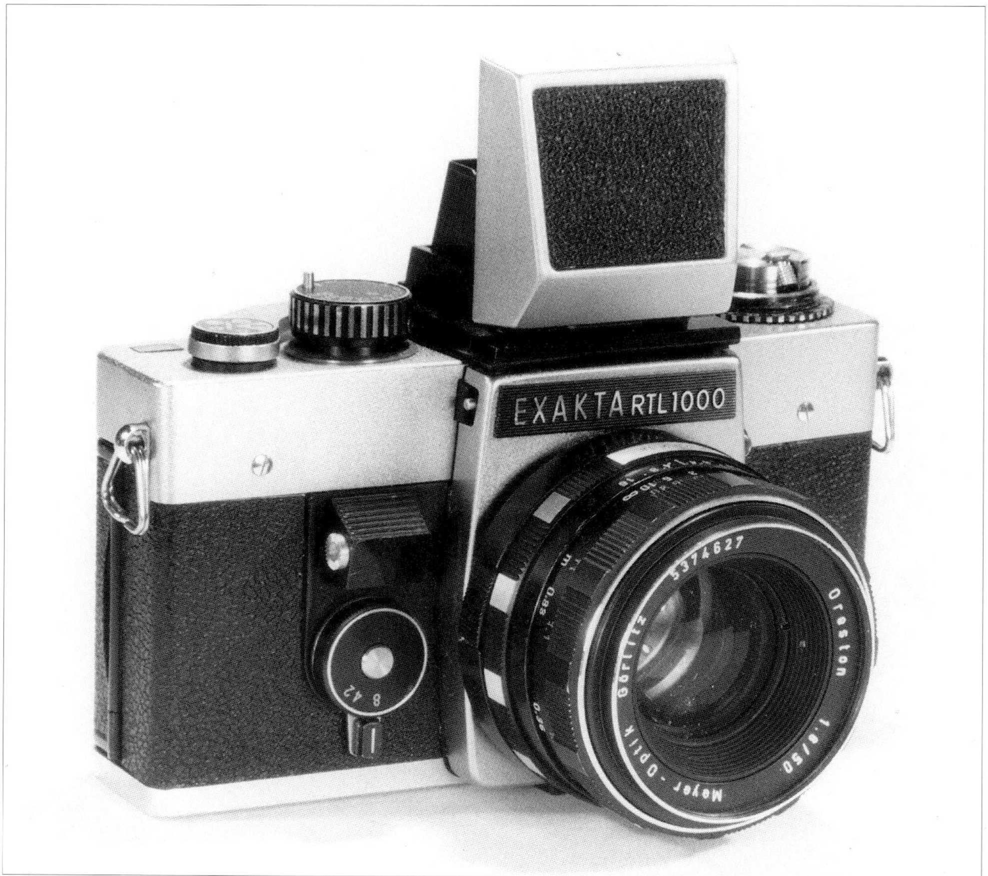

as something unworthy of consideration. Yet, in many ways, it's the camera's somewhat suspect parentage that actually makes it so interesting.

Right up until the launch of the RTL 1000 the shape of Exakta 35mm single lens reflexes still owed a lot to the original Exakta SLR launched way back in 1933 for 127 film and the 1936 Kine Exakta that was a 35mm version. They all had a similar body style, incorporating tapered ends that sloped away from the lens.

But the Pentacon-made camera is a slightly altered and relaunched version of the Praktica VCL - and Prakticas of that time were a lot squarer in shape. The result is a camera that looks like a Praktica of the late 1960s, but which still has a few original Exakta tricks up its sleeve.

Speeds of two, four and eight seconds were added to the Praktica specification, but their method of operation echoed the way Exaktas of old handled slow speeds: by setting the shutter to 'B' and adjusting the speeds on a separate dial on the front of the camera.

The RTL 1000 retains the Praktica's shutter release position, which was traditionally placed on the front of the camera, beside the lens, ready for the index finger of the right hand. But it adds Exakta's equally traditional left-handed shutter release on the opposite side of the lens as well, which echoes something of Exakta's history.

Right from the start, Exakta SLRs had left-handed shutter releases, situated on the front of the body beside the lens. Then, in 1954, with the launch of the Exakta Varex VX, Ihagee used this shutter release for a dual purpose. The lenses were equipped with plungers to close the aperture from its widest setting, used for focusing, down to the preselected stop needed for exposure. With the lens bayonetted into position, the plunger fell directly above the left-handed shutter release. So as the

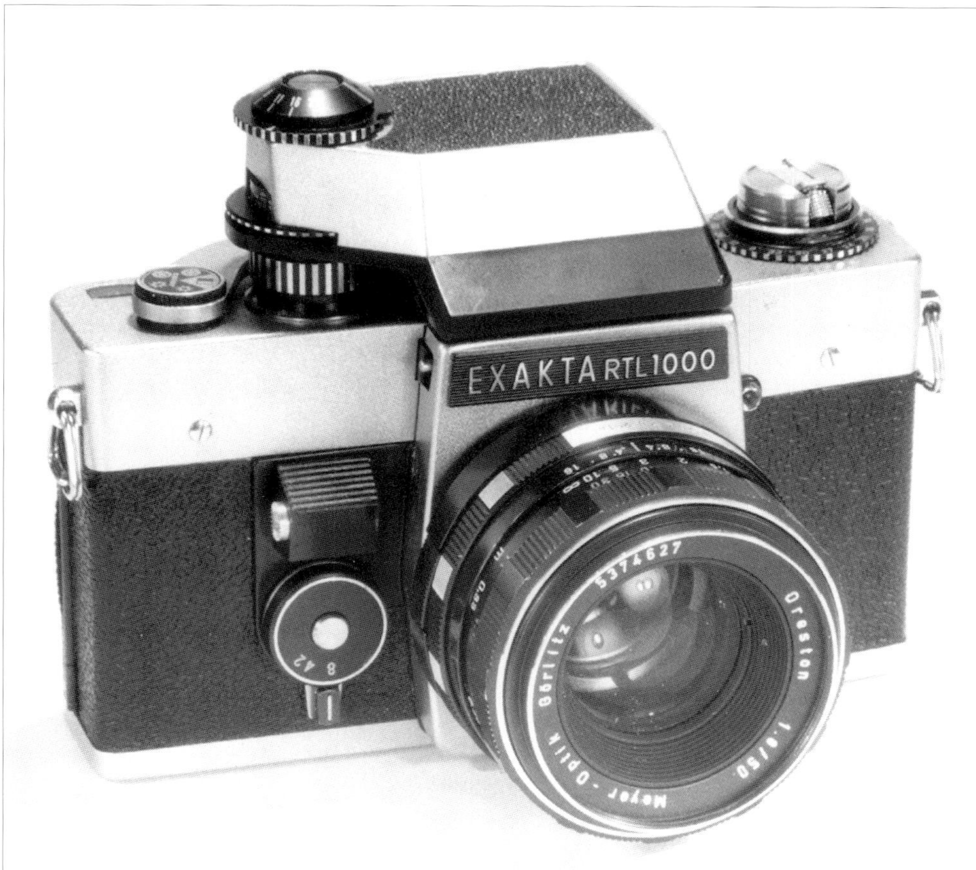

The RTL 1000 with its metered prism viewfinder in place.

plunger was pressed, the lens aperture first closed down to its preselected aperture, after which the plunger continued its stroke to release the shutter.

However, each of the two shutter releases on the RTL 1000 also activates a pin that pops out from the base of the body mount to link with the mechanism on newer Praktica-type lenses and so automatically close down the aperture. In this way, the camera allows the use of both the older Exakta Varex lenses and the newer Praktica-style lenses on the same body, providing automatic aperture preselection whichever lens is in place.

A new range of interchangeable focusing screens was launched with the camera, plus a range of viewfinders and, as a collector, it's worth looking for the camera, complete with its metered prism for eye level viewing, coupled with through the lens metering. Clicking the finder into position links its mechanism directly with the shutter speed control, which turns a similar dial on the top of the metering head as speeds are adjusted on the camera body. Against this dial a ring, engraved with aperture settings, is turned until a needle lines up with a circle in the viewfinder, thus indicating the appropriate aperture/shutter speed combination for correct exposure.

Early models of the RTL 1000 have the word 'Exakta' above the lens, later models substituted this for 'RTL1000' when the original owners of the Exakta name took legal action and Pentacon gave up using it. Apart from the name change, the cameras are identical.

Compact Stars of the Seventies

When a camera company launches a camera whose style is different from anything else on the current market, has not been seen before and won't be seen again, then what else can it be but a collector's item?

This was the time when autofocus was beginning to take off in compact cameras and, in fact, Olympus did show a small autofocus camera, behind glass, at Photokina in 1978. In style, it resembled a 35mm compact of the early 1970s, but it never went beyond the prototype stage. Instead, Olympus launched the XA in 1979.

The great - or rather, the small - thing about the Olympus XA is its size. For a full frame 35mm camera, it is remarkable for its time in measuring only 10 x 6 x 3 cm, comparing only with the Minox 35EL and Ricoh FF-1, both of which use a drop down bed that hides a pop-out lens.

The XA, on the other hand, has a simple sliding lens cover, making it just that little bit more compact. It's an aperture priority camera with a 35mm f/2.8 lens that closes down to f/22. The electronic shutter automatically adjusts itself with speeds from 1/500 second down to a full 10 seconds and focusing goes down to 0.85 metres. In the absence of autofocus, it has a coincident-image rangefinder in the viewfinder, activated by a focusing lever that rotates just below the lens. Other features include self timer, battery check and backlight control that adds 1.5 stops to the automatic setting. The camera has its own miniature flashgun, the A11, which fits to the side and couples with the camera's electronics.

This Olympus XA was the first of a range of

The original Olympus XA and the XA2 with its flashgun attached.

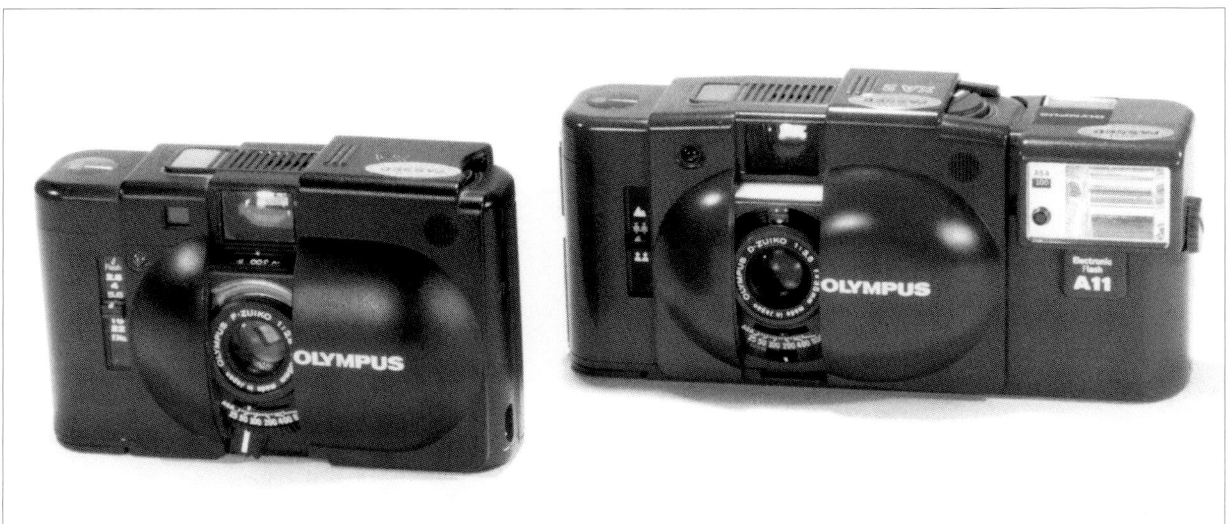

XA cameras, with different degrees of automation, all of which are rapidly becoming collectable.

XA1

The XA1 follows the same neat design as the original XA, but sliding back the lens cover reveals a Selenium type meter cell surrounding the lens, echoing a style used by Olympus in the Trip and Pen cameras. Film speeds are from ISO 100 to ISO 400 and there's a low-light warning in the viewfinder. The lens is a fixed focus f/4 D-Zuiko with automation programmed from 1/30 second at f/4 to 1/250 second at f/22. Flash is provided by the A9M flashgun, which fits to the side of the camera.

XA2

Sitting neatly between the very basic XA1 and the sophisticated XA, is the Olympus XA2. This too has programmed automation, more versatile than the XA1, but still not up to the standards of the original XA.

Film speeds can be set between ISO 25 and ISO 800, and the f/3.5 D-Zuiko lens can be focused, but only in three settings, designated by symbols that show mountains, full-length groups and head and shoulders groups. The XA2 takes the A11 flashgun, used with the original XA. It too has a low-light warning in the viewfinder and you'll find it in red as well as the original black.

XA3

DX coding comes to the XA range with the XA3, but manual film speed setting is also possible from ISO 25 to ISO 1600 for non-DX coded films. The lens is an f/3.5 and is focused by three zone symbols, as with the XA2. The camera features an easy film loading system, not seen before in the XA range and programmed exposure runs from 2 seconds at f/3.5 to 1/750 second at f/14. Flash is fitted in the same way as the other XAs.

XA4

The XA4 is unlike any of the other XA cameras in that it has a 28mm wideangle lens. Automation is programmed and film speed setting is by DX coding. Easy film loading is incorporated. The XA4 focuses closer than any of the other XAs, at O.3 metres and, to check close distances, the camera has a carrying strap that doubles as a focusing gauge, giving measurements of 0.3 metres and 1.7 metres. Parallax problems at close distances are solved by marks in the viewfinder for O.3 metre and 0.5 metre distances. Flash can be added in the same way as all the XAs.

The End of an Era

THE 1970s and early 1980s marked the end of an era for the 35mm single lens reflex. It was a time when the traditional shape of the SLR as it had been known almost since its inception, changed for ever. Once the changes began, they took off fast and, within a few years, 35mm SLRs moved into a new ergonomic era of very different shapes and designs in which mechanics gave way to electronics, metal bodies died and plastics reigned supreme. Even in the 1970s, metal was beginning to disappear from SLR camera bodies, chiefly around the top plate and pentaprism, although most manufacturers in this era did keep tradition alive by using plastic and polycarbonate that at least looked like metal.

Yet despite appearing old fashioned by today's standards, many cameras from this time offered new leaps in technology and innovations that pointed the way forward for the next generation of cameras, and so landmarks were forged which today have become collectors' items.

By the 1970s, the 35mm SLR market had become dominated by the Japanese and there was a select group of manufacturers that came to be known as the Big Five: Canon, Minolta, Nikon, Olympus and Pentax. This didn't necessarily mean that their cameras were better than the others; indeed, many of the smaller companies, like Ricoh and Konica to name but two, came up with some truly innovative ideas and designs during this decade, the like of which had never been seen before, or since.

So why did the Big Five prosper and why did the others fall by the wayside? The answer can be found in one word: marketing. Canon, Minolta, Nikon, Olympus and Pentax all had the power and the budgets to promote their equipment in ways that the lesser companies couldn't compete with.

So each of the Big Five produced a range of cameras which, today, are becoming of interest to collectors. But don't overlook those other, smaller camera manufacturers who were also producing 35mm SLRs at the same time. Despite the fact that their names tend to be much less associated with SLRs today, they did produce some very interesting cameras in the days before the traditional shape of the 35mm SLR came to an end.

Here's a selection that's worth a look.

Canon AE-1

Arriving on the market in 1976, the Canon AE-1 was the first 35mm SLR with a central processing unit - a computer chip that controlled all its functions.

The AE-1 looks like a traditional metal-made camera, but in fact the body is one of those that mixes metal and polycarbonates to still give the impression of a traditional, old-style SLR.

The camera uses a bayonet fit lens in the FD mount that first appeared on the Canon FTb in 1971 and went out with the Canon T90 in 1986. Before 1971, Canon SLRs used the FL mount whose lenses can still be fitted to the

AE-1, but which only work in the stopped down metering mode that was the norm when they were introduced. With FD lenses, metering can be carried out at full aperture. The early FD lenses, used on the AE-1, however, differ from other contemporary bayonet mount lenses in the way they fit to the body: the lens is placed in position, then a collar rotated at its rear, so the lens itself does not turn, reducing the risk of wear as the lens brushes against the body mount. The more traditional method of bayoneting arrived from Canon a few years later, but still with the FD mount.

The Canon AE-1 is a shutter priority SLR with match needle metering. With the lens aperture scale set to 'A', a shutter speed is selected and the camera automatically selects and sets the appropriate aperture, indicated by a needle in the viewfinder swinging across a scale. Taking the lens off its 'A' setting allows it to be used manually, with the needle in the viewfinder still indicating the aperture that now needs to be set by hand.

Shutter priority was unusual at this time since, in the early days of electronic automation, it was easier to build a camera that automatically adjusted its electronic shutter than to design one that had to mechanically close down an aperture. Most other single mode cameras of this time, therefore, used aperture priority.

The AE-1 spawned a number of variations which included the AT-1, for manual exposure only; the AV-1, for aperture priority and manual; and the AL-1, with a quick focus system in the viewfinder. This one uses two red LED arrows to show which way the lens needs to be turned to attain correct focus. When focus is spot on, a green LED lights up between them.

In 1981, the AE-1 was relaunched as the AE-1 Program, which added programmed exposure control and replaced the swinging meter needle with a scale of LEDs that lit up to indicate the appropriate aperture.

The culmination of Canon's A-series of cameras came with the A1 in 1979, which offers shutter priority, aperture priority, manual, programmed and stopped down metering modes.

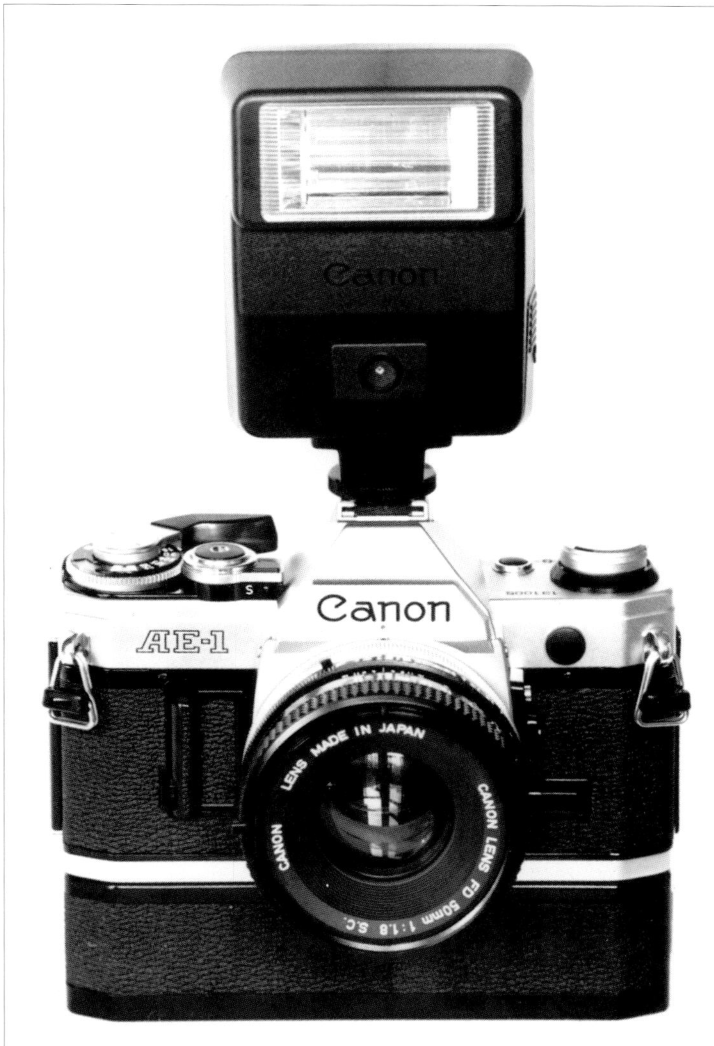

The Canon AE-1 was the first 35mm SLR with a central processing unit.

Minolta XD-7

Canon's A1 wasn't the first multi-mode SLR. That distinction goes to the Minolta XD-7, which is collectable because it was the first SLR to offer shutter priority, aperture priority and manual modes, all in the same camera.

As each mode is selected, using a switch around the shutter speed dial, the viewfinder information changes. In manual, the viewfinder displays the selected shutter speed and a recommended aperture. In aperture priority, the selected aperture is displayed in a corner of the finder and a red LED glows

The Minolta XD-7 was the first dual mode SLR.

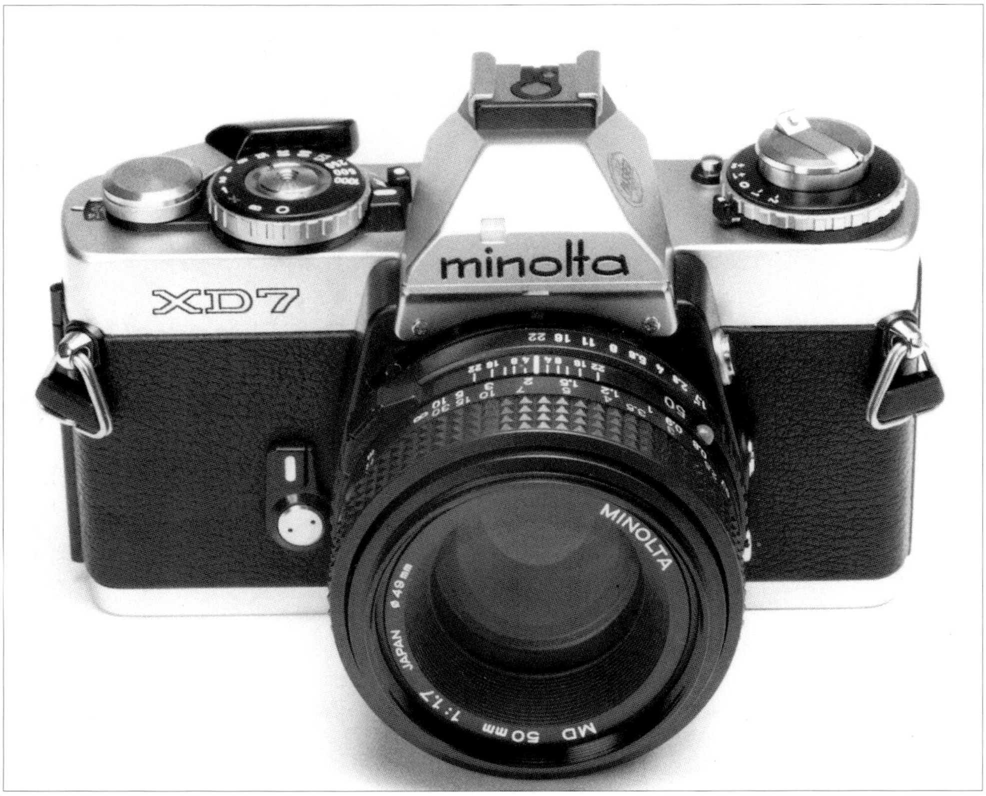

The Nikon EM was the company's first camera for the true amateur.

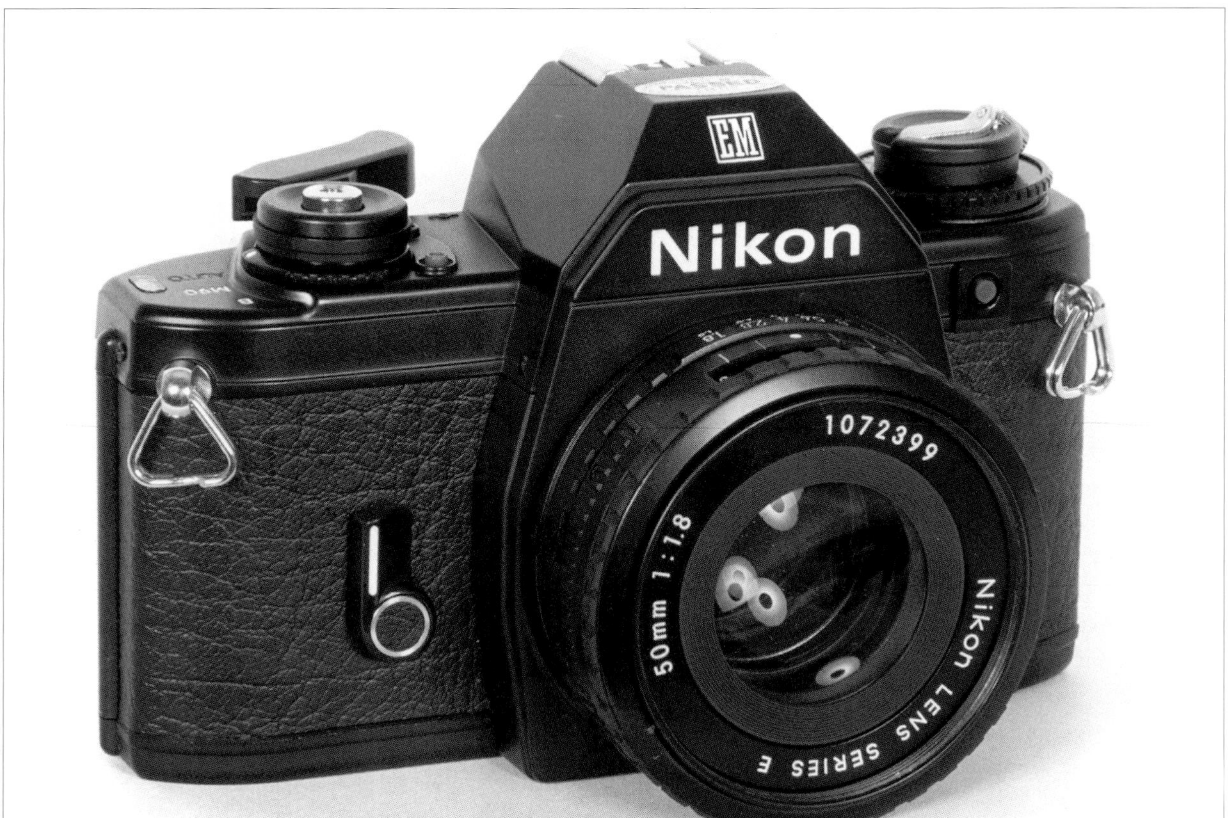

against the selected shutter speed on a scale to the right of the finder. Set the control to shutter priority and the speed scale changes to an aperture scale with the LED showing the selected f-stop.

The Minolta uses MD mount lenses, but it's possible to use older Minolta lenses too, right back to the first Minolta mount seen on the SR-2 in 1958. They can even be used with the aperture priority automation because the XD-7's meter uses a fast reacting silicon cell that takes its operational reading as the exposure is initiated and with the lens closed down to its working aperture.

All of which was pretty advanced for 1978.

Nikon EM

The reason why the Nikon EM is collectable is because it represented a radical departure for Nikon. Until then, the company's cameras had been aimed squarely at the professional or advanced amateur market. The EM, on the other hand was offered at a budget price for amateur photographers.

The camera, which was launched in 1979, accepts the range of prestigious Nikkor AI (standing for Automatic Indexing) lenses, but to keep the price down even more, it also accepts what was then a new range of low-price Nikon 'E' lenses.

The camera is an aperture priority model, but there is no shutter speed setting control and it does not have a manual mode as such. What it does have, however, is a 1/90 second mechanical shutter speed for flash, which allows a certain amount of manual exposure control. Other than that, there is only a 'B' setting and an auto setting to select. The rest is electronic and automatic.

The only other manual override is an exposure compensation feature, but just in case the camera should automatically set a shutter speed that is too slow for hand holding, an electronic signal beeps to warn of possible camera shake as soon as shutter speeds drop below 1/30 second.

Olympus OM-1

In the 1970s, there was a sudden craze among camera manufacturers for making much smaller single lens reflexes. The camera that started it all was the Olympus OM-1... although that wasn't the name Olympus originally wanted to call it.

The camera was launched in 1972 as the Olympus M-1 and straight away ran into problems, since Leica had originally registered the name as a trade mark. Olympus covered up their mistake on some of the very early models by adding a small logo panel to the front of the body. By the time the camera was into full production, however, the name had been changed to the Olympus OM-1, first of the compact SLRs.

But the OM-1 is notable for more than its trim dimensions. It's the basis for a true SLR system that, at the time of its launch, included two fisheyes, four super-wideangles, four normal wideangles, three standards, a mid-tele zoom, nine telephotos, four macros and a shift lens. It also allowed focusing screens to be interchanged and, soon after its launch, an OM-1md version arrived that accepted a motor drive that ran at five frames a second.

What was more, the motor drive operated at this fast speed without the need to lock up the mirror - and that was unheard of in 1972. It was something that tended to jam up some lenses made by independent manufacturers because they couldn't take the rate with which the aperture had to be continually opened and stopped down during exposure at such a speed.

Today, the Olympus OM-1 is collectable as the first of the compact SLRs. But if you find one with that logo panel stating 'Olympus Tokyo' just in front of the on/off switch, then you might just discover the original M-1 logo behind it - and then you've got a real collector's item.

Pentax ME Super

Remember this was the decade when manufacturers were beginning to test the water with

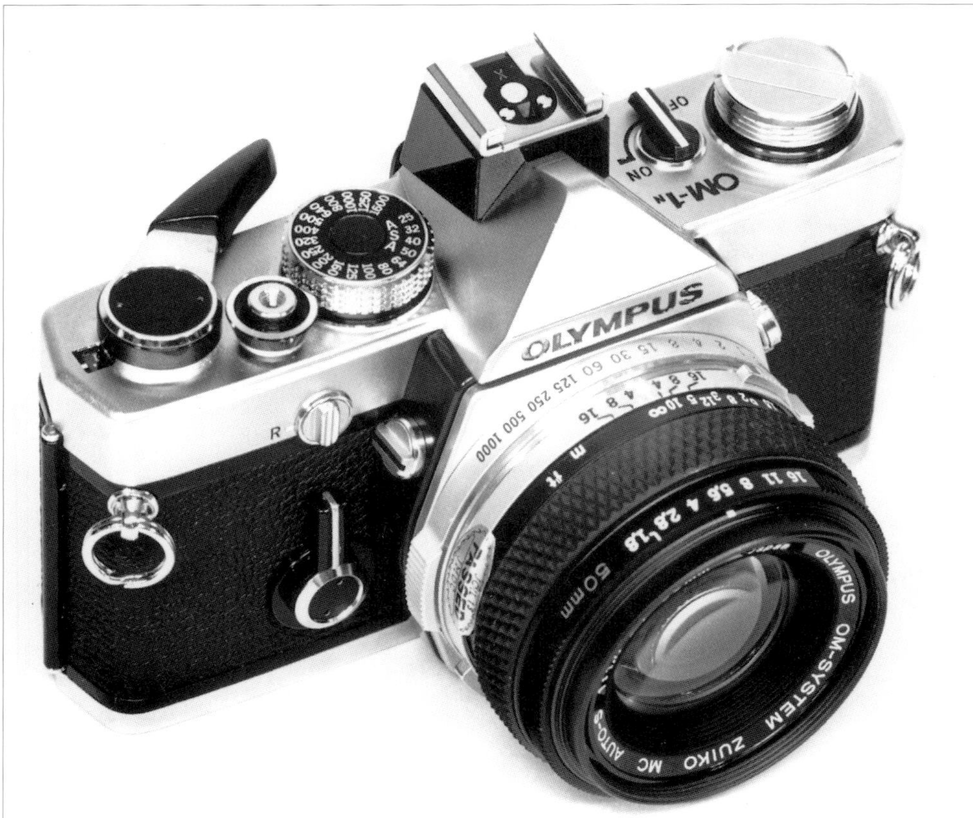

The Olympus OM-1: first of the compact SLRs.

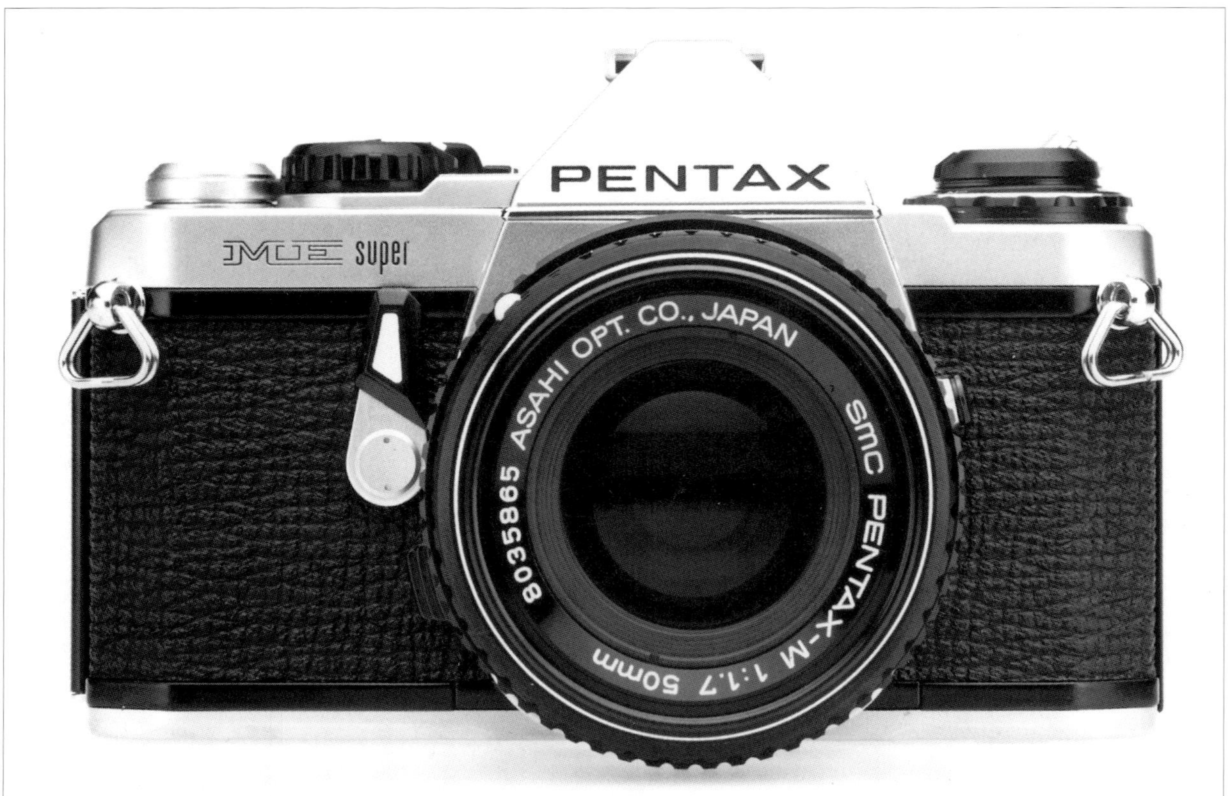

The Pentax ME-Super was unusual in its day for using electronic controls for shutter speeds.

simple forms of electronic control, replacing the more traditional knobs and dials - and that's what makes the ME-Super collectable.

The camera was an upgrade of the Pentax ME, launched in 1976 as one of the then popular range of compact SLRs. The original ME was a fully automatic camera, using aperture priority, with no shutter speed control and no way to use it manually. The ME-Super improved on that by adding manual control of the shutter, but not by the traditional knob or dial. In its place, the ME-Super has two small black buttons set into the top plate. Pressing one moves the shutter speeds progressively higher; the other takes them back down the scale, setting progressively slower speeds.

In use, the photographer holds the camera to the eye and presses one or either of the buttons, watching a display in the viewfinder as the speeds climb or fall. The ME-Super, like the original model, also has aperture priority control.

Konica FS-1

Photokina in 1978 saw the launch of the first SLR with a built-in electric motor drive. It was the Konica FS-1 and, as well as offering automatic film wind as each exposure was made, the FS-1 used its in-built motor to give automatic film load.

To load the FS-1, a standard 35mm cassette is slotted into the back, the film tab extended slightly and the back closed. The built-in micromotor then automatically threads the film and advances it to the first frame.

Konica was, in fact, the company that produced the first automatic SLR in the Konica

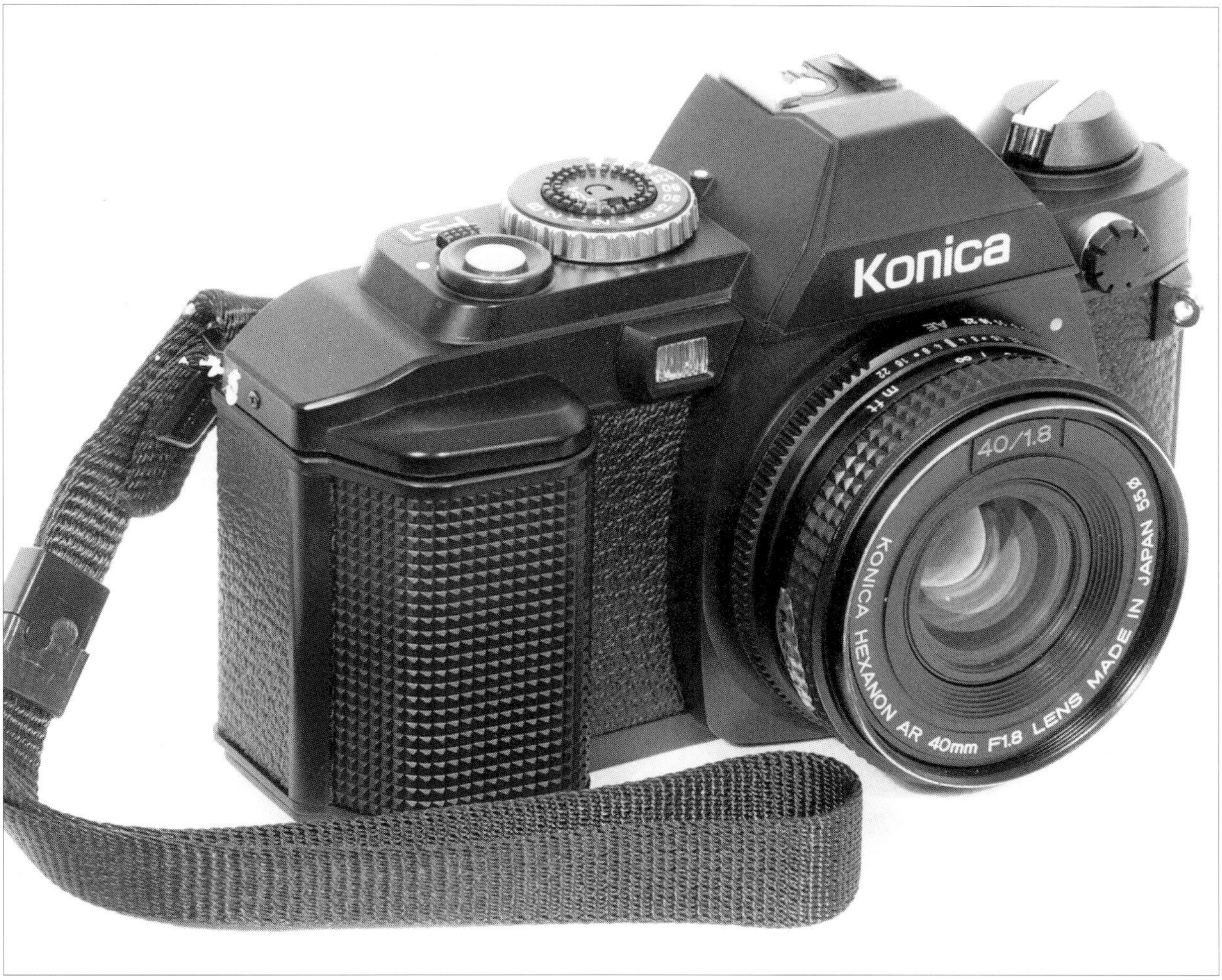

The Konica FS-1 was the first 35mm SLR with a built-in electric motor drive.

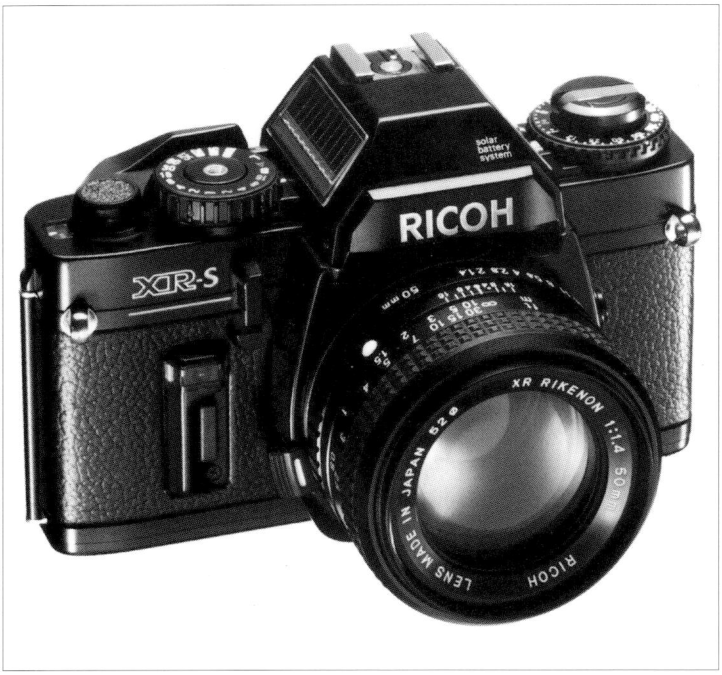

The Ricoh XRS uses solar panels to charge an internal battery.

Autoreflex of 1968. Unlike most of those that followed from other makers, it used shutter priority automatic, and that was still the case by the time the FS-1 was launched a decade later. It was also unusual at that time in having a totally electronic shutter that did away with mechanical gear trains and used, instead, twin micro solenoids to activate the first and second curtains. It's a Copal shutter that travels vertically, rather than horizontally.

Ricoh XRS

In the early 1980s Ricoh came up with the first (and possibly the last) camera to use solar panels in place of batteries. The camera in question was the Ricoh XRS which, apart from those panels, had all the features of a previous model called the XR-7.

The solar panels are situated on either side of the pentaprism and they are used, not as a direct source for the camera's electronics, but to charge an internal battery which was reckoned to function even in dim light for up to five years.

The camera is an aperture priority SLR with manual override.

Hanimex RF35d

Today, no self respecting SLR is without a built-in flashgun, but in the early 1980s, no maker even considered the idea - no one, that is, except Hanimex.

The Hanimex RF35d looks a little like a 35mm compact camera of the time with a pentaprism added, complete with a small electronic flashgun in exactly the place you'd expect to find it on a compact.

The camera is a manual model with a standard, non-interchangeable 45mm lens whose apertures run from f/16 to only f/2.8, relatively small for an SLR of the day.

So really, the RF35d is little more than a compact with a reflex viewing system, but the addition of a built-in flash for the first time in an SLR makes it a collector's item today.

Early Autofocus

The 1980s was the decade when autofocus arrived with a vengeance, but its beginnings were in the 1970s with the introduction, by Honeywell, of a module, made available to a number of different camera manufacturers and designed to automatically control the focus of a lens. The rush was immediately on to produce an autofocus camera and the company that got there first was Konica - so that's the one to collect.

Konica C35AF

At the UK press conference that launched the Konica C35AF, the distributors came up with an ingenious method of demonstrating its capabilities. In a darkened room, they placed a focusing chart within the film plane of the camera, then mounted the whole thing on the front of a projector, so the camera lens was now acting as the projector lens. A young lady

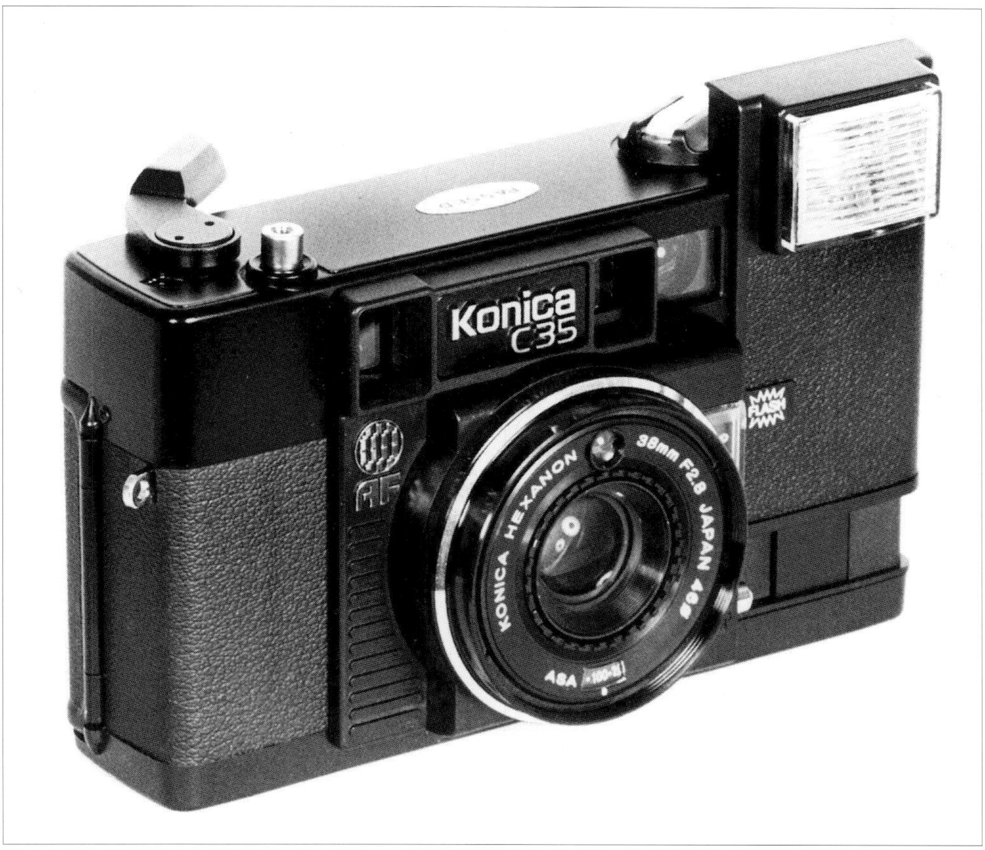

The Konica C35AF was the first autofocus compact.

dressed as a Japanese geisha then stood at one end of the room, holding a small white screen on which the camera automatically focused the chart.

She took a few steps forward and, of course, the image went out of focus. But as the camera's release was pressed, the image automatically snapped back into focus. They repeated the action all the way down the room and, all the way, the camera kept automatically readjusting the focus. The Honeywell module that made all this possible works like this.

The camera has two small windows beside the viewfinder and either side of the lens. One contains a fixed mirror, the other a pivoting mirror, rather like a traditional, old-fashioned manual rangefinder. Between them, however, is a prism that reflects light down to an electronic focus detector which, in turn, controls a tiny sliding lever that interacts with the movement of the lens. Winding the film racks the lens out to just beyond its normal closest focusing distance of 1.1 metres. Then, as the shutter is released, a spring pulls the lens backwards towards its infinity setting. At the same time, the windows of the electronic rangefinder look at the subject, which the photographer has positioned by means of a small bright frame in the centre of the viewfinder. The pivoting mirror begins to turn, reflecting its image into the prism, along with a secondary image from the fixed mirror. The electronics recognise when the two images coincide as a point when the image contrast is suddenly increased. At that point, a solenoid is activated which shoots out a tiny sliding lever that stops the lens in its tracks. Only then does the shutter release to take the picture. It all happens in about 80 milliseconds.

Other than its then revolutionary autofocusing mechanism, the C35AF is a fairly standard 35mm compact of its time: it features automatic programmed exposure which is also being measured and set while the autofocus mechanism is in action, shutter speeds from 1/60 - 1/250 second, 38mm f/2.8 lens, built-in flash and manual film wind.

The only problem with the C35AF was that,

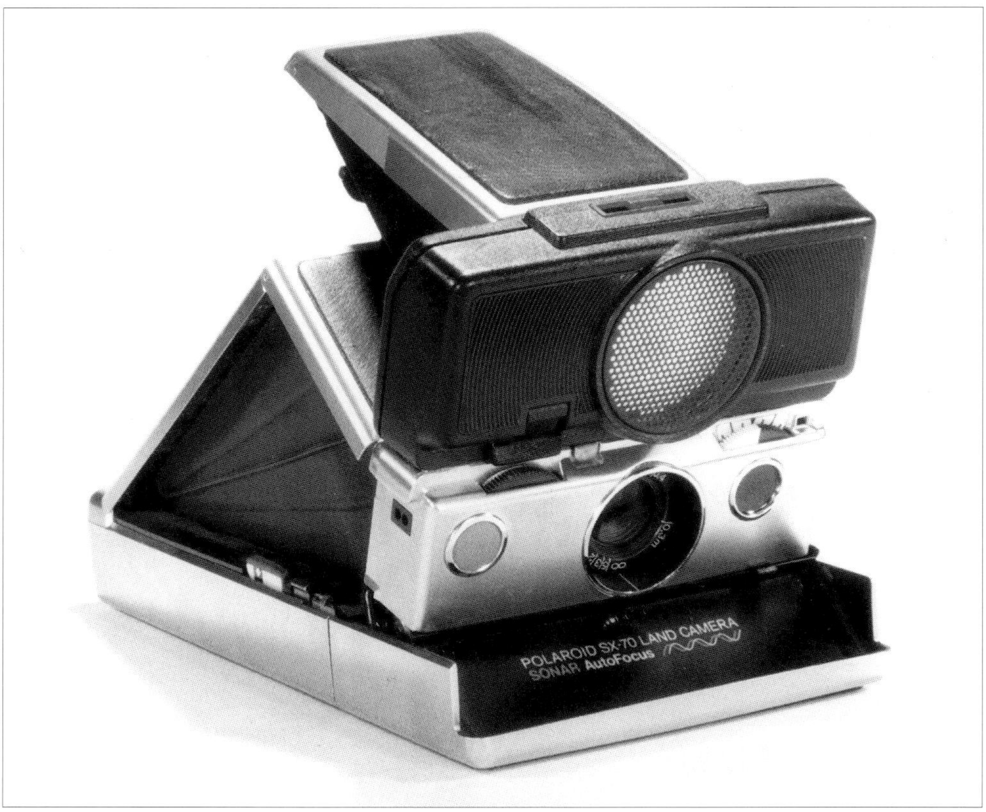

Polaroid's SX-70 Sonar Autofocus camera was the first autofocus SLR.

maybe in the rush to get the camera out ahead of competitors, the makers did not incorporate a focus lock, so sharp focus can only be attained when the main subject is in the dead centre of the picture area.

The next autofocus camera and the first with a focus lock arrived the following year. It was made by Yashica who called it simply the Yashica Auto Focus.

SX-70 Sonar Autofocus

The first autofocus single lens reflex came from a surprising direction. It wasn't made by any of the then top names in Japanese SLR manufacture, but by Polaroid.

The camera is the SX-70 Sonar Autofocus that was launched in 1978. It's an update of the original SX-70, first seen in 1972 (see page 134), but with the addition of a unit that emits patterned delays of sound waves, inaudible to the human ear, to determine distance, based on the time taken for the beams to bounce off the subject and back to the camera's receptor. The system then used the information to focus the lens and control the correct amount of flash required to light the subject accurately. The lens focuses automatically with first pressure on the shutter button.

The SX-70 Sonar Autofocus is a slightly larger version of the original SX-70 and folds in exactly the same way.

Autofocus SLR lenses

In 1980, two lenses arrived which could be attached to a standard SLR to convert it for autofocus. One was made by Ricoh in the Pentax K-mount; the other was made by Canon in its FD mount.

The AF Rikenon 50mm f/2 appeared first, allowing the manufacturers to claim it as 'the world's first automatic focusing system for the single lens reflex camera'.

It works very much like a manual rangefinder with a sensor taking the place of the human eye. Onto this sensor are projected two images of the subject, from two rangefinder-like windows, one of which incorporates a pivoting mirror. As the lens is activated, the mirror swings so that one image on the sensor moves in relation to the other. The sensor recognises when the two coincide as a point where contrast is at its maximum, relating the information to the angle of the mirror at the point of sharp focus. That information is then turned into a command that is passed to the motor which focuses the lens.

The AF Rikenon takes the form of a fairly normal looking lens, encased in a sleeve, topped by a large box that incorporates the autofocus mechanism. It focuses automatically down to 3 ft, although closer distances down to 1.5 ft can be achieved by switching to manual. Its K-Mount was pioneered by Pentax, but also used on several other SLRs of the time, including Ricoh, Cosina and Makinon.

The Canon lens, which was launched within a few months of the Ricoh at the 1980 Photokina, is the more sophisticated of the two. It's a 35-70mm f/4 zoom, reasonably compact for its day, with the small, box-like attachment that holds the autofocus mechanism fitted to the side. It works by a system

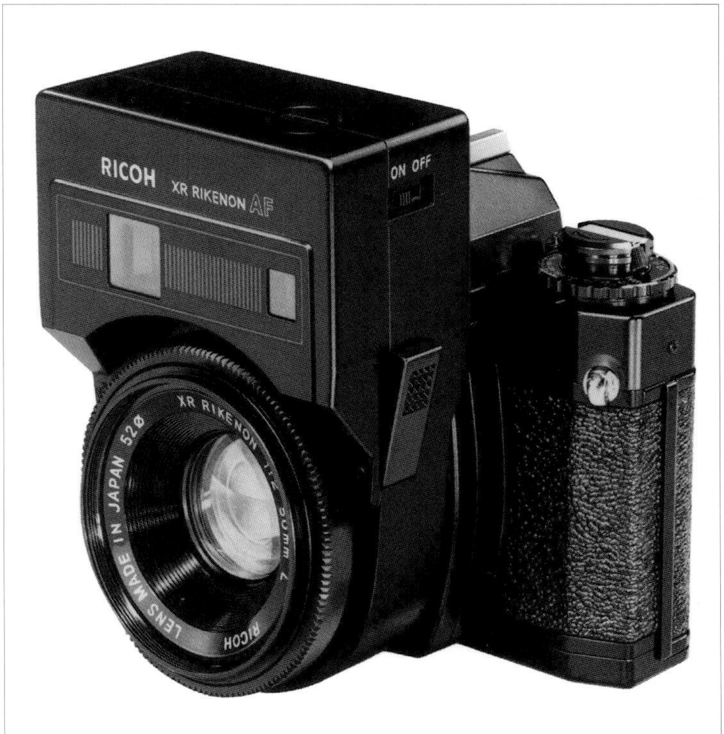

The now rare AF Rikenon autofocus lens for K-mount cameras

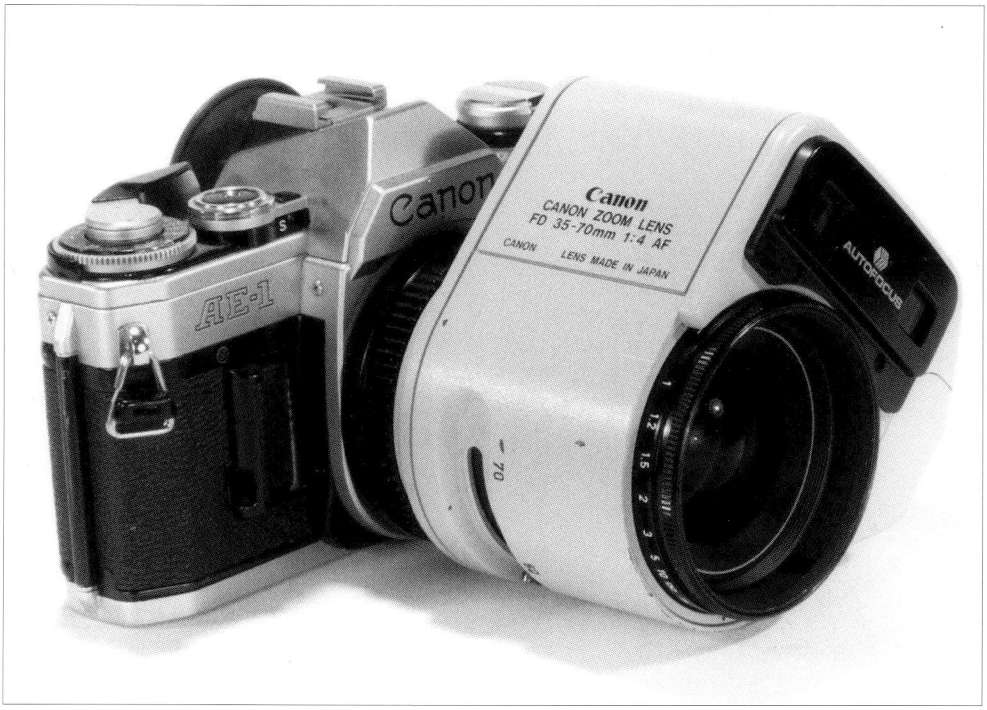

Canon's autofocus lens, attached to a Canon AE-1 converts a manual focus camera for automatic focusing.

that differs from that used in the Rikenon and which Canon called Solid State Triangulation. In this, hundreds of tiny sensors are arranged in a linear array and receive, side by side, two beams of light from the subject, by way of two windows on the front of the lens housing. One covers only the subject detail on which the autofocus spot in the viewfinder is centred. The other beam covers the entire scene, distributing close, medium and distant detail over the sensors. The centre spot image of the main subject falls onto different areas of the sensor array depending on its distance from the lens and, by comparing the separation between the two images, the system computes the angle of incidence between them and hence the distance. A motor then rotates the lens to the correct setting.

In use, all the photographer has to do is aim the camera and press a button on the side of the lens. The image comes into focus and can be checked by the rangefinder built into the camera. Removing the finger from the button then locks the focus in position, allowing the picture to be composed as desired without the focusing automatically changing again.

Neither lens was as accurate as today's autofocus and, in fact, Ricoh suggested that their lens should not be used at apertures wider than f/5.6, something that was emphasised by marking stops up to that aperture in green, wider stops in white. The idea was that, with smaller f-stops, depth of field should hide slight inaccuracies in the focus. Neither lens is too good in low light either, or with subjects that lack contrast, but the Ricoh has a slight edge over Canon in incorporating a bleeper that sounds when focus has failed. The Canon lens simply goes to infinity, whatever the distance if, for example, it is pointed at a white wall. Not too useful for a photographer of the 1980s, but an idiosyncrasy that adds charm as far as today's collector is concerned.

Canon T80

The natural progression from Canon's autofocus lens was to incorporate similar thinking into a purpose-built SLR. At this time, 35mm single lens reflexes were going through a new look, pioneered by Canon with the T50. The T80 follows that style and adds an autofocus lens as standard.

The Canon T80 has a built in microproces-

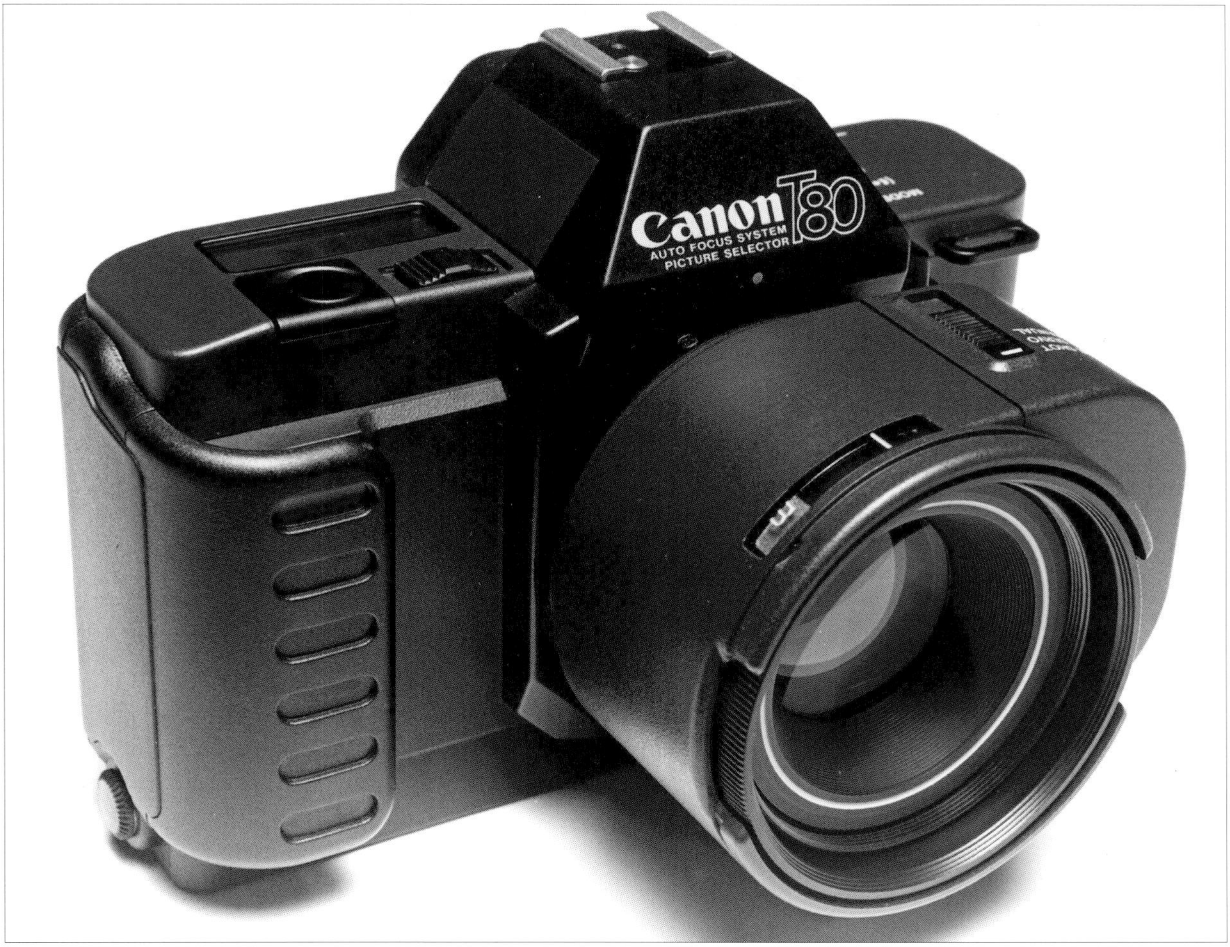

The Canon T80 was an early autofocus SLR.

sor that controls functions that include exposure and focus. In operation, as light passes through the lens, some of it is split off at the main mirror and passed down to the ranging sensor in the bottom of the mirror box. At that point, three charge coupled device line sensors detect focus sharpness and pass the information to the microprocessor. This compares the information from each sensor and, from that, computes the subject distance. Command signals are then sent out to the micromotor that adjusts the lens.

Nikon and Olympus

In 1982, two more major Japanese camera manufacturers flirted with the idea of autofocus with systems that died almost as fast as they appeared.

Nikon introduced a special version of the then current F3 and called the Nikon F3AF. It used a special interchangeable pentaprism viewfinder called the AF Finder DX-1 and provided autofocus only with specific lenses made for the job. They were the AF Nikkor 80mm f/2.8, and the AF Nikkor 200mm f/3.5 IF-ED. Each lens had built in micromotors around the barrel to adjust the focus. It made them a little more bulky than conventional lenses, but not nearly as unwieldy as the Canon and Ricoh autofocus lenses.

The special viewfinder could also be used on a standard Nikon F3 to assist manual focusing of virtually any conventional manual focus Nikon lens by means of its built in LED focus indicators.

The same year, Olympus came up with their version of an autofocus SLR, following the Canon idea with a special - and once again, rather bulky - autofocus lens to be used with

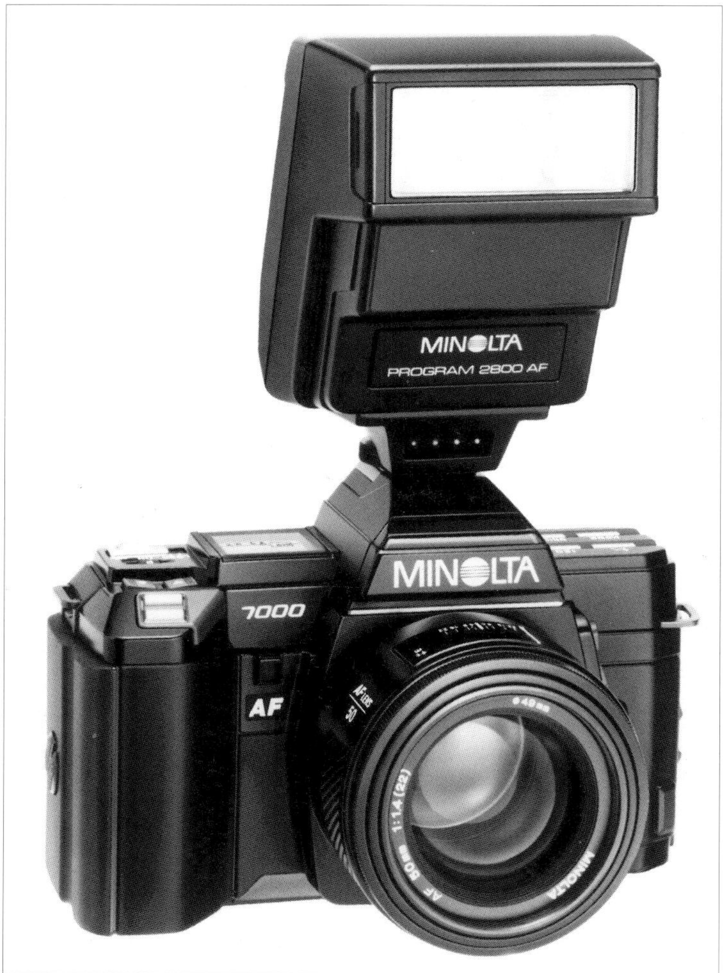

Making autofocus truly practical for the first time: the Minolta 7000.

the Olympus OM-30. The lens was a 35-70mm zoom with its autofocus mechanism built into an appendage below the lens barrel. The OM-30 could also be used to aid focusing with other Olympus OM-fit lenses, providing they had maximum apertures of f/4 or wider.

The OM-30's other claim to fame is what Olympus referred to as the world's first In-Focus Trigger system. Together with a motor drive or winder and a special adapter cord, automatic motor driven follow focus was claimed to be possible.

Minolta 7000

In 1985, 35mm single lens reflexes took a giant leap forward. This was the year that Minolta launched the 7000, the world's first body integral autofocus SLR. In other words, the mechanism that drives the focusing of the lenses is out of the lens and into the camera body. For the first time, autofocus lenses were just about the same size as manual lenses, although the camera's body was a little bulkier than some other 35mm SLRs of the time.

The Minolta 7000 was unique at that time in providing autofocus functions even in low light. It did this by utilising the camera's dedicated flash's near-infrared AF-assist feature to provide instant focus readings in conditions where it would be extremely difficult to manually focus a conventional SLR.

To quote Minolta's promotional material at the time: "This innovative system lets you shoot under virtually any and all lighting conditions - in candlelight or moonlight... in dim indoor scenes or outdoors in the evening... even in total darkness!"

Autofocus aside, the Minolta is an extremely sophisticated camera for its day, offering exposure modes that include standard programme, wide programme and tele programme. And if the photographer is confused about which of those to use, the camera has the world's first automatic multi-program selection. What that means in real terms is that the system takes data from the autofocus lenses and translates this into information that sets the most appropriate exposure mode. With a zoom lens, it also changes mode according to the focal length being used. On top of that, the camera has shutter priority, aperture priority and manual modes.

In 1985, the Minolta 7000 was about as sophisticated as it was possible for a camera to get. It marked the beginning of a new era in photography, both amateur and professional, and closed for good the days of the manual focus, manual exposure 35mm SLR.

Collecting Amateur Cine Cameras

THE interest in collecting cine equipment is on the increase. It's a branch of collecting that many collectors have shunned in the past, but the truth is that there are a lot of very interesting cine cameras around and - unlike still photography - the projectors too can be fascinating pieces of mechanical wizardry.

In many ways, collecting cine equipment today is a lot like collecting still cameras was just before the hobby took off in a big way in the early 1970s: there is not a lot of information about the subject; the cameras are harder to find; and, when you do find them, they are relatively inexpensive compared to still cameras. That last fact alone makes them worth considering and of strong interest to the collector on a medium size budget.

There are, of course, a number of early cine cameras and projectors which are way out of reach of the average collector and, indeed, there are a fair few specialist (and rich) collectors who have always been interested in this field. We're talking here about cameras such as the 35mm, wooden body, hand-cranked Prestwich Cinematographic Camera made by the Prestwich Manufacturing Company of Tottenham in 1897, which took 100-ft length films and which appeared within a year of the start of cinematography. A camera like this, which would be prized by any collector, could set you back many thousands of pounds. In fact, almost any cine camera made before the 1920s is an extremely specialised piece of equipment whose rarity is reflected in its high price as a collector's item.

For the more general collector, who wants to find an easy and relatively inexpensive inroad into this fascinating branch of collecting, a better bet is to concentrate on the amateur cine cameras and projectors which began to appear in the 1920s and continued to be made into the 1970s.

Let us pause here, then, to take a very brief look at how amateur cine equipment rose to popularity in the first half of the 20th Century.

Cine cameras have been around since the 1890s and, after 1900, a few of these were made for amateur use, notably those that used a 17.5mm film size. In 1912, the French company Pathé introduced a camera and projector for home use, which used 28mm film. But mostly the equipment of this time was all professional gear, used almost exclusively by film studios and a few brave explorers. Manufacturers experimented with many different film gauges, ranging from 10mm to 70mm, but the size that became the standard was 35mm, pioneered by Edison in America and Lumiere in France.

Then in 1923, two things happened that brought cine photography well and truly to the amateur film maker. In America, Kodak introduced a cine camera that took 16mm film and, in France, Pathé introduced one that took 9.5mm.

The introduction of 16mm was a great success. With a frame size of 9.65 x 7.21 mm, against 18 x 24 mm on 35mm film, the economies were immediately attractive to the amateur film maker. In real terms it meant that 1 ft of 16mm film lasted two and half seconds on the screen, as opposed to one second for standard 35mm; a 100 ft reel of 16mm, then, gave the same amount of film time as a 250 ft reel of 35mm. Furthermore, greater economies were made by introducing a film that could be processed as a direct positive, rather than as a negative that had to be reprinted before projection, as was the case with 35mm. With film costing £1 10s (£1.50p) for 100 ft, a seven second sequence - adequate for recording most situations - cost about 10d (4p), about the cost of shooting a film negative in a still camera of the time, developing it and making a small print.

You might see 16mm cameras of this period referred to as sub-standard models. This has nothing to do with inferiority of workmanship, but rather is a reference to the small film gauge, 35mm having been previously adopted as the 'standard' size for cine.

Pathé's introduction of a 9.5mm camera was even more cost effective. The French company had already produced a projector for the format back in 1912, in which the electricity for the lamp was generated by a dynamo connected to the hand crank that moved the film through the gate. It was introduced to project a library of films that had been reduced to the 9.5mm size from commercial cinema successes of the day. The idea was good, but it never really caught on. A little later, in 1922, the same company introduced the Pathé Baby projector, also for home projection of commercial films initially, but soon to become more popular for projecting films made by the first 9.5mm cine camera launched in 1923. Although the film was narrower in width than Kodak's 16mm, the image size of 8.3 x 6.5 mm was only marginally smaller, a feat that was achieved by placing the sprocket holes in the centre of the film, between frames, rather than at the edge, as was the case with 16mm, thus allowing the 9.5mm image to extend practically to the edge of the film.

With the popularity of amateur cine photography firmly established, Kodak went on to introduce even more economies in 1932 with the production of the first 8mm camera. The film was known as Double-8 because it was, in fact, double-sprocketed 16mm which was run through the camera one way, taken out, turned over and run through again, giving an image size of 4.37 x 3.28 mm. After processing, the film was slit down the middle and the two halves joined together. The new film was spooled in reels of 25 ft which, when processed, slit and joined, gave 50 ft with a running time, at 16 frames per second, equivalent to 100 ft of 16mm.

This was the film that became known as Standard-8, and it was the major amateur format until 1965, during which time, cameras were also made for Single-8, an 8mm film that was actually 8mm wide and run once only through the camera; and another 8mm film that was pre-loaded into cartridges.

In 1965, Kodak introduced Super 8, yet another 8mm film, this time sold pre-loaded in plastic cartridges that dropped straight into the specially made cameras and somewhat reminiscent of the company's Instamatic feature for still cameras introduced a couple of years before in 1963. Super 8 made cine photography easier for the non specialist and, with its slightly larger frame size of 5.31 x 4.01 mm made possible by smaller sprocket holes, it gave better quality. True cine enthusiasts, however, were heard to bemoan the fact that the film gate was now made of plastic and built into the disposable cartridge, a fact that they felt couldn't possibly give the same quality as a permanent metal plate built into the camera by a precision manufacturer. The cameras also became very sophisticated very quickly, adding electric motors in place of the more traditional clockwork of older cameras, sound on a magnetic stripe with a built-in microphone attached to a boom on the top of the camera, zoom lenses with extremely wide ranges and built-in auto exposure.

Concurrent with Kodak's launch of Super 8, Fuji introduced their own version, producing the same image size from a similar film but in a different design of cartridge. Of the two, the Kodak cartridge proved to be the one that other manufacturers adopted and, for a while, Super 8 reigned supreme. But it never caught the imagination of the amateur film maker in the way Standard 8 had and many cine enthusiasts, with a library of home-made films behind them on the old format, were reluctant to switch to the new one, even though dual format projectors were sold at the time. By the middle of the 1970s, amateur cine as a major hobby was beginning to die. Some blame the advent of video, but in fact good portable video cameras were still some 20 years in the future when interest in cine began to wane. Perhaps film making as a hobby died because the cameras just got too sophisticated and complicated to use. Maybe with the arrival of colour TV, film makers lost heart in ever being able to match what they saw every night in their living rooms. Or maybe it was just a hobby that had had its time. Super 8 was clever, but it didn't engender the pioneering spirit of early amateurs using 16mm, 9.5mm and Standard 8. It's those cameras, made mostly between the mid-1920s and the mid-1960s which are the most accessible and the most interesting to today's collector.

The following list of cameras and projectors is by no means a definitive one, but it should give the budding collector insight into the interesting facets of this branch of collecting, together with an idea of what is available and easily obtainable at minimum cost.

35mm EQUIPMENT

Photo Cine Sept

This is one of the few 35mm cine cameras available to the collector on a reasonable budget. Made by André Debrie of Paris in 1922, it was unusual in its day in being a 35mm movie camera that could be hand held, a fact that made it popular with newsreel photographers of the 1920s.

Loading 17 ft of 35mm film in special cassettes provided a 15 second burst of action, after which the camera had to be reloaded, an act made simple by the use of pre-loaded cassettes - or spool boxes as the makers called them - allowing daylight loading.

It is also reputed to have been used in the occasional feature film in places where a short burst of action required the use of a small, hand-held camera, rather than the much larger conventional cine cameras of the day.

Although originally sold as a short run movie camera, the Sept is actually a still camera too, and in that context it is a 35mm camera that pre-dates the Leica I, usually recognised as the first truly viable 35mm model. As a still camera, it takes around 250 pictures, 18 x 24 mm half frame size, either in a continuous sequence or one at a time, the clockwork motor winding the film automatically after each exposure. The single speed shutter provides instantaneous or time expo-

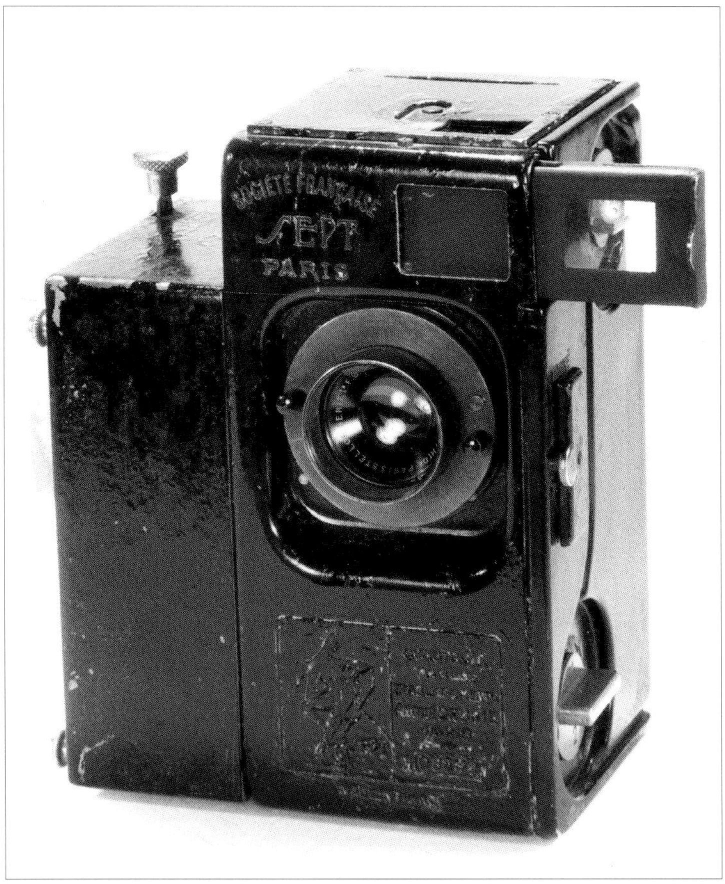

The Debrie Sept is a 35mm still and cine camera combined.

sures and it was quite possible to combine several still exposures with perhaps a 10-second burst of movie action all on the same length of film.

The camera, also known as the Debrie Sept was originally advertised as a three in one camera, because it takes snapshots, time exposures or movie sequences. But it has other functions too. With the opening of a panel at the back and the attachment of a light source, it can be used as a projector. Likewise, it can be used as an enlarger. With slots opened top and bottom, an unexposed film can be automatically fed through, alongside a developed film to expose a positive film strip. Add to all those functions the fact that it can be used in single or continuous exposure mode and you have seven different functions, from which the camera derived its name, Sept being French for seven.

16mm EQUIPMENT

Cine Kodak Model B

The Cine Kodak that introduced 16mm film to the world was a large, boxy affair that today is coveted by the specialist collector. But in 1925, the far more compact Model B was introduced and that is much easier to find on today's collecting market.

Shaped like a thin box camera, it takes either 50ft or 100ft spools of 16mm film and its trim size is aided by the way the spools are loaded. They actually lie on top of each other, separated by a hinged flap. The full spool drops into a lower chamber, the flap is closed and the film is then fed through a gap, around the gate mechanism and back to the take-up spool that

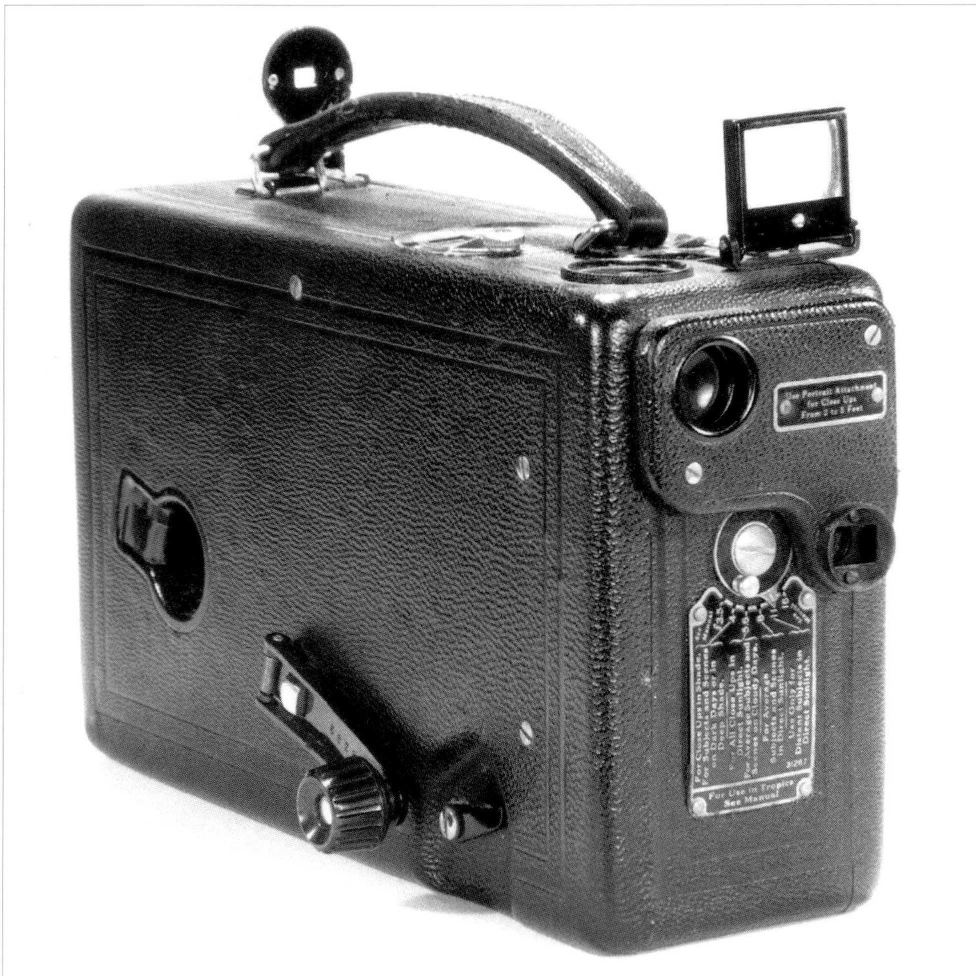

The Cine Kodak Model B, one of the earlier 16mm cameras.

rotates above the first spool on a spindle attached to the closed flap.

The camera sports both eye-level and waist-level viewfinders and has a fixed focus lens with apertures from f/3.5 to f/16, designated by subjects and weather descriptions. A clockwork motor drives around 20ft of film to one winding.

Keystone Criterion

Keystone was an American company originally founded to make projectors. In the 1930s, they made a series of 16mm cameras, including this one, the A9.

It's a large, oval-shaped camera, made of metal covered in brown leather and with the film taking the traditional path from top to bottom. Apertures from f/2.5 - f/22 are set on one side of the lens while, on the other side, the words 'bright', 'hazy' and 'dull' are engraved to be set against 'Summer' or 'Winter' settings, for those who are not so technically minded.

Shutter speeds, from a clockwork motor, are also adjustable with 16 frames per second for normal, 24fps for sound, 10fps for low speed and 64fps for slow motion.

Magazine Cine Kodak

This one, made in 1936, has a number of unusual features. First, its 16mm film is in cartridges, each one with a closed shutter over the film window that opens only when the cartridge is in the camera and the body is closed. In this way, cartridges can be changed mid-film without losing a frame.

The camera has interchangeable lenses from 25mm to 152mm and an adjustable viewfinder that alters the field of view according to the focal length in use by sliding a lens back and forth between the back site and the front window. It also has a facility for fitting a Reflex Focusing Finder. Reflex viewing was difficult to achieve while the film was running on a cine camera of this era, but for close-ups, especially when shooting titles, it was very useful, which is where this accessory comes in.

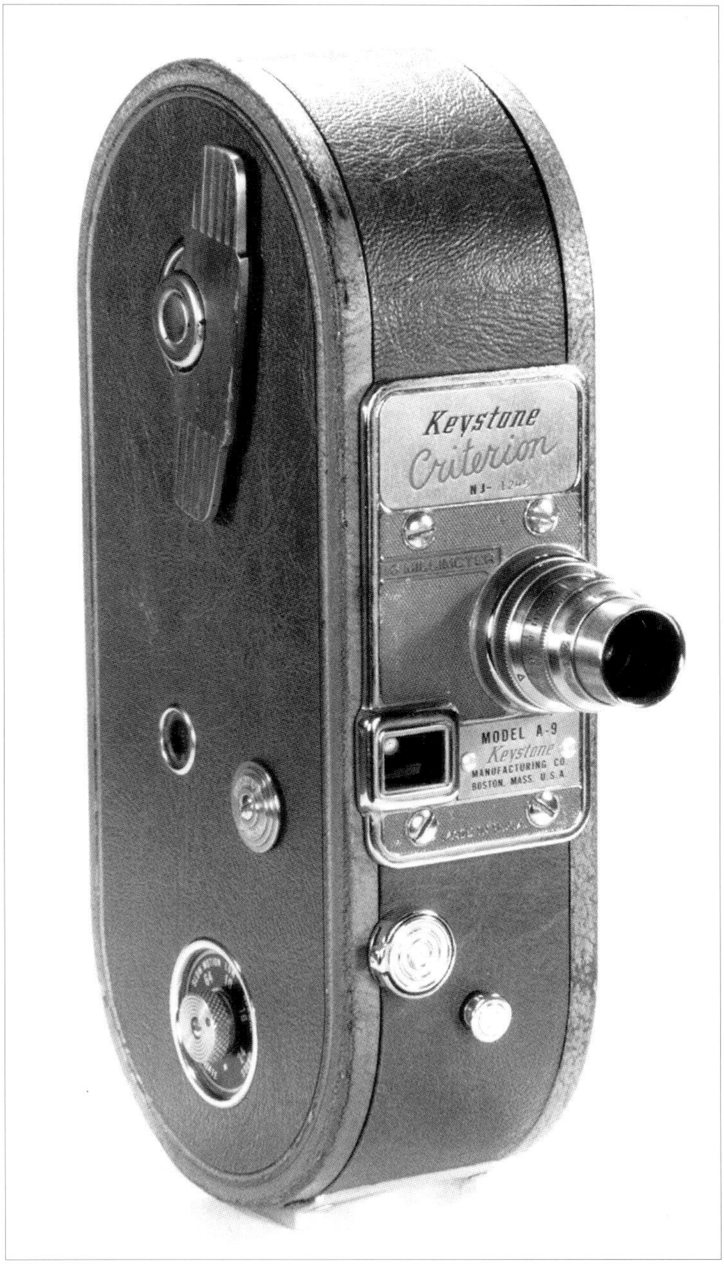

The Keystone Criterion.

With the camera on a tripod, the side of the camera is opened, the film cartridge removed and the Focusing Finder fitted in its place. The shutter can then be opened by means of a small pin-like device on a chain attached to the Focusing Finder and, looking into a separate viewfinder on the side of the accessory, it is possible to see directly through the lens. The camera is lined up on the close-up subject and its position locked on the tripod. The Focusing Finder is then removed, the film put in its

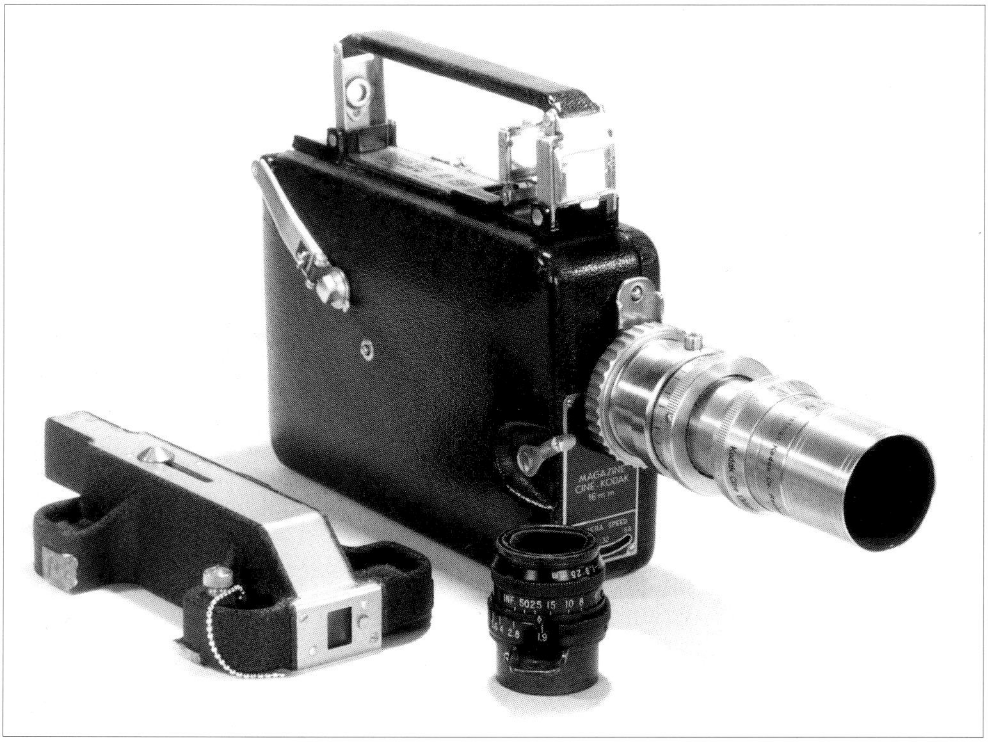

The Magazine Cine Kodak with its 63mm telephoto lens fitted, its special Reflex Focusing Finder and the standard 25mm lens.

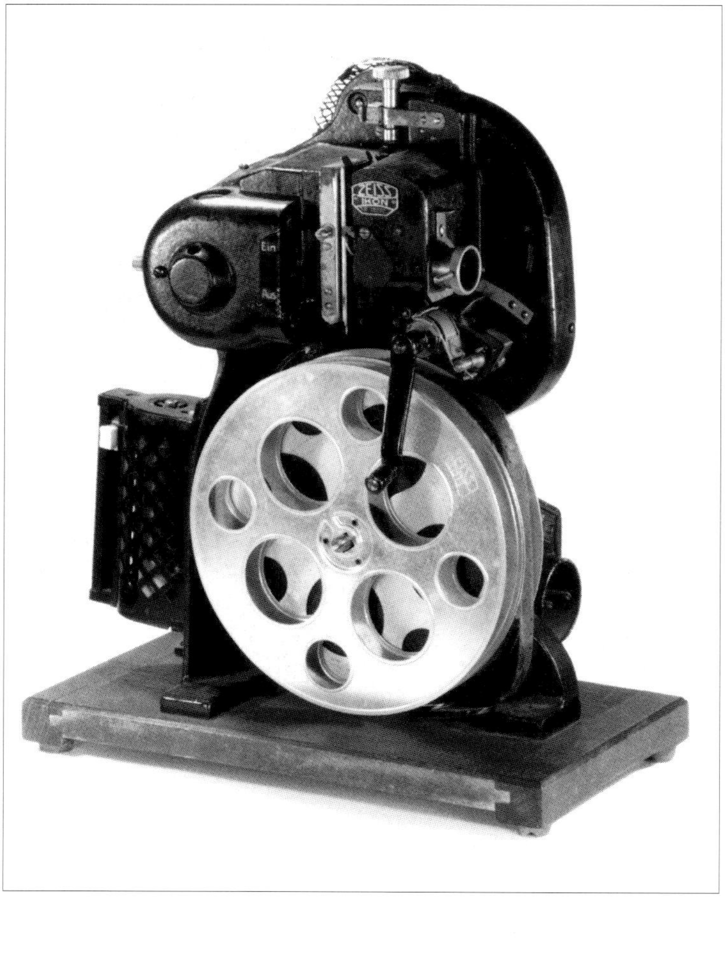

The Zeiss Ikon projector from 1930 is unusual in placing both film spools together beneath the lens.

place, the camera body closed and the film shot.

Zeiss Ikon projector

Made in 1930, this is an early entry into the 16mm cine projector market from Zeiss Ikon and, at the time, it was the only portable projector that could be carried in its case already threaded with film and ready for projection as soon as it was plugged into the mains. The carrying case also incorporates a small projection screen on an inner side that makes it possible to set up and show films in daylight within only a few minutes.

The ready anywhere, anytime feature results from the unusual step of placing the two film spools side by side on a common spindle below the lens, rather than one on each side of the lens as is more usually the case. The film runs from the inner spool in a loose loop, then brought down through the gate and onto the take-up spool. The projector has a rheostat built in to reduce mains voltage to 30 volts for the bulb

In 1931, the projector was upgraded with a

brighter bulb and a new condenser system that gave three times the illumination of the previous model.

Kodascope Model C

This projector, made by Kodak in 1926, is one of the more compact 16mm models, made possible partly by separating the rheostat from the projector and making it a separate plug-in unit. The Kodascope's folding reel arms, in more conventional positions than those on the Zeiss Ikon, take 400 ft reels.

In 1928, a slightly different version, called the Business Kodascope, was produced in a carrying case with a built-in translucent screen and two lenses of different focal lengths for either normal projection or rear projection.

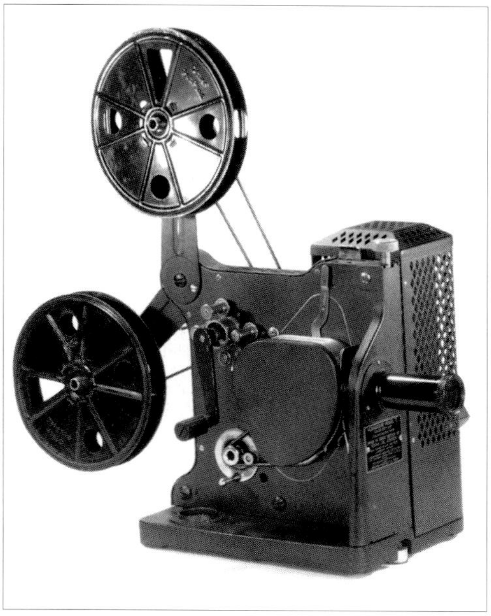

The Kodascope Model C projector is more compact than most 16mm models.

9.5mm EQUIPMENT

Pathé Baby

Here's the camera that introduced 9.5mm cinematography to Europe in 1923. The Pathé Bay was hand cranked and, according to advertising of the day, "brings home that old wish - to see ourselves as others see us". Other than strict instructions to turn the crank at no more and no less than two turns to the second, the only other control is the aperture whose scale runs f/3.5, f/5, f/7, f/10 and f/14.

A close-up device, incorporating a lens and wire frame can sometimes be found for this camera, used to clip on the front to make titles for films.

A few years after the Baby's introduction, Pathé produced two add-on clockwork motors, the Camo and the Motrix, allowing the film maker to use the camera hand-held, rather than with the tripod that was a necessity with hand cranked cameras. They also ensured more even exposure, since inadvertently turning the crank faster or slower would under- or over-expose the film.

The Camo was Swiss-made and exposed a complete cartridge of film at one winding, the French-made Motrix was less expensive and exposed only about two-fifths of the film to one winding.

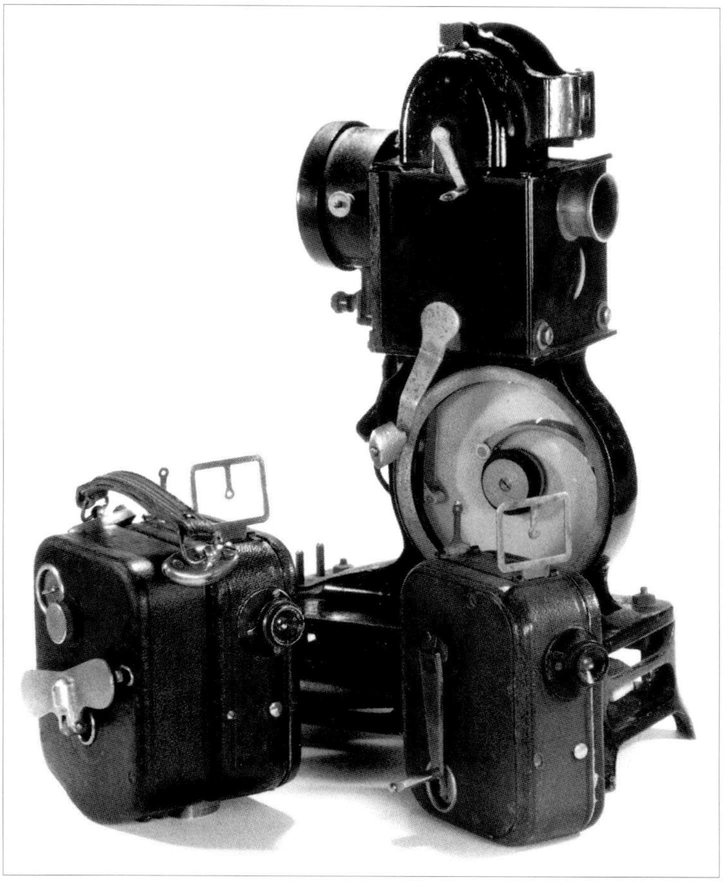

The Pathé Baby projector with two models of the Pathé Baby cine camera, one of which is hand cranked, the other with its add-on clockwork motor.

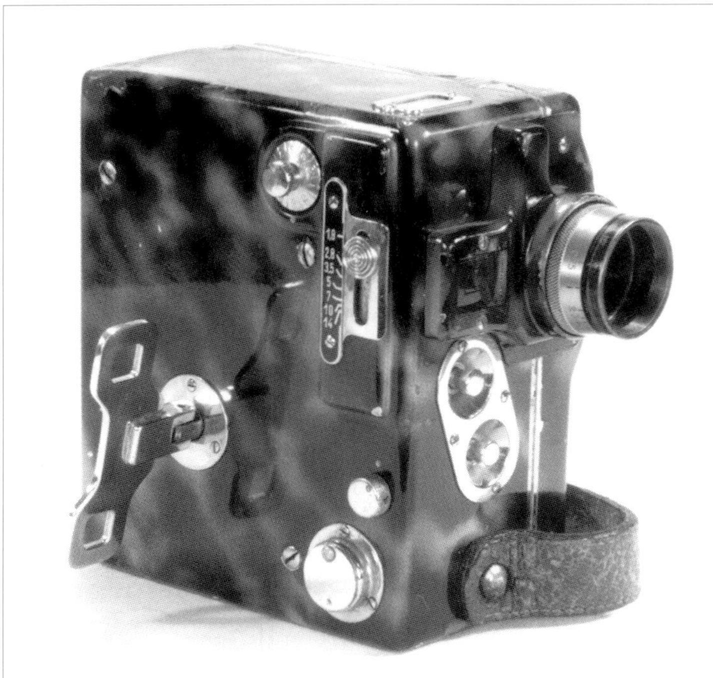

A Ditmar 9.5mm cine camera that is unusual for its tortoiseshell case.

A new version of the Pathé Baby, similar to the first model, but with a wider body to accommodate a built-in motor was introduced in 1926. It allowed a whole reel of film to be exposed at a single wind.

Pathé Baby projector

If you had been a 9.5mm cine enthusiast in 1923, this is the projector you would undoubtedly have been using. Introduced originally to show scaled down versions of current commercial films, it soon became adopted by amateur film makers.

Like its namesake camera, the Pathé Baby projector is hand cranked and has an unusual glass sided chamber into which the film is loosely wound from a reel on the top. It takes up to 60 ft of film at a time and is capable of throwing a picture 3 ft wide at a distance of

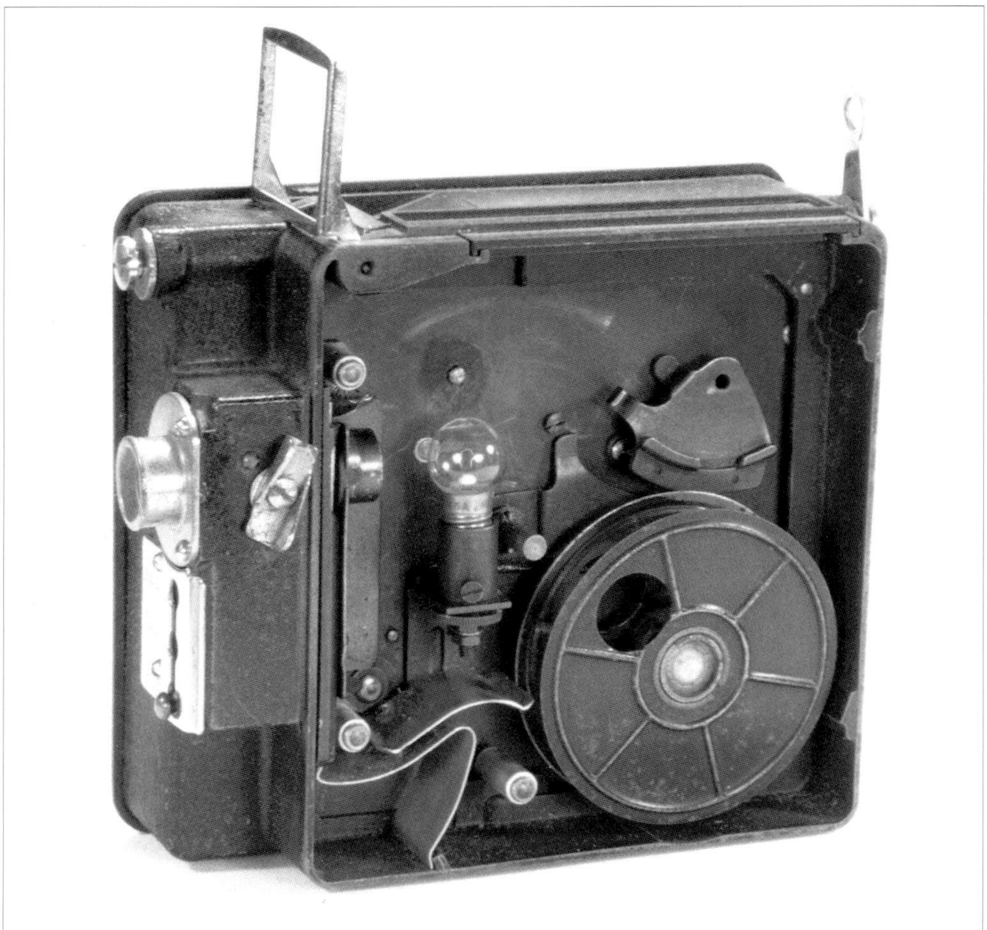

Inside the Campro, showing the torch bulb that allows the camera to double as a projector.

11ft from the screen. At the end of the performance, a second handle on the top reel is turned to rewind the film onto its original spool.

In the base of the projector is a dangerous looking electrical resistor to reduce mains power for the low voltage lamp, but this was made redundant by use of an add-on dynamo that lit a special 6 volt bulb, the current being generated as the crank was turned to advance the film through the gate.

Special notches on the film could be used to automatically stop it at any frame that the viewer wanted to look at in more detail and, if the dynamo was in use, pressing a catch on its side disengaged the drive to the projector, allowing the crank to be turned to generate the required current without the film advancing.

Instructions suggested clamping the projector firmly when the dynamo was being used to prevent vibration.

Ditmar 9.5mm

Ditmar cine cameras were made in Austria. Mostly they have metal bodies, covered in black leatherette, but this one is particularly collectable because it has an unusual and distinctive tortoiseshell type of lacquer over the metal.

The lens focuses from 0.5 metres to infinity, apertures are adjustable by a sliding scale on the side of the body between f/1.8 and f/14 and two separate shutter buttons give two different running speeds.

Campro

Home Cine Cameras Ltd was an English company and, in 1935, they produced a 9.5mm camera to take Pathé cartridges and which, to all outward appearances, looks like a normal clockwork driven cine camera of the time. But take the side off and behind the film gate there are two unusual additions. The first is a tiny condenser lens situated behind the film path; the second is a torch bulb.

Once shot and processed, the film was reloaded and, plugging a battery pack into a socket on the back of the body, the camera could be used as a projector. That's why the lens has three adjustable apertures, marked 'bright', 'dull' and 'project'.

Pathescope Prince and Princess

Even as late as 1959, Pathescope was still launching 9.5mm equipment and this camera and projector, designed to complement one another, represented a real departure from convention.

The Prince cine camera is a fairly simple affair, attractively styled in a matt grey die cast alloy case with a 23mm f/2.8 fixed focus lens. What sets it apart is the release which can be pushed either forwards or backwards to set-

The Pathescope Prince camera and Princess projector.

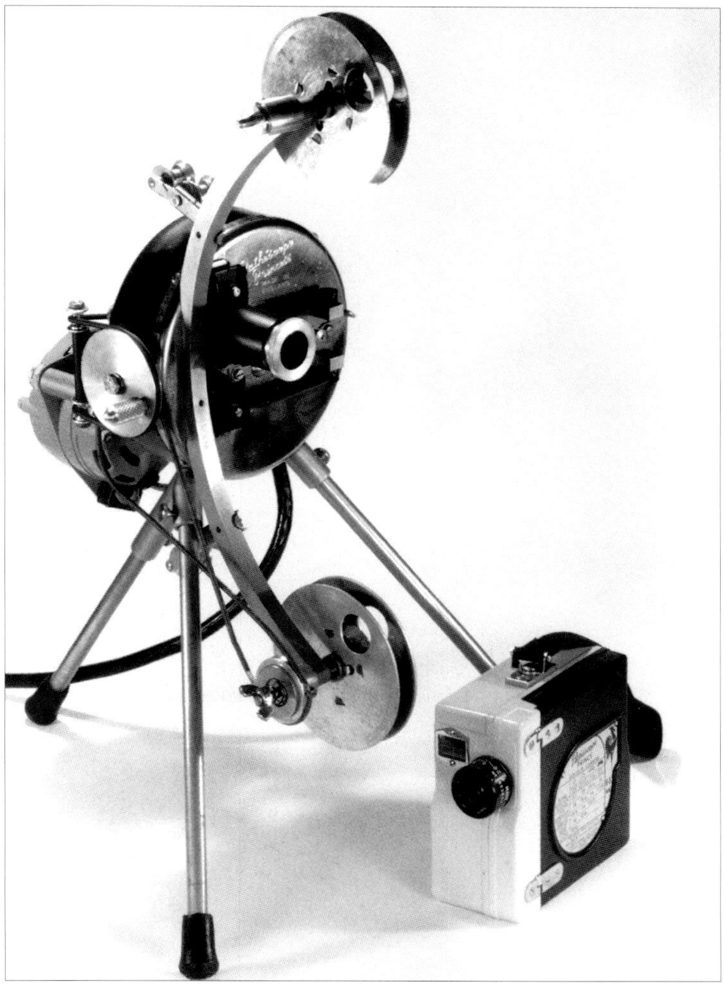

tings marked 'cine' and 'snapshot'. The second setting takes single frames one at a time.

There is nothing unusual about a single frame control on a cine camera, but this one is for use with the Princess projector, an unusual design that stands on three tripod legs that support a flat, drum-shaped lamphouse with a stainless steel front plate. Models were available for hand cranking or in a version that added a motor mounted behind the lamp house. In place of the usual sprockets around which film has to be looped, there are twin spring loaded rollers to give the film a smooth path through the gate.

Run in the normal way, the projector shows movies from any 9.5mm film. But then, by removing certain belts from the motor to the film driving mechanism and refitting other belts from a handle down to the take-up spool, the cine frames can be wound through one at a time to show the single frames taken in the Prince's 'snapshot' mode. To prevent the film burning when it is stationary in the gate, the heat of the 22-volt lamp is reflected back from the stainless steel front plate of the lamp housing.

Used in this way, a reel of 9.5mm film in the Prince camera was capable of producing more than 1,100 individual frames - more than enough for anyone's holiday snaps!

Inside the Cine-Kodak Eight, showing the large cogged wheel that feeds film to the top of the gate and takes it up again at the bottom.

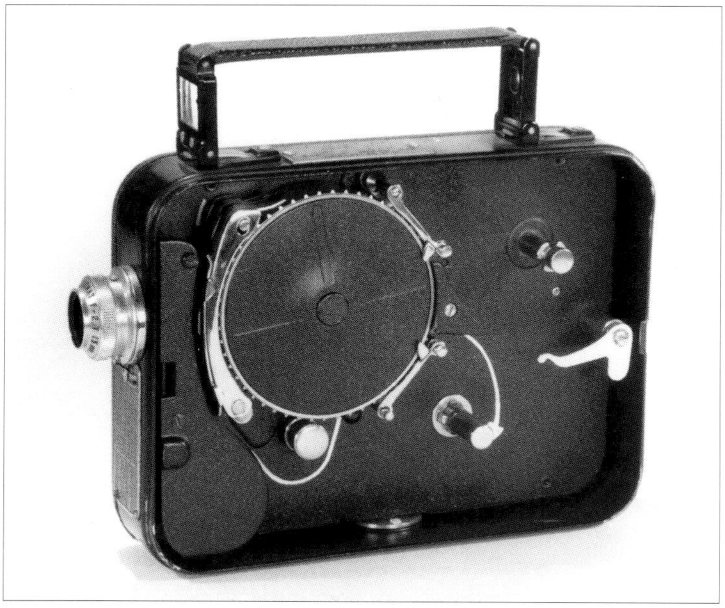

8mm EQUIPMENT

Cine-Kodak Eight

Here we have the camera that launched Standard 8 film in 1932. It's an extremely compact, clockwork-driven model fitted with a Kodak f/3.5 anastigmatic lens that stops down to f/22.

Amateur cine cameras of this era tend to have meagre specifications compared to still cameras of the time, but this one has two interesting features. The first is the viewfinder which is incorporated into the carrying handle and folds down like any camera strap when not in use.

The second is the way the film is fed through the gate. Most cine cameras feature two cogwheels, top and bottom of the gate, around which the film is looped. The Cine-Kodak 8 uses one large cogged wheel inside the body and behind the lens that serves to both feed the film into the gate and take it up again on the other side.

Keystone K-8

Dating from around 1935, this is a scaled down version of the 16mm Keystone cameras like the Criterion mentioned above. It sports an f/1.9 lens and a plate on the front of the camera suggests apertures down to f/16 for different lighting conditions, from 'heavy shade/bright interiors' to 'brilliant scenes' when shooting at the normal 16fps. Slower and faster speeds of 12fps and 48fps are also available. The camera has an optical viewfinder, plus a large wire frame finder on the side with two masks for the standard and an interchangeable telephoto lens.

The Keystone K-8, like its 16mm counterpart, is a tall oval shape and it is, in fact, very easy to get confused about which way up it should be used, particularly since the optical finder is beneath the lens towards the base of the body rather than above it. For that reason, one end of the camera has the word 'Top' embossed on it so there can be no mistake!

Movinette 8

The Zeiss Ikon range of Movinette and Movikon cameras are among the more unusual cine designs, shaped more like still cameras than cine. They were made between 1952 and 1959. Models include the Movikon 8 and 8B, and the Movinette 8 and 8B, distinguished by different shutter speed and lens combinations and the fact that the 'B' models have meters.

The cameras take Double-8 film, feeding it along a rather tortuous route that starts on the left of the body, running to the top of the gate, where it twists so that it is facing the lens, before twisting again as it emerges at the bottom of the gate to be taken up by the take-up spool on the right.

It's a lot like using a still camera, a similar shape that is held horizontally and with the shutter release on the top plate.

The Movinette 8 illustrated here has a fixed focus lens, single 16fps shutter, apertures from f/2.8 - f/16 and a depth of field scale engraved behind the clockwork winding key.

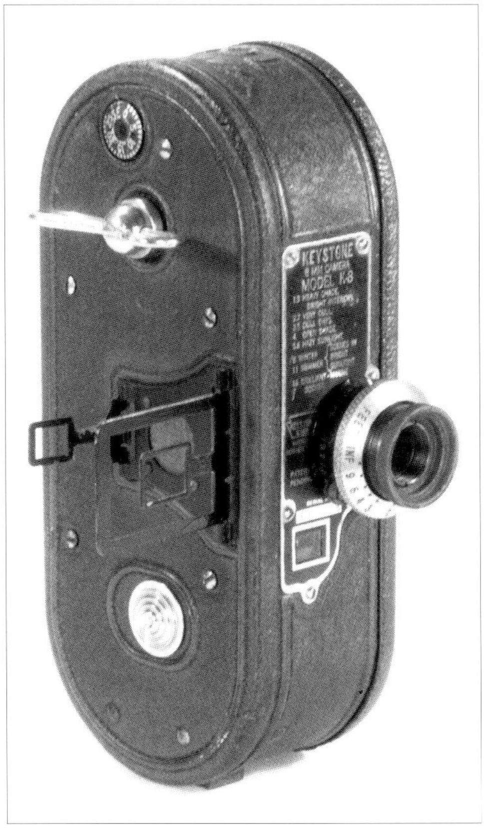

The Keystone K-8.

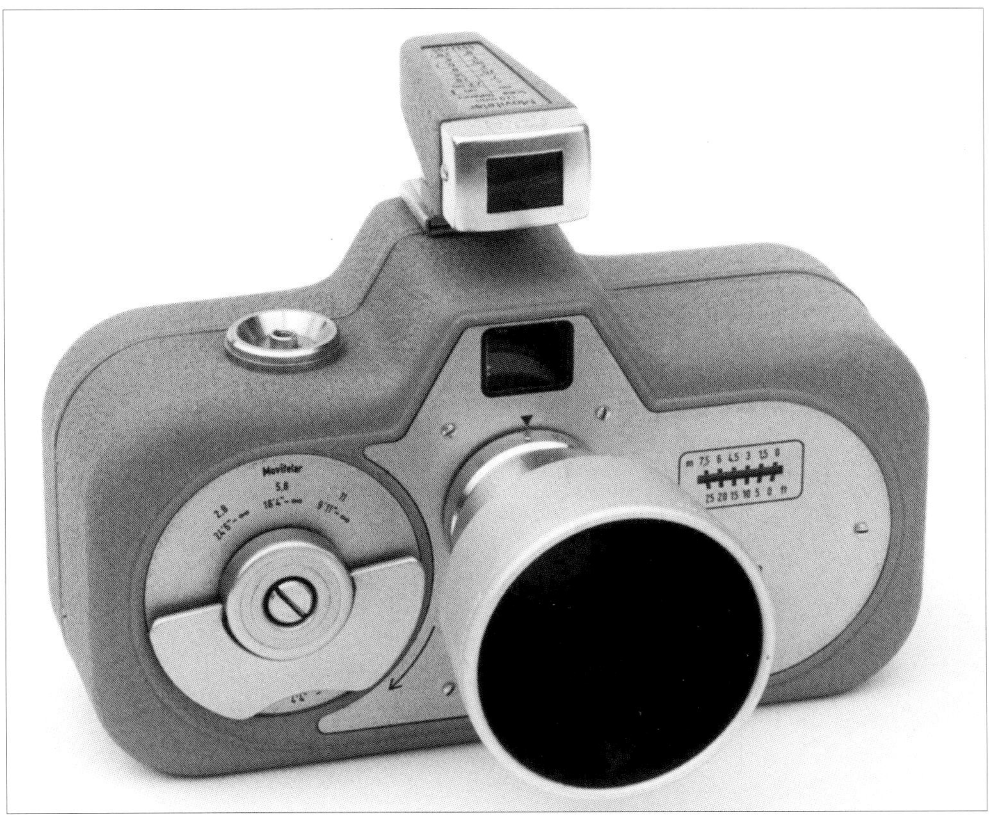

The Zeiss Ikon Movinette 8, equipped with its 2xf teleconverter, lens hood and accessory viewfinder.

The Univex A8.

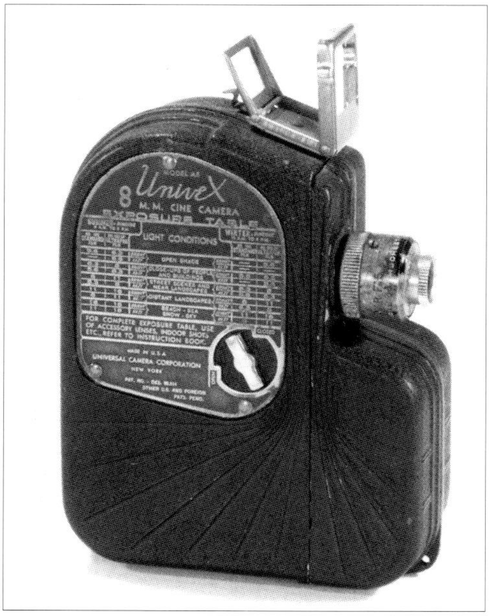

The 10mm focal length of the Movinette and Movikon lenses can be doubled up to 20mm by use of the Movitelar 2xf teleconverter, which was sold in a special case with its own lens hood and an accessory viewfinder that slips into the accessory shoe on the top of the camera. The viewfinder tilts and click-stops at three positions to compensate for parallax. On its top, a scale converts focusing distances on the original lens to new distances appropriate with the converter is in place.

Kodak even used their Brownie name on a small range of cine cameras.

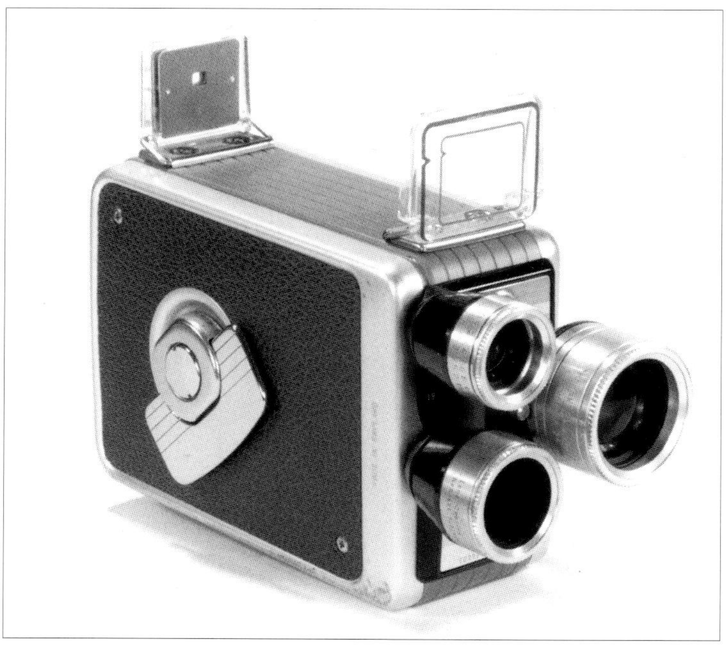

Univex A8

Made by the American Universal Camera Corporation in 1936, this was the camera that popularised Single-8 film, taking 30ft at a time on the company's own patented spools.

Consequently, the Univex A8 is one of the smaller cine cameras of its age, hardly larger than the palm of the hand and with an attractive art deco design etched into the body. It has an interchangeable f/5.6 lens and a comprehensive exposure guide engraved on a plate on the side, giving apertures for different lighting conditions.

Kodak Brownie

Collectors of still cameras will know the Brownie name as being synonymous with making photography simple and accessible to those on a budget, and in 1951 that philosophy came to cine in the Brownie Movie Camera.

A few years later, Kodak added a turret to the Brownie to give standard, wideangle and telephoto options, but the turret doesn't actually incorporate three lenses.

The 13mm standard lens is in the body behind the front panel and its turret houses only a hood. Giving the turret a twist, however, brings two converter lenses into play which work with the standard lens to give 9mm or 24mm focal lengths. In this way, the maximum aperture remains at f/1.9 for all three focal lengths.

The hoods are colour coded: red for standard, orange for telephoto and green for wideangle, and corresponding frames of the same colours are etched onto the direct vision viewfinder to show their coverage.

The Brownie takes Double-8 film and has a shutter fixed at 16fps.

Bolex B8SL

In the 1950s, Bolex cine cameras, made by Paillard in Switzerland, were among the best. This one is a twin turret model for Double-8 film. The standard lens is a 13mm f/1.9 and the tele lens is a 36mm f/2.8. The standard is a fixed focus lens, the telephoto focuses down to 1.75 ft, and coloured frames in the viewfinder indicate the field of view for each

The camera also has a built-in meter which is switched on by pressing a catch above the viewfinder, then matching two needles as the aperture ring of whichever lens is in the taking position is rotated. It automatically switches off again as filming begins.

Eumig C3R

The C3R, made in 1958 is an improved version of the Eumig C3 made between 1938 and 1955, and it represents an interesting non-reflex method of showing an accurate field of view for each of its three lenses as they are brought into play. The standard lens, fixed to the body, is a 12.5mm f/1.9. Two adapters, which rotate on the turret to sit in front of the standard lens convert it to double and half its focal length.

Twisting the turret to bring each lens into play also places another lens in front of the viewfinder to change its angle of view and so show a fairly accurate idea of what will appear on film.

The system was an obvious improvement over etching different frames, some of them extremely small, into the viewfinder.

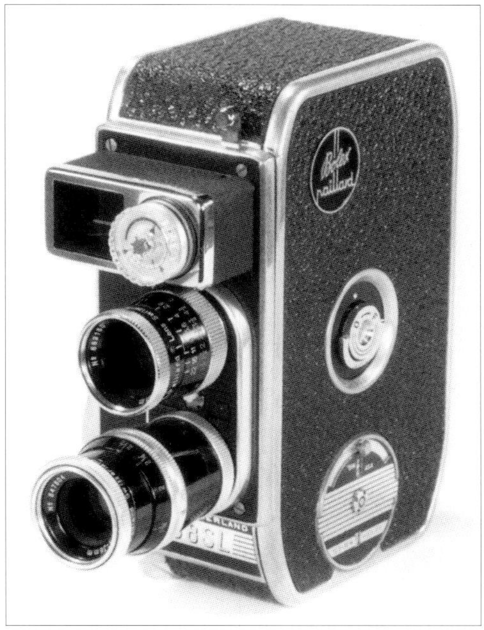

Bolex B8SL, one of the better made amateur cine cameras, much sought after in its time.

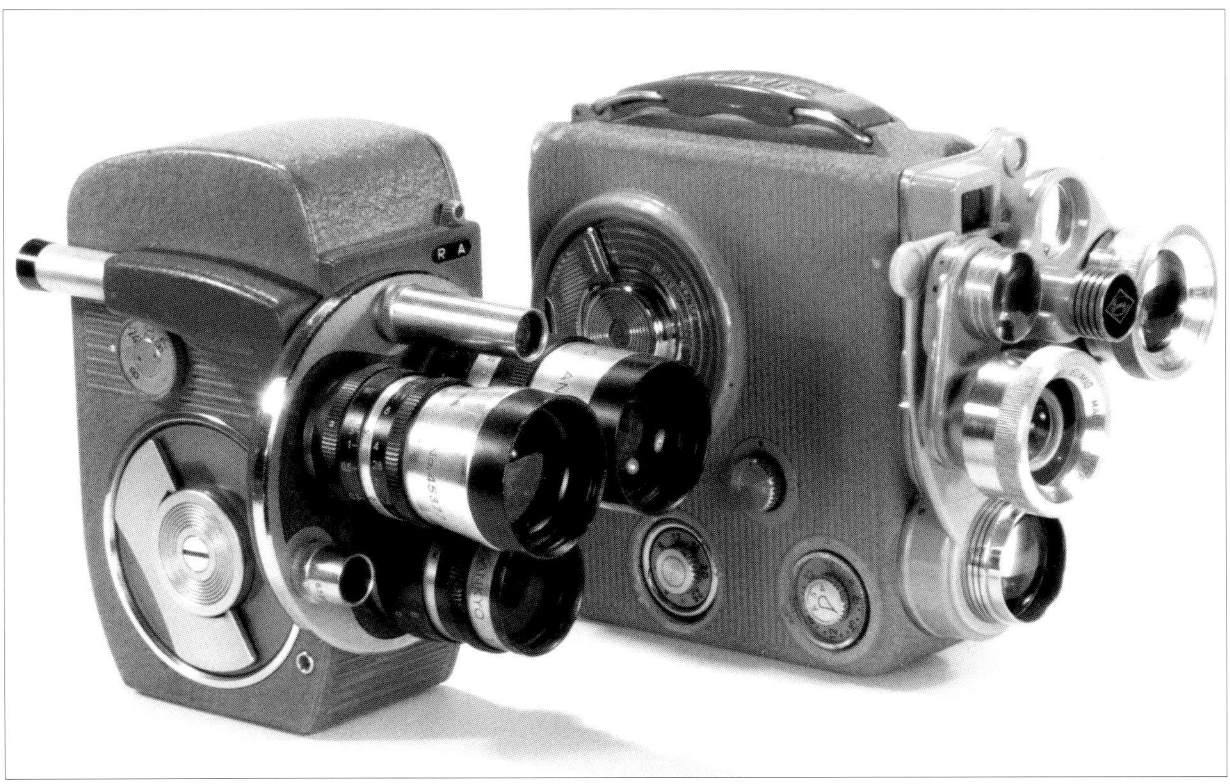

The Eumig C3R and Sankyo 8R, three-lens turret cameras that used unusual methods of viewfinding.

Sankyo 8R

This cine camera, made in the 1960s, also has a three-lens turret but is unusual in having two separate viewfinders. The first shows the view seen by the lens in use by means of a supplementary lens that comes into play in front of the viewfinder as the lens turret is rotated. The second is like a miniature telescope that looks through the lens to side of the one in use. This, then, can be used to focus the lens first, before it is twisted into position for actual use.

Sekonic Dualmatic Zoom

This model is unusual in providing a method of turning the film over after its first run through the camera without having to unload. The Double 8 film is loaded in the usual way and the first 25 ft run through. Then, pressing a catch on the body, allows the entire centre section to twisted through 180 degrees so that the film is immediately ready for its second run. As well as saving time and the sometimes tricky business of threading film, this prevents exposure to light of film allowed for a trailer at the end of one side and leader at the start of the other and so allowed a few more seconds of shooting time to every reel.

Bolsey 8

Manufactured in America in 1956, this was, at that time, the smallest cine camera ever made. It is actually smaller than a cigarette packet. The camera takes Single-8 film in its own special Bolsey cassette and sports a 10mm f/1.8 lens that stops down to f/22 and which can be focused down to 1 ft.

The shutter button has three settings, one which locks it, a second which runs the shutter at 16fps and a third which exposes single frames one at a time. The single frame adjustment wasn't uncommon on cine cameras, but what is very unusual in this model is that, with the shutter in this single frame mode, speeds are then adjustable in still camera increments from 1/50 second to 1/600 second.

So the Bolsey 8 cine camera doubles as a true subminiature still camera.

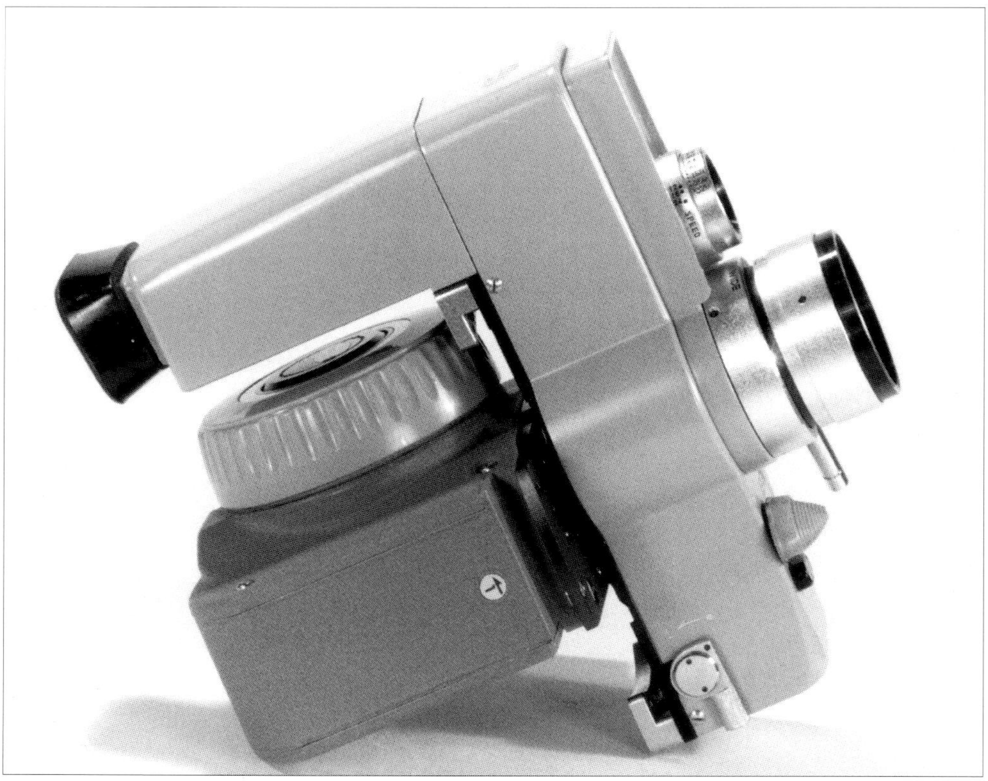

The Sekonic Dualmatic Zoom allows the film to be run through twice without opening the camera half way.

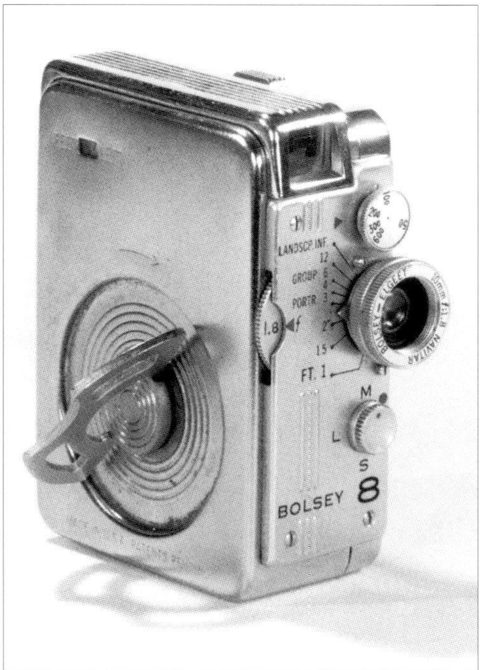

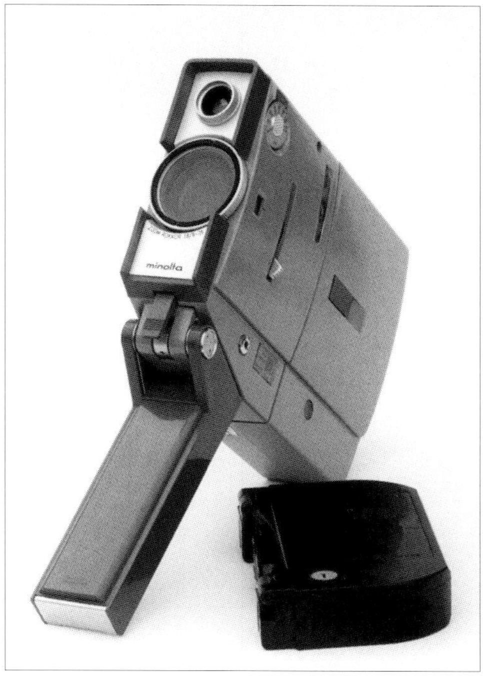

Far left: The Bolsey 8 doubles as a subminiature still camera.

Minolta's Minoltina camera with its reloadable Standard-8 film cartridge.

Minoltina

As the Standard-8 era drew to a close, Minolta set out to make life easier when it came to loading and half-way re-loading film. Their solution came with the Minoltina.

It's a single lens reflex that uses it own special cartridges into which the Standard-8 film is pre-loaded, not spool to spool as with most other 8mm cameras, but from the film spool to a built-in take-up spool, similar to that used in a still camera.

Once loaded, the cartridge is then inserted intact into the camera and, at the end of the first run, it is simply removed, turned over and re-inserted. At the end of the second run, the film, still in the cartridge, is found back on its original spool. Spare cartridges were supplied so that any number of films could be pre-loaded ready for action.

The Minoltina also incorporates a neat handle that, when not in use, folds up to form a lens protector.

The camera is battery-driven rather than clockwork, as was the case with the vast majority of Standard-8 models. Taking that into account, along with its reflex viewing and the film cartridge feature, the camera represents something of a transition between Standard-8 and Super-8.

Kodascope Eight

The Kodascope Eight was the first 8mm cine projector, introduced in 1932 along with the Cine-Kodak Eight. It uses a 100-watt bulb and incorporates a special mica screen that

The Kodascope Eight projector which, along with the Cine-Kodak Eight, introduced 8mm film.

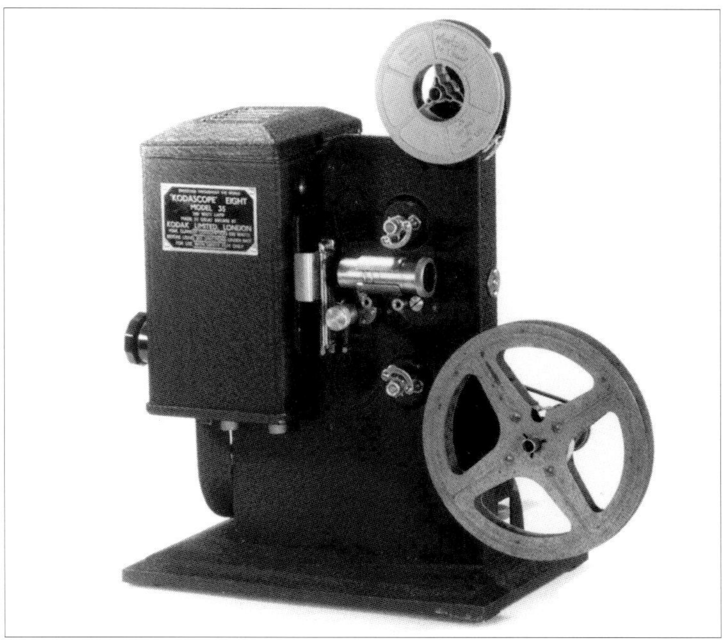

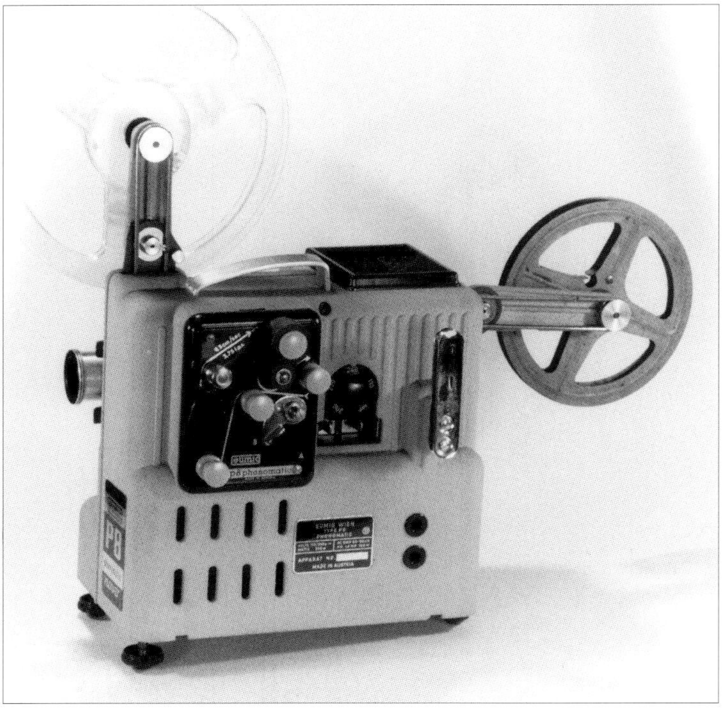

The Eumig P8 Phonomatic Novo with its sound synchronising device on the side.

automatically comes into play between the bulb and the film if the speed of the projector becomes sufficiently slow to damage the film.

Eumig P8 Phonomatic Novo

Made in 1963, this 8mm projector incorporates an unusual mechanism for synchronising film with a taped soundtrack. Set up beside a reel-to-reel tape recorder, the tape is fed from the first reel, through the recording heads in the usual way, then around a pivoting arm on the side of the projector before being returned to the tape recorder's second reel.

That pivoting arm is linked to a resistor that slows down and speeds up the projector according to its position and, as it is switched on, the tape holds the arm at the top of its throw, turning off current to the drive and bulb and preventing the projector from actually starting. Turning on the tape recorder and so feeding through tape, allows the arm to drop and the projector starts.

All projectors speed up and slow down slightly as they run and, although the effect is usually too subtle to be seen on the screen, it is enough to prevent a soundtrack, running on a separate tape from remaining in synchronisation. On the Phonomatic, however, any changes in projector speed mean that the consistent speed of the tape continually pulls the pivoting arm up and down, its resistor automatically and continually re-adjusting the speed of the film through the gate.

Although the system was not accurate enough for lip-synch, it was good enough for music and sound effects.

SUPER-8 EQUIPMENT

Agfa family

Agfa launched this unusual camera system in 1980 as movie camera that also takes still pictures. Looking more like a cine camera than a still one, it has only two controls: one for continuous shooting, the other for single frames. It takes Super 8 cine film.

Part of the system is the Agfa Family Monitor, which shows the moving pictures on its own, small, in-built screen. If the pictures were taken on continuous run, then they move on the screen. If the single frame control was used, then the film will have been coded by the camera and the Monitor automatically stops. The Monitor can also be stopped manually, or set to screen individual shots at three second intervals.

With the addition of a special printer, any single frame on the film could originally have been turned into a colour print on the spot, by use of the Kodak instant photography system... which these days is as dead as the Agfa Family.

Right: The Agfa Family camera with its purpose made Monitor.

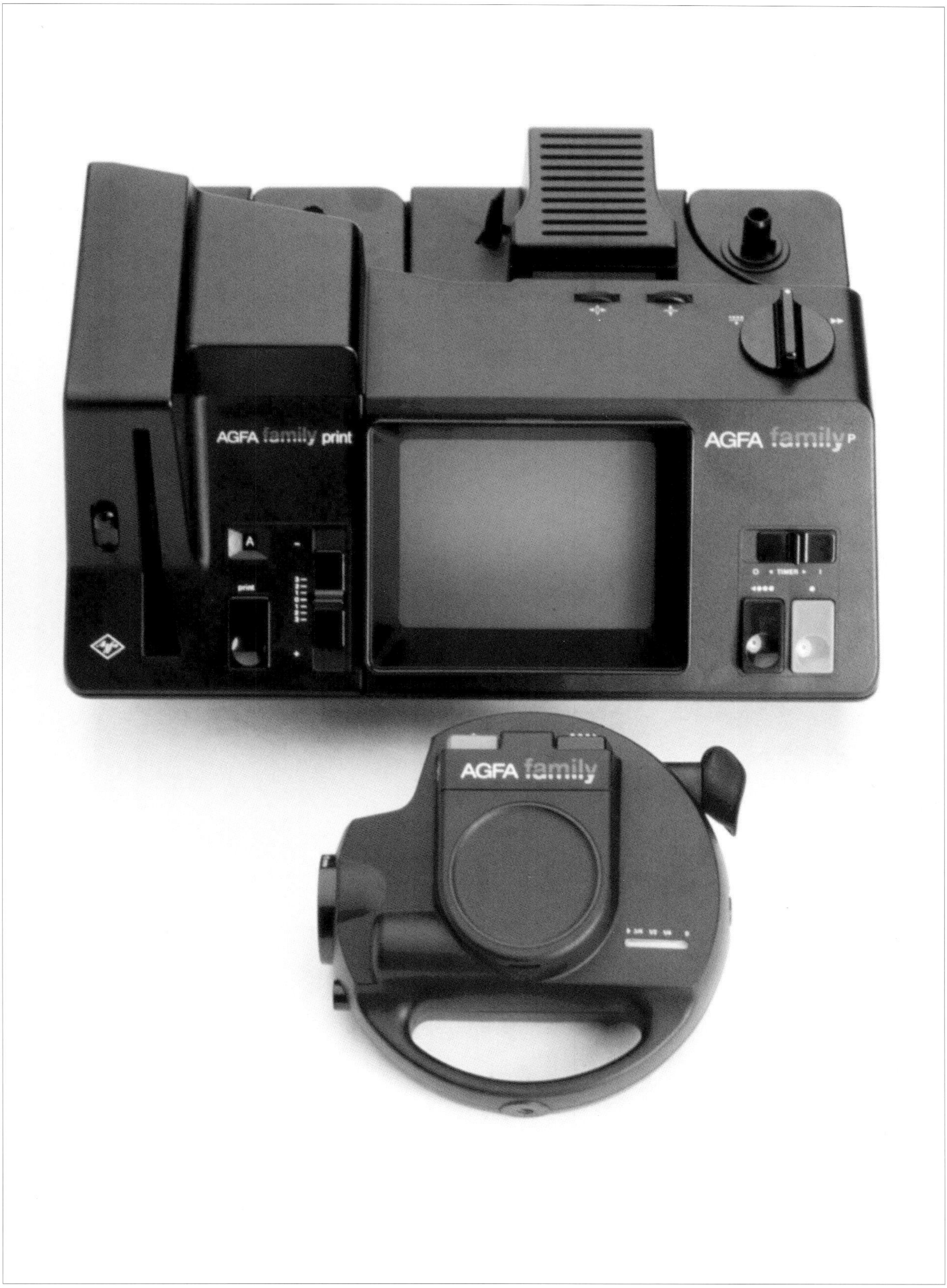
AGFA family print
AGFA family P
TIMER
print
AGFA family

Glossary

Accessory shoe: Clip on the top plate of a camera to accommodate accessories such as flashguns, exposure meters and rangefinders.

Amateur Photographer: Weekly British photographic magazine, originally known as The Amateur Photographer, first published in 1884 and still published today. Known to most photographers as AP.

AP: See Amateur Photographer.

Aperture: Variable opening to control the amount of light that is allowed through the lens and onto the film. Measured in f-stops.

Aperture priority: Form of automatic exposure in which the user sets the aperture and the camera automatically selects and sets the correct shutter speed.

ASA: American Standards Association, a measure of film emulsion speeds.

Auto exposure: A method of setting shutter speeds and/or apertures in a camera automatically to give the correct exposure for different levels of light.

Autofocus: Automatic lens focusing system.

'B' setting: Standing for brief time or bulb (from the days when camera shutters could be tripped by a pneumatic bulb on the end of a length of rubber tube). A camera setting in which the shutter remains open whilst the control is pressed and closes again when it is released.

Bed: Part of a folding camera that folds down from the main body to support the lens panel.

Between lens shutter: A leaf type shutter that is situated between the elements of a lens.

BJ: See British Journal Photographic Almanac.

Box Brownie: Generic term that has come to be accepted for any box camera, inspired by the Brownie series of cameras made by Kodak.

Box form: Description of camera that is basically box shaped.

Brief time: see 'B' setting.

British Journal Photographic Almanac: Established in 1860 and published annually thereafter with articles about photography, plus details of the latest advances and reviews of new equipment for the year. Collected for its value in the research of cameras and photographic equipment. Usually known to collectors as the BJ.

Capacitor: Part of a flashgun that stores electricity so that the flash is always fired by the same maximum voltage even when a battery is low.

Cassette: Container for film. Placed in a camera, the film is wound out of the cassette and back again at the end of the roll. Some early cameras featured cassette to cassette loading so that rewinding was unnecessary. Usually applied to 35mm film, but occasionally used in other sizes too.

CdS: Form of metering that relies on light falling on a cell and changing its resistance when a current is supplied from a battery.

Central processing unit: Computer chip in electronic cameras that correlates and controls functions.

Compound lens: Lens made up of individual elements in groups.

Concave: A lens that is thinner in its centre than at its edges.

Convex: A lens that is thicker at its centre than at its edges.

Depth of field: The amount of an image that is acceptably sharp on either side of the point at which the lens is actually focused. Varies with the use of apertures, focal length and camera-to-subject distances.

DIN: Deutsche Industrie Norm - German standards organisation, a method of calibrating film speeds.

Direct vision viewfinder: Eye level viewfinder that looks directly at the subject.

Disc: Film frames arranged around a rotating disc, used in place of the usual rollfilm in disc cameras.

Double stroke: Type of lever wind on a camera that takes two strokes to advance the film one frame.

DX coding: Method of automatically setting film speeds in electronic cameras, controlled by coded information on the cassette.

Electronic flash: Method of flash photography that incorporates a reusable flash tube in place of the older flashbulbs that could be used only once.

Elements: Individual lenses that go to make up a compound lens.

Enlarger: Darkroom apparatus for projecting a negative onto a sheet of printing paper and so controlling the size of the print.

EV: See Exposure Values.

Exposure meter: Apparatus that measures the amount of light falling on a subject and expresses it in terms of shutter speeds and apertures, according to a set film speed.

Exposure Values: Method of measuring exposure and expressing it as a series of numbers that refer to specific light levels irrespective of which shutter speed and aperture combination is used. For example, 1/30 second at f/11 is actually the same exposure as 1/60 second at f/8 or 1/125 second at f/5.6, but they all have an EV of 12. Derived by adding together the reciprocal of the shutter speed and the aperture in terms of powers of 2.

Flashbulb: Small bulb for use in pre-electronic flashguns, made for once only use.

Flashcube: Sealed cube with four flashbulbs embedded in it.

Focal length: The distance between the centre of a lens and its sharply focused image when the subject is at infinity. Used to calibrate and identify different types of lens. Long focal lengths indicate telephoto lenses, short focal lengths indicate wideangle lenses.

Focal plane: The place where the film is positioned in a camera.

Focal plane shutter: A shutter consisting of two blinds that run in the focal plane. As the shutter is released, the first blind begins its travel followed by the second. Shutter speeds are controlled by the speed of the travel in combination with the width of the slit between the blinds.

Focusing: Method of moving the lens in relation to the film to attain a sharp image when the subject is at different distances.

Focusing screen: Screen, particularly one made of ground glass, onto which an image is thrown for focusing, usually from the camera's lens, sometimes from an auxiliary lens.

Folder: Term used to describe a folding camera.

Frames (cine): Individual frames that record a series of still images that combine to give the impression of movement.

Fresnel lens: Lens that consists of concentric rings each with a convex surface. Used in the form of a plastic sheet behind focusing screens to enhance illumination.

Gate (cine cameras): The place where individual frames of a cine film are exposed. Incorporates a mechanism to draw the film into position, allowing it to remain still for the exposure before pulling the next frame into position.

Ground glass screen: Screen on which a camera's image is projected. Sometimes on the back of a camera, but also incorporated into the viewfinders of single and twin lens reflexes.

Hot shoe: Special form of accessory shoe which incorporates electrical connections that mate with a flashgun.

'I' setting: See instantaneous.

Instamatic: Trade name of Kodak which should only be applied to that company's 126 cartridge film cameras made from 1963. Often wrongly used as the generic term for any snapshot camera.

Instant return mirror: Front surfaced mirror incorporated in a single lens reflex to reflect the image from the lens into the viewfinder. The mirror flips up a fraction of second before the exposure is made. If it returns to its original position automatically straight away after exposure, rather than having to be wound into position as the film is advanced, then it is known as 'instant return'.

Instantaneous: Any shutter speed on a camera other than the 'B' or 'T' settings, but usually used to refer to a single speed of around 1/50 second on snapshot cameras.

ISO: International Standards Organisation, a method of calibrating film speeds.

Leaf shutter: Shutter that relies on iris blades opening and closing to control speeds, usually found between the lens elements or in the body behind the lens.

LED: Light Emitting Diode. Small device that glows brightly when a low current is applied to it, used to indicate information in a camera's viewfinder or on the body.

Lip synch: Term used in cine to indicate that the synchronisation between the picture and the soundtrack is perfectly matched.

M synchronisation: Type of flash synchronisation in which the contact is made slightly before the shutter reaches its maximum opening. Used mostly for photography with flashbulbs which need time to build to their maximum power.

Manual: Exposure mode in which shutter speeds and apertures are set by hand, rather than automatically. Also used to describe cameras in which the correct exposure is suggested by an in-built meter by means of matching needles or LEDs, though not set automatically.

Match needle metering: Method of measuring exposure in a camera by adjusting apertures and/or shutter speeds until two needles coincide or one meets a predetermined mark.

Meniscus lens: Simple lens consisting of a single piece of glass with one convex and one concave surface.

Monochromatic: Usually used to refer to black and white pictures, although it actually means any image which is composed of a range of different tones of the same colour.

Open aperture metering: Method of metering in which the reading can be taken at the lens's widest aperture, rather than at its taking aperture.

Parallax: The difference between the view seen by the lens and that seen by the viewfinder in non-reflex cameras.

Pentaprism: Device used in a single lens reflex to bounce the light around the viewfinder after it has been reflected from the reflex mirror and onto the focusing screen. The resulting image is the correct way round and right side up.

Photokina: Major photographic exhibition held in Cologne in Germany every two years.

Polarising filters: Filters which cause light to vibrate in a single plane only. Used to reduce or remove reflections in non-metallic surfaces.

Program exposure: Form of automation which sets both shutter speeds and apertures automatically.

Rangefinder: Device, either built into a camera or made to be fitted as a separate accessory. Compares the subject from two different angles and so assesses its distance.

Red eye: The effect that results from a flashgun's light being reflected off the retina at the back of a human eye and giving the impression of red pupils. Caused when the flashgun is set too close to the camera lens.

Red window: Small circular window in the back of a camera body through which numbers, printed on the film's backing paper, can be read.

Reflex: A method of reflecting an image via a mirror onto the screen of a camera's viewfinder. Found in both single lens and twin lens reflexes.

Rotary shutter: Circular disc with an aperture cut in it and which revolves behind the lens to control shutter speeds.

Selenium cell: Used in exposure meters. As light strikes selenium, it generates minute amounts of electricity which are used deflect a needle and so indicate exposures.

Self erecting: System in a folding camera that causes the lens to automatically spring into the taking position as the camera is unfolded.

Shutter: Device in a camera to control the amount of time light is actually falling onto the film.

Shutter blind: One blind of a focal plane shutter.

Shutter priority: Form of automatic exposure in which the user sets the shutter speed and the camera automatically selects and sets the correct aperture.

Shutter speeds: The times for which a camera shutter is actually open. Usually expressed in fractions of a second, but can run to whole seconds.

Single lens reflex: Camera which reflects the image from the lens directly to the viewfinder so that the image seen in the viewfinder is exactly the same as that which will appear on the film.

Single stroke: Type of lever wind on a camera that takes only one stroke to advance the film one frame.

SLR: See single lens reflex.

Snapshot camera: Any form of simple camera with the bare minimum of controls.

Sprocket holes: Holes along the edge or edges of still or cine film which are used to wind the film through the camera by way of a sprocket wheel.

Standard lens: Lens which gives a field of view approximate to that seen by the human eye. Its focal length differs with the size of the frame. On a 35mm camera, the standard lens is one of around 50mm.

Stereo: The effect of shooting two pictures from two slightly different viewpoints similar to the spacing between human eyes so that, when each image is viewed independently, one with each eye, an impression of three dimensions is produced.

Stop down metering: Method of metering in which the lens has to be stopped down to its taking aperture before an accurate exposure reading can be obtained.

'T' setting: Standing for time. A camera setting in which the shutter opens when the release is pressed and remains open until it is pressed again.

Telephoto: Any lens that has a focal length longer than that of a standard lens. Used to magnify the image and bring far subjects closer on film.

Through the lens metering: Method of metering which measures light actually through the lens of the camera.

Time exposure: Exposure in which the shutter is held open for longer than the normal fraction of a second. Very often manually timed and used with the camera's 'B' or 'T' settings.

TLR: See twin lens reflex.

Top plate: The top of the camera that houses controls such as shutter release, film wind, frame counter, etc.

TTL: See through the lens metering.

Turret (cine): A panel that holds two or more lenses and which can be rotated into position for filming. Also seen on a few rare still cameras.

Twin lens reflex: Type of camera with two lenses, one to take the picture, the other to reflect a similar, though not exactly the same, image to a screen in the viewfinder.

Viewfinder: Device for estimating what the image on the film will look like. Built into nearly all cameras, though missing from some specialist models. Rangefinder cameras without reflex viewing will often use separate viewfinders that fit into the accessory shoe when certain specialist lenses are in use.

Wideangle lens: Any lens that has a focal length shorter than the standard lens. Increases the field of view, allowing the picture to contain more at the sides, top and bottom.

X synchronisation: Type of flash synchronisation in which the contact is made exactly as the shutter reaches its maximum opening. Used mostly for photography with electronic flash which reaches its maximum power almost instantaneously.

Zoom lens: Lens of variable focal length.

PICTURE CREDITS

A great many of the cameras featured in this book are from my own collection, but for pictures of some of the more rare or exotic cameras, I am indebted to a number of people and organisations who have supplied pictures or actual equipment for me to photograph.

Thanks first to Christie's South Kensington, the world's leading camera and photographic auctioneers. Their photographic specialist Michael Pritchard can be contacted at 85 Old Brompton Road, London SW7 3LD - telephone 0171-321 3279, fax 0171-321 3331, Internet http://www.christies.com/cameras. A free brochure is available from them on request. From their auction catalogues, I have drawn pictures of the following cameras: Twin Lens Contaflex, Super Kodak Six-20, Graphic Jet, white Kodak Brownie 127, Leica M3, Leica M2, Ilford Witness, Periflex I, Hologon Ultrawide, Canon 7, Samocaflex, white Hapyucc, Tessina, Gemflex, Golden Steky, Stylophot, Hit cameras, Petie Vanity, Petie lighter cameras, Petal cameras and Roundshot.

At the time this book was planned, Classic Collection was one of Europe's finest independent stores for the camera collector, and the following cameras were first published in their catalogues: Exakta, Kookie, Mecaflex plus tele lens, Laqon-44, Walz Automat, Primo Junior, Toyoca, Arco, Wrayflex II, Mikroma, Slimax, View-Master Personal Stereo, View-Master Stereo Color, Widelux, Viscawide, Photogrammetry underwater panoramic camera, Rollei SL26, Snoopymatic, Kodak Instamatic Reflex and Minolta CLE. Classic Collection ceased trading in May 1998.

The Hove International Blue Book is a regularly published price guide to collectable cameras and I am grateful to the publishers for allowing me to reproduce pictures of the following cameras from its pages: Periflex III, Periflex Gold Star, Periflex Interplan, Nikon I and Nikon S.

My thanks also to David Hugill for the picture of Photographica, the annual photo fair organised by the Photographic Collectors Club of Great Britain; to Terry Scott who has contributed technical articles to the British photographic press for more years than either of us is prepared to admit and whose files produced the Nikon EM, Konica FS-1 and Canon T80; to Pentax UK for digging up what they reckoned to be the UK's last surviving publicity picture of an ME Super; to Photopia International for finding a picture of the long forgotten Ricoh XRS; to Dieter Scheiba whose collection provided pictures of the Agfa Family and the super rare Janus; and to my good friend Bob White who kindly allowed me to photograph several cameras from his own collection.

John Wade

Index

D

E

F

G

H

I

J

K

L

M

N

O

P

R

S

T

U

V

W

Y

Z

Other Titles Available from Hove Books

HOVE LEICA BOOKS

LEICA THE FIRST 70 YEARS
LEICA THE FIRST 60 YEARS
LEICA R COMPENDIUM
LEICA M COMPENDIUM
LEICA COLLECTORS GUIDE
MY LIFE WITH LEICA – WALTER BENSER
LEICA R8
LEICA R7
LEICA R6
LEICA R5– R3
LEICA M6 – M1 *2nd Ed*
LEICA DARKROOM PRACTICE
LEICA LEN PRACTICE *2nd Ed*

HOVE LEICA POCKET BOOKS

LEICA POCKET BOOK *6th Ed*
LEICA ACCESSORY GUIDE *2nd Ed*
LEICA INTERNATIONAL PRICE GUIDE *7th Ed*

HOVE COLLECTORS BOOKS

HASSELBLAD COMPENDIUM
JAPANESE 35mm SLR CAMERAS
CLASSIC CAMERAS 1945–85
NIKON COMPENDIUM
NIKON RANGEFINDER CAMERAS
CANON COMPENDIUM
CANON RANGEFINDER CAMERAS 1933-68
ZEISS CAMERA COMPENDIUM 1940-72
ZEISS IKON CAMERAS 1926-39
ZEISS CONTAX REPAIR MANUAL
SPYCAMERA - THE MINOX STORY *2nd Ed*
KODAK CAMERAS FIRST 100 YEARS
EXAKTA CAMERAS 1933-78
ASAHI PENTAX REFLEX CAMERAS 1952-89
HOVE INTERNATIONAL BLUE BOOK

HOVE LEICA INSTRUCTION BOOKS etc

LEICA GENERAL CATALOGUE 1931
LEICA GENERAL CATALOGUE 1933
LEICA GENERAL CATALOGUE 1936
LEICA GENERAL CATALOGUE 1955/8
LEICA GENERAL CATALOGUE 1961
LEICA GENERAL CATALOGUE 1975
LEICA INSTRUCTIONS FOR MODELS 111a, 250 etc.
LEICA INSTRUCTIONS FOR MODELS 11 & 111c, f & g
LEICA INSTRUCTIONS FOR MODELS M1, 2, 3, & 4
LEICA INSTRUCTIONS FOR MODELS M5, CL, Leicaflex
LEICA INSTRUCTIONS FOR REPRODUCTION DEVICES

HOVE BOOKS

Hove Books Ltd.
30 The Industrial Estate, Small Dole, West Sussex. BN5 9XR